Edith
Kurzweil

The
Freudians

A Comparative Perspective

YALE UNIVERSITY PRESS

NEW HAVEN AND LONDON

Set in Janson type by G&S Typesetters, Austin, Texas.
Printed in the United States of America by Vail-Ballou
Press, Binghamton, New York.

Library of Congress Cataloging-in-Publication Data
Kurzweil, Edith.
    The Freudians : a comparative perspective / Edith
Kurzweil.
        p.   cm.
    Bibliography: p.
    Includes indexes.
    ISBN 0–300–04009–1 (alk. paper)
    1. Psychoanalysis—History.   2. Freud, Sigmund,
1856–1939.   I. Title.
BF173.K83   1989   89–8897
150.19′52—dc20   CIP

The paper in this book meets the guidelines for
permanence and durability of the Committee on
Production Guidelines for Book Longevity of the
Council on Library Resources.

10   9   8   7   6   5   4   3   2   1

Contents

Preface

Psychoanalysis has been written about from every conceivable point of view. It has been celebrated and condemned, distorted and revised. But though endless clinical studies, new theories, exposés, histories, and biographies of many participants have appeared, there has been no serious attempt to compare the development of psychoanalysis in different cultures. While primary sources, both old and newly available, have been searched thoroughly, no one seems to have explored the underlying premises as they have been influenced by factors arising within specific national contexts. It has been assumed that, for better or worse, psychoanalysis as characterized by classical Freudians is all of a piece. This is particularly striking when one reads the secondary sources that I have relied on rather heavily in order to focus on local differences: these provide the clues to the various interpretations, priorities, and emphases historians and psychoanalysts themselves have placed on the original materials.

While working on a previous book, *The Age of Structuralism: Lévi-Strauss to Foucault* (1980), especially on a chapter about the French psychoanalyst Jacques Lacan, I noted that some Parisian Freudians (and not only Lacanians) hold a number of assumptions about Freud and psychoanalysis that their counterparts in, for instance, the New York Psychoanalytic Society would never accept. How was it, I asked myself, that bona fide members of the Société Psychanalytique de Paris and of the International Psychoanalytic Association are as certain of the truth of "their" Freud as New Yorkers are of theirs? After my book was published, some American Freudians asked me on occasion—often at a social event—to explain Lacanian psychoanalysis in a few sentences. Since these questioners were among the most respected members of the profession (and I was a mere sociologist), I speculated further about how and why specific Freudian theories flourish in one country or city and are rejected in another, and to what extent particular institutional conditions help or hinder their dissemination.

My own perspective is not that of a Freudian, nor do I employ the techniques of a psychohistorian. I am a sociologist comparing the courses taken by practicing analysts within the larger domain of psychoanalytic theory and practices. Historians and psychoanalysts have usually had their own interpretations of the past. As a sociologist, however, I do not offer a new psychoanalytic or historical view; rather, I have juxtaposed the most reliable and some of the more provocative histories in order to present a map of the landscape and to examine how psychoanalysis has permeated every aspect of modern culture—at the same time that individuals in psychosomatic medicine, literary and art criticism, political science, and politics have opened up, or restricted, the directions psychoanalysis would take in Austria, France, England, Germany, and the United States. (Given the scope of the project, I had to leave out the rest of the world.)

What seemed to be a terrible handicap during the time I grew up turned out to be helpful in writing this book. Because I was born in Vienna, had some schooling in Belgium before finishing high school in America, and later lived in Milan, I am quadrilingual, and I tend automatically to check translations and to compare cultural customs and phenomena. While studying sociology, I learned somewhat reluctantly to convert this personal habit into a professional advantage. I also observed over the years that people who have not had an analysis tend not to have a feel for the subject, so that my former personal difficulties also turned out to be an asset, at least in dealing with the complex, sometimes slippery issues raised by psychoanalysis.

Given the proliferation of writings in each of the areas psychoanalysis has penetrated and my need for an overview of them all before I attempted any sort of comparison, I relied on advice from a relatively few prominent psychoanalysts, primarily in New York, Cambridge, Frankfurt, Paris, and Vienna; I attended many meetings in New York as well as international gatherings in these cities and in Hamburg, Jerusalem, Montreal, and Boston—where I listened, observed, and spoke to Freudians. Most of all, I depended on the psychoanalytic literature—a literature so rich and immense that I could select only representative works by central figures; I had to forgo mentioning many important people and contributions and had to ignore all the fascinating clinical cases and vignettes.

The psychoanalysts I contacted generously fit me into their schedules and often told me about important theoretical and personal differences within their own institutes. Because of my need for a broad perspective, however, I focused on emerging institutional patterns rather than on evaluations or elaborations of distinctive "successes" and "failures," and I decided to examine the work of "dissidents" only insofar as it affected classical psychoanalysis. Moreover, because many excellent histories of specific organizations are now available (see the reference) and others are being written, I judged that I could afford to forgo conveying some of the flavor of institutional psychoanalysis in order to concentrate on comparing its development in specific contexts and cultures.

I might not have started this project had it not been for a Rockefeller Humanities Fellowship and a sabbatical leave from Rutgers University in 1982–83; and I might have taken longer to finish it had it not been for another sabbatical leave and a National Endowment for the Humanities Fellowship in 1987 and 1988. I am also grateful for resident scholarships at the Maison des Sciences de l'Homme (Paris), the Center for European Studies (Harvard), the Sigmund-Freud-Institut (Frankfurt), and the Sigmund Freud Gesellschaft (Vienna). During these six years, when invited to talk about the progress of the book in both Europe and America, I met hundreds of psychoanalysts, psychologists, historians, and sociologists whose questions and comments were often extremely helpful. Among them I want to thank particularly the Parisians Maria Torok, Alain de Mijolla, Janine Chasseguet-Smirgel, René Major, Piera Castoriadis-Aulagnier, Serge Lebovici, J.-B. Pontalis, Conrad Stein, Joyce McDougall, Françoise Pinaud, and Rachel Rosenblum (who became a close friend). In Germany, I am especially grateful to Margarete Mitscherlich, Alfred Lorenzer, the late Klaus Horn, Dieter Ohlmeier, Mechthild Zeul, F.-W. Eickhoff, and Karola Brede. When Karola Brede's late husband, Helmut Brede, invited me to teach at the Johann-Wolfgang-Goethe Universität in 1984, he provided me with yet another opportunity for research: I met with the analysts around Hermann Argelander and Peter Kutter, and Emma Moersch allowed me to participate in seminars with candidates. And in Frankfurt, the librarians Inge Pabel and Helmut Beireuther were helpful as was David Ross at the Brill Library in New York. Since I did not have the opportunity to visit England, talks during congresses, mostly with Pearl King, Dissona Pines, Edna O'Shaughnessy, and the Orfords pointed me to the most relevant literature by Kleinians and neo-Kleinians. In Vienna, Harald Leupold-Löwenthal opened the door that led to my six-week tenure at Freud's first office—an awesome and unforgettable experience. There I spoke at length to Hans Strotzka, Elizabeth Jäger-Jandl, Elizabeth Brainin, Kitty Schmidt, Peter Schuster, Wolfgang Berner, Eva Laible, Ernst Federn, and Hans Lobner. Sanford Gifford, Reuben Fine, Leo Rangell, Mortimer Ostow, Judith Kestenberg, Arnold Cooper, and Gail Reed sent me reprints when they heard what I was up to, and so did André Haynal, Anna Maria Accerboni, Alain de Mijolla, and Janine Chasseguet-Smirgel. (For reasons of space, I have cited no more than a few contributions by any one person.) My breakfasts with Alan Roland and my lunches with Marion Oliner, both of whose books (on Eastern and French psychoanalysis, respectively) were in progress at the same time as mine, provided encouragement. Peter Loewenberg not only discussed the manuscript with me every time I was on the West Coast but read it carefully and regularly supplied me with information about the lawsuit by American psychologists against the "medicalized" Freudians until the book went to press. Among the people at Yale University Press I want to thank my most competent manuscript editor, Cecile Watters, as well as Gladys Topkis for her encouragement and advice. Special thanks go to William Phillips, who patiently read several drafts and kept admonishing me to put psychoanalytic language into everyday English. I thank them all and hope they will find the book worthy of the interest they showed while it was being written.

Introduction

Every country creates the psychoanalysis it needs, although it does so unconsciously. For national traditions, interests, beliefs, and institutions influence both the general public and its avant garde, by conditioning a kind of collective unconscious. I do not mean to imply that psychoanalysts reflect what has been called "national character" (Inkeles and Levinson, 1954) or "social character" (Fromm, 1942) but only that even the best psychoanalysts, those who manage to cure their patients, inevitably function within the native philosophical assumptions, intellectual controversies, and fashions of their culture. And these ultimately affect not only the professional activities of the analysts but their larger intellectual concerns, such as human freedom, democracy, or war and peace.

This book deals with the roots of these local and national assumptions and with their impact on psychoanalysis itself. I focus also on the variables that tend to affect particular trends and views within psychoanalysis. Thus I trace not only how Freudian ideas evolved, took hold, and led to conflict or harmony but also how they are refracted in the mirror of several different cultures. Who listened to Freud, how his concepts were picked up, and how psychoanalytic therapies were institutionalized not only differed radically in Austria, England, France, Germany, and the United States but determined how psychoanalysis would continue to fare in the entire Western world. I also take account of how psychoanalysis changed these cultures and how such changes were sparked by the emigration of (mostly Jewish or "marginal") Freudians, whose ideas sometimes evolved in response to their new surroundings. Ultimately, my purpose is to show that the meeting of specific personalities and traditions at specific historical moments in various places led to a divergence in Freudian thinking, which no longer allows us to speak of a coherent psychoanalytic doctrine.

By now psychoanalysis has become ubiquitous, so that we tend to forget the tempest it once created, or that both praise and criticism, all along, would reaffirm and alter one or more of its many assumptions. Varying psychoanalytic traditions were created by Freud's loyal disciples, by those who broke with him, and by others who in turn broke with the disciples. Psychological and social issues were constantly being reexamined in the name of Freud, and many of the ideas of the disciples were picked up or dropped to inflate or deflate new claims. After World War II, for example, German psychoanalysts fathered a bevy of "analytic social psychologists" (to root out anti-Semitism and reeducate the population) while the Americans championed "scientific psychoanalysis" (by accumulating empirical data and case studies). It was as natural for the French to rally around the metaphoric qualities of psychoanalysis (whether or not they preferred to follow Jacques Lacan into their "French" unconscious) as it was for the Austrians to stay "on the surface" (by inadvertently turning Freud into a monument to their long-lost empire). And it was as necessary for Sándor Ferenczi's heirs to go into "internal emigration"—that is, to practice clandestinely or not at all—if they wanted to remain in Budapest after 1948 as it was for the Yugoslavs to claim that their "dynamic psychiatry" was more or less Freudian.

The divergent national psychoanalytic societies—all of them claiming direct and privileged descent from Freud—were bound to develop their own theoretical interests, accompanied by heated controversies, even as their roots remained interlocked in the International Psychoanalytic Association. The way the proponents advocated their own clinical views and theoretical positions at biannual meetings and managed to compromise without unduly compromising themselves will be addressed throughout this book.

Undoubtedly, it would be as difficult to pin down the Freudian unconscious—the aim of psychoanalysis—as it would be to learn about the transference, the relationship in which the patient casts the analyst in the perceived role of parent or sibling. The psychoanalysts, of course, always knew that these phenomena could not be fully explored, but they expected to learn more about them in the course of their treatment of patients and by discussing their observations at professional meetings. What they learned through investigating their patients' psychic mechanisms became the core of psychoanalysis rather than the juicier topics reaching the public and the media—such as whether *Wo Es war, soll Ich werden* (where id was there shall be ego) has been mistranslated or given the wrong emphasis, whether Jeffrey M. Masson is a charlatan or a genius, and whether Freud had an affair with his sister-in-law. Still, how, where, and when particular issues tend to surface are themselves indicative of current intellectual preoccupations in various cultures. They tell us more about the societies that foster these debates than about psychoanalysis, although ultimately the psychoanalysts are expected to, and do, relate to the interests of their publics.

As it is, each country (and each city) produced its specific cacophony of psychoanalytic discourse, its specific rereading of the history, specific emphases, interpretations, and controversies. These, in turn, relied upon elaborations following the thoughts of one or more favorite "sons" or "daughters," whose ideas would ebb and flow in line with contemporary concerns. But whether in its linguistically oriented French version, in its critical-theoretical German problematic, or in its Anglo-Saxon "scientism," psychoanalysts would question old orthodoxies and in the process end up with new ones. And the more established they had become, the more valiantly they would defend their turf. Even Jacques Lacan did so after having created a new school, or a succession of schools, in order to overcome what he called the deadening aspects of professionalism. So, as Freud's ideas increasingly flooded the Western world, the psychoanalysts' secessions and splits became the substance of psychoanalytic history. The analysts themselves could never agree on whether their disagreements resulted from legitimate theoretical differences or from subjective factors rooted in unconscious motives, and outsiders rarely gave them the benefit of the doubt.

My comparative perspective focuses on how psychoanalysis emerged and took hold and on the so-called determinants of group-shaping experience and knowledge.[1] The Freudian "group," however, was both national and international, so that allegiances often would shift. These shifts occurred from the very start, when analysts first "diagnosed" their opponents' neuroses in relation to particular cultural assumptions. To some extent, this practice was justified, as the psychoanalysts had to investigate how their patients' unconscious was formed or inhibited by society—by regressive regimes or by prevalent religious beliefs. This also explains the perennial attempts to integrate Freudian and Marxist tenets in the expectation of making good on the liberating promises of both. Even global views of history as dominated by breaks or by continuity or the vision of an ideal society could be explained by their proponents' personalities, while themselves reflecting temporal, local, or organizational interests, which these proponents often have overlooked or underestimated. In principle, I am sympathetic to the larger psychoanalytic aims, but I am as dubious that they will bring more than partial insights as Freud was at the end of his life. For no matter how many clinical break-throughs the psychoanalysts may make, much more besides a knowledge of individuals' unconscious processes will be needed to channel human aggres-sion and, in general, bring about a good society.

From the beginning, to grow or not to grow at the expense of theoretical purity was a central issue that sometimes distorted the nature of psycho-analysis.[2] Psychoanalysts, who inevitably had to concentrate on specific as-pects of psychoanalysis, could legitimately quote Freud to justify whatever facet or theoretical path they chose to pursue. Yet because the Americans, for instance, tended to generalize from their own immediate world, they would be aghast when French psychoanalysts (not only Lacanians) began to ques-tion their scientific stance or when some of the Germans criticized their bourgeois bias. In principle, many of the French would distance themselves from stressing the scientific aspects of psychoanalysis and the resulting jar-gon; the English would be taken up by the split between Kleinians and Freudians; and many Germans would fall back on Freud's sociological com-mentaries in order to revamp the earlier Freudo-Marxisms. All these efforts, of course, emphasize particular partial ideas of Freud's, revise or combine them with others, and, to a greater or lesser degree, lean on Austrian nostalgia.

The first part of this book, comprising four chapters, focuses on the re-ception of psychoanalysis, its early history, its basic ideas, and their applica-tions before 1945. Given the many conflicting interpretations of fin-de-siècle Vienna, Weimar Berlin, and the biographies of Freud and the early Freud-ians, I use these in order to examine how the emphasis on one idea or another, by historians and analysts, itself advances current thinking about psycho-analysis and its practices—practices responding to specific ideologies, philoso-phies, and social concerns. I also show how Freud's wish for an international association ended up by imposing impractical or even counterproductive rules on national associations and inevitably caused friction between and within them and that these frictions were exacerbated when psychoanalysts could not separate institutional, intellectual, and emotional concerns.

The second part of the book addresses psychoanalytic applications, and specifically the elaborations of psychoanalytic concepts in response to intel-lectual and political issues within each milieu. Chapter 5 deals with psychosomatic medicine—the original locus of Freud's discoveries—and its institutionalization within the various medical establishments. Chapter 6 examines the early uses of psychoanalysis in pedagogy, in Germany and Austria, and their misuses by the Nazi "therapists" during the Second World War. This chapter also discusses how psychoanalysis was used to help reeducate the entire German population and the general replacement of psychoanalytic pedagogy by the study of children and then of adolescents. Chapter 7 explores Freudian views on women and feminist views on Freud—from the early disagreements with Freud by such disciples as Karen Horney and Helene Deutsch to recent theories. Here, cross-cultural influences, particularly among France, England, and the United States, have been especially strong.

Chapter 8 analyzes the psychoanalysts' preoccupations with literary works and their authors. Following Freud, many psychoanalysts continued to study specific artists and writers in relation to their creations, although others considered such activities peripheral. The psychoanalytic interpretations of art and literature in the various countries and their polemical differences are perceived as reflecting temporal intellectual concerns—with the culture of narcissism, conceptualizations of the self, and theories of deconstruction.

The third part of the book looks at postwar psychoanalysis. After the Second World War, when the majority of European analysts had become "Anglo-Saxon," psychoanalytic theories and practices began to diverge more and more. Now, the so-called medicalization of psychoanalysis, which had won out over Freud's preference for the acceptance of lay analysis, became a bone of contention among German psychologists. At the same time it benefited nonanalytically trained psychiatrists everywhere. In England medicalization was more or less contained, but in America it helped limit access to psychoanalysis to the middle classes. German analysts, seeking the best of both worlds, have tended to attack it and in the process have revived the discussions among the early Viennese socialists and the Berlin society. (Psychoanalysis for the working class, delinquents, and marginal figures in society was a central issue in the polemics surrounding Freud's break with Alfred Adler.)

In chapter 9, the focus is on the problems facing the international organization after 1945. By then the so-called adaptive components of ego psychology had caught on in America, and in England they had found their echo in Anna Freud's theories of ego defenses. It was at this time that the controversy between Anna Freud and Melanie Klein and their institutional and intellectual rivalry for succession reached a climax. Increasingly, the "generation of the sons," led by two "daughters," was carried away by idealistic promises, rivalries, political priorities, and careerism—always in the name of

Freud. Had the Anglo-Saxons not dominated the International Psychoanalytic Association, for instance, French psychoanalysis, which in part rejected ego psychology or at least its required training period for candidates, might have gone in a different direction. As it is, we know that in America non-Freudian and neo-Freudian therapies co-opted certain popular ideas while the somewhat stricter Freudians turned steadily more orthodox, and that in France, classical analysts, many of whom had philosophical backgrounds, kept an eye on the Lacanian rereading they rejected. In Germany, psychoanalysis caught on after the treatment of mental and psychosomatic illness by psychoanalysts became reimbursable under the mandated health insurance system.

The impact of the Freudians' evolving ideas and therapies on the culture at large is explored in chapter 10, and chapter 11 provides an overview of the theoretical positions that are the bedrock of the Freudians' disagreements and of their factionalism. Chapter 12 focuses on the psychoanalysts' views of, and connections to, politics and notes the penetration of psychoanalysis into every aspect of the modern mind. By pointing to its impact on medicine, on the universities, and on the general culture—in response to new formulations, to political givens, and to the confusions caused by translations—it is possible to undercut preconceived notions and yet indicate that psychoanalysis has lived up to cultural peculiarities. Its French incarnation has an imaginative quality, uses elegant language, and is short on footnotes and indexes; its German counterpart is heavy, convoluted, and thoroughly documented; and its Anglo-Saxon branch is personality-oriented and tends toward scientific jargon. These are some of the issues I summarize in the conclusion.

Psychoanalytic concepts, of course, did migrate and in the process were transformed. They "remigrated" when former Europeans came to the United States from South America and brought along Kleinian syntheses, or when Lacanian ideas were adopted by American feminists and literary theorists. Thus psychoanalysis became internationalized when encouraging specific adaptations and reconceptualizations while, at particular moments, supporting local and ideological priorities. These priorities, in turn, depended upon each society's stage of development. And ultimately psychoanalysis did not do away with the intellectual habits of the modern world, as Freud in some euphoric moments thought it might.

When Freud linked personality and cultural factors, he combined his insights with a dynamism none of his followers possessed. After the Second World War, only two, in their own fashion, even came close: Alexander

Mitscherlich in Germany and Jacques Lacan in France. Both were charismatic figures, which meant that their leadership engendered some sort of religious feelings. The extent to which such charisma interfered with or bolstered the psychoanalytic transference again transformed a cultural question into a therapeutic one. This, in turn, leads us to wonder to what extent the upsurge of analysis in Germany and France was caused by these "great men," and whether the more pedestrian quality of American psychoanalysis in recent years can be ascribed to the absence of visionary individuals or to the fact that it had entered the mainstream.

Clearly, there were and are too many cultural and institutional variables to draw narrow or categorical conclusions. The radical profundity of Freud's thought, its intimate roots in his own analysis, in his Jewishness, and in fin-de-siècle Vienna, legitimate the many interpretations and reevaluations. That is why Freud's correspondence, gradually being released, and the letters and diaries of his disciples deserve the enormous attention they are receiving: in fact, the fertility and promises of Freud's ideas have been reaffirmed by the revelations of the archives throughout the West. Still, the controversies are bound to multiply as we question whether Anna Freud, for instance, withheld passages from the Fliess letters, or entire letters, to protect her father, her own theories, or the movement; whether Maria Torok (1984) is correct in maintaining that Freud took some of his ideas from Sándor Ferenczi; or whether Manes Sperber is justified in believing that some of Freud's concepts were borrowed from Adler. Whatever the final verdicts, they not only might uncover these and other skeletons but will reflect national and cultural priorities. Looking at some of these priorities comparatively reveals local and institutional biases and highlights both the enormous advances and the blind spots of the different theoretical constructs explaining the human unconscious.

In 1908, Ferenczi divided psychoanalysis into the era of Freud's isolation and discoveries, the era of the pioneers' cooperation, and the coming era of organization. He could not know the consequences of his farsighted prediction. I would add a fourth one, the current era of the reevaluations of Freudiana by academics and Freudians. Some of them provide interesting tidbits; others are on their way to creating as tedious a specialty as Marxist studies; and yet others are rewriting psychoanalytic history, thereby challenging Freudian theory and therapy. Yet despite these theoretical flights, psychoanalysts are actually healing patients and gaining new clinical insights. The reports of their cases are more plausible than their generalizations about culture—which a hostile press is always eager to tear apart.

Unfortunately, in a book painted with as broad a brush as this one, I cannot convey even the flavor of any of the case studies. But they often demonstrate the many ways in which the unconscious may determine human behavior. What the Freudians learn from their patients, they translate into clinical theories, which, ironically, continue to contribute not only to psychoanalysis but to many of the popular therapies denouncing Freud.

Part One

PSYCHOANALYSIS
BEFORE 1945

Chapter 1

The Reception of Freud's Theories

The history of psychoanalysis presents unique problems, for not only are psychoanalysts likely to be subject to the customary theoretical biases of other social scientists, but their views of the past are shaped to a large extent by the kind of psychoanalysis they practice. Thus classical Freudians tend to follow Ernest Jones, who, as one of Freud's earliest disciples, was the standard-bearer of Freud's own "On the History of the Psychoanalytic Movement" (1914d). Jones maintained that psychoanalysis was born in 1900 with the publication of *The Interpretation of Dreams* and that Freud's earlier works, such as the "Studies on Hysteria" (1893) and the *Project for a Scientific Psychology* (1895)—written during the "period of gestation"—led up to it. He argued that psychoanalysis would have had more immediate impact if the scientific journals had not waited so long before reviewing the *Interpretation* (Jones, 1953–57, 1:360–61). Jones, of course, based his contention on Freud's own recollections of his isolation and loneliness (1914d) before the publication of the *Three Essays on the Theory of Sexuality* (1905).

Hannah S. Decker's (1977) investigations, however, support skeptics such as Henry Ellenberger, who maintains that Freud was not as "settled down . . . on [his] desert island" during these years as he claimed because he already was "acquiring a reputation" (1970, pp. 445–47). And Frank J. Sulloway, with a bit of irony, writes that Freud's "splendid isolation" had been brief (1979, pp. 484–89). But Ellenberger had to inflate the importance of the period before 1900 in order to demonstrate that Freud had been no more than a link in the chain of dynamic psychiatry, and Sulloway was seeking to establish Freud's credentials as a "crypto-biologist" who had never given up on physiology.

French traditions for the most part have not led to speculation about Freud's alleged isolation. The French have been more interested in their own history of psychoanalysis and have referred to Ellenberger's and Sulloway's theses only for support of specific views about "American" ego psychology, whose ascendancy, some of the French Freudians have argued, has drawn attention away from Freud's larger contributions and has transformed his art into pseudoscience. They have focused on the prepsychoanalytic period to investigate the relationships between Freud and the disciples or to emphasize the ideas he picked up from Jean-Martin Charcot, a neurologist and famous teacher at the Salpêtrière, and Hippolyte Bernheim, a professor of internal medicine who used hypnosis. Or they have examined the impact of Paris on the young Freud. The Austrians, on the other hand, have continued to boost the influence of fin-de-siècle Vienna, that intellectual hothouse which had produced such figures as R. von Krafft-Ebing and Morris Benedikt, whose explorations of the links between hysteria and sexuality had preceded Freud's; and they have underplayed Freud's feelings of isolation and his ambivalence toward Austria. Some Germans, more inclined to corroborate Freud's loneliness, have cataloged the details surrounding specific slights and the motives behind them to support the isolationist theme. The Londoners have accepted Jones's version, although most Kleinians among them have ignored Freud's history altogether. In fact, Freud was not as isolated and embattled as some Freudians claim, nor was he overly popular.[1]

Freudians generally are committed to what Sulloway calls the hero myth and the history of the perilous journey. Even Freud's detractors must admit that he was a pioneer who won out against overwhelming odds. Still, each country has its own story to tell. The loyalty of German Freudians has led them to emphasize the glories of the Berlin organization and its everlasting influences on training; the French point to the prominence and reputation of their psychiatric and philosophic traditions; the Viennese glorify the pioneers' socialist aims; the Hungarians stress Freud's special devotion to Sándor Ferenczi and his hope that his daughter Anna would marry him; and the Italians regret the influence of Catholicism (and later of fascism), which kept psychoanalysis at bay. Clearly, all these approaches are culture-bound. Psychoanalytic history cannot be as value-free as the history of mathematics or of physics, if only because psychoanalysis ipso facto incorporates cultural and personal history, as well as interpretation which affects the writing of this history. Cultural, professional, and personal attitudes color both friendly and hostile histories and biographies. And because these investigations also contain notions borrowed from psychoanalysis, the difficulties of arriving at some kind of objectivity are compounded.[2]

The reception of Freud's new psychology itself reflected the assumptions of the time. According to the Freudians, *The Interpretation of Dreams* (1900) was being ignored by the "major technical medical weeklies" because of ingrained mores and entrenched beliefs (Brodthage and Hoffmann, 1981, pp. 135–47). But Ellenberger points to enthusiastic reviews in the popular press (1970, pp. 783–84). Freud apparently was upset by attacks from psychologists by whom he had expected to be praised. It was a long time before he distanced himself enough to attribute "misperceptions" to the fact that psychoanalysis has three "missions"—the investigation of mental processes, the treatment of neurotic disturbances, and the construction of general psychological insights (*S.E.*, 1:145–57). But Freud also played down the extent to which his frequent reconceptualizations, which in part were a result of new knowledge about his own complex personality, would make for further misperceptions.

Because psychoanalysis owed so much to Freud's self-analysis, his person, his family background, and his early relationships are fair game for interpretation. This is why Ellenberger, for instance, by emphasizing the period between 1894 and 1900 as the time of gestation and of Freud's "creative illness"—an illness following a period fraught with feelings of isolation and depression, with neurotic and psychosomatic symptoms—could hold that what came after the *Interpretation* were merely addenda. But Freudians, who also exaggerate the master's suffering, have argued that this ordeal transformed him because he "conquered" his psyche and thereby discovered the roots of the unconscious. For them, the *Interpretation* is the cornerstone for an unending succession of psychoanalytic discoveries.

Perhaps the clue to this period is Freud's relationship to Wilhelm Fliess. Freudians tend to play down Fliess's role as Freud's mentor (he himself nearly expunged Fliess from the record) and point to the foolishness of Fliess's beliefs that unconscious psychological mechanisms manifest themselves in seven- or twenty-eight-day cycles and that psychosomatic symptoms often are centered in the nose. Until the recent publication of the complete letters of Freud to Fliess (Masson, 1985), they rarely acknowledged how much power Fliess had over him. But Ellenberger's thesis that Freud was no more than a long moment in the history of dynamic psychiatry did get a boost from his emphasis on the Freud-Fliess connection. And the release of Freud's letters (Fliess's have been destroyed) as the first record of a transference—and at that the transference that was to become the prototype for all psychoanalyses—legitimately sparked reevaluations of Freud's contributions and his relation to his disciples.[3]

Inevitably, new interpretations, demystifications, and exigeses will be determined by specific traditions: in France these may serve, once more, to demonstrate that psychoanalysis is not as "scientific" as the Americans like to think and that Freud had learned more from F. A. Mesmer or A. A. Liébeault than he ever acknowledged in his works on hysteria (Roussillon, 1984, p. 1368). In the German-speaking countries, some scholars will search for clues to the "excessive" adaptivity of psychoanalysis; others will find evidence to prove the hostility of Freud's medical contemporaries; and still others may assign more importance to Freud's humanistic inquiries. On the other hand, the renewed interest in the origins of psychoanalysis has already inspired international and interdisciplinary meetings which ultimately may help transcend the national prejudices and ideological gaps that most Freudians have tried to ignore.[4] (This is more likely to occur in the academy, where such cooperation currently is encouraged, than in psychoanalytic institutes, where the emphasis is on specific therapeutic practices.)

As the Freudians were learning more and more about psychological ambivalence, they were not always able to separate psychoanalytic "science" from gossip. This is why the records of the early days are a treasure trove for historians, enabling them to check faulty reconstructions and sort out confusions and passions. But we cannot possibly mediate between prejudices in an evenhanded fashion since there is no final "psychoanalytic truth." Interpretations based on speculation cannot be given the same weight as historical research that is aware of the pitfalls of reminiscence or parti pris biases.[5] And since psychoanalysis aims to view subjectivity objectively, it is not surprising that the battle over its past rages on. Each faction believes that the group that controls this past will control its future.

Freud and the Viennese

Both Freud's followers and his detractors have had trouble separating his expectations from the actual situation—that is, from professional ambition and personal rivalries—and in unraveling his ambivalence toward his anti-Semitic surroundings and his professors (Theodor Meynert, Ernst Brücke,

Hermann Nothnagel, and his mentor Josef Breuer). In the battles between supporters and detractors, their positions on whether or not the disciples exaggerated Viennese anti-Semitism and anti-intellectualism and whether or not sexuality and parent-child relations were taboo subjects also are central.[6]

The salience of Freud's Jewishness continues to be a point of contention among historians. Certainly he was troubled by his own ambivalence as well as by anti-Semitism and resented the negative impact on his career. He particularly objected to having psychoanalysis called a Jewish science, for such a label, in the Viennese ambience, was bound to harm the movement and militate against its growth. But in fact, all seventeen of the first disciples, between 1902 and 1906, were Jewish, so Freud was especially pleased when Carl Jung, a Christian, not only became a psychoanalyst but started a group at the Burghölzli clinic in Zurich. (Later, Ernest Jones and several other Anglo-Saxons became part of the movement.) He reportedly was embarrassed by Otto Rank's "Jewish" looks, which were thought to confirm the "Jewishness" of psychoanalysis. Yet in 1930, in a letter to A. A. Roback, an American Yiddishist and psychologist, Freud stated that not only had he not had a Jewish education but he regretted this lack (E. L. Freud, 1960, pp. 393–94), and he wrote to Marie Bonaparte in 1926, after B'nai B'rith had honored him on his seventieth birthday, that, contrary to some rumors, he had never denied being Jewish (p. 367). According to the historian Dennis B. Klein (1981), the many contradictory reports about Freud's attitudes to his Jewishness reflect the biases and (conscious or unconscious) aims of revisionist historians, narrow-minded theologians, categorizing sociologists, apologetic assimilationists, and belligerent Judaists. Klein rather credibly showed that the attitudes of Freud and his contemporaries originated in the short-lived period of liberalism between 1860 and 1880, which had spawned extremely open political polemics and intellectual and artistic excitement, and that although reactionaries cut it short they could not destroy its progressive ideas. Freud, who belonged to this German culture as well as to the Jewish one, had naturally incorporated all the conflicts and ambivalences such a dual "allegiance" was bound to foster. Klein, by exposing the inherent contradictions between being Austrian and being Jewish and by mediating between the opposing "assimilationist and dissimilationist reconstructions," expected to get rid of the various "fictional" reconstructions.[7]

Klein did not blame Freud's ambivalence on his psyche but compared him to his Jewish compatriots who alternately acknowledged and ignored their religion: they dealt with anti-Semitism in accordance with their status, circumstances, political preference, and provocations. Freud's reactions, of course, were more consequential than those of his peers since they were being incorporated into psychoanalysis. Most recently, Peter Gay (1987) has argued convincingly that psychoanalysis could not have been conceived by anyone but an atheist and that Freud's secular Judaism and his status as an outsider allowed him to talk of sexuality more boldly than an insider could have done.

In this context, Freudians often cite Freud's recollection of a childhood experience and its reappearance in one of his dreams. At the age of ten or twelve, he recalled in "Material and Sources of Dreams," he was walking with his father, and Jacob Freud, wishing to indicate to his son how much better things had gotten for the Jews, particularly in Vienna, told Freud about an incident in Galicia, when a gentile who had come toward him had knocked his hat into the gutter and yelled at him to get off the pavement. "What did you do?" Sigmund asked his father indignantly. "I stepped into the gutter and picked up my cap," Jacob replied calmly, while Freud compared him unfavorably to Hannibal's father, who had made his son swear that he would take revenge on the Romans (Brill, 1938, p. 260).

Some (including Freud) considered this incident and its reappearance in a dream during the self-analysis as central to Freud's disillusion with his father. Like Freud himself, they connected it to his (fantasy) identification with the Semitic warrior-king Hannibal, who had fought against the power of the Catholic church, and to his desire to go to Rome. The more eclectic Freudians linked it to his repeated psychoanalytic investigations of Moses. But few of the many inquiries into Freud's delicate relationship to Judaism have addressed the fact that anti-Semitism was a daily reality he had to live with—whatever his unconscious reactions might have been. No one, of course, would think of asking questions about the gentileness of Freud's contemporaries Brücke, Meynert, or Charcot, who did, after all, live in a gentile world. Yet Freud as well as his disciples not only had to investigate the weight of conscious and unconscious guilt and denial about the Jewish past and about assimilation and accommodation but also had to live with anti-Semitism and with the politics in which it was embedded.

Freud's pessimism, his customary depression upon returning from abroad, and his inertia about leaving Vienna before the Anschluss in 1938 are usually said to have been rooted in his unconscious. Although such interpretations certainly are valid because Freud was Freud, too little attention has been paid to the fact that every Viennese Jew of his class felt ambivalent and had internalized the Austro-German culture along with its anti-Semitism. (Vienna was home; even under the most auspicious circumstances emigration would entail insecurity and anxiety.) Thus they were bound to believe that assimilation in dress, speech, and manner and "acting like a gentile" would reflect positively on all Jews and would bring about more general and genuine acceptance and tolerance by the Viennese. All in all, personal and professional factors were confused by everyone, so that the acceptance of Freud's person and of psychoanalysis remained as inseparable as the two sides of a coin.

Freud's medical colleagues—whose careerist and scientific prejudices inevitably mirrored some of the prevalent anti-Semitism, which went hand in hand with chauvinism—multiplied the ambiguities. They automatically questioned the French connections that Freud highlighted and his enthusiasm for Charcot's teachings. To what extent was Meynert rejecting the French rather than the sexual nexus when, on the occasion of Freud's lecture on male hysteria before the Vienna Society of Physicians in 1886, he is said to have noted that Vienna did not produce cases of the sort Charcot had treated in Paris?[8] And to what extent did this provincial attitude exacerbate Freud's ambivalence toward Vienna?

Jones for the most part underestimated Viennese anti-Semitism before the 1930s. It is unclear whether he did so because he was gentile, because he was diplomatic, or because he was too far away to understand. Moreover, the Freudians by then were routinely examining every slight as a source of psychic resistance, jealousy, or affective defenses. This habit allegedly made Freud's colleagues as suspicious as did his reluctance to belong to an "acceptable" medical specialty. But subsequent events proved Freud to have been correct: most Austrians welcomed the Nazis more readily than the Germans had and soon outdid them in committing anti-Semitic acts. And by now it has been amply documented that anti-Semitism *did* play a role in holding up the promotion by the ministry that would determine Freud's status, earning power, and general reputation.[9] In sum, objective conditions legitimated Freud's "double identity," as a Viennese and a Jew. And this would allow commentators to stress whichever identity they preferred and to substantiate whatever judgment of psychoanalysis they already held.

Most historians agree that the Viennese were hostile to psychoanalysis and that this hostility was part of a pervasive and often unexpressed anti-Semitism. Psychoanalysis was a threat to bourgeois values. Undoubtedly, general suspicions of Jews and foreigners grew as the Austro-Hungarian Empire was being dismantled (again, by foreigners), and these events further contributed to the Austrians' rejection of psychoanalysis. Until recently the Austrians did not even bother with psychoanalytic history, and when they did, they seemed motivated more by patriotism and nostalgia than by an interest in psychoanalysis itself.[10] But nowhere else had the psychoanalytic critique of creed and country applied so directly, nor had other environments allegedly produced neuroses as dramatic (and as treatable by psychoanalysis) as Vienna. Thus both Freudians and anti-Freudians agreed with Freud's remark to a tax collector that his reputation began only beyond the Austrian borders. His fame, in fact, was born in America, and from there was re-exported to Europe.

The Reception in German-speaking Territories

Hostility to psychoanalysis in German-language areas came from psychologists, sociologists, theologians, and philosophers, in addition to psychiatrists. They ignored or dismissed psychoanalysis as unscientific and immoral or as undermining Christian ethics. According to Johannes Cremerius (1981a), professor of psychosomatic medicine and psychotherapy, the members of these more or less entrenched academic disciplines felt threatened. Neither Max Weber nor Leopold von Wiese tried to apply psychoanalysis to enrich his own sociological theory—respectively, *verstehende Soziologie* and *Beziehungslehre*.[11] But in citing all the familiar justifications for resistance to psychoanalysis—its acceptance of sexuality, masturbation, and premarital sex, its threats to persons "participating" in the oedipal triangle and to male authority—Cremerius did not pay much attention to the fact that Freud's contemporaries, in discrediting psychoanalysis as tantamount to the paranoid babble of old wives' tales, as masturbation of the soul, or as a product of the talmudic imagination only madmen and fanatics could practice (p. 9), were protecting the status quo. Decker (1977), however, pointed to the other side: the favorable appraisals and mixed reactions. Focusing on physicians who tried to practice psychoanalysis, she chided Freud for his reluctance to disseminate his ideas to *all* German-speaking psychiatrists and defended these psychiatrists by pointing out that they had to function within a milieu that disdained "philosophic" medicine and felt threatened by "theatrical" demonstrations such as Charcot's. So whereas Cremerius indicted the German academics' suspiciousness of Freud, Decker was inclined to excuse them. By looking at the larger German milieu rather than just the professional one, she explained why so many German doctors, along with their compatriots, continued to believe, for instance, in "the superiority of their own genes over French ones" (p. 56) or in French decadence.

Essentially, Cremerius, though exploring early attitudes toward psychoanalysis, also wanted to find out whether these were the same attitudes that later had allowed the Holocaust. He separated the early reception by the various disciplines—sociology, psychology, theology, and philosophy—but did not distinguish among Austria, Germany, and Switzerland in what occurred.

The sociologist Hans-Dieter Brauns (1981), who examined the political biases and religious affiliations of prominent sociologists at the turn of the century, found that ethnologists had given so much attention to *Totem and Taboo* (*S.E.*, 13:1–162) that some sociologists had to pay heed. But most of them judged Freud's hypothesis about human origins implausible: he had not substantiated how the memory of this primordial event—the killing of the father by his sons—is retained in the human unconscious and then surfaces in neurotic or mob behavior. Yet because the ideas of Darwin and their application to anthropology by J. J. Atkinson were in vogue and were quoted by Freud, it was thought that Freud had furnished still another inductive theory about human origins.[12]

According to Brauns, only one sociologist, F. Müller-Lyer, wrote in a psychoanalytic vein, but all he did was to state that his own results resembled Freud's (1981, pp. 40–41). Brauns could not say why Müller-Lyer's explanations went no further.[13] He also did not attribute the relative "popularity" of Freud's *Group Psychology and the Analysis of the Ego* (1921; *Massenpsychologie und Ich-Analyse*) to its timing: this work appeared at a moment when public discussions of the emotional relationship between masses and their leaders were at a peak.[14] Still, Robert Michels, the political theorist and activist, took note of Freud, although he misconstrued the intent of *Group Psychology* by equating the concept of libido with erotism and sexuality (Brauns, 1981, pp. 60–63). The sociologist Werner Sombart, on the other hand, argued that this work was unclear and thus decided to ignore the rest of Freud's ideas (pp. 58–59); Theodor Geiger, another sociologist, acknowledged his own skepticism and distance by arguing that it is permissible to be open to suggestivity but not to suggestion (pp. 75–76). All in all, by the mid-1920s, the sociologists had dropped Freud's mass psychology. Ultimately, Brauns concluded, most of them dismissed Freud without ever having read him. They felt threatened by the idea that fantasy is responsible for the construction of reality. Instead of judging their neglect as symptomatic of the "irrational barrier against psychoanalysis" (pp. 50–54), I would maintain that the sociologists, who had been fighting the historicists, were concerned primarily with establishing themselves as a scholarly discipline, and psychoanalysis was even less scientific than sociology itself. Also, both sociology and psychoanalysis were trying to gain a modicum of institutional power and professional turf.

Psychoanalysis fared no better in relation to German psychology (Brodthage and Hoffmann, 1981, pp. 135–253). Around 1900, many universities had established chairs in psychology (or in psychology and philosophy). Psychologists either published on narrow topics in their own professional journals or addressed the larger psychological questions of humanity in the general press. Their approaches originated in philosophy (that is, the verstehende psychology of Wilhelm Dilthey, E. Spranger, or Ludwig Klages) or in physiology (the natural-scientific, "nomothetical" models of Gustav Theodor Fechner, Wilhelm Wundt, or Ernst Mach). But this division often was fudged since some psychologists added various twists to their inquiries. They competed with one another, but they also wanted to avoid the bad reputation that had befallen philosophy for being speculative (p. 141). Hoping to establish their subject as a science, the psychologists were too busy fighting the disintegration of their discipline to bother with psychoanalysis. (Psychological publications then were frequently changing direction, along with their names and editors.) They kept their distance and objected to Freud's claim that psychoanalysis was yet another branch of psychology.

Basically, psychology and psychoanalysis developed on parallel tracks. Psychologists of all denominations had intellectual origins different from those of psychoanalysts; they spoke another language, embraced other premises, and defended other interests. Although they did not directly compete with psychoanalysts for institutional positions, the psychologists were on the defensive when the two groups eventually engaged in dialogue. This was true, for instance, in the *Zeitschrift für Psychologie*, which, unlike the *Psychologische Forschung* and the *Psychologische Studien*, periodicals that ignored Freud entirely, had reviewed him scathingly as early as 1900. (Psychology textbooks also ignored him.) Even the authors who had read Freud carefully called psychoanalysis stubborn, unscientific, and subject to fantasies about repression.

There were very few reviews of *The Interpretation of Dreams* (1900) in the serious psychological journals before 1910 (Cremerius, 1981, p. 158), and these few were nasty: the theory was wrong, unacceptable, not scientifically proven. Many psychologists followed Wilhelm Wundt's "nonanalytic" *Völkerpsychologie* to show that psychoanalysis could not prove its claims and compared it to the old dream mysticism. Others thought that anyone taken in by psychoanalysis was prone to hysteria and sexual pathology (Brodthage and Hoffmann, 1981, p. 154). The friendliest psychologists credited Freud for his "clear and illuminating presentation of dreams"—the "watchman of sleep." Nevertheless, they concurred that his notion of the unconscious was unscientific and that therefore psychoanalysis was "unworthy of rebuttal" (p. 158).

The *Three Essays on the Theory of Sexuality* (1905) fared even worse than the *Interpretation*, and *The Psychopathology of Everyday Life* (1901) was barely mentioned: psychologists rejected childhood sexuality as pure speculation or as a sickness (Brodthage and Hoffmann, 1981, p. 158). One of them argued that the subject of sexuality was to be avoided at all costs; another suggested that psychologists should study Freud but had better warn parents against him; and another criticized him for focusing on content rather than form—that is, on Gestalt (pp. 158–64). Ludwig Klages, although claiming to respect Freud, found that the "confessional elements" of psychoanalysis were ineffectual and had added little to the knowledge of hysteria. Wilhelm Stern considered psychoanalysis to be a disease that had emanated from Vienna and Zurich; it was being spread by Freudians "lacking every true disciplinary competence" (p. 158). Altogether, the psychologists agreed to reject Freud's method along with the idea of childhood sexuality. They did not even believe that he had cured "Little Hans."

When during the 1920s the psychologists started to realize that psychoanalysis was more than a flash in the pan, they began to dispute its claims rather than merely write two-line dismissals. In the early 1930s they were surprised that psychoanalysis had been thriving between 1900 and 1933 while consensus about psychology was vanishing and its general appeal fading. Indeed, they thought the success of psychoanalysis was unjustified (Brodthage and Hoffmann, 1981, p. 176). Essentially, psychologists and psychoanalysts had begun by competing for the same "truths," but by the time the Nazis took over, they were already competing for some of the same university positions.

According to the philosopher Carl Eduard Scheidt, his colleagues did not accept psychoanalysis either. This was due to prevalent ideologies on both the right and the left, to the challenge psychoanalysis presented to accepted paradigms, and to the dominant discussions between those who advocated naturalism and those who supported idealism. These disagreements about the roots of cultural conditions and the resulting subsumption of psychoanalysis under naturalism meant that the idealistically oriented circles which were controlling "school philosophy"—that is, what students would be taught—could not allow a favorable reception of psychoanalysis. The critiques surrounding Freud's cultural contributions especially kept reiterating that psychoanalysis is based on biological monism, which denies the specificity of mind (*Geist*) and culture and reduces them to biological drives. It was not until 1945 that German philosophers opened up to the psychoanalysts' empirical findings and started to address them. Scheidt noted that this change led to a permanent "identity crisis" of philosophy itself (1986, pp. 7–13).

The theologians, who had been losing ground to scientists since the beginning of modernity, discarded psychoanalysis as antithetical to religion. Had it not been for Father Oskar Pfister, a liberal Protestant Swiss, they might not even have bothered to reject it as a natural science, for the division of spheres into natural and spiritual put psychoanalysis outside their purview. But Pfister tried to persuade his colleagues that precisely because psychoanalysis was a science, it was worth learning about and co-opting. Since psychoanalysts and theologians controlled the formation of sublimation, he argued, religious morals and psychological complexes were cut from the same cloth. He urged theologians to accept psychoanalysts, to cooperate with them and discard their own moral prejudices. By adapting psychoanalysis and especially the transference, Pfister also discredited Catholicism (Scharfenberg, 1981, p. 264). Now, he attacked priestly celibacy and sexual abstinence as furthering maximal repression of natural instincts. He thereby elevated Protestantism: it "had anticipated psychoanalysis by getting rid of celibacy and monkhood" and thus "already had· *put the instincts to primary use* through sublimation." Pfister "substantiated" this claim by paralleling the irrational demands parishioners make on their priests with those patients make on their analysts and those the early Christians had made on Jesus. He even argued that psychoanalytically trained theologians would make better psychoanalysts than doctors—an argument one still hears today.

In Jesus' day, Pfister said, Jews had suffered from a nationally induced compulsion neurosis because Mosaic law had demanded the massive repression of sexual instincts. But by advocating the direct love of God, Jesus had sublimated his own command for repression and liberated Eros. Hence he had overcome the fear deriving from repressed libido. Those of his followers who had not yet seen the light, Pfister continued, could get rid of their defenses against love with the help of psychoanalysis (Scharfenberg, 1981, p. 269). Nevertheless, he insisted that psychoanalysis stood above religion: religion "cannot be analyzed." Compulsion and coarse sexualization are neurotic distortions and turn into "religion" only after love (with the help of religion) has helped the individual overcome fear. True religion is progressive. When Freud sent him *The Future of an Illusion*, in 1927, Pfister criticized it as "populist" and as pitting psychoanalysis against hallucinatory wishes. But he continued to champion psychoanalytic transference as a useful tool.

Although Pfister kept reiterating that belief in God incorporates morality, humanism, and knowledge and that psychoanalysis could enhance the development of each of these, he did not convince other theologians. Pfister remained almost alone in believing that psychoanalysis was not too "quick in absolving people of their sins" (Scharfenberg, 1981, pp. 256–58). In defense of intransigent theologians, some historians have held that in the Weimar Republic they needed to bolster their followers' identities to enable them to stand up against totalitarian influences, particularly fascism. But the growing political liberalism had been hostile to all religion, and psychoanalysis threatened the fiber of religion along with the theologians' status. They defended their credos, were afraid to examine heresies, and considered the theory of sexuality dangerous. They fought both the relativization of norms and values and the notion of repressed impulses. So German theologians held firm, arguing that dream analysis would require more knowledge of the human psyche than they possessed and might propel priests into precarious contact with the female members of their churches. They leaned more toward Jung's mysticism (Scharfenberg, 1981, pp. 275–77).[15]

Apparently, then, none of the disciplines welcomed psychoanalysis in Germany, and the critiques by psychologists, philosophers, sociologists, theologians, and doctors must have reinforced one another. Nevertheless, in spite of the rejections, Freud's ideas did take root. Hence we must conclude that though the Freudians' specific complaints of neglect might have been correct, there were other forces at work. The early setbacks undoubtedly impelled Freud's followers to close ranks, and this, I believe, contributed to the success as well as to the "castelike" qualities of the movement.

America Opens Its Doors

Psychoanalysis underwent a sea change when it crossed the Atlantic. Freud's trip in 1909 was an immediate success, and the acclaim he received for his lectures at Clark University (later published: 1910a) made him famous overnight. Still, this instant popularity was probably part of the American propensity to welcome everything new.

The historian Nathan G. Hale, Jr. (1971), in describing the cultural atmosphere surrounding the Clark lectures, indicated that the growth of the movement and the theory was conditioned by American society. This society, Hale argued, was dominated by a civilized morality—a coherent system regulating economic, social, and religious norms, defining correct behavior, prescribing a unique regime of sexual hygiene, even stipulating models of manhood and womanhood. "This moral system tried to coerce a recalcitrant and hostile actuality" (p. 25) and was congruent with a fierce passion for business success, upward mobility, and the acquisition of wealth. But the high value accorded to premarital continence, religious purity, devotion to hard work, and even to marital celibacy were inducing "mental problems." Furthermore, "higher creations" were thought to emanate from transmutations of physical and sexual energy (which functioned like electrical energy). Quacks sold secret remedies against all sorts of "sexual ailments," including masturbation, and no one, including physicians, knew how to deal with either the ailments or the palliatives. To Americans beset by a romantic sentimentality that divorced body and mind, love and sexuality, psychoanalysis was yet another healing agent to help overcome these dilemmas. A number of American psychiatrists and neurologists had visited Jean-Martin Charcot and Hippolyte Bernheim in France, and Pierre Janet in 1906, at Harvard, had argued that hysterics inherit a weakened ability to synthesize their experiences. Thus some American physicians had already experimented with hypnosis for cases of hysteria. Psychoanalysis, they had vaguely heard, might be more effective, so they invited Freud (and Jung and Ferenczi) to teach them how to eradicate mental and sexual ailments.

Freud's lectures were attended by the introspectionist psychologist Edward Bradford Titchener; by A. A. Brill, Freud's first translator; by the psychologist and philosopher William James; and by the psychiatrist Adolph Meyer (who had come directly from the meetings of the newly created National Committee for Mental Hygiene, dedicated to eradicating mental disorders). The anthropologist Franz Boas, who had already demolished doctrines of racism; the Boston Brahmin James Jackson Putnam, one of America's foremost neurologists; and Emma Goldman, the anarchist leader, were among the large general audience. The heterogeneity of this group as well as its aura of expectancy appear to have inspired Freud to give an extended synthesis of psychoanalysis that was singularly appropriate for the Americans: he simplified psychoanalytic theory, emphasized practicality and optimism, and included discussions of sublimation. By concentrating on examples of trauma and catharsis, he appears to have stressed the efficacy of psychoanalytic treatment and exaggerated the potential of rational choice. He also took a bold yet highly ambiguous stand on reforming conventional standards of sexual morality. This appealed to those who were pushing for a new approach to mental disturbance, at a time when psychoanalysts had not yet dealt with the vicissitudes of sexuality, narcissism, and the death instinct, or with the division of the personality into id, ego, and superego (Hale, 1971, p. 6). Had he developed these concepts, the Americans might have been less enthusiastic.

Clearly, the Americans' enchantment with psychoanalysis inspired Freud to formulate radical generalizations and to organize scattered insights into a coherent and brilliant synthesis (Hale, 1971, p. 14). But by stressing the idea that repressed unconscious wishes may result in neurotic symptoms and by defining sublimation rather vaguely, he encouraged simplistic interpretations of psychoanalytic theory and superficial applications. In the Clark lectures,

Freud took unwitting stands on American issues—on the relations between mind and body, and heredity and environment, and on the question of how physicians ought to treat their patients. And he could not have known of the strange links between American popular and professional cultures that account for the speed with which new ideas tend to spread. At first he was pleased with the press coverage: news about psychoanalysis was disseminated in hyperbolic and accessible fashion.

To Emma Goldman, Freud had proved that sexual repression had crippled the intelligence of women. The neurologist Morton Prince, with the help of hypnosis, had already discovered the unconscious, and Putnam had argued that "consciousness, including the subconscious, was the ultimate reality" (Hale, 1971, p. 133).[16] And investigations into functional psychiatry, psycho-pathology, and psychological problems of childhood sexuality (linked to clinical observations by Boris Sidis, Edward Cowles, and Adolph Meyer) had prepared doctors to listen to what Freud told them. So the professional and cultural climate had been ripe for him, and his lectures, in turn, contained enough ambiguity for people to interpret them in a variety of ways. Freud felt vindicated by his success. Soon afterward, on December 5, after his return to Vienna, he wrote to Putnam that "most people demonstrate that they do not intend to accept anything new; . . . I know that you are free of such habits of mind, and therefore I assume that gradually you yourself will become convinced even of what may at the moment still appear inconceivable" (Hale, 1971a, p. 90). He was glad that Putnam had begun to practice psychoanalysis and that other Americans welcomed it so readily. The cases they described invariably corroborated his theories, and they almost outdid the Viennese disciples in dismissing his critics as neurotic, ignorant, and unable to master the psychoanalytic method.

These attitudes, however, fomented opposition in the culture at large. Every journalist, philosopher, medical celebrity, and religious leader now defended his turf against encroachment by psychoanalysis in the popular media. Havelock Ellis, though arguing that Freud had restored the sexual emotions to their role in the etiology of hysteria (Hale, 1971, p. 261), also maintained that sexual intercourse was a private matter and that sexual liberty would foster the independence of mind that could combat civilized morality. Vice commissioners testified that the social evil of prostitution was ubiquitous, particularly in cities, and was furthered by foreigners, drinking, and dancing. At least implicitly, psychoanalysis was being indicted. Such disapproval, however, only united the friends of psychoanalysis, and the public polemics themselves helped spread the new concept.

Some of the American followers, many of them doctors, maintained personal relationships with Freud through correspondence. He analyzed a number of them on long walks during congresses and "supervised" their cases by mail. The American disciples mostly focused on the curing potential of psychoanalysis and adamantly opposed the crackpots, quacks, and mental healers who claimed to be analysts.

As we know, Freud and the Americans soon disagreed over the question of lay analysis. Freud expected lay healers to be admitted into psychoanalytic organizations in order to raise the ethical and intellectual level of the groups and to make psychoanalysis something more than a medical specialty. In a letter to Pfister on November 25, 1928, he wrote that he perceived a "secret link between the *Lay Analysis* and the *Illusion*. In the former I wish to protect analysis from the doctors and in the latter from the priests . . . [in favor of] a profession which does not yet exist, a profession of lay curers who need not be doctors and should not be priests" (Meng and Freud, 1963, p. 126).

European Freudians now quote and requote this passage to discredit the ensuing American medicalization of psychoanalysis. But they tend to forget that Freud was opposed also to the type of lay analysis that began to be practiced in America. Although he had felt flattered by the American reception, he worried about the facile applications: "Americans came too easily by truths others had struggled to discover . . . and were too easily satisfied with superficial appearances" (*S.E.*, 20:177–258). The American acceptance triggered Freud's ambivalence: just as in Europe, where the movement was being weakened by Jung's and Adler's "superficial" approaches, he could no longer control its direction. But how could the American situation have been anything but superficial in Freud's eyes? The extensive press coverage alone was bound to have major repercussions. As Hale noted:

Between 1915 and 1918 psychoanalysis received three-fifths as much attention as birth control, more attention than divorce, and nearly four times more than mental hygiene. The popular image of the cause of neurosis had discarded environmental stress, had strengthened the existing emphasis on trauma located in childhood, and had added the menace of suppressed sexual and aggressive desires. . . . The unconscious had become a Darwinian Titan and dream analysis the road to its taming. (1971, p. 397)

Since public interest in mental healing had now spread to psychoanalysis, journalists asked the Freudians about their cases. Eager to proselytize, some of them would brag of miracle cures. Ultimately reporters' clichés were being wedded to exaggerations and heightened by enthusiasm. Around New York, the psychoanalysts went so far as to offer courses on sexual hygiene and on the "newer psychology" in extension classes, summer schools, and "girls' colleges" (Hale, 1971, pp. 398–400).

It is impossible to ascertain to what extent Freud had anticipated that his Viennese charm, together with a simplification of the theory, would seduce his American listeners. Nor is it clear why the lectures he presented at the University of Vienna in 1916 had many listeners at the beginning but few at the end. Thus both Freudians and their detractors continue to speculate about the extent to which the Austrian and American cultural climates with their distinctive native preferences and prejudices determined from the outset the impact of psychoanalysis.

The French Door Is Closed

"How can we measure the distance separating Vienna from Paris at the turn of the century?" asked the Parisian analyst Victor N. Smirnoff in 1979. He went on to recall that the French had neither attacked nor exploited psycho-analysis but had chosen to ignore it. Apparently French chauvinism and xenophobia, along with traditional French modes of thinking, were threat-ened by psychoanalysis (1979, p. 21). Smirnoff's comments, however, ad-dressed not only the actual situation but the Parisians' current fascination with early psychoanalytic history. At least in quantity, their reinterpretations by far outstrip the history itself.

At the turn of the century the French still explained mental illness as a form of possession. In addition they had a strong psychiatric and neurological tradition, so that psychoanalysis did not appeal to the doctors and was not presented to the public (Roudinesco, 1982, p. 68).[17] Hysteria was being treated with suggestion, hypnosis, or magnetism (see chapter 5), and physicians from all over the world were descending on France in order to learn these meth-ods. Thus most French historians tend to agree with Ellenberger that the dominant psychiatric tradition—from Pinel to Délasiauve, from d'Esquirol to Magnan—was as much an obstacle to the acceptance of psychoanalysis as was the tradition of rational, introspective, and humanistic psychology. (Un-like their German counterparts, French psychologists did not have to battle a rigid psychophysiology.) Faith healers such as Augustus Ambreuse Liébeault (1823–1904) had already fallen out of favor. But Hippolyte Bernheim, a phy-sician and leader of the Nancy School, whom Freud had visited in 1889, con-tinued to treat his patients with the help of suggestion. (Freud had read Bernheim's paper *De la Suggestion dans l'Etat Hypnotique et dans l'Etat de Veille* [1884], in which he distinguished between hypnotic suggestion and hypnosis in the treatment of hysteria.)

The greatest opposition to psychoanalysis in France came from the psy-chology of Pierre Janet. His dynamic theory, which took into account a psychogenic process deriving from life experience, from fixed ideas, and from an organic substratum, had philosophic support in Henri Bergson's ideas (Ellenberger, 1970, pp. 377–86). According to Ellenberger, Bergson's notion of "attention to life" was similar to Janet's *fonction du réel*, and his focus on the spearhead of life (as the avant-garde of evolution) was close to Janet's concepts of "psychological tension." Janet, furthermore, was bound to retain an edge over Freud because he belonged to the French intellectual community Freud had described so well in his letters to his fiancée, Martha Bernays.

In fact, Janet, who was three years younger than Freud, had been listening to Charcot at the Salpêtrière at the same time as Freud. Ellenberger credited Janet as the first to found his own system of dynamic psychiatry, which Janet consistently upheld against psychoanalysis. (In a letter to Jung, who was about to meet Janet in London, Freud warned him of Janet's antagonism and suggested a possible mode of argumentation [McGuire, 1974, pp. 32–33, Letter 20F]). But Roland Jaccard, a French psychoanalyst and historian of psychoanalysis, has recently argued that Janet was not sufficiently interested in psychoanalysis to take note of any of Freud's theories after the *Studies in Hysteria* of 1895 and that the French critics' sympathy for Janet even led them to substitute Janet's terminology for Freud's to the point of using "the term subconscious which Freud never used" (Jaccard, 1982, 2:13).[18]

After his appointment to the Collège de France, Janet blocked psychoanalysis rather directly. He argued that Charcot's lectures on traumatic neuroses and his own ideas had inspired Freud, but that Freud had misconstrued them: in particular, Janet claimed that Freud had taken his own early studies of unconscious phenomena in hysterics too seriously.[19] In any event, Freud rejected Janet's contention that the splitting of consciousness was a primary trait of hysteria because he and Breuer had noted it as a secondary condition—as images arising during hypnosis and cut off from consciousness (*S.E.*, 2:41). Thus he denied Janet's influence on psychoanalysis, although he went out of his way to acknowledge Charcot's. And Freud alone is credited with turning observations on hysteria into a "theoretical edifice" (Lorenzer, 1984).

The French did not malign psychoanalysis as did the Austrians and Germans, nor did they "adapt" it like the Americans. Instead, they kept their distance. Nevertheless, current French histories inflate the French influence on Freud in order to explain their early indifference. They emphasize the importance of Freud's presence at Charcot's lavish receptions, where he met *tout-Paris*, and they quote Jones's paraphrase of Freud explaining that Charcot had aroused Freud's interest in hysteria and in psychopathology and thereby made him rethink Breuer's observations, to the benefit of psychoanalysis

(Jones, 1953–57, 1:74). The French also inflate the importance of Freud's prefaces to and translations of Charcot's *Lectures* of 1886 and 1892–94 (*S.E.,* 1:19–22, 113–43) and of *Bernheim's Suggestion* (*S.E.,* 1:71–85).[20] Some French historians glorify Charcot by insinuating that Freud had introduced Parisian ideas in order to advance his career in Vienna. Others have quoted Freud's recollection of Meynert's chauvinistic remarks when he presented Charcot's concepts (in his seminar on *l'hystérie masculine,* October 15, 1886) in order to conclude that the Viennese did not appreciate either Charcot's or Freud's genius because they could not stomach French thinking.[21] Actually, both the French and the Austrians were relatively immune to foreigners' ideas, routinely proclaiming their national self-sufficiency and importance.

In spite of the mutual distrust between Paris and Vienna, there *was* an exchange of knowledge on a small scale. Freud clutched at every straw: each visit or written word led him to think that the French were becoming more receptive to his ideas. In 1910, for example, he was overjoyed about a letter of December 3 he received from Dr. Morichau-Beauchant of Poitiers (McGuire, 1974); in a letter of December 13 Jones informed Freud that the Frenchman from Poitiers planned to send a contribution to the *Zentralblatt*—on homosexuality and paranoia (pp. 224). Soon Freud wrote to Abraham about the "solid support in Poitiers" and about "a letter from a student of Régis in Bordeaux" (Abraham and Freud, 1965). Indeed, few of Freud's early works were available in French. "Les Diplégies cérébrales infantiles" (1893) and "Obsessions and Phobias: Their Psychical Mechanism and Their Aetiology" (1893h) were translated for the *Revue Neurologique,* but these translations were as inconsequential as the references by several Swiss authors (inspired by Jung rather than Freud): Théodore Flournoy had written a note on *The Interpretation of Dreams* in 1903; Alphonse Maeder commented on interpretations of dreams and parapraxes in 1907 (Barande and Barande, 1975, p. 40; Roudinesco, 1982, p. 12); and Théodule Ribot mentioned psychoanalysis (Barande and Barande, 1975, p. 40).

Janine Chasseguet-Smirgel (1981), no doubt intrigued by the current curiosity about this history, recently found a 1907 article by Schmiergeld, de Lodz, and Provotelle explaining that Freud's new psychology relied on "a reeducation of the mental state of psychoneurotics and hysterics" and that he induced patients to return to an earlier mental state by plunging them into forgotten memories. But they immediately compared Freud's view of mental illness (he took account of hereditary factors and thought that patients retained their intelligence) to Janet's conceptions (he perceived mental disintegration). And they went on to judge Janet's analysis of his patient Marie (her symptoms were related to shame) as superior to psychoanalysis. These authors did concede, however, that psychoanalysis demonstrated the symptomatic links between psychic and organic life (p. 1405), and they noted that Freud's method could benefit persons of superior intelligence rather than the intellectually handicapped. Just the same, they concluded that psychoanalysis was exaggerating "the symbolic manifestations of sexual desire" (pp. 1390–91). Evidently, they knew that Janet had published his case histories—on Lucie (1886), Marie (1889), and Marcelle (1891)—before Freud had reported on Anna O., although she had been treated between 1880 and 1883.[22] In any event, Schmiergeld, though giving a fairly sympathetic rendition of psychoanalysis, could not help but side with Janet. Others, it seems, were even more afraid to step outside their Zeitgeist. But Ellenberger and a number of French historians also take Janet's side by attributing Freud's feud with him to Freud's desire for fame. Classical analysts, on the other hand, have countered with comments on Janet's nasty character and have tended to recall Freud's warnings to Jung about him (McGuire, 1974; see letter of April 14, 1907).

In general, reconsiderations of the early French controversies blame resistances to Freud on cultural chauvinism. Freudians, for the most part, explain the hostility as irrational defenses, whereas historians focus on rival practices, from the continuing pull of magnetism and mesmerism to the use of hypnosis or the so-called medical glance.[23] But French commentators tend to inflate the influences *on* Freud and to exaggerate the Parisians' contributions. Even Freud's remark to his fiancée that the self-satisfied Parisians attributed every important idea or invention to themselves is quoted at times in a manner that turns this reproach into a back-handed compliment.

The British Branch

British psychoanalysis was started by Ernest Jones in 1913. Freud had met him at the First Psycho-analytical Congress in Salzburg in 1908 and liked his paper on "Rationalization in Everyday Life." In 1909 Jones had settled in Canada, after a number of differences with the British Medical Association. There too he had been somewhat abrasive, a sort of enfant terrible; he allegedly had sexually assaulted a woman patient and, shocking the rather provincial Ontarians, lived openly with his mistress (Grosskurth, 1986, p. 157). But then Jones followed Freud's advice and was analyzed by Ferenczi in Budapest (twice a day for two months). Soon after his return to London in 1913, he not only called together fifteen colleagues to form the London Psycho-Analytical Society but also became a member of Freud's "Committee of the Seven Rings" and later president of the International Psycho-Analytical Association (IPA).

Undoubtedly, Jones's importance to the movement as an Englishman and a non-Jew, as well as his disapproval of Jung's ideas, led Freud to rely on him. In fact, when the other senior London analyst, David Eder, expressed Jungian views, Jones dissolved the original London Psycho-Analytical Society. He reinaugurated it almost immediately (in 1919) as the British Psycho-Analytical Society, when he found twelve people who satisfied IPA membership requirements. The caliber of these founding members and of those who soon joined—among them James and Alix Strachey, Ella Sharpe, Joan Riviere, James and Edward Glover—gave psychoanalysis a certain cachet.

By 1925 there were fifty-four members and associate members in the society. Like the Viennese, they represented various disciplines. Nearly all of them, however, came from a Scottish, English, or Welsh Christian background and had a strong bias toward agnosticism and humanism (King, 1988, p. 128). Jones was publishing the *International Journal of Psycho-Analysis* (1920); the IPA had founded an International Psychoanalytical Library (1921) and soon would set up a clinic (1926); and James Strachey began translating and publishing Freud at the Hogarth Press (1924) (Kohon, 1986, pp. 27–28). In other words, psychoanalysis was being firmly established—not in the culture at large, but among an elite.

The Bloomsbury contingent was not typical of the members of the British elite. According to George Homans, in Britain gentlemen as a rule do not question the motives of other gentlemen, and class distinctions are protected by the habit of accepting social performances on their face value as long as they do not become embarrassing to the specific circle (Hampden-Turner, 1983, p. 63). The early London psychoanalysts belonged either to the dissident elite or to the Jewish bourgeoisie, and members of the traditional elite would have felt superior to them. This isolation did not encourage the spread of psychoanalysis to the public, and thus for a long time it was restricted to more or less intellectual circles.

Since England was a liberal country, there were no bitter divisions between the ruling classes as in France between Catholics and anticlericals and no right-wing movements as in Germany and Italy. The English valued their stable democracy, humane tolerance, compassion, and respect for human rights and legal equality. They felt no "need" for psychoanalysis. Hence the analysts were opposed by the majority of the public, the church, the medical and psychiatric professions, the elite, and the press. After they had made minor inroads, an open fight erupted within the British Medical Association.

A number of wild accusations led to the formation of a special committee to investigate psychoanalysis. When Jones had spent two years fighting these "psychologically illiterate" opponents (with little help from his frightened colleagues), he got the official committee "to respect the claims of Freud and his followers to the use and definition of the term 'psychoanalysis,' as applied to the theory (and technique based upon it) devised by Freud, who was recognized as having been the first to use the term" (Kohon, 1986, p. 29). The committee further agreed that its own members did not know enough about psychoanalysis to pass judgment; in time, both claims and criticisms would be tested.

The historian of British psychoanalysis Gregorio Kohon concludes that this report brought favorable consequences for the psychoanalytic movement, but he points out that because of the committee's refusal to approve or appreciate the claims of psychoanalysis, its verdict fell far short of acceptance (1986, p. 30). Whatever acceptance there was, it must be added, was found in London rather than the country overall.

The Faces of Freud

In Hungary, Italy, and Russia, psychoanalysis had a relatively early start, but for a variety of political or religious reasons, it remained a minor movement or was nipped in the bud altogether. In Japan a few adherents introduced psychoanalysis into psychiatry in 1919 (Takahashi, 1982, p. 481). There, as everywhere else, the reception of psychoanalysis depended on the features of the society that would tend to make psychoanalysis plausible, on its norms, and on its means of diffusing new knowledge (Berger, 1981, pp. 59–60). Since psychoanalysis contradicted taken-for-granted customs and threatened the culture's dominant thinkers and ideas, it inevitably challenged conventional wisdom, dogmas, and traditions everywhere. That Freud's therapy was perceived as a threat to doctors, priests, and psychologists almost ensured organized opposition.

The views of Sulloway, Cremerius, Roudinesco, and others about the reception of psychoanalysis reflect specific biases. Moving Freud's biology and neurophysiology to the center of his system devalues its humanistic content; concentrating on political repression underlines its sympathy to Marxist ideals; stressing the contributions of the disciples implies questions about Freud's originality. Thus, assumptions about the unconscious and childhood sexuality will be inflated or deflated according to one's aims. This does not mean that one thereby denies that Freud "systematized" the unconscious but only that one is rethinking questions about the scientific nature of psycho-analysis, its impact on individuals and society, and its curative potential.

Organizational histories of psychoanalysis (the subject of the next chapter) recount its development in numbers—of members, of topics presented at meetings, of ever more rigorous training requirements, of patients and types of patients served—for this is how we measure progress. Such histories also compare clinical and institutional factors under various cultural conditions and influences. But Freudians, who usually do not worry much about statistics, tend to glorify their past. Thus when C. P. Oberndorf reminisced about American psychoanalytic history between 1909 and 1929, he recalled it primarily as integral to medical theory and practice and as going off in different directions. He thought that Freud's openness to lay analysis had been due to the valuable contributions of a few Viennese and to "more personal unconscious reasons" (1949, pp. 153–61). Sándor Lorand, on the other hand, compared the reception of psychoanalysis in Europe and in the United States:

In 1925, when I came to America, I found a different attitude in New York toward psychoanalysis from that of Europe. Whereas European physicians and psychiatrists generally showed great resistance and intolerance toward analysis, in New York many were ready to listen to analysts and a sizable segment of the lay public seemed eager to learn about psychoanalysis. There was, to be sure, no lack of criticism and resistance . . . but the general atmosphere was far different from the rigid antagonism prevalent in Europe. (1969, p. 589)

Lorand's view may not have been too objective, but the record seems to support him.

During the past sixty years, the differences in theoretical approaches to psychoanalysis from country to country have grown. This is not to say that professional cooperation across national boundaries has weakened but only that the modes of inquiry or the underlying theoretical premises in each country were responding to the same traditions of thought and institutions that had conditioned the reception of psychoanalysis. In this light, even the Americans' recent interest in Freud's neurophysiology and biology, the French stress on the prepsychoanalysis, the Germans' preoccupation with anti-Semitism and fascism, the British respect for the young child, and the Austrians' nostalgia are extensions of earlier concerns. And the Italians' recent reminiscences about Edoardo Weiss, the lone follower of Freud in Trieste (he moved to Rome in 1932 and to Chicago in 1939), or the Hungarians' revival of Ferenczi are among other things manifestations of national pride. Many historians of psychoanalysis praise their native sons first—so the French reminisce about their princess, Marie Bonaparte, and the Germans about Karl Abraham.

Freud's ideas arose from a specific conjuncture of theoretical and practical conditions and elicited a variety of responses. In Central Europe, what is roughly called "modernism" was nearing its height. Industrialization and bourgeois culture had become successful enough to allow more and more individuals to focus on matters beyond the essentials for survival. These conditions themselves had helped promulgate the notion that science and rationality were supreme and that more science and rationality would lead to more progress, maybe even to utopia. If psychoanalysis had not emerged, another psychological explanation would have been found for the unhappiness of the affluent in spite of their possessions and for the tendency of the poor, even though hard working, to remain poor. Capitalism could explain the economics, but religion no longer fulfilled its emotional functions: as every theorist since Saint-Simon had shown, it had been replaced by a belief in science, had become delegitimated or at least questioned by ever larger numbers of people whose lives were changing, who were exposed to new ideas, to travel, to technical inventions. Because religious leaders had fewer answers and fewer followers, psychoanalysis, with its belief in personal autonomy and in the possibility of "salvation" through individual initiative, was particularly suited to modern living. Even the priests were reacting to their own increasing impotence. Reluctantly, they were picking up and adapting psychoanalytic ideas.

Insofar as Freud located irrationality—personal and societal—in the human unconscious, the progress of psychoanalysis depended upon the eradication of irrational thought and action. In its claim to being scientific, therefore, it reflected the belief in scientific norms, yet retained humanistic values. Still, institutions that were slow to relinquish their traditions would only slowly accept the idea that the unconscious was the personal locus of those traditions. But on the societal plane, it was believed, however vaguely, that psychoanalytic insights might further democratic notions of human liberation by freeing many individuals of their neuroses.

Chapter 2

From Informal Group to Formal Structures

B y 1906 Freud had published five books and about seventy articles. His *Three Essays* had been reviewed in Europe and America. He had established contacts with the English sexologist Havelock Ellis and the Swiss psychiatrist Carl Jung. He received letters from around the world every day, but there were still no more than a handful of people in his immediate entourage. Some of them intended to form a network to spread the word, but none of them dreamed that the organization they were about to create would eventually, like the proverbial dog's tail, wag the body of its host, psychoanalysis.

The Wednesday Society

Between 1902 and 1906, Wednesday evenings were set aside for meetings in Freud's study. The participants welcomed anyone who showed up: enthusiasm for psychoanalysis was their bond. Given their own eagerness, the disciples assumed that psychoanalysis would catch on and that their passions and efforts alone would spread its truth. They did not envision the need for a formal organization. Nor did they imagine that they would be guiding a large movement or that they soon would be heading rival groups. And they did not anticipate that someday Freud's closest adherents would be accused of having become a community of believers or that Freud would be held responsible for such a development.

In effect, Freud had requested total allegiance from his pioneers. He felt protective of them and expected them to extend psychoanalytic research, which he would synthesize. How, then, did organizational priorities gradually intrude upon, and even come to overshadow, substantive considerations? Did they really ensure the power of an elite, as detractors have maintained, or did the organization save "the gold of psychoanalysis," as Freud had expected? In other words, how did the Wednesday Society become transmuted into the IPA, and how did it maintain its power after Adler, Jung, Stekel, and others had formed rival groups? And if psychoanalysis was being subverted and overly bureaucratized, how had this happened over Freud's putative objections? Did the disciples countermand his explicit sanctions against formalization (which he feared would constrict the free play of their minds) or was organizational growth inevitable?

While the psychoanalysts met informally on Wednesdays and could all fit into Freud's study, they were extremely casual. So it seemed natural that when they had to move, two of the four suggestions for bigger quarters were for coffeehouses. But as soon as they had rented a meeting hall, they behaved with more decorum: there were more participants, they were more aware of their importance, and they wanted to keep track of their discussions, for scientific purposes or with an eye to posterity. Thus Freud employed Otto Rank, a brilliant but unschooled locksmith whom he had taken under his wing, to take notes.[1] The pioneers were certain that their honest interactions and even their arguments would actually promote the advancement of the science (Nunberg and Federn, 1962, pp. xix–xxi)—overlooking the fact that the explosive character of their relationships was anathema to organizational cooperation.

In 1902, when they started to meet, all of Freud's followers—Alfred Adler, Rudolf Reitler, Isidor Sadger, and Wilhelm Stekel—lived in Vienna. Soon Max Kahane, Paul Federn, and Edward Hitschmann joined them. They read Arthur Schnitzler, Hugo von Hofmannsthal, and Rainer Maria Rilke; they championed liberalism; and they actively participated in everyday politics. They supported the leftist ideals of their fellow intellectuals and expected psychoanalysis to help advance them. Rank's *Minutes* give the flavor of these meetings, with their random observations and references to political events, and they convey a sense of excitement and independence as well as the biting humor and inordinate curiosity of the participants.

To encourage total openness, Freud tried to keep rules to a minimum. He was especially cordial to guests. And whoever would present a paper, the rite of initiation, was accepted as a member. After preliminaries were disposed of, each meeting began with such a presentation. Then the group would break for coffee, reconvening to discuss the paper. Everyone was expected to talk, the members drawing numbers to decide who would go first; but Freud decided what aspect of a topic would be stressed, and he was rarely overruled or interrupted. He had the first and the last words, in part because he had the knack of converting casual comments into theoretical hypotheses. (Even his detractors have admired Freud's intellectual facility, maintaining that it went a long way toward making psychoanalysis plausible.)

Recent biographies of the disciples have pointed to the seeds of their subjects' later theoretical pursuits in these early presentations. The disciples often thought their different styles and interests ultimately explained their disagreements with one another. But their differences also expressed their neuroses and their personalities. From the *Minutes* one can conclude that Rank tended to be pleasant but somewhat arrogant; Wittels, righteous and obnoxious; Federn, acquiescent; and Stekel, disruptive and disagreeable. Such characteristic behavior also became theoretical grist in the psychoanalysts' mill. Later, after it had become de rigueur to expose all conflicts, in the name of science, as manifestations of unconscious processes, this reductive habit would cause organizational headaches (see chapter 10).

During the early period, the Freudians expected that exposing their strongest emotions, fantasies, and dreams and permitting the group to interpret them would clear the air and unite them more strongly than before. Yet, as early as 1912, Lou-Andreas Salomé, Freud's confidante, noted in her diary that the unavoidable fights were unpleasant. She sympathized with Freud, who "no longer had the peace he [allegedly] enjoyed until 1905"; but she was certain that the "arguments were beneficial" for the future of psychoanalysis and would further the movement (1958, p. 98).

Undoubtedly, it did not help that some participants took to posturing when their comments began to be recorded—particularly after they started thinking of themselves as a vanguard. Now, a few people, with posterity in mind, wanted to be credited for their original formulations and insights, so that Federn even proposed that they abolish "intellectual communism" and forgo using new ideas without permission from their authors (Nunberg and Federn, 1962, p. 299). Essentially, they zigzagged between exploring their unconscious, expressing their solidarity with the group, and engaging in heated polemics. And as they pooled their speculations, reported on cases, and insulted one another, the Freudians seem to have cast Freud as their oedipal father and one another as rivalrous siblings.

Consequently, historians can read all sorts of things into the *Minutes* and elevate the contributions of their favorites. Nevertheless, Freud dominated. French commentators now depict him as the "father" who always had the ultimate word in disputes between his "intellectual sons," and they demonstrate how he enforced civility as well as organizational rules. German psychoanalytic historians frequently have focused on how he decided on the line of inquiry: some of them note that these meetings seem to have been forerunners of group therapy, others admire Freud's tolerance and his levelheadedness in dealing with wild conjectures, and still others marvel at his ability to balance praise and criticism.

When in 1907 Max Eitingon, the first foreigner to visit the group, arrived from Zurich, he remarked on the pioneers' lively and contentious spirit. He had come as an emissary from the Burghölzli clinic to get advice about a particularly difficult case. Working with Jung, Franz Riklin, Karl Abraham, and Eugen Bleuler (the Burghölzli director), Eitingon had responded to Freud's call: he had become a "practicing psychoanalyst." He was said to be full of trepidation upon entering this illustrious circle, which by then included Fritz Wittels and Alfred Meisl, as well as Kahane, Reitler, Stekel, Adler, and Sadger. Rank and Federn had just become members (Wulff 1950, p. 75). The record shows that Eitingon attended twice (on January 23 and 30, 1907), and that twelve and ten people, respectively, were present. Eitingon's questions were to the point: he wanted to know what causes neurosis, what therapy—and especially the transference—consists of, and what becomes of hysteria after psychoanalysis. Rank noted, rather naively, "This evening's discussion is devoted to answering these questions" (Nunberg and Federn, 1962, 1:1, 93).

After the International Congress of Psychoanalysis was held in Salzburg in August 1908, attended by forty-two people, the Viennese analysts decided to organize more formally. They realized, in retrospect, that meetings should be carefully planned, set up in advance, and paid for through dues. They moved to constitute themselves as an international professional organization, for they expected to conquer the world by legitimating their enterprise and uniting against hostile medical and political establishments. Soon, as psychoanalysis spread to more and more countries, the IPA was extending its authority over its members.

In April 1908 the Wednesday Society was transformed into the Wiener Psychoanalytischer Verein (WPV), and between then and 1911 the movement made rapid strides, only to suffer a setback when Adler broke away. Tensions had been mounting. Adler had been pushing for immediate application of psychoanalytic theories in the community while Freud maintained that such applications were counterproductive to the search for the unconscious. After

Adler set up a rival organization, the Verein für Forschung an Individual-psychologie, the members of the WPV, in a close vote, expelled him (see chapter 12). As a result, organizational life changed drastically, and relations among the followers became more formal. The Freudians began pointedly to ignore Adler's Individualpsychologie, and Freud became more involved in the IPA. But by writing off Adler (who increasingly saw neuroses as manifestations of larger sociopolitical forces), Freud had established a precedent for handling "deviants."[2] Still, Adler inadvertently paved the way for more general acceptance for all of them. By convincing Austrian officials of the value of psychoanalytic principles even when used in fairly superficial and pragmatic ways, he rose in the Social Democratic hierarchy and managed to influence social policy: he introduced psychoanalytic ideas into the Austrian school system, mental health clinics, early childhood education, and rehabilitation centers for delinquents (Reichmayr and Wiesbauer, 1979, p. 16).[3]

Because Jung's departure two years later caused particular problems (he had to be replaced as president of the IPA and as publisher of the *Jahrbuch*), Freud set up rules for handling "dissenters": from now on they were to be judged by a special IPA commission, which would depersonalize such situations.

Since organizational precedents had been established when Jones was recording these events, he was in a position to embellish or to play down the unpleasant issues that had surrounded Adler's departure. In contrast, Stekel's departure did not cause much disruption in the WPV, in part because Jones managed to smooth things over, and in part because Stekel had no organizational functions. Whether or not Jones was being overprotective of the movement, as is often argued, is moot. All the Freudians were political enough to know that whoever controlled their organization would be in a position to take charge of its theoretical direction and its dominant ideas—and that included Freud himself.

Germany's Organizational Talents

A series of events combined to make Berlin the center of psychoanalysis. Karl Abraham had decided to leave the Burghölzli for Berlin and asked Freud for advice and help. (As a foreigner and a Jew, he felt that his professional future in Zurich was limited.) Freud, who had read Abraham's paper "About the Meaning of the Importance of Sexual Dreams in Adolescence to the Symptomatology of Dementia Praecox" (1907) and had liked his direct references to psychoanalysis, was pleased by the prospect of a German branch and encouraged him to go. "If my reputation in Germany grows," Freud wrote, "this will be helpful to you, and if I may designate you directly as my pupil and follower—you don't seem to be the man who would be ashamed of it—then I can energetically take your side. On the other hand, you yourself know with what enemies I still have to fight in Germany" (Abraham and Freud, 1965, Oct. 8, 1907). He went on to warn Abraham against Berlin psychiatrists (who were arguing about the validity of hypnosis) and German doctors in general and advised him to go directly to the public.

Many psychoanalytic historians speculate that Freud's advice to Abraham was colored by his disappointment in Fliess and thus in his earlier hopes for a psychoanalytic society in Berlin. But all of them describe Abraham's triumph. He immediately contacted every German psychiatrist and neurologist who had shown any interest in psychoanalysis, and they soon "flocked" to his apartment (Maetze, 1976, p. 1147),[4] which became the center for the lively discussions of the Berlin Psychoanalytische Gesellschaft. Magnus Hirschfeld and Iwan Bloch—who had praised the *Three Essays* in 1906—came to the first meeting, in August 1908. So did Heinrich Körber and Otto Juliusberger, who had presented a "Beitrag zur Lehre der Psychoanalyse" (Comment on Teaching Psychoanalysis) at the Berlin Psychiatrischer Verein in 1907. Later they were joined by Ernst Simmel, who soon founded the first "polyclinic" (in 1934 he started the psychoanalytic society in Los Angeles, where he was joined in 1938 by Otto Fenichel), and by Otto Binswanger (his patient Irma, whom he sent to his nephew Ludwig, became a classic case: "Versuch einer Hysterienanalyse"; it appeared in the same volume of the *Jahrbuch* as Freud's famous case of "Little Hans").

Abraham was a gifted proselytizer. For example, he organized a lively "Freud-debate" at the Dalldorf Clinic of his former professor Hugo Karl Liepman (Maetze, 1976, p. 1147), and he set up courses for doctors to inform them of the most recent theories about neuroses and dreams (Abraham and Freud, 1965, p. 45). Since Freud appreciated his dedication, they became friends and correspondents. They discussed organizational problems and exchanged manuscripts, and Freud "supervised" Abraham from a distance. Thus, Abraham read Freud's "Character and Anal Erotism" before it was presented in Salzburg and predicted that it would have the effect of a small bombshell—a prediction that came true during the congress.

The Psychoanalysts Unite

At the IPA meetings in Nuremberg, in August 1910, Sándor Ferenczi, the foremost Hungarian Freudian, brought up "The Need for a Closer Cooperation among the Followers of Freudian Thought and Suggestions for the Formation of an Ongoing International Organization." Ferenzci proposed that opponents of the movement as well as self-proclaimed psychoanalysts be treated by analyzing their unconscious motives; in this manner they would be brought around or silenced (1955, pp. 299–301). Their critiques of psychoanalysis, he pointed out, were contradictory, manifesting behavior as "neurotic" and defensive as that of patients in treatment. Ferenczi also traced the historic path of psychoanalysis and outlined its future. But in his enthusiasm, as he was recapitulating the "heroic" era, the era of the "guerrilla war," and glorifying the coming "organizational" age, he predicted, naively, that the psychoanalysts would avoid the frictions inherent in other organizations: after all, they had insight and self-control. (This speech exemplified the increasingly arrogant manner in which Freud's disciples dismissed their opponents, explaining why the latter would become so inflamed.)

At these meetings, the psychoanalysts decided upon the structure of the International Psycho-Analytical Association: it was to be a loose association of local (national) psychoanalytic societies, each headed by someone approved by Freud. They agreed to meet at biannual congresses and to communicate by mail in the interims. Endorsing Ferenczi's high expectations, they agreed that they needed no rules beyond those required by incorporation and that they would add new statutes when necessary. They wanted the IPA to operate as informally as possible.

At first, the Freudians did not realize that the IPA's broad international scope would be the cause of uncontrollable conflicts and that its loose mandate—to spread psychoanalysis—would clash with a wide variety of local constraints and traditions. In fact, psychoanalysis was the only profession to have an international base before local organizations were in place, which permitted the Freudians to ignore local and national customs, peculiarities, and laws. Later, these would impose themselves when, for instance, it came to professional acceptance and to the licensing of nonmedical analysts. At the time, however, Freudians simply assumed that psychoanalysis would automatically overcome such "artificial" obstacles as national boundaries and licensing laws, and underestimated the impact existing regulations would have on the diffusion of their ideas.

The Freudians also paid little attention to the mundane questions of organization because no one then realized the greediness of all organizations—that is, their propensity to expand and take over (Coser, 1974). Instead, they shared the cosmology of their day—the belief in progress, which meant to them that with the help of psychoanalysis "humanity" ultimately and inevitably would transcend "nationality." In this way, they justified ignoring administrative details: they perceived their organization primarily as a means to spread their message. The Freudians' organizational center was to move with the IPA's presidency from Zurich to Berlin and then to London, but Vienna would remain the intellectual center because Freud lived there.

The early psychoanalysts spoke German, and so it was natural that after the Nuremberg congress the group met in Weimar (September 1911) and in Munich (September 1913). It planned to meet in Dresden in September 1914, but the First World War interfered. By then, the movement had taken some long strides: *Imago*, begun in 1912—published by Freud, printed by Hugo Heller, and edited by Rank and Hanns Sachs—had become an important organ; so had the *Internationale Zeitschrift für Psychoanalyse*, which replaced the *Zentralblatt für Psychoanalyse* edited by Stekel (he continued it as *Zentralblatt für Psychoanalyse und Psychotherapie*), and the *Jahrbuch für Psychoanalyse* edited by Jung. Nevertheless, Adler's and Jung's defections bothered Freud enough that he felt it necessary to assure Ferenczi that he was as certain of possessing the "truth" as he had been fifteen years before (Cremerius, 1984, pp. 27–28).

Although the rupture with Jung had been in the air for some time, it was not certain that Abraham would succeed him as president of the IPA or as editor of the *Jahrbuch*. When the leading analysts became apprehensive about the impending rift with the Zurich contingent (they knew that the Munich group would follow), they started to correspond with one another about the problem. In fact, the coming break led Freud to rely more and more on Abraham, Ferenczi, Rank, Sachs, Jones, and later Eitingon; they were his committee, the heirs and guardians of psychoanalytic purity—even when they could not agree on whose theory was the purest.

Since Freud's chosen descendants now felt justified in perceiving themselves as his legitimate successors, it was natural for them to assume that they in turn were to select their heirs. Much later, when this practice was attacked as too elitist and traditional, dissenters maintained that the committee, even between 1913 and 1914, had functioned like a "religious" community. (Some opponents said that its spirit had passed on from the father to the sons.) This would lead the members of the IPA, the so-called Freudian establishment, to dig in their heels and insist that they were protecting the heritage. Their opponents, however, would accuse them of ever greater conservatism.

World War I

The more successful the international movement became, the more the Freudians ignored politics. While preparing for their Dresden congress in

1914, for example, they remained oblivious to Europe's explosive political climate and the impending war. It took Freud until August to write to Abraham that they would not meet, that war was inevitable. Infused with patriotic feelings, he felt "like giving this not very hopeful Empire another chance" (Abraham and Freud, 1965, p. 184). But Freud was upset that "England was on the wrong side." Jones had used his personal connections to help Anna return to Vienna with the Austrian ambassador, via Portugal, after the war's outbreak, and yet Jones "belonged to the enemy" (p. 188). Actually, the psychoanalysts had been so preoccupied with their organization that they seemed to blind themselves to the prevailing climate of international tension and uncritical patriotism.

As soon as they overcame their annoyance over the war's interfering with their congress, however, they could note its horror, and they started to put psychoanalysis to use. Abraham, who soon joined the army, was the first one to examine war neuroses psychoanalytically. He wrote to Freud: "The psychoanalyst in me watches in wonder, as I operate on hydrozeles, or perform a rib section" (Maetze, 1976, p. 1151). By 1915, he had resumed his psychoanalytic inquiries and was treating war neuroses with psychotherapy.

In any event, the Freudians for the first time realized the split in their loyalties between nation and movement. By the 1930s they resolved this conflict by appealing to higher principles—human advancement, peace, freedom. The focus on this larger goal sometimes would justify their paying even less attention to political factors and forces (see chapter 12). But during the First World War, psychoanalytic politics did not yet encompass public declarations or antiwar resolutions. Instead, the Freudians mainly pursued their scientific investigations and nurtured their organization. They continued to publish the *Internationale Zeitschrift für Psychoanalyse:* Abraham alone published twelve articles between 1914 and 1918, and Ferenczi's "Über zwei Typen von Kriegsneurosen" appeared in the journal. When government officials asked the psychoanalysts to try curing soldiers of the neuroses the war had caused, they were pleased. But they realized also that such an endeavor would require large numbers of persons' taking crash courses in psychoanalysis. Abraham was opposed, fearing that psychoanalysis would become fashionable on false grounds and that charlatans would pretend after the war that they were real psychoanalysts (Abraham and Freud, 1965, p. 268).

The idea that psychoanalysis might help troubled soldiers inspired the Berlin physician H. Oppenheim in 1915 to publish "Der Krieg und die traumatischen Neurosen" (in *Berliner klinische Wochenschrift*) and Ernst Simmel, director of a special clinic for war neurotics, to write *Kriegsneurosen und psy-*

chisches Trauma in 1918. According to Freud, Simmel was the first German doctor to use psychoanalysis as a matter of fact and without condescension. Therefore, he suggested that Abraham review the book and induce Simmel to join the movement: "I think a year's training would turn him into a good analyst" (Abraham and Freud, 1965, p. 255). That was how Simmel became Abraham's analysand after the war.

Success in Berlin

The analysts' war experiences gave psychoanalysis a broader scope and inspired them to open the first polyclinic, in Berlin in February 1920. People responded favorably in a generally open political climate, and the clinic flourished. Before long a room was furnished for play therapy and a woman doctor trained for this new activity. But though the patients kept coming, Abraham complained to Freud that the clinic was not attracting enough young people. Clearly, his eye was on the future of the movement as much as Freud's was.

At this juncture, the members of the committee communicated regularly through *Rundbriefe* (letters circulated among them all). Freud, now sixty-five, said he wanted to give up the business end of the movement, but he remained its guiding spirit and cosigned all letters with Rank. They mostly dealt with practical problems—rules, statutory changes, payment of membership dues, training programs, meetings and congresses, and quarrels (especially between Rank and Jones) over questions of publication and copyright rather than science.

From these letters we learn that the Berliners almost succeeded in getting psychoanalysis accepted by the mainstream academics. At one point, they nearly bested the German psychologists when they tried to have Abraham appointed to a university chair, but the plan ultimately foundered. The hoped-for professorship didn't materialize, for the faculty opposed the request. Later the question was raised again, and it was implied that Abraham might be appointed if he were to convert; he, however, refused (Abraham and Freud, 1965, pp. 255–300). But even if Abraham had won the post, there would have been other complications. Since professors were obligated to examine students in their specific field, medical students would have had to be tested in psychoanalysis. But how could this be done if they were not offered an analysis? And should they want to be analyzed, the facilities were lacking. These worries, however, were premature, and the Berliners designed their own training program.

According to the German historians, it was the superior psychoanalytic climate in Berlin that attracted many analysts. But the letters of Alix and James Strachey (Meisel and Kendrick, 1985) and the biography of Melanie Klein (Grosskurth, 1987), for instance, suggest that the liberal climate of Weimar's Berlin and its nightlife were other drawing cards. In any event, Hermione von Hug-Hellmuth and then Hanns Sachs came from Vienna in 1920 to offer courses in psychoanalytic pedagogy and to set the ground rules for training analyses. Soon, Karen Horney (1922–24), Helene Deutsch (1923–24), Melanie Klein (1921), and Karl Müller-Braunschweig (1922) arrived as trainees and analysts. Sándor Radó and Franz Alexander (the first person to receive a full training analysis; he was accepted as an analyst in 1925) came in 1921. (The influx of the Hungarians also was triggered by the persecution of Jews and their expulsion from the universities and the professions in the aftermath of Béla Kun's Communist regime.) Siegfried Bernfeld left Vienna for Berlin in 1926; so did Otto Fenichel. Theodore Reik arrived in October 1928 and Wilhelm Reich in 1930. Anna Freud taught at the institute in 1929, as did Hugo Staub, a former Viennese lawyer. When the Seventh International Psychoanalytic Congress met in Berlin in 1922, the Berliners proudly demonstrated to their visitors how the polyclinic supported both clinical work and research.

In 1928, Franz Alexander, Karl Müller-Braunschweig, and Sándor Radó created an official curriculum. They were able to attract candidates from a variety of professions without compromising psychoanalytic purity. Eitingon, in particular, opposed all quicker therapies and shortcuts. Thus, by 1930, aspiring analysts in Berlin were required to have a training analysis before being initiated into the theory or admitted to the seminars, and they had to handle a case under supervision before graduating. Candidates would discuss theoretical and methodological problems relating to their cases in a setting that to some extent re-created the interactions within the Wednesday Society (Alexander, 1930).

Such seminars among fellow candidates, under the guidance of a training analyst, soon became the norm in psychoanalytic institutes. Ultimately, the Berliners' methods were emulated all over the world. The analysts who had been trained there spoke of its glories long after they left Berlin. But others— those who would end up attacking "scientific" psychoanalysis—accused those at the polyclinic of having introduced rigidity and narrowness. And Melanie Klein, whose analyses of young children went against the Berliners' grain and who therefore felt increasingly isolated, moved to London in 1926.

Indeed, the seemingly organizational problems—how to select candidates, what to teach them, and for how long—were confronted as part of psychoanalysis itself. Later on, the perennial issues of medicalization versus lay analysis and of its cost to analysands would be traced primarily to the Berliners: the purer psychoanalysis became, the costlier the training, the higher the class origin of candidates—and the stronger the attacks against elitism.

In the early 1920s, however, these issues had not yet become explosive. By the fall of 1928, some 66 analysts had graduated in Berlin, and 34 others were on their way. By 1929, 711 persons had attended courses. By 1930, 94 therapists had worked at the polyclinic, 1,955 consultations had taken place, 604 analyses were completed, and 117 were ongoing. The institute now offered more courses, attended by theologians, graphologists, nurses, and social workers. In sum, the success of this enterprise turned it into a model for all other psychoanalytic organizations. And after Abraham died in 1926 and Eitingon took over (Ernest Jones replaced him as president of the IPA), these activities continued.

The Berliners' exemplary practice had been a boon to both therapy and theory, so that Gregory Zilboorg, an American born in Russia, declared that its graduates made up the bulk of "Who's Who in Psychoanalysis": "There is no place in America or Europe where the 35 years of psychoanalytic research were more carefully systematized, more clearly crystallized, and offered to the beginner with such seriousness and devotion" (Maetze, 1976, p. 1168). Clearly, Ferenczi's hopes for a "superorganization" had materialized, although he himself soon would deem its rules too rigid. And Anna Freud, in her posthumous Festschrift for Eitingon, reaffirmed the early rules by reiterating that duly appointed IPA committees were to be the arbiters of what constituted "true" psychoanalysis. These arbiters, of course, had had the "training analyses" the Berliners had "invented" (Alexander, [1930], 1970, p. 1).

Histories of psychoanalysis in Germany tend to deal almost exclusively with Berlin and scarcely mention the societies in Heidelberg (where Frieda Fromm-Reichmann had a small private clinic), Dresden, or Hamburg. And they barely note that Karl Landauer and Heinrich Meng had contacts with the Institut für Sozialforschung in Frankfurt, which furthered Freudo-Marxist syntheses. Perhaps the Berliners' prominence so overshadowed the other centers they could not attract potential members and thus grow beyond the status of societies (these did not have training centers); perhaps many leftist intellectuals preferred Berlin so they could participate in the liberation of working-class polyclinic patients with the help of psychoanalysis.

The Viennese psychoanalysts, of course, were also on the political left. But most of them were not active, or conversely, they were too active to organize as the Berliners had. In 1927, Wilhelm Reich, for instance, joined work-

ers who were protesting the wanton shooting of a man and a young child by
the Heimwehr (dominated by the Christian Socialists), and he indignantly
noted that the Social Democrats did not call out their Schutzbund to fight
the police who were shooting the demonstrators (Sharaf, 1983, p. 85). Yet,
even though his strongest sympathies then were for the Communist party,
Reich nevertheless was involved primarily with his patients and with the Vienna Psychoanalytic Polyclinic. As in Berlin, they analyzed farmers, students,
workers, and others who could not afford to pay for treatment. Together with
Otto Fenichel, Grete Bibring, Siegfried Bernfeld, and other members of the
so-called *Kinderseminar*, Reich pushed for socialist ideals. Thus the activities
of the polyclinic, which in some sense had been anticipated by Adler, as well
as by August Aichhorn's and Siegfried Bernfeld's experiments with delinquents and Anna Freud's kindergarten, indicate that some of the Viennese
were as politically engaged as the Berliners. Still, the Berliners' ambience,
the fact that they were not vying for Freud's attention on an intimate basis,
helped them get along better among themselves.

The Advent of Hitler

Soon after Adolf Hitler took over the country, the Nazis co-opted the
Berlin institute. First, the Aryan members Felix Boehm and Karl Müller-
Braunschweig induced the Jewish members (a majority) to withdraw "volun-
tarily" from the Deutsche Psychoanalytische Vereinigung (DPV). According
to Jeanne Lampl-de Groot, who joined Freud when the two men came to Vienna to talk with him, they did not get Freud's consent to this move as they
pretended they had. In spite of their claim that they wanted only to preserve
their institute's structure, however, they subverted the organization and lived
up to the expectations of the Nazis. Once again, the Freudians were so preoccupied with their movement that they shut out political realities. In fact, at
the Lucerne congress in 1934, Ernest Jones asserted that Eitingon "could not
possibly have foreseen [in 1932] the incredible developments of the following
months" (*Bulletin*, 1934, p. 486). A year later, many Jewish analysts, though
assuming that Hitler would soon be toppled, had nevertheless left Germany.

Most of the Freudians believed that placating the Nazis would save psychoanalysis. To that end, they elected Boehm and Müller-Braunschweig sole
members of the executive committee, and anticipating more direct Nazi
pressure, the German contingent withdrew from the IPA. Now, Freudian psychoanalysis was being denounced as Jewish while some of its ideas were being
converted into their Germanic counterparts: they all called psychoanalysis,

for example, *Seelenheilkunde*, "healing the soul." By 1936, the Berlin institute had become part of the Reichsinstitut and was attached to the Deutsche Allgemeine Gesellschaft für Psychotherapie, headed by Prof. Mattias Heinrich Göring, an Adlerian and cousin of Hermann Göring.[5] This organization published the *Zentralblatt für Psychotherapie* and originally derived much of its legitimation from its association with and support by Jung. Actually, Jung was using this opportunity to get back at Freud, claiming that Freud had applied "Jewish categories to Christian Germans or Slavs . . . [by considering] the precious secret and the creative roots of Germanic man a childish, banal morass, while suspecting [Jung] of anti-Semitism" (Grunert, 1984, p. 871). He now asserted that the difference between German and Jewish psychology no longer should be glossed over (Jung, 1934, p. 9). Although Jung soon distanced himself from this position, he undoubtedly added legitimacy to the Nazis' despicable acts, although certainly the atrocities would have occurred without his blessing (see chapter 4).

In 1938, the Wiener Psychoanalytischer Verein (wpv) was reduced nearly overnight from 88 members (104 if candidates are included) to 2 and became another one of Göring's Reichsinstituts. Freud, who had advised against emigration until shortly before the Anschluss, fled the country along with most Jewish members and a number of others. Although this was a traumatic step for Freud, organizational activities were relatively unaffected, for most had already been moved to London. The annexation of the wpv followed the pattern that had been established in Germany. It was ironic that the remnants of the Viennese and Berlin organizations were being joined just as psychoanalysis was being scattered. Now, the so-called Gruppe A (between four and fourteen people) in the Berlin Reichsinstitut, which was said to have remained loyal to Freudian ideas, operated in more or less clandestine fashion. Although we will never really know the extent to which it was co-opted, the organization in 1945 had over two hundred therapists, so that the Freudians were at best a small minority.

The wpv was never formally dissolved. One of its two remaining members, Alfred Freiherr von Winterstein, was *rassisch belastet* (racially tainted): he had one or two Jewish grandparents and thus had to shun public life. Alfred Aichhorn, like Freud before him, held meetings in his home, but they were now clandestine. And another small group met between 1944 and 1945 under the direction of Victor E. Freiherr von Gebsattel, who was not friendly to the regime but was not a psychoanalyst either.

In recent years, a few survivors of the Reichsinstitut have reported on therapists' activities between 1933 and 1945 as if they flourished in those years. But they have had to be careful about their claims because whatever research they took part in was aimed at implementing Nazi policies. So whether we believe those who tell us privately that without compromises and collaboration psychoanalysis would have died (thus admitting that what was practiced was not psychoanalysis) or those who think that the existence of the group itself was proof of its subversive stance, we cannot speak of a continuing psychoanalytic structure. After the war, new activities were grafted onto the skeletons in a number of cities, among them Berlin, Vienna, and Munich, and psychoanalysis was resurrected and relegitimated (see chapter 9). The Viennese, however, whose country was occupied by the Russians until 1955, actually did little more than go through the motions of reviving their organization until pushed by the student movement in the late 1960s.

Speaking of the period before Hitler, we can superficially characterize the Austrians as having retained their early informal structure even after the formation of the IPA and a polyclinic and the Berliners as having created an exemplary formal organization. Psychoanalysts, of course, tend to attribute these structural differences to Freud's dislike of organization versus Abraham's and Eitingon's talents along this line. But this view ignores the influences of the two social and political milieus, which exerted their own pressures on the participants and broadened or closed their options. These pressures may also have been responsible for what Wittels called the specific milieu-oriented neuroses; or these might have been both cause and "proof" of Wittels's prejudice against Berlin (Nunberg and Federn, 1962, 1:373).

The Americans Organize

The dissimilarities between the two German-speaking psychoanalytic groups were less striking than their differences from their counterparts in the United States, where psychoanalytic terms such as *defenses, Oedipus complex, fixation,* and *reaction formation* were already becoming household words. Local psychoanalytic societies in America were fending off candidates and patients instead of seeking them and had to "defend" psychoanalysis against wild analysts, quacks, faith healers, and charlatans. Eventually, some of these defenders became more Freudian than Freud.

After their visit to America, Freud, Ferenczi, and Jones had stayed in touch with a number of American followers and had urged them to organize outside the Psychopathological Association instead of setting up a branch within it. In response, A. A. Brill founded the New York Psychoanalytic Society in 1911 (it was granted autonomy at the Third International Congress in 1914);[6] James Jackson Putnam set up the Boston Psychoanalytic Society in

1914; and in the same year a number of people dispersed all over the country formed the American Psychoanalytic Association (APA) (Hale, 1971a, p. 318).[7] All the APA founders were doctors, but they did not explicitly restrict membership to physicians. According to Nathan G. Hale, Jr. (1971a, p. 318), these organizations were started to please Freud and to strengthen the international movement. In addition, they made it possible for members to exchange information *en famille*.

For the most part, Americans had learned about psychoanalysis through reading, and they were also influenced by proselytizing analysts and by neurologists and psychiatrists who had gone to Vienna and Zurich or had listened to Freud at Clark University (Hale, 1971a, pp. 319–24). Their social background, says Hale, differed from that of the Europeans in that most of them were from a slightly lower social rung than the average business person; thus becoming doctors had meant upward mobility. Only a small proportion was Jewish. Most of them had bachelor's degrees, and those who turned to psychoanalysis were self-selected and self-trained. Until the late 1920s, they entered the profession after a self-analysis, helped by reading, discussion, and correspondence. At the outset, Freud had encouraged these means of training, but he soon recommended that everyone copy the Zurichers, the first ones to require that analysts be analyzed by another. (Later on, this was stipulated by the American Psychoanalytic Association but not the New York group.)

The American analysts were more democratic than the Europeans: they saw a greater proportion of factory workers, secretaries, poor artists. Still, most of their hours were filled by middle- and upper-middle-class patients. They soon had their own publications and often printed daringly speculative articles in the *Psychoanalytic Review*, edited by William Alanson White. The *Psychoanalytic Quarterly* was founded in 1933 in order to feature the more orthodox contributions. Their organizations and their interactions were heterogeneous and informal. They kept scant records, particularly when compared to Rank's *Minutes* or the detailed logs of the Berliners. (There were American notices in the *Zeitschrift*.)

After World War I, the discrepancies—particularly in medicalization and training requirements—between the APA and the IPA had grown, so that the APA had begun to push for independence. This attitude was sparked partly by anti-German feeling as well as by the wish for autonomy. As White put it, American psychoanalysts had to free themselves "from the Pope in Vienna," but White's motion was defeated. Many of the Americans realized that they knew rather little about clinical practice. Hence, they asked Freud to spend six months in New York giving courses and conducting analyses.

When he refused, a number of them journeyed to Vienna or Berlin to be analyzed. According to Gregory Zilboorg, they reportedly were overwhelmed by the rigor, the sophisticated concepts, and the new clinical techniques, particularly those of the Berlin institute.

Now, American psychoanalysis made another spurt: in 1924, the Boston society, after having dissolved in 1918, reconstituted itself; and the Washington Psychoanalytic Association was founded. But the Americans were not yet aware that the Europeans were far from united. They did not realize that Melanie Klein had left for London because she had strayed from the Berliners' interpretations of Freud's death instinct and from their understanding of primal anxiety, or that Rank was already distancing himself from the rigor the Berliners were perfecting. Rank unwittingly upset the Americans when he presented them with "a new viewpoint, introduced by me," and when he argued that short-term psychoanalytic therapy often was effective and even preferable (Lieberman, 1985, p. 229). The Americans already felt too pressured by the many quacks and healers claiming to do brief "psychoanalyses" and by the conflicts over lay analysis and short-term therapy.[8] Actually, Rank and Ferenczi were increasingly deviating from Freud's method: they geared their analyses less to uncovering traumatic events in the patient's past than to the activity of the analysis—that is, to the therapeutic dialogue—an approach Harry Stack Sullivan would incorporate into his interpretive psychiatry. Freud, who in the beginning was less orthodox, now backed the Berliners and their followers, so that in 1924, he officially rejected Rank's ideas and became estranged from Ferenczi, a few years before the latter died in 1933.

The Rise of the American Psychoanalytic Association

The American organization was especially threatened by the lay analysts, because the public was unable to distinguish them from imposters. At least initially it was this problem rather than the need for more knowledge that led APA members to press for uniform professional criteria. Medicalization, it was argued, might keep out some qualified humanists, but that would be a lesser evil than the proliferation of wild practices. The Freudians called upon the IPA's training commission to resolve this issue. They failed to realize that the IPA could control access to its own membership but could not possibly influence American policymakers on who would be allowed into the healing professions. In 1926, for instance, after the New York society had asked the New York State Board of Charity for permission to establish a psychoanalytic clinic, the state, supported by a powerful physicians' lobby, passed a law forbidding nonmedical people to practice medicine. This meant that lay analysts, whatever their training, were barred from practice and that the APA, which had lay members, was denied its request for a psychoanalytic clinic.

Legal decisions, however, could not settle whether medical training is necessary for, or even improves, the practice of psychoanalysis, and as we know, this issue remains central. Neither then nor later would analysts agree on the best way to conduct a psychoanalysis (see below and chapter 11). At the time, it did not help that Ferenczi, while visiting at the New School for Social Research, held private seminars at the APA which nondoctors would attend and that his listeners later on would call themselves psychoanalysts. (Rank and Adler did the same.) This controversy became the central topic of the Tenth International Congress in Innsbruck, in 1927, where twenty-eight papers were presented on the question of lay analysis. A high point was reached when Anna Freud, referring to herself, asked whether a regular lay member of the WPV would be admitted to the APA or the NYPA and C. P. Oberndorf said no (1953, p. 136). (It is interesting to note that Oberndorf, upon seeing Freud for the last time before he died, wondered why Freud was cool toward him [1949, p. 161]). But organizational disagreements did not stop there. Americans could go to Vienna or Berlin to become lay analysts and thereby get around American rules. They finally forged a truce: the Europeans agreed not to train lay candidates who had not already been approved by an American society, and the Americans promised to consider accepting nondoctors.

By 1929, a number of local societies (New York, Boston, Washington, and Chicago) had begun to hold seminars, offer theoretical courses to candidates, and institute control analyses. In 1931, the New York Psychoanalytic Institute was opened, with Brill as president. In 1932, the first German analysts—led by Karen Horney, who joined Franz Alexander in Chicago—came to America.[9] During the same year the APA was dissolved and reconstituted as a federation of local organizations. The new federation had few functions because training and membership decisions were made by the locals, and analysts who were accepted by a local society automatically became members of both the APA and the IPA. The latter was to have ultimate authority and to approve every decision taken by the APA's Council on Professional Standards.

Lay Analysis in London

During the 1920s, the British Society was confronting its own problems with lay analysis. These were compounded by the fact that, although Jones was a doctor, 40 percent of his colleagues, whose work he respected, were not. After endless debates, the Society's Sub-Committee on Lay Analysis, headed by Jones, decided in 1927 that "most analysts should be freely admitted provided that certain conditions are fulfilled" (Kohon, 1986, p. 31). Jones did not, however, elaborate on these conditions—how medical schools were to choose future candidates or how the patients of nonmedical analysts were to be "inspected by a physician." Clearly, the decision could not satisfy Freud, who insisted ever more strongly that would-be psychoanalysts should be trained in psychoanalysis rather than in medicine—which, he said, "gives people a false and detrimental attitude."

Jones was torn between his conviction that the medical outlook would be a boon for future analysts and his wish to please Freud. He had just entrusted the analysis of his own two children to Melanie Klein, a lay analyst. Even the term *lay analysis*, which to Freud meant nonmedical, in England could just as readily mean nonprofessional or nonlearned. And this semantic confusion invited yet more prejudices. In any event, whatever Jones's own preferences were, he protected his lay colleagues and made certain that a high proportion of analysts in the British Psycho-Analytical Society would not be doctors (Kohon, 1986, p. 36). His insistence also may have furthered the prestige of the child psychoanalysts, few of whom were doctors, as well as research in that area by Melanie Klein and her circle and later by those around Anna Freud.

The Immigrants Arrive

In America, medicalization was accepted by 1927, after Bertram Lewin, presiding over the New York Council on Professional Standards, convinced the analysts that he was not trying merely to gain his own ends but was responding to pending legislation: were lay analysts admitted to the New York Institute, it might be closed. Franz Alexander and Karl Menninger talked of similar conditions in Chicago.

Gradually, the Americans became even more resentful of the Europeans, and at the International Congress in Marienbad in 1936, they announced they would veto any resolution that in any way addressed American issues. The Europeans were losing their hold as a result of political events. Those who had come to America softened their views in response to the dislocation they had undergone: they were both grateful to and at the mercy of their hosts. Earlier differences diminished as they cooperated for the sake of psychoanalysis and as the former Europeans came to realize they had underestimated the weight of local conditions and the Americans' preference for pluralistic control—for federation over centralization (see chapter 9).

By 1938, the APA had formulated its own rules for "minimal training of physicians" at psychoanalytic institutes and societies; it spelled out proper conduct for its members; and it prohibited the training of laymen. The rules, however, could be amended with the consent of local organizations. The Americans then submitted their resolutions to the IPA and declared that in the future they would cooperate on scientific matters alone. In practice, the new rules meant that a few lay analysts, such as Ernst Kris, Siegfried Bernfeld, Erik Erikson, and Otto Fenichel, whose reputations towered over those of most of their American colleagues, would be appointed honorary members, but most of the others would have to be doctors.

Events in Europe soon transformed the American organization, and it grew steadily with the influx of European analysts:

Year	Number of APA Members
1932	92
1938	157
1940	192
1942	230
1944–45	247
1946	273

From R. P. Knight, "The Present Status of Organized Psychoanalysis in the United States," *Journal of the American Psychoanalytic Association* 1, nos. 1–4 (1953): 207, table 1.

The Americans set up a committee to welcome the Europeans. At first, fearful of competition, they asked them to move to the interior of the country rather than settle in New York. Nevertheless, by 1945 there were four times as many analysts in that city than at the beginning of the war. Wherever they ended up, the immigrants' abilities bolstered psychoanalysis as a whole. Between 1939 and 1946, new teaching institutes were created in Washington-Baltimore, Topeka, Philadelphia, and San Francisco, along with societies in the last two cities and in Detroit. The influx of famous European analysts increased the demand for psychoanalysis. But it did not take long before the controversies over lay analysis that had been played out between the IPA and the APA surfaced within the APA itself. (Within this confusion, each local American society developed in its own way, under the aegis of specific personalities responding to specific issues, compromises, and rifts. The story of each society, I have been told, would fill a book.)

The Psychoanalysts at War

Karen Horney's *The Neurotic Personality of Our Time* (1937) and *New Ways in Psychoanalysis* (1939), which stressed the importance of cultural impact on individual development, were the first challenges to the turn toward ego psychology (see chapter 3). They caused a furor within the APA, although Horney, after many debates, was barred "only" from teaching. In response, she resigned from the New York Psychoanalytic Society and founded the Association for the Advancement of Psychoanalysis, where in 1941 she was joined by Clara Thompson, Erich Fromm, and Harry Stack Sullivan. When Horney refused to teach lay people, Sullivan left and started the William Alanson White Institute, which was not recognized by the APA. Another group, led by Judd Marmor, left Horney in 1944 because she chose not to train candidates of the New York Medical College. (Marmor's institute did not ask for APA recognition, and its members lost the benefits of belonging.)

In 1942, some members rebelled against the "authoritarian tendencies" in the APA. Led by Carl Binger, Abram Kardiner, J. P. Millet, and Sándor Radó, they formed the "Columbia group," but without resigning from either the APA or the IPA. Thus substantive issues, which inadvertently included leftist and rightist politics, once again were being settled through organizational moves: new institutes abounded, but basic questions remained unresolved.

J. P. Millet was annoyed that the European analysts and their students increasingly dominated the APA in the 1940s. He claimed that they were trying to establish the IPA's authoritarian style of leadership by virtue of their former relationship to Freud (1966, p. 558). But the APA had decided not to admit more than one institute per locality, so that analysts, although they might be engaged in bitter disputes, were constrained to cooperate with one another. (In fact, at the first postwar meeting, in 1946, the APA dropped this geographic rule.) But regardless of whether the analysts belonged to the same institute, they did not follow Freud's wish that they "roar or howl together in chorus and in the same rhythm, instead of having each one growl in his corner," as he had suggested to Groddeck (Honegger, 1988, p. 76).[10] Even the increasingly loose mechanisms of control did not engender harmony, nor did the reaffirmation of allegiance to the IPA.

Actually, psychoanalysis had been transplanted to Anglo-Saxon territory: its physiognomy had been altered, and it had become legitimated among many intellectuals. Moreover, by 1952, 64 percent of the IPA members were American (the next largest contingent were the British). Hence, the Europeans ipso facto no longer dominated.

By then, Anna Freud had become the symbolic heir, although she lacked Freud's authority, and circumstances were changing. She could not blame organizational dissent on bad character traits or neurosis, as her father had done. And psychoanalysts no longer considered personal criticism a boon to their science, as they had on those Wednesday evenings in Vienna; rather, they took it literally and were offended. Furthermore, when the disciples thought of each other as equals, their quarrels increased. In order to neutralize their "sibling rivalry," it was imperative that impersonal criteria be adopted: organizational matters now would have to be decided on merit alone. But in the struggle for intellectual dominance and leadership, the analysts could not agree on a definition of objectivity.

The Tardy French

Because the French had not taken to psychoanalysis, their organization before the war was small and informal. Only two of its members—Marie Bonaparte and Eugenie Sokolnicka—were in close touch with Freud. Basically, Janet's and Bergson's understandings of the unconscious had won out over Freud's, and the relatively strong psychosomatic tradition had also militated against the acceptance of psychoanalysis. Hence, the French did not take much notice of it until 1919, when René Laforgue wrote an essay on the psychoanalysis of schizophrenics. And only in 1921 did Sokolnicka (she had been analyzed by Freud and had studied with Jung and Ferenczi) manage to start a movement (Barande and Barande, 1975, pp. 43–44).

When the Société Psychanalytique de Paris (SPP) was registered in 1926, it had ten members, and even these were not fully committed. Laforgue, who together with Eduard Pichon and two others had formed another organization, Evolution Psychiatrique, the year before, inevitably had split loyalties. For a long time, he refused to put Freud's name on the masthead of the *Revue Française de Psychanalyse* and said that he "disliked the mentality of the psychoanalysts around Freud" (Roudinesco, 1982). (It has recently been established that he wrote to Hermann Göring after the fall of France, suggesting cooperation [Mijolla, 1987].) Laforgue and Pichon usually offered to treat most of their neurotic patients medically before suggesting psychoanalysis. Such a "choice," of course, further curtailed psychoanalysis.

Even without these obstacles, expansion would have been difficult: only four of the members—Laforgue, Raymond de Saussure, Charles Odier (both analyzed in Berlin by Alexander), and Rudolph Loewenstein (from Berlin and reportedly analyzed by Freud but actually by Hanns Sachs)—were qualified to take on and train candidates. The situation was slightly improved when René Spitz and Heinz Hartmann, in transit to the United States, analyzed a few people. (By then the French had argued over translations of Freud, had started the Conference of French-speaking Psychoanalysts, and had joined the IPA, by whose regulations they more or less abided [Mijolla, 1982, p. 28].) Still, in 1939, after thirteen years, the SPP had only twenty-four full members.

During those years, it seems, French psychoanalysts were rather free-wheeling. Relationships with candidates and patients were determined by personal preference rather than rules. The resulting informality kept organizational problems to a minimum, and when they arose they could be handled in privacy. In fact, Roudinesco's (1982), the Barandes' (1975), and Jaccard's (1982) histories do not deal with organizational matters except in reference to the IPA. Roudinesco praises the lack of formality as a boon to individualism and is especially astute in pointing to the many contradictory attitudes: Pichon, for example, was strongly for medicalizing French psychoanalysis. This pitted him against Marie Bonaparte, who advocated lay analysis. Nevertheless, the two agreed that candidates needed a didactic analysis (it had become an IPA requirement), though Pichon denounced everything else this body stood for (Roudinesco, 1982, p. 302). At the same time, Pichon rejected Freud's elevation of psychoanalysis above nationality and reaffirmed French superiority, expecting to analyze away the "German" characteristics of this "Viennese theory" (p. 304). This stance was somewhat ludicrous in view of the fact that two of the founding members of the SPP were Swiss and a few others spoke French with a Russian accent. Mijolla, however, attributes these tensions to the heterogeneity of the founders of the SPP: doctors and non-doctors, a Bonapartist princess and a monarchist, nationalists and emigrants, alienated Catholics and didactic Jews, a medical professor in transit, convinced Freudians and amateurs, and even one who was drawn to astrology and homeopathy. Somehow these analysts needed each other; they were ambivalent toward Vienna and did not have the talent to mobilize others (1982, p. 29). How could they do serious and original work? Inevitably, the French contributions could not rival those of Ferenczi, Rank, or Abraham. Even Marie Bonaparte, Freud's most ardent champion, aside from her essays on Edgar Allan Poe, did no more than disseminate the ideas of others.

The SPP's statutes differed from those of other IPA locals in that the French opted to admit two sorts of members—titular and associate. The former were senior analysts, and they elected the executive committee. Candidates were to be granted associate membership and upon graduation were to be promoted to titular membership. But the titular members had much leeway: Pichon and Laforgue deviated more from IPA rules than did Bonaparte and Loewenstein, although none of them took these rules too seriously. According to Roudinesco, their disagreements did not prevent the French analysts from meeting over many a dinner, especially in the elegant homes of Laforgue and Bonaparte. There, they

spoke incessantly of sexuality, morals, "strange" troubles and madness. Their clinical stories furnish intimate details about the lives of their analysands. But this did not stop some of the practitioners of the unconscious from being puritan bourgeois, scandalized by the sexual practices of their patients. One would think that in their social lives, the subversive effects of the rediscovery of sexuality favored the outbreak of moralism. (1982, 1:354–55)

Roudinesco is not the only historian of French psychoanalysis to revel in such details or to speculate on the consequences of personal alliances and dislikes. But whether these historians stress early events to show that the French had good reason to ignore psychoanalysis or that the prehistory set the stage for the emergence of Lacan, it is clear that the SPP's organizational life by 1939 had not advanced beyond that of the Wednesday Society before 1908, and that its focus on science was minimal.

After the Second World War, even the embryonic French organization was gone: Pichon and Allendy had died; Sophie Morgenstern had committed suicide when the Germans arrived; Borel had left the field. And Hartmann, Loewenstein, and Spitz had established themselves in America. The remaining Parisian psychoanalysts, therefore, had to regroup and recruit new disciples. Whatever followed would be a beginning.

The Watershed

Freud's death in October 1939, so soon after his emigration from Vienna, coincided with the beginning of the *drôle de guerre*. Since political events had forced adherents of the practice of psychoanalysis to move from the Continent to America and England for the duration of the war, both the ideas and the organization were bound to undergo fundamental changes. But psychoanalysis, once the charismatic leader was dead, would have had to be reorganized even if the Nazis had not tried to stamp it out. No matter what the political reality, Freud's followers would have had to adapt to the new situation.

With Freud gone, factionalism increased. That he himself had initiated the pattern of breaking relations with opponents justified the many organizational ruptures over ever narrower issues. In fact, the more widely accepted psychoanalysis was in a given country, the more numerous would be the splits and the more diverse the organization. The "sons" and "daughters" might claim they had been closest to Freud or had understood him best, but they now used their organizations to implement their own ideas.

During the first forty-five years of psychoanalysis's history, its practitioners had become professionalized, and the pioneers had become the gurus of the profession. Freud's deputies, Ferenczi, Abraham, and Jones, were now the driving forces in their respective countries. There, as leaders of the movement, they with their followers negotiated with medical and legal authorities, pushing for the general acceptance of psychoanalysis, although not without a good deal of frustration. It was difficult, for example, to explain psychoanalysis to lawmakers who could not understand its basic premises. Thus, they were forced to adapt and occasionally to bend to the customs, rules, and legal codes of the various countries. Their followers no longer had close ties with one another and thus felt less attached to the IPA. But having pledged to conform to IPA criteria and benefit from the association, the analysts would often feel torn between the demands of country and profession.

It had been imperative to formulate professional codes in order to exert control, especially while new national or local organizations had too few members to separate personal and political prejudices from professional practices. But national authorities often expected to wield the same type of control over the analysts that they exerted over other professionals. The Americans resolved these problems by restricting access to the profession to physicians; the Germans, by accepting psychologists under very special conditions; the Austrians, by eventually reuniting with Adlerians; the British, by compromising; and the French, by favoring hospital affiliation for analysts.

Paradoxically, none of the national regulations would deal with what psychoanalysts themselves gradually came to indict as malpractice: bad countertransferences that were due to analysts' failure to resolve their personal conflicts. The Freudians realized they themselves had to enforce ethical standards upon their members. On the other hand, full disclosure of unacceptable practices could interfere with psychoanalytic precepts of privacy and confidentiality—if the damaging information had been received "from the couch." If it was thought that a respected colleague had not been "abstemious," that the analyst had taken advantage of a patient either emotionally or sexually, public exposure could harm the profession. Moreover, since patients' reports might easily be the product of unconscious wishes and their accusations no more than fabrications, the Freudians knew only too well that airing these issues in public would be counterproductive, for outsiders would not understand. Under the circumstances, it was difficult to impose sanctions on those who had transgressed. Thus questions about criteria for admission in the first place became central and screening committees more powerful. The practitioners spent much time trying to predict what character traits eventually would make for the best analysts. Such a task is difficult for any profession anywhere, but it was almost insuperable for psychoanalysis, given the need to protect the privacy of its dialogue—a dialogue that must not be monitored after a candidate has graduated.

After the Second World War, some of the members of regional organizations, such as the federations of German- or French-speaking psychoanalysts, started to address the enforcement of ethical codes. Although these organizations were supranational in scope, their members found it easier to cooperate with colleagues speaking the same language. Moreover, since membership in these organizations overlapped with memberships in local societies and the IPA, the members could get to know one another more intimately. The repeated exposure to colleagues would not only make for a more trusting climate, it was argued; their meeting again and again on the many committees would dissolve distrust of strangers—an inevitable problem in the IPA with its large membership.

After a while these federations too would become bureaucratic, however, for the Freudians have had to continue imposing bureaucratic solutions to resolve the questions arising from the tensions between learning more about psychoanalytic therapy, elaborating on theoretical issues, and advancing the psychoanalytic movement. But these solutions inevitably are compromises based on culture-bound assumptions which then impose themselves on the IPA. Thus, ever since Freud's death, consensus has been riddled with more and more compromises translated into more and more rules—rules that cannot avoid reining in the spontaneity psychoanalysis is built on.

Chapter 3

From Therapy
to Theory

American interpretations of the genesis of psychoanalytic theory stress historical, clinical, or biographical factors. But whether they support the classical Freudians' claim that psychoanalysis started with *The Interpretation of Dreams* (1900) or the contention of Ellenberger and Sulloway that the "Project for a Scientific Psychology" (1895) is the root of Freud's oeuvre, most historians tend to assume that Freud's thinking before 1900 was shaped by his relation to Fliess as well as by his work in neurology. Still, commentators cannot agree on when his explorations of the roots of brain damage—aphasia, paralysis, blindness, lameness, tics—shifted to a new investigation. But at some point in the course of his inquiries Freud noticed that the symptoms of many diseases, including syphilis, were like those of hysteria, and he began to speculate on what linked these diseases to the symptoms of neurotic ailments, such as depressions, phobias, obsessions, and paranoia. His "Project," in fact, addressed the connections between the sexuality of *all* his patients and their physical disturbances. Some of his admirers, however, stress his determination not to reduce physical symptoms to psychic ones or vice versa, whereas others are likely to play down the importance of the "Project" because of its affinity with Darwinism.[1]

Whatever we think about Freud's ambitious undertaking to pinpoint the biological roots of psychic processes, we know that he abandoned it because

61

it did not work. He had expected "to furnish a psychology that would be a natural science; that [would] represent psychical progress as quantitatively determinate states of specifiable material particles, thus making those processes perspicuous and free from contradiction" (*S.E.*, 1:295). Even James Strachey, Freud's English translator, who was not much interested in the "Project" itself, thought it provided an "extraordinarily ingenious working model of the mind as a piece of neurological machinery" (*S.E.*, 4:xviii). The fact that Freud *did* try to construct a neurological model of the psyche has led some physiologists to trace the ideas advanced in the "Project" through all of psychoanalysis and others to concentrate on one or another of his specific points. But still others argue that Freud dropped the entire endeavor as irrelevant to psychoanalysis: did he do so in order not to take time out from psychoanalysis, or because the "Project" reminded him of the painful relationship with Fliess he was trying to forget?

Early Insights and Practices

When Anna O., relieved of her illness, embraced Freud, he guessed that she was not taken by his charm but was expressing a "false rapport": that she was transferring previously repressed emotions onto him. Breuer, we recall, had treated her from December 1880 until June 1882. He had listened to her descriptions of symptoms and had used suggestion during hypnosis, thereby bringing about what he called "catharsis." But after this daily treatment had led her to feel attached to him, to the point of "finding herself in the contractions of a hysterical birth (pseudocyesis)," Breuer went on a trip (or fled) and turned her over to Freud. As Freud listened to her story, he connected her symptoms to the relationship she had had with Breuer. In fact, Freud turned the traditional doctor-patient relationship upside down—that is, he did not tell her what to do.

In his "History of the Psychoanalytic Movement" (*S.E.*, 14:3–66) Freud recalled that he had given in to his curiosity for a number of reasons. He had heard Breuer talk of a nervous woman patient who had related her suffering to the *secret d'alcove*, the marriage bed. Charcot had held that a woman's affliction customarily was due to *la chose génitale*. And his Viennese colleague Chroback had referred to a patient's sexual anxiety. Taken together, Freud reminisced, these clues had shown him his path. According to Ellenberger and Sulloway, the "History" was written to further the movement and encouraged the Freudians' "hero myth." Therefore, they played down Freud's inventive listening—the *écoute* the French analysts have been exulting over for the past couple of decades.

Still, whatever the current interpretation, Freud *did* allow Anna O. to question him and to tell him what she chose to. And the formalization of this change in roles *did* remove her hysterical symptoms, at least temporarily. When he treated Frau Emmy von N., who was unable to nurse her newborn infant, Freud could already explain that she was linking emotions to fantasies of expectation, with all the meaning she attached to their fulfillment and to the insecurities that permeated these meanings (*S.E.*, 1:117).[2] Since he apparently did cure her, it was somewhat unfair for Ellenberger to fasten on the fact that Freud had done so by combining hypnosis and suggestion and that this was closer to the methods of faith healers than to those of physicians. Clearly, Ellenberger did not appreciate, as the Freudians do, that Freud managed to generalize from this case to a series of cases involving the influences of the psyche on bodily functions and that he learned to differentiate between symptoms of hysteria, neurosis, and cases of *hysterie d'occasion* (*S.E.*, 1:123).

Nor have the detractors been very much impressed by Freud's innovative method. At first, he asked his patients to lie down and close their eyes in order to encourage unconscious memories to surface. When free associations did not seem to occur, he would become impatient, would press his hand on the patient's forehead, and would "lead" her. But after Fräulein Elisabeth von R. reproved him for interrupting her train of thought by questioning and prodding, he learned that silences were particularly useful (Jones, 1953, pp. 243–44). Gradually, he stopped guiding his patients' minds, and by 1892 he had completely given up hypnosis.

From then on, he increasingly advised his followers to let the patients lead them; the analyst was to practice "psychoanalytic abstinence," to avoid loving, sexual, and hostile relations with patients as well as social and business relations. Freud had also noted that patients' physical symptoms increased when unpleasant memories came up, when recall stopped, when they became afraid of dependency, or when they felt neglected or angry. This made him wonder how best he could deal with the resistances (he soon called them "transferences") that seemed to be induced by the psychoanalyst. This was why Freud began to delay interpretation, to keep quiet and stay out of the process as much as possible. Step by step, he decreased his active involvement. First, he stopped touching the patient's head; then he placed his chair behind the couch in order to avoid eye contact.

Over the years, American Freudians have elaborated on this push toward a "neutral" psychoanalytic setting, which both internal and external critics at times have deemed exaggerated. In fact, we now have a history of psychoanalytic abstinence as a concept in technique and a subliterature on the controversy, including a "classical" position which expects the analyst to remain totally incognito and the patient to refrain from major life decisions such as change of career or spouse during the analysis (see Lipton, 1977). But analysts arguing against abstinence, such as Heinz Kohut, held that "to remain silent when one is asked a question . . . is not neutral but rude" (1971, p. 89). In any event, there is no doubt that Freud had established the rudimentary conditions and techniques for psychoanalysis before 1900 and that these were expected to pave "the road to the unconcious."

In Dreams Begin Theories

Freud's early followers, inspired by *The Interpretation of Dreams* (1900), were drawn to his new explanations of hysteria, which rejected both purely physical theories and those that relied on the power of suggestion or on trancelike states. But most of the disciples knew much less neurology than Freud. Thus they were more likely than he to explore the unconscious of their patients through language alone rather than fall back on the unfathomable links between psyche and biology. In any event, he had formulated his basic ideas about infantile sexuality by 1895 and had recognized that the capacity for bisexuality was universal. Furthermore, he had noted the differences between infants' and adults' sexuality and that some behaviors that in children are "interests" (voyeurism, exhibitionism, sadomasochistic impulses) in adults are "perversions." He also had wondered about problems of sleep and memory, and especially about the reasons for repressing painful memories (*S.E.*, 2:352).

Theories of repression invariably are based on one or another component of Freud's self-analysis (Jones, 1953; Isbister, 1985, pp. 73–76). But aside from the more obvious substantive questions the so-called prehistory presented yet another problem to Freud. Since he relied greatly on his own dreams and their interpretation as the basis of his new science, he was bothered by the need to explain the "story-telling" aspects of this material to a scientific audience, his medical peers. So, when reporting on his first full-length analysis (Fräulein Elisabeth von R.), for instance, he went to great lengths to prove that he was being scientific and was not making up stories:

I have not always been a psychotherapist. Like other neuropathologists, I was trained to employ local diagnoses and electro-prognosis, and it still strikes me myself as strange that the case histories I write should read like short stories and that, as one might say, they lack the serious stamp of science. I must console myself with the reflection that the nature of the subject is evidently responsible for this, rather than any preference of my own. The fact is that local diagnosis and electrical reactions lead nowhere in the study of hysteria, whereas a detailed description of mental processes such as we are accustomed to find in the works of imaginative writers enables me, with the use of a few psychological formulas, to obtain at least some kind of insight into the course of that affliction. (*S.E.*, 2:160–61)

These preoccupations would persist. Nearly every time he was attacked for moving too close to philosophy, Freud would insist that he was ignorant of that field: he claimed not to have known of Schopenhauer's interpretation of insanity until Rank told him about it and played down what he had read by Nietzsche in order to prove that psychoanalysis was derived from empirical observation alone. Some recent German historians have been trying to prove that he was much more familiar with these philosophers than he admitted and that his early defensiveness was unwarranted. They have done so rather effectively by digging into Freud's correspondence, political involvements, and school records.[3] Freud simply wanted to distance psychoanalysis from the bad reputation philosophy had among doctors, natural scientists, and psychiatrists. Freudians excuse his subterfuge as an innocent forgetting for the sake of the movement. Actually, Freud felt compelled to prove that he was a doctor—one who cured hysterical symptoms by uncovering fictitious traumas and fantasies.

Originally, Freud thought that the recollection of trauma alone would cure the patient. When this turned out to be just the first of many abreactions and new insights engendered only temporary relief, he was disappointed. This led him to explore the circumstances and feelings surrounding the trauma and to attempt to develop the best method for uncovering it. As Freud became more and more aware of the impact on adults of repressed childhood memories, particularly those surrounding sexuality, he explained the relative absence of sexuality during latency as being due to repression. (The existence of a latency period is currently being challenged.) And he spoke of the transference of painful memories and of erotic libido onto the psychoanalyst as the only means to remember this past:

There is only one power which can remove the resistance, the transference. The patient is compelled to give up his resistance to *please* us. Our cures are cures of love. There would thus remain for us only the task of removing the *personal* resistances (those against the transference). To the extent that transference exists—to that extent can we bring about cures: the analogy with hypnotic cures is striking. It is only that in psychoanalysis, the power of the transference is used to produce a *permanent* change in the patient, whereas hypnosis is nothing but a clever trick. The vicissitudes of the transference decide the success of treatment. The only thing the method still lacks is authority; the element of suggestion must be added from without. But even so, the need of the unconscious for liberation meets us half way. The neurotic does not fall ill again because we have made conscious the infantile content. (Freud, 1912b; Nunberg and Federn, 1962, 1:100–02)

The more he focused on the direct connections between repression and transference, the more Freud began to look for internal differentiations. Thus he distinguished between positive and negative transference. In fact, he began to conceptualize the *transference*. He suggested that the analyst, instead of concentrating on the patient's utterances too closely, should trust his own "unconscious memory" (*S.E.*, 12 : 111–20). Such a focus also was to "save" the analyst from indulging the patient's sexual (and other) fantasies about himself, which by the very nature of this intimate setting seemed to occur routinely. As we can note, for instance, from Freud's letter to Jung, on June 7, 1909, in reference to Sabina Spielrein, Freud too had grappled with this problem:

Such experiences, though painful, are necessary and hard to avoid. Without them we cannot really know life and what we are dealing with. I myself have never been taken quite so badly, but I have come very close to it a number of times and had *a narrow escape*. I believe that only grim necessities weighing on my work, and the fact that I was ten years older than yourself when I came to psychoanalysis, have saved me from similar experiences. But no lasting harm is done. They help us to develop the thick skin we need and to dominate "countertransference," which is after all a permanent problem for us; they teach us to displace our own affects to best advantage. They are a *blessing in disguise*. (McGuire, 1974, pp. 230–31)

A year later, Freud talked more extensively of the irrational feelings of the analyst toward the patient as *countertransference* (*S.E.*, 11:141–52). And he became more and more adamant about the danger of personal involvement with patients, especially when Ferenczi increasingly advocated it. Soon he would postulate that the *disposition* to love the analyst depended upon the *predisposition* of the patient's personal history, insofar as his early libidinal emotions had been turned into unconscious fantasies and then were made available for projection onto the analyst by the psychoanalysis itself. The transference became part of the neurosis, and no one any longer suggested that the analyst might have caused it.

Actually, the Freudians soon realized that every new insight would affect clinical work as well as theory. At first, for example, Freud wondered why the childhood sexual experiences his patients were reporting had been repressed to begin with and then expressed as symptoms. Then he thought this had happened because these feelings had been prematurely aroused when the child was in an otherwise latent state and could not handle them. But soon he connected the memories to the feelings of anxiety and guilt that had originally accompanied them and realized that the memories were not usually factual recollections. Instead, they were elaborations of fantasies based on erotic wishes about significant persons in the child's life, particularly its parents.

Thus infantile (sexual) wishes, rooted in the oedipal complex, were perceived to be at the core of unconscious wishes in every individual's later life. When Freud perceived, in 1897, that not every patient who produced such fantasies had been seduced by her father, he abandoned the seduction theory. But the events surrounding this change of heart, of which he informed Fliess when he wrote on September 21 that he no longer "believed in his *neurotica*," have led to the most varied interpretations (Masson, 1985, p. 264). The most extreme is by Jeffrey Masson, who claims that Freud abandoned his original theory in deference to, and under the influence of, Fliess.

The new locus of seduction in the daughter's fantasy life should have made psychoanalysis more acceptable. But, again, because this insight had originated in Freud's self-analysis, both early and later disciples, and especially "revisionists," could justify questioning it, as they did everything derived from or related to the period of Freud's exemplary cure—the foundation of their discipline.

Theoretical Unity

During the early years, the Freudians pooled their intellectual and clinical resources and speculations; hence we cannot yet speak of the influence of different milieus. Vienna was the milieu for those who chose to follow Freud. When in their deliberations on Wednesday evenings the Freudians attributed specific neuroses to national customs or prejudices, they rarely wondered how such customs, in turn, might affect the occurrence and the nature of transference and countertransference. Thus, when they agreed that Viennese neuroses were the most susceptible to psychoanalysis and the most useful, they did not question whether attitudes toward childhood sexuality or resolutions of the Oedipus complex, for example, might differ from one culture to another. The assumption that these phenomena were universal led them to assume that their own experiences would be applicable everywhere. This made sense for a number of reasons.

First, since every human being now was thought to share a common (unconscious) past, psychoanalysis was believed to reaffirm the universal bond between races and creeds. True, this was an assumption about culture (see chapter 4), but it was based on the a priori experiences of individuals within specific cultures. And the origin of dreams, which had been hidden for thousands of years, was to be clarified by the members of the Wednesday Society (*S.E.*, 4:29). As the *Interpretation* (1900) together with the *Three Essays on Sexuality* (1905) became their bible, the Freudians did not doubt that they would eventually penetrate to the roots of civilization by mining their patients' unconscious, finding materials transcending not only all cultural artifacts but time and space.

Second, data derived from case studies, through a combination of scientific method and innovative reasoning, were to prove the theory and fill in the gaps. By "psychoanalyzing" literary characters and tracing their traits to the lives of their authors, they dramatized their clinical findings. The conclusions analysts derived from their literary studies appeared to corroborate their therapeutic assumptions.

Third, as Freud realized that patients amenable to hypnosis also would be likely to cooperate in free association, he kept systematizing this method as the most viable route to the unconscious. Now he conceptualized the transference and later the countertransference. These elusive processes, which needed constant watching and were to illuminate the mechanisms of the unconscious, also were considered universal.

Fourth, when the "chimney sweeping" of Anna O. (Bertha Papenheim, who later became a leading figure in social work) had led Freud and Breuer to formulate the psychophysical dynamics of hysteria, they were not yet aware of how fortunate they had been in having a patient intelligent enough to talk herself into a state of health by describing the details of her day and how these, in turn, were affecting her feelings. When few of their subsequent patients turned out to be so "ideal," they started to wonder about who would or could develop into an ideal patient—or even into an ideal analyst. Still, in his most euphoric moments Freud thought that nearly everyone was qualified to fill both roles; in his depressive moods he doubted ever finding a patient with a "perfect" neurosis.

All in all, the Freudians' inductive reasoning often would corroborate what they had set out to prove. But after they had agreed that wishes, fears, hopes, and anger are accessible through dreams and that these would lead to the unconscious, they argued only about the specific paths. And, given the nature of psychoanalysis, their deliberations became part of the scientific data. That was how this brilliant assortment of mavericks shared in the excitement of discovery. In their enthusiasm, they were helping to "provide Freud with the greatest satisfaction any man could experience" (*S.E.*, 3 : 11–23; Obituary of Charcot). And before long, the disciples knew that the exploration of a particular mind was teaching them about mind.

Roots of Later Theoretical Conflicts

In the beginning, Freud embodied psychoanalysis. He developed or appropriated new ideas, incorporated them, and with the group explored their implications for patients. The disciples presented their own cases and hypotheses, which, in turn, led to controversies and to improved practice. But the need for ongoing reinterpretation and for open-endedness also encouraged wild conjectures. Such conjectures later could be justified by quoting Freud, as Marxists quote Marx or Kantians Kant. In this way, some of his ruminations and epigrammatic statements were turned into basic doctrines.

Freud's "History of the Psychoanalytic Movement" (1914) gives us the first glimpse of the theoretical complications that were dividing the disciples. Until about 1913, Freud thought he would be able to prevail over his followers and hold them within his intellectual orbit. He reportedly wrote this essay in order to save psychoanalysis from dilution. But he seemed unaware that in trying to preserve unity (by fighting Adler and Jung), he was actually sowing the seeds of further divisions. In fact, he inadvertently set the stage for the major directions his movement would take when he insisted that he "knew best what psychoanalysis [was], and how it differ[ed] from other ways of investigating the life of the mind" (Nunberg and Federn, 1965, 3:148). Essentially, he had already lost Adler, and although at the time he thought he still might hold on to Jung, according to Ferenczi, the "History" itself was the ultimate "bomb" leading Jung to resign.

When Freud wrote his "History," he was fighting for the survival of his ideas—that is, for the centrality of *unconscious* phenomena. To save this focus, he felt impelled to get rid of all dissidents' therapies of commitment[4] and to turn his most loyal disciples into a sort of executive committee. Thus he made an organizational decision to enforce his theoretical position about the centrality of the unconscious. From then on, the followers would defend his doctrine not only against Jung's and Adler's deviance but against all those who would water it down.

The long-range future of psychoanalysis was being decided then. Freud not only rejected Adler's and Jung's ideas but boosted Abraham's, so that Abraham, helped by Eitingon, would be in a position to take the lead. The two other major disciples, Ferenczi and Rank, would have other disagreements with Freud—Ferenczi as the forerunner of the so-called Budapest School, Rank as the advocate of short-term therapy.

Jung's central concepts of "psychic intertia," "non-fulfillment of the life-task," and "being above or below," as well as Adler's "masculine protest," "inferiority complex," and "positive tendency" contradicted basic components of Freud's theories. All these formulations helped move the unconscious and sexuality to the sidelines: legitimating them ipso facto would do away with the essence of Freudian psychoanalysis. If Jung was correct and "the basis of 'incestuous' desire is not cohabitation but . . . the strange idea of becoming a child again . . . of entering into the mother in order to be reborn through her," then Freud's "biological" premises would not hold up (Brome, 1978, p. 142). And if universal symbols could be traced to archetypes, as Jung claimed, the Oedipus complex would have to go. Rather than confront these issues directly, the Freudians tended to explain them in psychoanalytic terms: they accused Jung of having given in to pressure from the Swiss citizenry who condemned their iniquitous ideas about sexuality as Viennese. They denied that "psychoanalysis had changed over the years" (Brome, 1978, p. 145) and that sexuality had been wrongly conceptualized. Instead, the disciples backed Freud, who had stated in *Über Psychoanalyse* (*On Psychoanalysis*) (1913) that psychoanalysis had nothing to do with mysticism. By implication they rejected Jung's ancestral archetypes and refused to accept his redefinition of libido as general rather than sexual. Ultimately, they would call him a mystic and dismiss him as paranoid.

Before long, in *Totem and Taboo* (1912–13), Freud developed his own explanation of the beginnings of civilization, which ostensibly demonstrates its oedipal roots. And in "On Narcissism: An Introduction" he would attack Jung's assertion that originally there was unity of all the instincts: "The Libido has been withdrawn from the external world and has been directed to the ego, and thus gives rise to an attitude which may be called narcissism. . . . [And] we see also, broadly speaking, an antithesis between ego-libido and object libido" (*S.E.*, 14:75–76). Later on, he would add that "the name of libido is properly reserved for the instinctual forces of sexual life, as has hitherto been our practice" (*S.E.*, 16:413).

As Jung went on to pursue his "mysticism" (and Adler his "socialism"), Freud increasingly battled them on theoretical grounds. Repeating that sexuality was central, he called it "the single function of the living organism which extends beyond the individual and is concerned with his relation to the species" (*S.E.*, 16:413). Though earlier, in order not to lose Jung, Freud had hesitated to support Abraham, who maintained that dementia praecox occurs when the libido tries to obtain satisfaction through objects or sets the subject's own ego in its place, he now irrevocably rejected Jung's explanation that a toxin or poison causes the fixation of the complex and injures the psychic function as a whole (Brome, 1978, p. 96).

One of the most plausible recapitulations of Freud's breaks with Adler and Jung has been offered by the German psychoanalyst Alfred Lorenzer (1984). He reconstructed the events to show that Freud at first took a middle-of-the-road position between them. Since they both "theoretically rejected the sexual moment" and led psychoanalysis in opposite directions—Adler

stressing the rational psychic components and Jung the irrational ones—
Freud, in trying to prevail against them both, arrived at what Lorenzer calls a
dead end. But all "three schools of psychoanalysis"—Freud's, Adler's, and
Jung's—Lorenzer found, held onto the notion of the unconscious. Even
Adler located "the stimulation for attention not in consciousness but in interest which remains unconscious . . . where human strength and the line of life
develop. Only its reflection exists in consciousness" (Adler, 1929, p. 76).

Actually, Adler thought that "attention," "interest," "factor," and
"strength" depend upon the unified personality whose "character traits are
comparable to a guideline sticking to the individual like a template" (p. 126).
But these character traits are outward appearances, stated Lorenzer (1984),
since dreams derive from attitudes toward life, and the underlying tensions in
the "life plan" result from the conflict between "feelings of community" and
the "wish for power." These were of equal importance to Adler, Lorenzer
noted, and were represented in both his conscious and unconscious. But to
remain a practicing Marxist, Adler had to stress the reflection of social influences. The devaluation of unconscious motivation, however, *had* to be rejected by Freud. Nevertheless, he did use a weakened version of Adler's
autonomous aggressive drives in his concept of reaction formation—a com-
pensatory force of the ego and of ego functions. Since Freud had rejected
such an idea in 1908, Adler would be angry at him for the rest of his life
(Ellenberger, 1970, p. 517; Sperber, 1972).

Jung, on the other hand, located the unconscious in the archaic-collective
unconscious "and with unbounded tolerance watched every fog, *numen* or
taboo that rolls around in it" (Lorenzer, 1984, p. 3). Just as Adler moved the
contents of the unconscious into the reservoir of ego drives, Lorenzer noted,
so Jung found it in the roots of archaic-irrational emanations. And whereas
for Adler the irrationality of the unconscious disappeared in favor of a totally
socialized self, Jung dissolved the self in favor of an "ont/ology of the unconscious." To put it simply, Adler's unconscious functioned as an appendage of
the conscious, and Jung's conscious as an appendage of the unconscious.

Lorenzer, a neo-Marxist, thought the relation between conscious and unconscious was being simplified because social influences internalized in the
unconscious themselves militate against resisting existing norms. Insofar as
the Adlerian individual remains free to make his own decisions, said Lorenzer,
these result from rational and reflexive processes. Jungians, on the other
hand, by dividing conscious and unconscious, had to insist that the unconscious is behavior-determined and separate from both conscious and action-
oriented language. Freud, however, incorporated two approaches, the physio-

logical and the psychological, and related them to each other by means of his theory of sexuality (Lorenzer, 1984, pp. 162–98).

The only way Freud could both compromise and build a consistent theory against Adler and Jung, concluded Lorenzer, was to postulate three structures—id, ego, and superego. This led Freud to talk of the "true symbol" which arises from the unconscious; according to Lorenzer, this was reconcilable with Jung's symbols (even if strictly separate from the "constant" and "supraindividual" assumptions about symbols), as well as with "ego psychology."

In Roudinesco's version, the theoretical controversies that surround these formulations, which generally are conceived as breaking with previous ones, are less decisive than is the prepsychoanalysis. According to her, Freud had followed Kraepelin's explanation of paranoia over Bleuler's ideas of schizophrenia, whereas Jung postulated that there was an "autonomous *dementia praecox*; and he did not call it schizophrenia." Freud, she writes, reportedly said that Jung could believe in the existence of dementia praecox if he wanted to, but "it does not exist, there is only obsessional neurosis and paranoia" (Roudinesco, 1982, p. 126).

Ellenberger gave less credence to such verbal exchanges. Concerned with restoring the history of dynamic psychiatry, he focused on Adler's and Jung's long-range agendas: Adler wanted to change society—that is, to alleviate neuroses, psychoses, and criminal behavior—by perfecting his *Menschenkenntnis*. And Jung even before meeting Freud had been a successful psychiatrist at the Burghölzli. Neither of them was a defector, Ellenberger argued against the American Freudians; they simply had left to pursue old interests.

Clearly, these different versions of the theoretical arguments among the early Freudians now are being reinterpreted to further specific viewpoints. In sum, what happened in the beginning is being revived to buttress specific perspectives and local allegiances, or to over- or underinterpret specific theoretical or clinical factors.

The Structural Theories

Freud, as we know, kept refining some of the main ideas he had formulated in the *Three Essays on the Theory of Sexuality* (1905). There he had located drive in bodily sources, distinguishing between its aim (the discharge of sexual tension) and the object through which satisfaction is achieved (*S.E.*, 7:125–245). Because the erotogenic zones are connected to vital functions (the oral one to eating, the anal and urethal to defecating and urinating, and the genital to reproduction), he linked the satisfaction of all drives to erotic arousal and pleasure. (Later on, satisfaction was found to be sought for its own sake.) Sucking at the mother's breast therefore was said to be the prototype of every later satisfaction to which fantasy keeps returning (*S.E.*, 16:314). As the primacy of the oral drive gives way to the anal (sphincter control), to the phallic (awareness of the penis), and then to the genital (at puberty), the libido was found to be associated with more or less appropriate aims and objects. (All of these eventually would be elaborated in contradictory ways by Freud's descendants.) Frustration of the drives, it was realized, would give rise to aggression. Oral aggression would be expressed in wishing to bite or devour; anal aggression would be demonstrated in wanting to expel, poison, or hurt with feces; and phallic aggression would be expressed in the wish to penetrate, tear, and cut. But libido also was fickle: it was found to move easily from object to object and get fixated at an early stage, such as autoeroticism or narcissism. Furthermore, each experience was said to produce its own accompanying fantasies, and these, in turn, were traced to the roots of future conflicts, both intrapsychic and with the external world.

Freud described and took for granted the pressuring characteristics of these drives. When he attempted to define them, in "Instincts and Their Vicissitudes" (1915), he noted that the four major components of a drive—pressure, source, object, and aim—had to be examined separately and then related to one another (*S.E.*, 14:111).[5] So during the period when Adler increasingly was basing his theory on observations of personality and Jung was stressing archetypal influences—both culturally and more or less "consciously" determined—Freud became ever more involved in elaborations of the unconscious sources of both personality and culture.

As Freud kept expanding his theory of drives, he constantly redefined the properties or functions of the four components and the dynamics or relations among them. These ideas later would invite exploration of therapeutic techniques, narcissism, object relations, and the specific controversies surrounding each of them. (Ultimately, these issues would dominate the theoretical discussions; see chapter 11.) But, again, cultural and personality factors combined when American Freudians preferred to pursue the ego components of these theories at the expense of drives, or when German psychoanalysts and Lacanians accused them of misunderstanding the centrality of libido. In fact, this was why Lorenzer, for instance, had wanted to go back to the earliest formulations about drives: he believed that these opened the way for a more "radical" psychoanalysis than ego psychology, though not necessarily as radical as Wilhelm Reich's.[6] Drives do not allow for "adaptation," Lorenzer maintained, and thus are capable of reaching back into the individual's earliest development—to the roots of anti-Semitism, leader-follower dynamics, and their symbolizations. Such an emphasis implicitly deflates American ego psychology.

The French psychoanalysts Jean Laplanche and Jean-Bertrand Pontalis, on the other hand, wanted to do justice to *all* the conceptualizations and controversies surrounding the definition of *drives* and their nuances:

The Freudian approach . . . tends to overturn the traditional conception of instinct. It does so in two contrasting ways. In the first place, the concept of "component instinct" underscores the idea that the sexual instinct exists to begin with in a "polymorphous" state and aims chiefly at the elimination of tension at the level of the somatic source, and that it attaches itself in the course of the subject's history to representatives which determine the object and the mode of satisfaction; initially indeterminate, the internal pressure faces vicissitudes that will stamp it with highly individualized traits. But at the same time, far from postulating—as the instinct theorists so readily do—that behind each type of activity there lies a corresponding biological force, Freud places all instinctual manifestations under the head of a single great basic antagonism. What is more, this antagonism is derived from the mythical tradition: first, between Hunger and Love, and later, between Love and Discord. ([1967] 1973, p. 216)

Clearly, Laplanche and Pontalis, though faithful to Freud's intent, nevertheless allowed for a number of different readings. Still, they betrayed their French location. By emphasizing both the break with traditional concepts of "instinct" and an openness to a mythic past, they inevitably contradicted Ellenberger's stress on the continuity of Western modes of thought—with Freud as one link in a long chain. Furthermore, Laplanche and Pontalis focused on the comparative aspects between object-cathexes based on early experiences and instinct, theories rooted in physiology, whereas Ellenberger compared Freud's theories to those of contemporaries sharing his preoccupations. The French, however, are attached to their philosophy: in France, notions of "individualized traits" long have been central (as defining an individual's existential situation); such traits do not even appear in Ellenberger's otherwise extensive index. Objectively, these positions, along with many others, can be extrapolated from Freud's writings. To stress the antagonisms between hunger and love, or between love and discord, however, is to take seriously Freud's distinctions between Eros and Thanatos, which goes against the grain of the ego-centered theories of Anglo-Saxon psychoanalytic "science" (see chapter 11).

Roots of Ego Theories

When Freud wanted to prove to Jung that there was no general drive, he focused on the psychic manifestations of the sexual drive. And when he found that he could not easily separate such drives as love, fear, anger, or hate—that is, what he came to refer to as "libido"—he postulated that these were partial drives that later on would coalesce into specific structures. These structures were said to function either alone or in conjunction with the sexual drive. The sources of these partial drives were bodily organs, especially the erogenous zones. Other bodily functions, though possibly contributing to the libido in early human ontogenesis, Freud found, seek their own satisfaction. Furthermore, when he stopped postulating libido as a general source of energy and separated the drives, he also laid the foundation for his developmental stages: oral (the infant's mouth is central), anal-sadistic (the function of elimination predominates), and genital (the partial drives are organized under the primacy of the genital zones).

After having postulated his theory of drives, Freud wondered how the psychosexual steps get integrated, and at what crucial moments psychopathology gets started. (This made it easier to pin down patterns of psychopathology.) So he examined connections between the evolution of partial drives and specific phases of psychosexual organization. He noted that when a pathological transformation of the sexual drive had thwarted normal development, mental sickness would set in. Therefore, in neurotic patients this drive was thought to have been altered rather than lost: they were continuing to hold onto the primary sexual object or its infantile replacement. This insight spoke to the psychiatrist's preoccupations as well: it allowed for examining the links between mental health and illness as well as for a differentiation between neurosis and psychosis. Now, the Freudians were in a better position to convince psychiatrists of the curative powers of psychoanalysis for neurotic trauma.

While systematizing the drive theory, Freud also began to examine and conceptualize narcissism. Ellenberger maintains that the concept of narcissism was designed to incorporate the ideas of Havelock Ellis (in England) and Paul Naecke (in 1899 in Germany). But many American Freudians have considered "On Narcissism: An Introduction" (1914) the turning point in psychoanalysis, as a near-refutation of drive theory and the basis of ego psychology. (Ellenberger adds that Freud now adapted Jung's explanation of schizophrenia as resulting from an "introversion of libido" and Adler's emphasis on self-esteem [1970, pp. 510–11].) At that time Freud described narcissism as a specific form of sexual deviation in which the individual is in love with himself (*S.E.*, 16:416). He noted too that it is possible for the libido to withdraw its cathexis (as Abraham had shown in dementia praecox) from the object. And in the Schreber case, where he elaborated the links between homosexual drives and paranoia and spoke of the subject as "taking himself, his own body, as his love-object (*S.E.*, 12:65)" or "loving himself," he both altered previous formulations and anticipated later ones.

Essentially, the works of 1914–15 are the basis for many theoretical elaborations. But most classical Freudians maintain that narcissism was anticipated in 1910, when Freud explained homosexuals' object choice as the result of their wanting to love someone resembling themselves, and then recathecting this object into the ego. "An original libidinal cathexis of the ego . . . fundamentally persists and is related to the object-cathexes much as the body of an amoeba is related to the pseudopodia which it puts out" (*S.E.*, 14:75–76). Freud went on to postulate a balance between *ego-libido* (attached to oneself) and *object-libido* (attached to the mother or her substitute) and then maintained that using one depletes the other. Clearly, he followed an energy model. This led Ellenberger to conclude that Freud was influenced by Fechner's topographic concepts of the mind. (Fechner had established a mathematical relationship between the intensity of stimulation and the resultant sensation.) Sulloway expanded on this influence and thereby "proved" that Freud remained the "biologist of the mind" he had been when he wrote the "Project" (1979, pp. 66–67). A number of French psychoanalysts, however, and not Lacanians alone, would conclude from this monograph that "narcissism must be defined *structurally*: instead of appearing as a stage in development, narcissism now emerges as a damming up of the libido which no object cathexis can completely overcome" (Laplanche and Pontalis, [1967] 1976, p. 255). In other words, excessive narcissism blocks further psychic growth and needs to be analyzed.

Lorenzer, once more considering these contradictory conclusions from the perspective of German psychosomatics, suggests a synthesis by assuming that "an underlying teleology [is] . . . imbedded in a biological system whose . . . organization cannot be apprehended through mechanistic categories" (1984, p. 126). Only the new *"ars interpretandi"* (the interpretive act par excellence reconnecting bodily and physical symptomatology)—that is, clinical understanding—could treat manifestations of narcissism. He suggests that psychoanalytic theory be dealt with in the same way as other productions of the unconscious.[7] This synthesis, once more, would allow Lorenzer to remain within the Freudian fold, to pursue his body-mind "hermeneutics," and to remain open to Marxist possibilities. But by implication Lorenzer must now accept the conceptualization of homosexuality as a developmental state accessible to curative efforts. This idea, however, contradicts the argument that homosexuality is *socially* determined; and in its implicit bias it gainsays Lorenzer's own Freudo-Marxism, which supports the primacy of formative influences. Lorenzer, however, was not the only one to extend the concept of narcissism to cultural issues: Marcuse (1955) and Lacan ([1966] 1977), Sennett (1977), and Lasch (1978), as we will note in chapter 12, did so as well.

In general, the cultural elaborations tend to ignore Freud's distinction between "primary narcissism" (the early state when the child cannot yet distinguish between itself, its libido, and the outside world) and "secondary narcissism" (a turning back of libido previously withdrawn from others into its own ego). Yet, these are the working distinctions psychoanalysts make in their clinical diagnoses and treatments. Secondary narcissism (which appears in schizophrenia and some extreme forms of regression, and as a structural feature of the subject) allegedly is superimposed upon primary narcissism. Less easily demonstrated than primary narcissism (which manifests the infant's unadulterated desire for gratification), secondary narcissism postulates a balance of energy between object-cathexes and ego-cathexes. It also assumes that the narcissistic formation of the ego-ideal (in which the ego serves as its own ideal and incorporates the infantile illusion of omnipotence) has never been abandoned. Freud, who essentially considered infantile libido (at birth) to be free-floating, explained it in relation to the pleasure principle: as the child becomes physically detached from his parents, its infantile libido disappears when the Oedipus complex is resolved. But according to Ferenczi this period could end much sooner, and according to Melanie Klein it occurs at around the age of four months, when the child works through what Klein called the depressive position (see chapter 11). This happens when the parent is accepted as an "other," as a reality. Such a theory rejects a state of primary narcissism, although, according to Phyllis Grosskurth, Melanie Klein hesitated to say that her system would not allow for it (1986, p. 371).

Primary narcissism is open to so many interpretations because Freud often changed his mind: between 1910 and 1915 he said that primary narcissism occurred between the stages of primitive autoerotism and object-love; later, he used the term to mean the first stage of life, prior to ego formation (life in the womb) (Laplanche and Pontalis, [1967] 1973, pp. 337–38). Therefore, not even the classical ego psychologists could ever agree on whether the formation of the ego is analogous to the establishment of a psychic unit and, if so, whether this happens when the baby is born or when it becomes conscious of itself. And they could not agree on the extent to which early perceptions of interhuman relationships themselves become incorporated into ego structure (see chapter 11).

Narcissism is one of the central concepts on which international Freudians focus in order to disagree. When narcissism is highlighted, the drive theory that German Freudo-Marxists put forth becomes less important. And when perceived as elaborating ego psychology, narcissism ipso facto would have to be considered "adaptive." Lacan's adherents, on the other hand, although they are as eager as their German colleagues to restore the radical stance of psychoanalysis, would assume a sort of "constitutional narcissism" as normative.

Another controversy grew up around Freud's views on ego formation as presented in the *Introduction to Metapsychology* (1917).[8] Now he argued that the melancholic's self-reproaches are between the self and the internalized father with whom he identifies and that melancholia therefore is different from normal grieving for a loved one: it is self-reproaching, self-destructive, and ends up in delusional expectations of punishment (*S.E.*, 17:244).[9] Here was yet more food for controversy, particularly after the duality of life and death instincts was elaborated differently by Melanie Klein. Essentially, the libido now came to be identified with the sexual expression of the life instinct and as such was being opposed to the death instinct. The latter allegedly derived from the organism's biological need to return, ultimately, to its inorganic state: threatened by death, our inevitable fate, the organism fights back through aggression. But whereas some Freudians, especially in America, have rejected this concept as a product of Freud's pessimism, his cancer, or his impending death, it provided Klein, who did not bother too much about biology, with the dialectical structure of opposites—love and hate, and the later paranoid and schizoid depressive positions (Grosskurth, 1986, p. 191).

From Amateurs to Professionals

The most controversial concepts were intricately linked to the psychoanalysts' clinical work. Whereas later the question of child analysis would be the battleground for Anna Freud and Melanie Klein, now *all* analysts debated, for instance, the theme of regression, especially during the analytic session. Freud had commented on it, in *Remembering, Repeating, Working Through* (1914), when he noted that the child often misconstrues its experiences and then repeats them when grown without knowing what these experiences represent. By then, however, such repetitions include subsequent ramifications in the form of inhibitions, attitudes, and character symptoms. Looking at these manifestations in the transference neuroses of his patients, Freud discussed them in relation to psychoanalytic methods. He was more and more convinced that erotic transference had to be dealt with by means of nongratification, neutrality, and attentiveness. Thus he suggested that these feelings be analyzed as "unreal."

Classical analysts such as Serge Lebovici would point out that this was the first time Freud had tied transference neurosis specifically to libidinal regression. Lebovici focused on this regression and related it to the resistance it elicits—a resistance that leads the libido (instead of following a "progressive" path) to be attracted to and "fixed" by the earlier unconscious infantile conflicts (1980, pp. 786–87). Aside from the theoretical consequences, such a stance itself must militate against the analyst's involvement in this conflict and thus supports a totally noninterventionist analytic style. The followers of Ferenczi or of Melanie Klein would have to reject this line of argument if only to uphold their more interfering or supportive methods and techniques. But they discovered other elements in Freud's works that would back up their clinical methods, for in searching for the proper technique he had often changed his approach. The transference at times was described as mere repetition (*S.E.*, 12 : 147); it also had to be traced to its specific past (*S.E.*, 12 : 154); and it could be described as "an intermediate region between illness and life . . . but of a provisional nature" (*S.E.*, 12 : 154). Another time he found transference love to be genuine, though unrealistic and full of idealizations, less free and adaptable than its normal counterpart, and belonging to resistance (*S.E.*, 12 : 159–71). In *Beyond the Pleasure Principle* Freud again elaborated on the reliving of early sexual experiences to reflect a forgotten past (*S.E.*, 18 : 7–64) and implied that they must not be gratified in the erotic transference. (The year before, he had advised Ferenczi against taking an active part in the analysis of a patient or even offering general emotional satisfaction.)

Many psychoanalysts have considered Freud's noninterventionist stance as most relevant and a boost to ego psychology because it invited a focus on method. A number of others interpreted it as reaffirming the analytic role between a patient who presents subjective experience and a doctor who facilitates the analytic process—in the working alliance. Nevertheless, the separation of roles at times has been attacked as elitist and potentially authoritarian. In the clinical situation, however, it is the personalities of the protagonists that make for the dialogue in the actual coalition between analyst and analysand. This interaction *is* more or less an authority relation, although it too takes its cues from the culture at large. The principle of reaching the unconscious through the transference remains the same everywhere. For Freud was certain that by being subjected to the psychoanalytic method of treatment analysands' repressed history could be revised and they thus would learn to deal more adequately with inner conflicts. But because this method relies entirely on subjective, confidential interaction, it has remained the major bone of contention for all analysts.

The method, we recall, had been operationalized by the Berliners, who had prided themselves on implementing Freud's ideas. In fact they expected more of their recruits than Freud did. But given the differences of personalities, each institute would develop its own character based on the style and theoretical preferences of its senior members and of the culture. And everywhere, as Ferenczi wrote in 1932,

> the analysis of the analyst [was] becoming more important. Do not let us forget that the deep-reaching analysis of a neurosis needs many years, while the average training analysis lasts only a few months, or at most, one to one and a half years. This may lead to an impossible situation, namely, that our patients gradually become better analyzed than we ourselves are ([1932] 1949, p. 226).

Because it no longer was possible to believe that "neurosis was the passport for becoming a psychoanalyst," or that personalities such as those of the Zurichers lacked the "necessary neurotic ingredients" (Nunberg and Federn, 1967, 2:468), the IPA increasingly had to function as the Freudians' collective conscience. Its representatives were to legislate on the thin line between "professional hypocrisy" (such as the analyst's toleration of the patient's projection of early hostility onto him) and sincerity and empathy. But is it really possible for psychoanalysts, any more than for anyone else, to maintain a totally objective attitude? What personality types promise to make the best psychoanalysts? Who is best equipped to invest his or her whole being to learn how to turn a technique into an "art"? Thus it is difficult to predict who will most benefit from and best assimilate psychoanalytic training.

Also, because the early patients were more innocent of psychoanalysis, they had not built up defenses against it. James Strachey's vivid account to his brother Lytton after going into analysis with Freud is exemplary of what a psychoanalysis was:

> Each day except Sunday I spend an hour on the Prof's sofa (I've now spent 34 altogether)—and the "analysis" seems to provide a complete undercurrent for life. As for what it's all about, I'm vaguer than ever but at all events it's sometimes extremely exciting and sometimes unpleasant—so I daresay there's *something* in it. The Prof himself is most affable and as an artistic performer dazzling. He is a good deal rather like Verall [James's favorite classicist at Cambridge] in the way his mind works. Almost every hour is made into an organic aesthetic whole. Sometimes the dramatic effect is absolutely shattering. During the early part of the hour all is vague—a dark hint here, a mystery there—then it gradually seems to get thicker, you feel dreadful things going on inside you, and can't make out what they can possibly be; then he begins to give you a slight lead; you suddenly get a clear glimpse of one thing; then you see another; at last a whole series of lights breaks in on you; he asks you one more question; you give a last reply—and as the whole truth dawns upon you the Professor rises, crosses the room to the electric bell, and shows you out the door.

That's on favorable occasions. But there are others when you lie for the whole hour with a ton weight on your stomach simply unable to get out a single word. I think that makes one more inclined to believe it all than anything. When you positively feel the "resistance" as something physical sitting on you, it fairly shakes you all the rest of the day. (Meisel and Kendrick, 1985, pp. 29–30)

Surely, we cannot expect even the best supervising analyst to be as certain as Freud was or to know whether a specific moment in a patient's resistance—with its obstacles to memory, its fears of emerging unconscious thoughts, and abreactions—has been dealt with optimally by himself or by the person supervised. These difficulties, in fact, are the same around the world, and they continue to haunt psychoanalytic theory. Where did Freud venture too far or associate too loosely? Was he entirely correct in his interpretations of the "Wolf-Man," and if not, what did this mean in terms of this case, subsequent cases, the theory? Where did he bend his theories in order to advance the movement? And was he too quick in trying to solve all the riddles psychoanalysis posed? Psychoanalysts around the world have been trying to answer these questions, but in spite of themselves, they cannot escape being influenced by their personal beliefs and surroundings.

They were justified, I think, in assuming that fundamental sexual characteristics would not be different in Vienna, Paris, Hong Kong, or Lagos, whatever cultural sanctions might interfere. But how they approached the manifestations of repressed sexuality depended upon how psychoanalysis challenged accepted knowledge or doctrines, which, in turn, would influence their clinical practices. For who could prove that the "family romance" was universal, or that every child passed through its own Oedipus complex? In the early years there were signs that the development of psychoanalysis might take different turns in line with different cultures, but these were faint, and their directions became truly visible only later on. Actually, when the advances of psychoanalysis themselves influenced symptom formation, when some countries bred their own gurus, and when it became clear that neuroses were not going to disappear, theoretical and clinical formulations would go off in many directions—all trying to capture the future Freud had promised.

Chapter 4

Promises to Culture

Freud was a physician whose visions soared far beyond the ills of his own patients to those of humanity. He expected to penetrate to the roots of human nature and to improve the lot of society. This ambitious project seemed not too farfetched at a time when Darwinism was riding high and more and more people, including Freud, assumed that "savages and halfsavages represented an earlier stage in our development." Freud added only that the modern psyche, with all its neuroses, also had evolved from that of primitive peoples (1912–13).[1] And since such disparate philosophers as Auguste Comte, Edmund Burke, and J. S. Mill had already established the infallibility of scientific progress, and psychologists were generalizing about humanity, Freud's excursions into all of culture and into the roots of human origins and religion belonged to his Zeitgeist. So the issues addressed in *Totem and Taboo* (1912–13) and in *The Future of an Illusion* (1927) were as topical as are our current preoccupations with "star wars," nuclear physics, and salt-free diets. In fact, Freud kept returning to questions of human genesis and updating his hypotheses in line with his evolving theories. After he had conceptualized the superego as the transmitter of culture, for example, he told his critics:

It is not true that the human mind has undergone no developments since the earliest times and that, in contrast to the advances of science and technology, it is the same

82

today as it was at the beginning of history. We can point out one of the mental advances at once. It is in keeping with the course of human development that external coercion gradually becomes internalized; for a special mental agency, man's superego, takes it over. (*S.E.*, 21:57–145)

Thus Freud connected his own theories with human history, which furthered his movement. This already had its own momentum and increasingly was leaving its imprint on the culture it reflected.

As psychoanalysis began to catch on, philosophers and anthropologists took notice of the cultural essays, and some of them used psychoanalysis as a new tool. Those who accepted the superego as the locus of morality (and with it the universality of the Oedipus complex) gradually incorporated psychoanalytic notions into their own specialties. But Freud expected them to help verify the oedipal hypothesis and to corroborate his philosophical assumptions. He wanted them to agree that man is unhappy because society imposes too many intolerable frustrations in the form of taboos, laws, and customs impeding sexual life, and that this happens because civilization requires us to turn our aggressiveness onto our own egos.

The philosophers, however, had their own quarrels. They were divided between the Kantians, who were defending the power of rational judgment; the Hegelians, who were debating the nature of spirit and freedom; the Marxists, who foresaw social change via reform or revolution; the Nietzscheans, who debated questions of power; and all those who tried to mediate between two or more of these doctrines. Thus the philosophers would approach psychoanalysis from their own specific perspectives. The psychoanalysts, in reaction to the philosophers, moved from clinical observations to large conjectures. But since they continued to legitimate themselves via medicine and lacked the philosophers' facility at argumentation, the philosophers usually managed to get the better of them. The disciples, whose Kant and Hegel were more rusty, tended to respond with quotes from Freud. Thereby they would almost invite opponents to ridicule the speculative and utopian aspects of the cultural essays and to go so far as to dismiss *all* of psychoanalysis.

Paradoxically, the intellectual public was fascinated by these debates and by the larger questions Freud's more venturesome monographs addressed. For the psychoanalytic movement grew not because people believed in childhood sexuality or in the invidious power of unconscious thought but because they hoped that psychoanalysis might uncover some of the enigmas of existence. How had humanity begun? What motivated individual behavior? Could religion still provide any answers, and, if not, then what could science offer? Precisely because the philosophers had no ready replies, the public looked more and more to the newly emerging disciplines such as anthropology and psychology. Freud was not the only one to discuss the anthropologies of J. J. Atkinson and W. Robertson Smith, who themselves were accepting the tenets of Darwinian evolution.[2] And the public wondered also about the various new theories explaining psychic behavior—Karl Bühler's notions of Gestalt, Ludwig Klages's characterology, Wilhelm Stern's personalism. Since each of these psychologists also was linked to a larger worldview, none of them could accept Freud's notion of a savage horde (*Urborde*) as the original locus of civilization. But their attacks on psychoanalysis led some outsiders to think that it was yet another anthropology, yet another supposition about cultural origins that was in the air—assuming that human history began when humans started to walk upright, when they invented fire or language. Thus Freud's cultural excursions belonged to the cosmology of the day, and intellectuals accepted or rejected them according to their own theoretical and emotional investment.

The disciples' contributions in these areas were inspired either by Marxist and humanist ideas or by those of the early cultural anthropologists. The former group, represented by Alfred Adler, Otto Fenichel, Siegfried Bernfeld, and Erich Fromm, sooner or later addressed the social goals psychoanalysis was to further. The latter, represented by Abram Kardiner, Sándor Radó, and Geza Róheim, were more focused on psychosocial interactions, in order to learn about optimal child rearing: happy and uninhibited children were bound to build a better society. In other words, both the more and the less radical psychological-anthropological inquiries promised a better world.

These promises would vary in the different countries and over time. But they always hinged on the degree of openness to new ideas within the society and on the mechanisms for their diffusion to the larger public. The atrocities of war, for instance, perpetrated by supposedly decent individuals, led some psychoanalysts to look for the unconscious dynamics of aggression, and these endeavors attracted a good deal of attention. (This was why, as we will see in chapters 6 and 10, German psychoanalysts in the 1960s would reinvestigate the works of the early "culturalists"—to understand the Nazi era—and why French psychoanalysts would focus on the spontaneous student uprisings of 1968.) Thus, when during the First World War the psychoanalysts cured a number of neurotic soldiers, they not only improved their clinical skills and learned more about aggression but imagined themselves closer to curing the world. Their optimism, among other things, would make psychoanalysis attractive to larger and larger audiences.

Early Excursions into Culture

In *Totem and Taboo* (1913), Freud's first long cultural monograph, which is anticipated in part in "Obsessive Acts and Religious Practices" (1907), he argued that both obsessional neuroses and religion are founded on the suppression or renunciation of certain instincts and on a sense of guilt. (In neuroses, the sensual instincts are repressed, whereas in religion egoistic impulses have been projected onto the higher goals [*S.E.*, 9:115–27]). We note that the preface to *Totem and Taboo* also spoke to issues in social psychology (*Völkerpsychologie*); that Freud proposed to correct the "deficiencies" of Wundt's behaviorism and of Jung's "mythical cosmology" (p. xiii); and that he wanted psychoanalysis to become more acceptable to the intellectual public. In the process, he also was rebuking his American colleague James Jackson Putnam, who had suggested at the Weimar congress (1911) that psychoanalysts address their patients' *conscious*, their ethics, and their social conscience as well.

Other parts of *Totem and Taboo* were anticipated in "Sexuality in the Aetiology of Neurosis" (1898), where Freud showed that sexual frustration could cause all sorts of neurosis and discontent. Unconventional behavior and particularly sexual liberation, he implied, might eventually eliminate such neuroses. Indeed, it now seemed only a short step from freeing women who were subjugated to their husbands to freeing everyone. For Freud argued that for the sake of humanity and in the "interest of the general public men [ought] to *enter upon sexual relations with full potency* in order to make civilization compatible with the claims of sexuality" rather than perpetuate the spread of neurasthenia (Freud's italics; *S.E.*, 3:278).

Basically, Freud wanted to convince the world that what goes on in our unconscious determines what we know consciously. Hence he hoped to turn German social psychologists into intellectual allies by providing them with "ethnological ammunition." They all were reading about tribal practices around the world in Richard Thurnwald's *Zeitschrift für Völkerpsychologie und Soziologie* (Journal for Social Psychology and Sociology). The data from the many case studies demonstrated that tribal societies had many different rites and practices and a variety of origins but did not fit into an overall framework. Freud, however, came up with an integrative theory by maintaining that all societies have descended from a savage horde dominated by a leader who owned all the women and had been killed and eaten by his sons. In order to get along with one another, and to survive, people needed the incest taboo. Furthermore, by concluding that every boy passes through an incestuous love for forbidden objects—his mother and sister—the Freudians offered the anthropologists an explanation for the "universal" incest taboo, as well as a theory that could unify all sorts of disparate anthropological data (*S.E.*, 13:25–29). In addition, psychoanalysis was to supply the followers of such anthropologists as J. G. Frazer with a method of investigating the fates of discarded or altered totems and taboos. Their work, in turn, would help legitimate psychoanalysis.

Written just before the works on metapsychology, *Totem and Taboo* differed, in part, from Freud's later cultural contributions, but anthropologists have questioned the validity of its assumptions. Clifford Geertz, for instance, found that "Freud's parallel between personal rituals and collective ones (along with Weber's *verstehende* methodology, Malinowski's exploration of the distinction between religion and common sense, Durkheim's nature of the sacred) . . . [continues to] dominate cultural anthropology to the point of parochializing it" (Geertz, 1973, p. 88). Malinowski (1927) disputed the theory of the Oedipus complex when he reported that male children in the Trobriand Islands "hated" their mother's brother rather than their father. Critics of psychoanalysis went along with Malinowski, but its defendants, such as Jones and Róheim, responded that Malinowski had discovered only that defensive feelings had been displaced, without having touched the unconscious roots of these feelings.

Melvin Spiro (1965b, pp. 155–56), an anthropologist who investigated what happens to the Oedipus complex in the Israeli kibbutz, where children from many families live together and are raised as brothers and sisters, found that sexual tensions brought about by proximity were being repressed in at least two-thirds of the children. Spiro, after bringing in other anthropological findings, concluded that "individuals who live together (whether they are family or nonfamily members) . . . develop and retain sexual feelings for each other unless they are inhibited by countervailing social and cultural pressures" (p. 157).

Historian H. Stuart Hughes dismissed *Totem and Taboo* as "one of Freud's successive infatuations"—along with his brief advocacy of cocaine therapy, his admiration of Fliess, his acceptance of his patients' seduction fantasies—and argued that it had been "a vast anthropological fantasy" aimed at establishing the Oedipus complex as "the key to all psychological riddles" (1958, p. 129). "It was not until the last decade of his life," continued Hughes, "that Freud turned his attention explicitly to the problems of man in society . . . beginning with *The Future of an Illusion*" (p. 136).

Hughes was addressing the American discussions of the 1950s, when psychoanalysis was popular with intellectuals. Some of them were arguing that Freud was a philosopher and tracing his descent from Plato through Hegel, while some humanists, such as Lionel Trilling and William Phillips, were applying psychoanalysis to literary criticism. Many social scientists were insisting that Freud's two interlocking metaphors, the Oedipus complex and the primal crime, could explain group behavior. Hughes considered him a "special kind of determinist" who had pushed the determining forces from the conscious to the unconscious (1958, p. 133).

Sociologist Talcott Parsons, however, whose ideas contributed much to these discussions, had taken off from Freud's theory of personality. In fact, he conceptualized interaction as built upon object relations which themselves are influenced by the internalization of *all the components of the common culture.* So even though Parsons maintained that Freud had overemphasized the importance of the superego as the agent of internalization and had neglected the systems of cognition and symbolism, he nevertheless postulated the superego as the bridge between the theory of personality and the analysis of culture and of the social system ([1952] 1970, pp. 17–33). But all those who believed that unconscious elements are dominant forces in personal and political life—that is, those who accepted Freud's views—believed also that any personality theory assuming an as-yet veiled central dynamic would replicate this dynamic in the cultural sphere as individual impulses took on a social character. They further believed with Freud that these impulses bind mankind and that the forces of civilization, which require greater and greater repression of instincts, thus induce an ever increasing sense of guilt (*S.E.*, 21:144).

On Wednesday Evenings

The Freudians who met on Wednesday evenings were enthusiastic at the prospect of liberating individuals and society from repressions and aggressions. Because Freud had located the key to history in the unconscious, they felt justified in applying clinical insights to anthropology and in arguing that cultural and family environments (along with biology) "determine" both the form and the content of literary works, as well as the psychic makeup of their authors. Freud, of course, who had a command of Western thought, could "legitimate" all sorts of psychoanalytic free associations and speculative theses. But some of his followers, whose talents were limited in comparison to Freud's, were less convincing, particularly when they reduced cultural phenomena to psychological ones, such as interpreting every tree or umbrella as a phallic symbol. Unsympathetic philosophers, sociologists, and anthropologists felt entitled to ridicule the Freudians. Art and literary critics as well did not appreciate the Freudians' incursions into their domains (see chapter 8).

In October 1906, Rank presented a provocative paper on the central literary themes of psychoanalysis, showing how the incest in Sophocles' *Oedipus Rex* was disguised. He went on to interpret the transformations of incest in literary works ranging from the Bible to *Hamlet* and Schiller's *Don Carlos*. By attributing these transformations to unconscious mental processes, Rank was not only bolstering psychoanalysis but convincing the disciples to look for psychoanalytic themes in the classics. Now the Freudians pointed to the similarities among neurosis, artistic creation, and dreams, and maintained with Freud that the artist is not by definition neurotic. Members of the group brought in their own free associations, let their imaginations roam, and, at the same time, attacked Rank for some of his generalizations. Later commentators would interpret such "constructive criticism" as manifestations of envy, dislike, or narcissism.

By now, the relations among these pioneers have become the subject of postmortem psychoanalyses. Still, at one of their meetings, Freud praised Rank for having ventured into literature, even though he thought Rank's argument was weak, his subject too broad, his examples inadequate, and the results not clear. Freud himself used the issues Rank had raised to generalize about repression, suppression, and defenses. That is why Rank's biographer James Lieberman (1985) holds that Rank did not get enough credit, although he agrees with historians who believe that Freud was protective of Rank. And even though Philipp Frey, another participant, belittled Rank's psychoanalysis of artists as vague, Reitler criticized it for ignoring paternal hate, and Hitschmann considered it a superfluous extension of the Oedipus situation, it led Freud to establish the theoretical distinctions between conscious repression (defense) and unconscious organic repression (repression) (Nunberg and Federn, 1962, 1:15–19). Furthermore, it was at this meeting that Freud for the first time referred to the Oedipus complex as the "family romance."

Thereafter, Freud wrote a great deal about the similarities between neurotic symptoms and cultural myths and their expression in socially acceptable behavior. But, as Phillip Rieff (1963a) reminded us, psychoanalysis had not been accepted at the time. It was widely believed that both religious observance and obsessive acts stemmed from the fact that individuals had attributed their evil and asocial impulses to the gods. Psychoanalysts hoped, however, that comparative psychoanalytic explorations of tribal cultures—by providing a better look at more primitive religious practices—might solve the riddles of modern consciousness (Rieff, 1963a, pp. 9–13).

When the disciples started to look for the cultural manifestations of psychoanalysis they found them everywhere. Some analysts followed Sadger, Sachs, and Reitler, who were analyzing oedipal themes in literary works by

Shakespeare, Heine, and Wedeking, or those who were finding them in biblical stories, fairy tales, and mythology. A number of followers applied Freud's generalizations by linking children's play to adult mental processes because such spontaneous activities as play and daydreaming had been found to draw on unconscious images. Others explored the creative process itself and the relation between a writer's work and his neurosis: they tried to generalize from the psychic content of literary works to the mental health of their authors and to literature as a whole. Years later, the cultural critic William Phillips noted, "The common denominator of all the [psychoanalytic literary] studies is that there is no common denominator" (Kurzweil and Phillips, 1983, p. 2).

In the beginning, the Freudians tried to "prove" the universality of the Oedipus complex; later on, they took it for granted. Ultimately, they no longer spelled out the reasons for the pervasiveness of childhood sexuality and its consequences in the cultural monographs: they all accepted it.

Such essays as "The Moses of Michelangelo" (1914), which Freud wrote primarily for a broader public, are now of interest largely to Anglo-Saxon art critics. But this work had a particular interest for Freud because he was romantically attached to everything Italian. When he first saw the sculpture, he could not get it out of his mind. He was attracted not only by its beauty but by the numerous and contradictory treatises the *Moses* had elicited. By focusing especially on the place of Moses in the Bible and noting such revealing details as Moses' fingers playing with the locks of his beard and the Tables of the Law turned upside down, Freud depicted Michelangelo as the creator of "a character-type embodying an inexhaustible inner force which tamed the recalcitrant world" (Kurzweil and Phillips, 1983, p. 91). Freud observed not only Moses' rage at the Israelites worshiping the Golden Calf but his control of his rage for the sake of civilization.

As Freud speculated about Michelangelo's intentions, he concluded that none of the many interpretations could have caught the artist's unconscious motives and that even Michelangelo "is no less responsible than his interpreters for the obscurity which surrounds his work" (*S.E.*, 13:236). And just as Freud thought that Michelangelo's *Moses* was inspired by his relationship to Pope Julius II—whose tombstone it was to crown—so Freud scholars have wondered to what extent his own rage at Jung, in 1914, had made him focus on and interpret Moses as he did. Still, Freud's interpretation has been challenged by art historians. It may have provoked some of the continuing scholarly studies of Moses and the increasingly psychoanalytic turn much art criticism would take.

Just before his death, Freud returned to the figure of Moses in *Moses and Monotheism* (1939). But now he saw Moses as an aristocratic Egyptian who had imposed on the Jewish people the worship of his own deity, Aten, as the single god. Because the Jews could not tolerate such restrictive belief, they were said to have killed the tyrannical young pharaoh; and when they needed a religion to unite them, they revived monotheism by worshiping Yahweh. By then, the Mosaic ideas were being codified along with the ethical demands and prohibitions against magic, which are fundamental to all religions. And Freud advanced the theory that the killing of the oppressive pharaoh paralleled the murder of the original father of *Totem and Taboo* and the guilt of the murderous sons. This essay underlined once more the link between monotheism and the Oedipus complex and argued that religion, along with other "illusions," is connected to psychic needs. Freud had explored these topics before (in "Reflections upon War and Death" [1915], "The Theme of the Three Caskets" [1913], and "A Religious Experience" [1928]). But *Moses and Monotheism* pulled all these themes together, at a time, it might be noted, when Freud, like Moses, was an old man and had to flee his homeland because he was a Jew.

Psychoanalysis in America

When Freud came to America he had not yet written *Totem and Taboo*. Indeed, his trip stimulated many of his comparisons of cultures and of religions. In his concluding remarks at Clark University he stressed the cultural claims of psychoanalysis as well as its potential usefulness:

A certain portion of the repressed libidinal impulses has a claim to direct satisfaction and ought to find it in life. Our civilized standards make life too difficult for the majority of human organizations . . . [and] consequently encourage the retreat from reality and the generating of neuroses, without achieving any surplus of cultural gain by this excess of repression. We ought not to exalt ourselves so high as completely to neglect what was originally animal in our nature. Nor should we forget that the satisfaction of the individual's happiness cannot be erased from among the aims of our civilization. (*S.E.*, 11:54)

The Americans were attracted to these promises of optimal personal gratification and the reduction of individual anxiety. Eager to do away with the mental and psychic havoc caused by sexual hypocrisy, the double standard, and the fear of venereal disease (prostitution was widespread and uncontrollable), they did not object even to the unpalatable Oedipus complex. They simply ignored it.

After the Clark lectures, Freud, accompanied by Ferenczi and Jung, visited James Jackson Putnam at his Adirondack camp. During the week they spent there, Putnam sized up his visitors and Freud learned about American customs. He discovered, for example, that Americans loved to spend vacations in wilderness retreats, which they stocked with "hidden comforts," and he wondered whether such habits might derive from dominant mores and beliefs (letter to his family, Sept. 16, 1909). This intimate contact, it seems, set the stage for Putnam's analysis, which consisted of a six-hour meeting with Freud at the Weimar congress in 1911. Actually, this was when their friendship began.

Even so, Freud's antireligious bias could not be reconciled with Putnam's "pragmatism," which made psychoanalysis a handmaiden of religion (Hale, 1971b, pp. 56–59). Typically, Freud analyzed Putnam's ideals in relation to their psychological roots (p. 42) and separated Putnam's psychoanalysis from his philosophy. The latter, he remarked to Jones, reminded him of a "decorative centerpiece [that] everyone admires but no one touches" (Jones, 1955, 2:86). Putnam, on the other hand, thought that Freud was reducing man's thirst for God to the need of the helpless infant for a protecting father (p. 24). Nevertheless, they respected each other personally, and this more than anything else turned Putnam into the most ardent advocate and promoter of psychoanalysis in America (Hale, 1971b, pp. 25–26).

According to Nathan G. Hale, Jr., Putnam read the copy of *Totem and Taboo* Freud sent him "with pleasure and admiration," although he realized it was an unacknowledged response to his own position (p. 56). Nevertheless, the argument did not convince him. All in all, it must have been difficult for both of them to bridge the inevitable gulf between a Central European and atheistic Jew and a self-assured and professionally successful Boston Brahmin. Their letters attest to their differences as well as to their common search for the roots of personality and culture.

In retrospect, we realize that Freud's interaction with his American followers was the first intimation that cultural factors would loom so large. In America his listeners responded enthusiastically, and the press instantly disseminated his thoughts. The new disciples were very different from the founders of the Wednesday group.

Since almost none of the American pioneers was Jewish, they helped move psychoanalysis from something dismissed as a "Jewish science" into mainstream thought. This pleased Freud. But he had some difficulty tolerating the Americans' loose applications: they came too easily to truths that others had to struggle for. And Freud was chagrined by the fact that some

Americans seemed to prefer Jung's ideas to his own. Had Jung found so much acclaim because he was a Protestant or because he played down childhood sexuality? Such conjectures made Freud ever more curious about the role of religion in the construction of every individual's unconscious. This may well have been why later on, after he had thought further about Protestantism and Calvinism, he concluded that all religions were illusions (*S.E.*, 21:1–56). Still, that was just before the Americans passed the Prohibition amendment, backed by the power of organized religion: "They are trying . . . to deprive people of all stimulants, intoxicants, and other pleasure-producing substances, and instead . . . are surfeiting them with piety" (*S.E.*, 21:51). Freud went on to observe that, like narcotics and childhood neuroses, religious consolation works against resolution of the oedipal dilemma (and hence against psychoanalysis).

Although Freud conceded to both Pfister and Putnam that there might be a "moral" affinity between psychoanalysis and Protestantism, since both were searching for "ultimate" truth, he always remained ambivalent about religion. He fought every illusion that might allow individuals to escape from reality: "The voice of the intellect is a soft one," he insisted, "but it does not rest until it is heard" (*S.E.*, 21:51). In 1927, however, Freud did not consider that this voice itself is informed by cultural traditions, that it too expresses specific worldviews, and that it too belongs to a particular social and cultural context.

Psychoanalysis and Anthropology

In the beginning, the psychoanalysts looked at tribal societies as the least "contaminated" by civilization and thus closest to instinctual life, which led them to assume that the mental and biological roots of primitive peoples are more readily accessible than those of modern men. Hence, they decided to join with anthropologists in doing research into earlier forms of civilization. Geza Róheim was the first psychoanalyst to subject primitive societies to psychoanalytic observation. In his book *Spiegelzauber* (1919) (*The Magic Mirror*), he elaborated on Freud and anticipated many of the subsequent anthropological-psychoanalytic syntheses, concluding:

We find the key to all collective ideas and rites, centering around the mirror, in the second ontogenetic level of the psychosexual development, in self-love (narcissism). In the same way as the individual [goes through] this stage in . . . childhood, so the [tribal] taboos grouped around mirrors concentrate to a great degree around the child; [and] the motivations of the taboo betray the unconscious knowledge of the true [oedipal] meaning. The petrification and conservation of the infantile psychic constellation is characteristic for the sorcerer predicting from mirrors, and the mirror-looking of kings. The resuscitation of infantile narcissism takes place in the average person when he finds in his children his own infantile self, and with, and in, his children relives his own childhood; in other words, *Spiegelschau* (mirrorsight) leads to reincarnation [and] the negative form of the ritual of mirror-gazing is partly the autosymbolic expression of a reaction directed against narcissism, partly horror of *self-knowledge;* [and] the demon appearing in the mirror corresponds to a projection of repressed fantasies. . . . Breaking of mirrors is also a motoric expression of feelings with negative connotations: it denotes a break with narcissism, as a way to object cathexis, and also with the object of libido, the original alter ego, who is thus killed via *Analogiezauber* (magic of analogy). . . . Mirrorgazing is considered dangerous for the dead, consequently forbidden (in popular superstition). (Róheim, 1919, pp. 260–61)

Clearly, Róheim had extended Freud's then recent formulations on narcissism and applied them to tribal practices. By the time a festschrift for Róheim was published (1951), the clinical ramifications of the psychoanalytic themes had already become commonplace assumptions. These themes would become central in Lacan's concept of the mirror-image and to a lesser extent in Heinz Kohut's extensions of narcissism to theories of the self (see chapter 11).

Studies of "basic personality," by observing family interactions, put childhood discipline at the center of cultural institutions and constellations (Kardiner, 1945). Because children introject parental patterns of behavior along with religion, folkways, and ideologies, personality was considered the product of these processes and thus became the means of comparing tribal cultures. Anglo-Saxon anthropologists in particular began to accept the idea that social environment and early experiences were incorporated in the superego. Ruth Benedict (1934), for instance, showed that inconsistencies in child rearing made the Alorese of Indonesia "generally distrusting" and that the Comanche values of warfare, conquest, and plunder allowed individuals "a high degree of freedom . . . [for] criminal ends." Margaret Mead's controversial studies of sex-role behavior in Samoa and her comparisons of the Tschambouli, Arapesh, and Mundogumor accorded with Benedict's view that culture is "individual psychology thrown large upon the screen, given large proportions and a long time span" (Mead, 1935). Later, Gregory Bateson concluded that people participating in similar cultural behaviors have similar character structures (Bateson and Mead, 1948, p. 131).

When these principles were applied to large-scale societies, sociologists and anthropologists spoke of "national character," which they defined as "relatively enduring personality characteristics and modal patterns" (Inkeles and Levinson, 1954, p. 983). But the concept of "national character" soon ran into trouble since it failed to account for class and other differences within a society and for the vast array of personality differences among individual members of any industrialized society. The "psychoanalytic" anthropologists attributed such variations increasingly to biology, disposition, adaptation to family expectations, birth order, or sexual drive, so that "personality" began to incorporate most of culture, and culture itself seemed to become an adjunct of personality.

In this scenario, traditions and functional needs dominated. And the generalizations—based on the sociopsychological formation of character structures, projective systems, or permissible reactive patterns—tended to result in rather vague categorizations. Thus both the sharpness of psychoanalytic insights and the specifics of tribal customs were being dulled.

After a while, critics started to question the glorification of the noble savage and the notion of pure primitive societies untouched by civilization. To some extent, these views had served as antidotes to the missionaries' interpretations of bare bosoms or fertility rites as expressions of lewdness and immorality. Psychoanalytic explanations, of course, provided a rationale for those who had sided with the missionaries as well as for those who had stressed the qualities of primitive life by postulating the primitive horde of *Totem and Taboo*, on the one hand, and spontaneous natives, on the other.

According to Geertz, psychoanalysis remained the preferred tool for tribal studies and for those who thought that patterns of child rearing determine cultural aggression and passivity. The British anthropologist Mary Douglas, however, found that by 1982 this type of anthropology had peaked. Indeed, she noted that psychoanalysis itself was in decline, that its "theory seem[ed] too much like a ship at anchor, once fitted out for a great voyage, but sails now furled, ropes flapping, motion stilled. It is not as if theoretical winds were lacking to drive it. But the motive to go somewhere is missing" (1982, p. 14).

At present, psychoanalysts and anthropologists rarely cooperate in searching for cultural and human origins: they drifted apart when their earlier inquiries did not yield the expected treasures. Most Anglo-Saxon Freudians went on to delve into object relations, and Erik Erikson, after having studied the cultural conditioning of Dakota and Yurok Indians, focused more and more on the psychogenetic development of identity. Many Anglo-Saxon anthropologists, however, continue to use some psychoanalytic notions when observing tribal societies that are disappearing or urban ones.

The divorce between anthropologists and Freudians could have been predicted: when psychoanalysts did not unveil the innermost roots of unconscious mechanisms, the anthropologists were bound to be disappointed. In Europe, a very few, such as the doyen of psychoanalytic anthropology, Georges Devereux and his adherents Mario Erdheim, Fritz Morgenthaler, and Paul Parin (see chapter 10), continued to compare cultures, but most anthropologists moved into narrower field studies.

Freud's *Civilization and Its Discontents* (1930a) provided an impetus to anthropological investigation much as anthropological data had stimulated Freud's explorations of irrationality. For the assumption that prehistoric crises of the human species were paralleled by neurotic crises among historical men meant, in turn, that the uncovering of original neuroses would reveal the original prehistoric crises. Freud's critics questioned this causal linking of historic truth, clinical method, and neurotic conflict and pointed to the inability to document such events. But most of his followers tended to accept the parallel between individual neurosis and historical origin.

In Anglo-Saxon countries, the cultural works gradually became removed from clinical concerns. Indeed, as the psychoanalysts Abram Kardiner and Sándor Radó increasingly shifted toward anthropology, they broke with Heinz Hartmann, Ernest Kris, and Rudolph Loewenstein (1951, pp. 16–17) and other colleagues who now were elaborating a scientific psychology which they expected to extend to the analysis of cultural conditions. Since the individual's immediate surroundings influence his behavior in conflict situations, Hartmann, Kris, and Loewenstein maintained, defense mechanisms (such as repression, projection, identification) and both conscious and unconscious motives (such as conflict, anxiety, fear of object loss or castration) ought to be analyzed directly rather than through the instinctual aspects of these conflicts (p. 21). Essentially, the global aspect of such concepts as "basic personality" and "character structure" (Kardiner, Ralph Linton), of "national character" (Benedict, Geoffrey Gorer, Mead), or of "social character" (Fromm, 1942, p. 25) went against the grain of the insurgent ego psychologists whose concerns were primarily intrapersonal.

Psychoanalysis and Sociology

While Kardiner cooperated with the anthropologists in applying psychoanalysis to tribal societies, the leading ego psychologist, Heinz Hartmann, began to look at mental health from a more sociological perspective. During his stay in Paris en route from Berlin to New York, Hartmann had observed that societies do not define what is healthy or normal in the same way, so that what is considered average or passable in one society may be deemed sick in another, and that personal values are affected by cultural and social conditions (Hartmann, 1939, p. 309). Since cultural factors impinge on personality formation whether traumatic experiences are "imprinted" on the body as psychosomatic symptoms or are taken in stride, Hartmann suggested that psychoanalytic diagnoses should take these factors into account. He noted that neurotic features may even determine individuals' careers: some take up nursing, for example, because they need to be in "superior" health; others turn to surgery to control sadistic tendencies; and some who become psychoanalysts project their own problems onto their patients. Hartmann essentially said that deviance is relative. To prove his point, he analyzed his colleagues' judgments and found that their own past experiences colored their views. Why else would some analysts diagnose the capacity to achieve and enjoy a sign of mental well-being while others would postulate all sorts of theoretical standards of health and still others would focus on types of intervention that might turn their patients' irrational thoughts and actions into rational ones (p. 318)? Apparently, few psychoanalysts thought that individuals' neurotic symptoms might be responses to conflicting expectations by their communities (p. 320).

Karen Horney had made a similar argument in *The Neurotic Personality of Our Time* (1937). Instead of tracing neuroses back to biological drives, she had emphasized the influence of life circumstances, and particularly the role of affection in childhood (p. 19), and she had denounced "theoretical paths . . . [that lead] into blind alleys . . . [and to] a rank growth of abstruse theory and a shadowy terminology" (p. 21). Clearly, Hartmann, whose formulations were increasingly convoluted, was one of her primary targets.

Erich Fromm went even further. By postulating the dynamic of the individual psyche (with its desires, fears, passions, and reason) as the basic entity of social process, he emphasized the conflicts of modern man (1956, p. 362). People assumed they were free, Fromm maintained, because during the past few hundred years a number of dictatorships had been overthrown, the church had been deprived of its domination, and nature had been mastered with the help of industrialization. But freedom, Fromm claimed, turned into a psychological burden: individuals afraid of isolation search for a sense of belonging, which is hard to come by under modern conditions of work. According to Fromm, this was why the Germans had been so eager to surrender their freedom to the Nazis or at least had failed to fight for it—they had wished to escape from it (1956, p. 3).

Such paraphrasing of Marxist alienation extended Fromm's previous work as a member of the Frankfurt School, as he used psychoanalysis to further radical politics. But his analysis of fascism incorporated a critique of Freud: as a product of his own culture, Fromm found, Freud had been "handicapped" in the attempt to understand irrational phenomena in the lives of normal individuals and had down-played individual and cultural dynamics. (In fact, Fromm's larger focus was a "study of the whole character structure of modern man.") From this perspective, Fromm tried to explain German authoritarianism and to understand how potential fascists (in democracies) may turn into real ones. Influenced by his new American milieu, he toned down his former radicalism. Moreover, his idealism to some extent converged with the American ideal of the individual as the mover of society, so that Fromm—however ambivalently—at that time also began to take to America.

In the 1940s, some American intellectuals of the left, who in principle were against going to war, ignored Hitler as long as possible. Their Marxist ideals had led them to be antifascist but less critical of Soviet totalitarianism. When the Soviets became America's allies these issues were further confused. When knowledge about the atrocities of the concentration camps and the gulag could no longer be ignored, many American intellectuals did not know where to turn. Some of them were attracted by Fromm's psychoanalytic insights coupled to his Marxist humanism as a means of escaping their dilemma. That intellectuals found plausible Fromm's explanations that the chaotic conditions in the Weimar Republic and massive unemployment had led Germans to follow Hitler and to fear freedom fed into the general concerns about the war and the psychological preoccupations surrounding it.

Many Americans, for instance, knew about the success of German psychological warfare and thus believed their government needed it also; a few had heard that the American army was underwriting Kurt Lewin's studies of small groups to understand the spontaneous emergence of leadership and the conditions that furthered it. (His stress studies, conducted under army auspices, were not known to the public.) The extensive investigation of *The Authoritarian Personality* by Adorno and his team (1950) got less publicity than Fromm but ultimately was disseminated as well. In any event, Fromm was popular because he both praised American society and wanted to protect its freedom. Later, in *The Sane Society* (1956a), he would become more critical of America's educational system, its political apathy, and the inequality of opportunity. But by then he had become an ardent reformer who expected to ameliorate the alienating aspects of American life by pointing them out—much as David Riesman had done in *The Lonely Crowd* (1950).

The classical Freudians, however, emphasized the divisions between psyche and body rather than those between psyche and society. And they thought the culturalists were renouncing the intrapsychic world as well as the psychoanalytic dimension of sexuality and aggression. Eventually, Fromm looked to "the end of 'humanoid' history . . . when things will have truly become man's servants rather than his idols . . . and when human energy will be in the service of life rather than in the service of death" (1956, p. 362). This sort of hope was yet another attack on the Freudians, particularly on the notion of the death instinct. "If it did exist," Fromm had already argued in 1942, "we would have to assume that the amount of destructiveness either against others or oneself is more or less constant" (p. 157). Instead, he pointed out, the amount of destructiveness varies among different social groups and societies.

Russell Jacoby (1983), when analyzing the *Rundbriefe* Otto Fenichel had sent to a group of left-wing Freudians between 1935 and his death in 1946, maintained that the adjustments by Fromm and the other "neo-Freudians" had been deplorable. Yet, Jacoby also argued that Fenichel and his friends had been afraid to admit their Marxism or their leftist orientation. But Fromm, it seems to me, did not appear to suffer from that fear. Indeed, he continued to explore social problems from an adversarial, "neo-Marxist" perspective.

Later on, Fromm went back to psychoanalysis proper, but unlike the classical analysts, who focused on ego theory, he elaborated Freud's earlier emphases on drives and his topological theories. By then he was addressing the revival of German left-oriented psychoanalysis (see chapter 10). Now, he differentiated even more between sexual instincts, which can be modified and adapted to reality and are relatively postponable and repressible, and instincts for self-preservation, which cannot be made unconscious, postponed, or sublimated. Thus he further rejected Freud's distinction between the instincts of love and death. According to Fromm:

drives toward self-preservation must be satisfied by real, concrete means, while the sex drives can often be satisfied by pure phantasies. A man's hunger can only be satisfied by food; his desire to be loved, however, can be satisfied by phantasies about a good and loving God, and his sadistic tendencies can be satisfied by sadistic speeches and phantasies. (1970, p. 140)

Fromm ultimately expected that the sex drive would be sublimated by changing men's relations to work and to their ideals. This emphasis, of course, contradicted Marx's theory of class polarization and Fromm's former assumptions of stark differences between tribal and modern societies. Still, by assuming that relations between the masses and the ruling classes were on a "neurotic-healthy" continuum, he concluded that socialism would come about through reform (1956, p. 2) and that he had been influenced by the optimistic aspects of American culture, such as the popular beliefs in upward mobility and happiness. Now, attacks on his relatively simplistic conceptions of personality came from all sides: according to Herbert Marcuse, Fromm had neglected "repressive desublimation," and radical Marxists found him not revolutionary enough. For classical Freudians he was too utopian. But by then, they had almost completely abandoned Freud's preoccupations with culture.

French Disregard of the Cultural Unconscious

Since the French had all but ignored psychoanalytic therapy until after the Second World War, they had not thought of its possible cultural applications. In fact, insofar as these ramifications were discussed, it was by philosophers refuting Freud—that is, by those whose own views would shine more brightly by contradicting him. I noted in the previous chapter that Janet's concepts of "psychological analysis" and the "subconscious" had won out over Freud's "psychoanalysis" and "unconscious"; that the French had confined classical psychoanalysis to a ghetto; that it had remained uninfluential; and that it was dismissed before 1939 as an aspect of the "inferior German psyche." "Cultural psychoanalysis" had served as an intellectual scapegoat, although for a brief moment Georges Politzer, a young philosopher, had attempted to put it to Marxist ends. He had been associated with a group of "young Hegelians" and with the surrealists, who championed art that had its roots at least partly in the unconscious. (Jacques Lacan was close to them in the 1930s.) But because Politzer also was a communist and thus had moved more or less underground, this type of psychoanalysis fell by the wayside.

In the 1970s Lacan's early forays into Hegelian philosophy were being celebrated by his followers. Only after he had become central to French intellectual discourse was it recalled that he had been a friend of the poet André Breton, who had postulated a future "surreality"—the resolution of reality and dream. These associations would give credence to some of Lacan's assertions about the "politics of the *imaginaire*" (see chapter 11) and their usefulness to Marxist theory.

Both Lacan's radical politics and his eccentric theoretical thrust had upset his Freudian colleagues. At the IPA meetings in Marienbad in 1936 he had advanced the view that the child's first recognition of its own reflection was central to its future personality, that if the impact of this event on the Oedipus complex were ignored, the clinical developmental picture would remain incomplete. (Later he postulated the mirror stage as the core of the Oedipus complex itself; see chapter 11.) During the following seventeen years his theory was not developed further: Hitler, the Second World War, and postwar conditions intervened. Lacan's subsequent attacks on his colleagues, however, were based on this long-standing theoretical conflict, aggravated by what he termed their adaptation to the IPA, their "neo-Gaullist political stance" (which he confused with being independent of America), and their anticommunism. Anti-Americanism also had an impact on the larger French intellectual milieu, which helped "create" and nurture its "French Freud."

The Lofty British

The British Psycho-Analytical Society flourished in the 1920s over the opposition of the church, the public, and hostile medical and psychiatric establishments (Kohon, 1986, p. 28). Most members of this society belonged to the intelligentsia, a group that was used to dealing with ideas. According to Gregorio Kohon (1986, p. 48), the London analysts bolstered psychoanalysis by relying upon three basic characteristics: they all suffered from a certain degree of psychological disturbance; they were immensely curious intellectually; and they were not given to moralistic judgments. Some of them, such as James and Alix Strachey, Adrian Stephen (brother of Virginia Woolf and Vanessa Bell), and his wife, Karen, were part of the Bloomsbury group. But others, such as Joan Riviere (next to James Strachey the most important translator of Freud), were part of the elite as well. They also were socially conscious and expected psychoanalysis to reach out to the masses.

Everywhere, individuals who became psychoanalysts had had either medical or academic training in philosophy, pedagogy, anthropology, or literature. But since the Londoners who took up psychoanalysis had been part of the leisured elite, most of them did not have to work and could pursue psychoanalysis as a pastime. In the process, however, they became extremely involved. Alix Strachey's letters to her husband from Berlin (where she was analyzed by Abraham, met all the analysts professionally and socially, and above all became Melanie Klein's friend) are a mixture of admiration, condescension, and trenchant insights into the eccentric ideas, behavior, and views of the psychoanalysts. These letters also describe how very much the Berlin analysts were part of the spirit of Weimar—its hedonist excesses as well as its social-democratic ideals.

Given the Londoners' social origins and their celebration of idiosyncracy, it is no wonder that they remained an insular group and that they celebrated independence. Leonard Woolf, for example, started publishing Freud's work in 1924, without ever trying to persuade Virginia to enter psychoanalysis; Jones, in 1943–44, managed to settle the "controversial discussions" (see chapter 9) without breaking up the society. Still, it was not long before they had adherents among important nonconformist middle-class sectors, such as Donald Winnicott and Harry Gunthrip, and Scots, such as Ronald Fairbairn and John Sutherland. In any event, James Strachey translated Freud's works, Jones published the *International Journal of Psychoanalysis*, and Freud relied on Jones to guide the entire movement. Thus London's central place within psychoanalysis was assured even before Freud and Anna Freud settled there. The position so many of the leading British analysts enjoyed within their own milieu was decisive in establishing psychoanalysis in spite of strong objections by many doctors, psychologists, and those members of the uneducated public who were less aware of psychoanalysis.

The Entrenchment of Psychoanalysis

By the time Freud died in 1939, psychoanalysis had become entrenched in the various countries in response to the intellectual interests of specific groups and individuals—subject to administrative rules and to public acceptance. The very adaptability that made for its appeal would make its adaptation within each milieu possible. Although the open-endedness of the unconscious would encourage disagreements about the correct interpretation, it went a long way toward securing Freud's place in history. For psychoanalysis, as a therapy for both individuals and society, was thought to come closer to solving the contradictions of modern culture and modern lives than purely philosophical systems, insofar as its investigations continued to be attached to medicine—that is, to a science. Thus, the psychoanalytic movement would climb to ever greater heights in the years after Freud died. By the 1940s it would have been inconceivable to compare psychoanalysis to other practices of mental healing. Its ideas were so appealing and so convincing that they soon permeated American culture and then the rest of the modern world. Even if, to use Mary Douglas's metaphor, the psychoanalytic ships were sailing in tumultuous waters and were passing each other by, they left their wakes. Psychoanalytic knowledge tended to pervade cultural and intellectual life. Although it did not deliver miraculous cures, psychoanalysis influenced a Babel of therapies as well as general thinking. Freud's ideas became ubiquitous. The ways in which they undercut the central concerns of religion and philosophy transcended national interests. And everywhere the extent to which Freud's works received attention or were ignored reflected dominant ideas about nation, religion, and family.

Gradually, something like a culture of psychoanalysis was being established. In America this occurred by the 1950s, when the intellectual public for the most part no longer frowned on personal psychoanalyses; when they lost interest in psychoanalyzing tribal cultures and concentrated on child studies; and when prominent Freudians were working in hospitals. Almost simultaneously, the application of Freud's ideas without acknowledgment—by "deviant" analysts, quack therapists, anthropologists, educators, cultural critics—became widespread. In this climate it became de rigueur to discuss theories of other-directedness and of psychological man, and to examine the culture of narcissism and the "me" generation—often without even mentioning Freud.

Part Two

APPLICATIONS OF PSYCHOANALYSIS

Chapter 5

Psychosomatic Medicine

Psychoanalysis was conceived when Freud and Breuer discovered that conversion hysteria could be cured if the patient verbalized its traumatic roots; it was born when Freud found a systematic method to elicit the thoughts that had caused the conversion. By 1895, he distinguished among patients who deflect unwelcome or forbidden impulses and temptations through obsessive or compulsive actions, those who convert these impulses into hysterical symptoms, and those who turn them into physical illnesses. But unlike shamans and witch doctors, who had also been known to remove some such symptoms, Freud expected to eliminate their psychological roots and thus to effect more or less permanent cures. Far from blaming the strange behavior of patients on possession by devils or on bad humors, he helped them reconstruct the traumas of early development and the turning of forbidden (sexual and aggressive) impulses back upon their bodies.

Since doctors alone were licensed to heal bodies, psychoanalysis would have to be legitimated through medicine, even after analysts started to focus primarily on neurotic ailments. Within medicine they had to compete against more scientific doctrines, and against psychiatry. How they would do so depended largely upon the institutional possibilities within each country and upon the reception by prominent physicians. The psychoanalysts would either have to defer to them or themselves become physicians. But when the

Freudians went to medical school, they would be trained in psychiatry—at the beginning of the century one of the least prestigious medical specialties. Because they already had difficulties proving their scientific mettle, psychiatrists wanted to keep their distance from the psychoanalysts lest their "scientific" reputations suffer even more.[1]

Psychiatrists were aware that patients have ingrained prejudices against recognizing mental illness and that they more readily accept diagnoses of physical rather than mental ailments. So the more similar the psychiatrists were to doctors who prescribed medication and bed rest rather than to those who delved into unwelcome thoughts, the more patients they were likely to attract. But they also realized that symptoms have cultural roots and that neurotics in some cultures are more likely to somatize their disorders (Mezzich and Berganza, 1984, pp. 436–38). Such differences were most glaring at the turn of the century and were being reinforced by the medical profession. Indeed, Freud himself noted that Austrian doctors tended to attribute their patients' ailments to physical rather than mental causes. He envied the French, who were experimenting with hysterical patients while maintaining a fairly reputable psychiatric tradition. In America, however, neurologists were the ones who searched for "acceptable" cures of the mind, and in Germany psychologists led the scientific investigations into mental behavior. But everywhere, the fate of psychosomatic medicine ultimately rested with psychiatrists and hospital administrators. Ruled by institutional priorities and the need for experience and expertise, these men shared the prejudices of their environment. Hence they could not apply psychoanalytic ideas until these had achieved a certain general plausibility—that is, until they had taken hold in the collective consciousness (Cremerius, 1981a).

In essence, then, the practice of Freudian psychosomatic medicine everywhere depended to a large extent on the whims and beliefs of the psychiatric establishment as well as on the politicians who appointed administrators and allocated the funds for mental health care. Still, psychosomatics turned into a medical specialty whenever empirical investigations of the body-mind connections became fashionable. And soon thereafter, general practitioners learned to diagnose chronic psychosomatic ailments as well as acute ones. At that point, the history of psychosomatic patients was reappraised. In the 1950s, for instance, when neuroses no longer were considered unintelligible figments of the imagination or minor physical debilities, Ernest Jones stated that Freud alone deserved credit for having defined the "extremely complicated structures . . . [that] express biological and social difficulties" (1957, 3:433). But Ellenberger contradicted him by citing earlier approaches to psychosomatics, such as healing through the gratification of frustrated wishes, exorcising ceremonials, hypnosis, and magic. The new psychosomatic medicine, he claimed, was different only from its immediate forebears: the advent of modern science alone had "separated" body and psyche; until then extrascientific healing by shamans, faith healers, medicine men, and wizards had been the norm. These were to Ellenberger the true "ancestors of dynamic psychotherapy" (1970, pp. 3–52). To take Freud down yet another notch, he reminded us that the Viennese physician Moritz Benedikt had "systematized the knowledge of the [sexual] pathogenic secret" before Freud had, and he praised both Jung and Pfister for having "cured sick souls" (p. 46).

In the 1950s, however, American physicians were already diagnosing over half of their patients' symptoms as psychosomatic, psychoanalytic thinking already was being taken for granted, and psychoanaysts were promising to alleviate or cure their patients' symptoms (Jones, 1957, 3:434). Furthermore, psychosomatic medicine had penetrated into hospitals: boosted by psychoanalytic research, on the one hand, and by sophisticated machinery and biochemical advances, on the other, more and more investigators sought to pinpoint the exact moment when a patient's psychic disturbance had turned into a physical symptom. The Freudians expected to discover the meaning of each causal trauma and to come up with a blueprint that would explain them all. These activities also drew them closer to the scientific community. Psychosomatics was turning into a reputable medical specialty.

Soon, psychoanalysts had more and more in common with the psychiatrists, who sometimes deferred to them; and as they gained in legitimation, they increasingly spoke in medical language. (This was especially true in America, where nearly all psychoanalysts had studied medicine.) Franz Alexander, a brilliant Hungarian who had been analyzed by Ferenczi in Budapest and then in Berlin, set up the first American psychosomatic clinic, in Chicago in 1929. Over thirty years later, he commented on the widening gap between psychoanalytic "humanists" and "scientists" and on the fact that psychoanalysts gradually had lost interest in literary and cultural questions and were adjusting to society rather than criticizing it (Alexander, 1957, p. 11). Psychosomatics was getting too scientific and descriptions of symptoms too metapsychological, he noted (1962, pp. 13–24)—thereby offending the classical Freudians (who justified their scientific language by anchoring it in the *Standard Edition*) as well as the "culturalists" (whom he likened to primitive men expecting to influence the gods, the weather, and people's health).

Alexander's comments would be recalled in the 1970s, after psychosomatics had passed its peak in America. By then, psychiatrists were relying on more cost-effective cures such as endocrinologic and neurophysiologic treatment and behavior modification. Because psychoanalytic therapy required private practice and rich patients, and epidemiological and biological causes for mental disorders were increasingly being investigated, the classical Freudians were losing out to psychiatrists. A number of them would adapt to the unpleasant realities by learning to use shock and drug treatment along with psychoanalysis.

Links between Psyche and Body

Practical questions once more activated research into the history of psychoanalysis, into Freud's person and his milieu. We can assume, I believe, that Freud knew of Benedikt's work, which appeared between 1864 and 1895, and of Anton Mesmer's (1734–1815) sensational cures. (Mesmer had treated deranged individuals with a magnetic fluid and later on with laying on of hands and suggestive stares.) In fact, Mesmer's reputation was so widespread that Freud probably adopted his method when he sought to activate his patients' unconscious by touching their foreheads and looking into their eyes (Ellenberger, 1970, p. 69). So Ellenberger's connections of Freud to the healers cannot be rejected; but neither can Jones's view that Freud was unique, since he was the first person to make a science out of free association.[2] Clearly, Freud knew that the success of Mesmer's public performances had discredited hypnotism as a medical practice and that doctors who hypnotized their patients ran the risk of losing their scientific reputations. This restriction was widely accepted.

Still, Freud was impressed by the adventurous bent of French psychiatrists, such as Auguste Ambroise Liébeault (1823–1904), who hypnotized some of his patients and, after inducing them to feel sleepy and slightly dazed, told them that their symptoms would disappear. Although Liébeault could not cure pulmonary tuberculosis or ulcers in this manner, his more modest therapeutic miracles convinced the physician Hippolyte Bernheim (1840–1919) to use "suggestion" at the school he had established in Nancy. Bernheim, in turn, converted Freud, who was as taken with his performances as he had been with Charcot's. Hypnosis was a reputable practice at French teaching hospitals, with more respectability and credibility in France than in other countries, where it was lumped with the feats of traveling circus performers. Particularly in Germany and Austria, hypnosis was beyond the pale, so that Freud's colleagues could feel justified in looking down their noses at the speculative experiments that "only the French were willing to tolerate."

In the 1880s, Charcot had experimented with new drugs just as Freud

had explored the positive effects of cocaine—increasing awareness, anima-
tion, energy—and its anesthetic qualities. Freud's enthusiasm, we know,
at first led him to overlook the addictive components—an oversight that
brought deserved criticism. Jones proposed all sorts of unconscious reasons
for Freud's overenthusiasm: this discovery would make him famous in a
hurry, and it would provide him with the money he needed to establish himself in order to marry Martha Bernays. In fact, Freud was angry at the physician Karl Koller to whom he had spoken of the properties of cocaine. Koller
had used it successfully as a local anesthetic for eye operations and was being
credited with the discovery. Most Freudians referring to this episode and
many historians maintain that Freud's anger at Koller was justified; they tend
to emphasize his overwhelming desire for recognition (Gay, 1988, pp. 42–44).
Some biographers also cite the cocaine experiments as illustrative of Freud's
extraordinary talents and curiosity, and some Freudians insist that Freud's biochemical research proved the links between psyche and soma and therefore
must continue to remain a legitimate concern of Freudian psychosomatics.

The "cocaine episode" certainly indicates that Freud's ambitions before
the creation of psychoanalysis were anchored in the competitive milieu of
Viennese medicine. Jones, however, plays down this episode because it occurred before the self-analysis—Freud's "heroic" endeavor. But Ellenberger,
arguing that Freudians exaggerate this "hero myth," considers Freud's neurophysiology as part of dynamic psychiatry and maintains that this prehistory
of psychosomatics belonged to Freud's state of "creative possession"—the
period in which he formulated new syntheses. I would add also that his medical training and his humanistic education helped in the development of his
view about the body-mind connections.

As long as psychoanalysis remained in disrepute, Western governments
paid little attention to it. However, French laws, which protected the traditional psychiatric establishment, in themselves were something of a hindrance to psychoanalytic approaches. In America, the abuses resulting from a
rather laissez-faire atmosphere led to the medicalization of psychoanalysis
(see chapter 9). In Austria and Germany, the attitudes of the psychiatric establishment militated against empirical investigations into the psychosomatic
roots of illness. And in England, where psychoanalysis took hold among an
intellectual elite, it seemed natural to neglect psychoanalytic psychosomatics.

Establishing American Psychosomatic Medicine

Although psychosomatic medicine was born in Vienna and was built on such
earlier ideas as dipsychism and polypsychism (Ellenberger, 1970, p. 168),

it did not mature until the émigrés came to America. By 1939, Freudians who had crossed the Atlantic had demonstrated that psychoanalysis could relieve certain somatic symptoms. But they had not yet been able to prove the actual links between mind and body. At this time, Heinz Hartmann's suggestion that "psychological problems might be more readily apprehended from the perspective of ego theory rather than that of the id" was taken seriously (Hartmann, 1939, p. 320). This led the Freudians to concentrate, for the most part, on Freud's structural theories (*after* "The Ego and the Id" [1923]) and to investigate the id and superego components that might be responsible for somatic symptoms. This shift came around the same time as the publication of Weiss and English's *Psychosomatic Medicine* and Flanders Dunbar's *Psychosomatic Diagnosis*.

These books, both published in 1943 and read by every medical student, synthesized and helped disseminate psychosomatic thinking. Today, of course, one is struck by the fact that it was not always taken for granted that "bodily changes may be brought about by mental stimuli and by emotion just as effectively as by bacteria and toxins, [or] that physiological changes accompanying emotion may disturb the function of an organ in the body" (Dunbar, 1943, p. 9). Actually, observations of chemical and electrical changes taking place between cells and their environment and ever more sophisticated measurements of such phenomena as levels of blood sugar and clotting time had shown the importance of the emotional factors addressed by psychoanalysts and had also enhanced the prestige of psychologists, physiologists, and psychiatrists who could demonstrate these processes scientifically. Psychosomatic medicine became their common ground: here they would cooperate for the sake of science and here they would vie for professional supremacy.

It is ironic, of course, that psychoanalysis was to lose ground to the more cost-effective treatments so soon after it finally had become acceptable. During World War II, the American government supported all research that might lead to the alleviation of war-related psychosomatic symptoms. And the psychoanalysts asked the most crucial questions. According to Dunbar, the cornerstones of psychosomatic medicine had been laid by Freud's contributions on conversion hysteria (the discovery that inadmissible thoughts turn into bodily symptoms), by Alexander's "dynamic direction of impulse" (it is controlled by an individual's emotional tendencies to incorporate, eliminate, or retain), by Kardiner's "action syndrome" (resulting from the interaction between ego and environment), and by French's investigations of the physiological changes accompanying dreams.[3] According to Dunbar, the fact that so renowned a man as French advocated the use of psychoanalysis changed the entire mental health field (1943, p. 660). The routine administration of Rorschach tests helped as well.

Most theoretical contributions to psychosomatics have been made by classical analysts, whose insights are based on relatively few longitudinal, in-depth studies. Ulcerative colitis, anorexia nervosa, dermatitis, and asthma, they now found, had their origins in infancy or early childhood. And they observed that in addition to psychological treatment patients whose bodily organs had been extensively damaged needed medical attention. This fact induced the psychoanalysts to separate psychological and medical therapies.

Soon, various medical specialists who could treat bodily damage were introduced to psychoanalysis. But Weiss and English urged that psychosomatics be integrated into every branch of medicine (1943, p. 15). To implement this plan, psychoanalysts were recruited as instructors. Nearly overnight, the Freudians became consultants, professors, and administrators. With the exception of a few who had emigrated from Europe, the American Freudians had gone to medical school and so shared a medical vocabulary. This wholesale cooperation with general practitioners seemed to turn them all into one happy family—at least for a short time. Psychiatrists, when introduced to psychoanalytic techniques, enlarged their horizons. More likely to treat psychotic patients than neurotics, they now supplemented shock therapy with psychotherapy. But when psychiatrists took on psychoanalytic patients the psychoanalysts were perturbed. For the psychiatrists had not gone through the proper training at an accredited institute, nor had they been fully analyzed. Still, they were licensed in psychiatry and thus could not be accused of malpractice.

Because psychoanalytic psychosomatics promised new cures, it entered mainstream medicine, and every ailment was examined from its perspective. As the status and prestige of psychoanalysts soared, they not only tightened requirements for professional access but occasionally made high-handed extraclinical judgments. (I was told that the psychiatrists frequently objected when Freudians treated psychotics as if they were neurotics, for by then it was generally agreed that psychotics, who for the most part were hospitalized, belonged to the psychiatrists and neurotics to the Freudians.)

One of the milestones in psychosomatics was Max Schur's case of a young woman suffering from extremely generalized eczema—a woman who when she entered treatment could barely talk and could not recall the childhood fears that had been reactivated when she married. Painstakingly, over a period of four years, she learned how her reactions to psychological conflicts literally were being played out on her skin—psychic stimulants led to itching and then to new lesions. Step by step, Schur helped her reconstruct the parallels between the development of her skin disorder and that of her neurosis and demonstrated the readiness of the organ system (in this case the skin) to respond to emotional stimuli by "interpolating the neurosis between environmental traumatization and the responding organ" (Schur, 1955, p. 157).

Generalizing from this case, Schur drew an intricate diagram showing the possible paths any trauma could take—from innate disposition to disease—when somatic, reactive, and external stimuli interact with mental and emotional ones. This chart was to serve as a sort of blueprint for physicians who wanted to diagnose the genesis of their patients' psychosomatic ailments. Schur had also noticed that some of his patients' repressed memories were "close to secondary process, to fantasies, daydreams, etc." (1955, p. 160). This observation, however, did not accord with Freud's dictum that somatic disturbances are rooted in very early repressed trauma.

When Franz Alexander had "gone against" Freud by dealing with bodily symptoms rather than their psychic roots (to avoid yet more irreversible organic damage caused by recurring emotional stress), he broke away from the classical Freudians. But Schur managed to stay within the fold: the "establishment" was willing to water its wine. Schur continued to treat both somatic and psychological roots of symptoms, but he backed the now "deviant" Alexander by maintaining that psychosomatic patients might profit from less extensive psychotherapy or from group therapy (pp. 160–61). (Later, strictly biological interventionists would augment their treatment with group therapy as well.) In fact, Schur helped legitimate the use of psychoanalytic therapy in place of orthodox psychoanalysis when he argued that psychosomatic patients might benefit from a reduction in the number of weekly sessions and from occasional interruptions in the therapy. Such a change of technique inevitably added more grist to the debates about training and practice as well as to the criticisms of classical analysis. But the promise of less expensive and shorter treatments also inclined hospital administrators to ask the Freudians to help instruct new breeds of health professionals, such as social workers and occupational therapists. So, at the apex of the acceptance of psychoanalysis, in the late 1940s, some simpler and more superficial therapies already were being accepted.

Psychosomatics in Germany

At the first congress of the International Committee for Mental Hygiene, in 1948, American psychoanalysts informed the world of psychosomatic advances. The participants were aware of the sociocultural influences on mental health practices and expected to help shape the policies of their own governments in this area (Mead, 1959). When these psychiatrists, psychoanalysts, social workers, nurses, psychologists, sociologists, and anthropologists got home, however, their national health associations refused to cooperate: policymakers "translated" their suggestions either into studies of feasibility or into philosophy. Nevertheless, psychosomatic diagnoses in principle began to be accepted. In practice, most administrators still had to be convinced of the legitimacy of each psychosomatic ailment—on a case-by-case basis—before allowing mandated reimbursement.

Outside the United States, the problems were compounded by the scarcity of psychoanalysts and by disagreements on what constituted a "cure" (Middendorp, 1956). German-speaking analysts could not even agree on a definition of psychoanalysis and were debating the social consequences of separating private and clinic patients. When Verena Middendorp, in 1956, interviewed sixty individuals three to six years after the termination of their treatment, she found that they had not undergone any fundamental changes in personality, although a number of them had started to live somewhat fuller lives and got along better at work or at home.[4] Some reported that therapy had helped ward off isolation, and others that they had become more sociable because they had shed the symptoms that disturbed the people around them.

In another study, Annemarie Dührssen (1962) asked 1,004 patients who had been in psychoanalytic therapy in Berlin's Zentralinstitut für psychogenische Erkrankungen whether they thought they had been helped. Eighty percent of her 900 respondents reported in the affirmative, 12 percent had "hardly improved" or "gotten worse," and 8 percent were critical of psychotherapy. (The 0.3 percent who had been misdiagnosed and the 1.7 percent who had changed symptoms were among the latter.)

In postwar Germany, research focused on specific psychosomatic ills such as interruption of physiological function, damage to a bodily organ, the "choice" of symptoms, and techniques of treatment. Since every psychoanalyst must try to determine what traumatic incidents caused a patient's original disturbance, medically plausible diagnoses are difficult to come by. For often the reality-oriented components of a neurosis remain functional while hiding psychic conflicts, thus keeping people from seeking psychoanalysis. "Functioning" neurotics don't ask for help as long as their symptoms remain "useful." And patients who most fear mental illness come to see psychoanalysts only after all other physicians have failed them.

In Germany, psychoanalysts examined their patients' symptoms in relation to their "functionality" in the post-Nazi milieu. Since symptoms must retain their plausibility even as they keep altering, psychoanalysts belonging to the same milieu as their patients are able to empathize with these symptoms, and this empathy to some extent serves as their basic therapeutic tool. But the German situation was complicated by the fact that the Nazi past consciously or unconsciously was being "avoided" by one or both partners in the therapeutic alliance. And because German psychoanalysts were also expected to treat patients from the lower socioeconomic classes, they could blame the patients' avoidance on lower verbal ability. Still, working-class patients usually did manage to overcome their customary inhibitions with therapists from their own milieu but felt less comfortable in the presence of medical psychoanalysts.[5] That they had to submit to "official" diagnoses for the purposes of reimbursement was still another hurdle. It always is difficult to predict psychosomatic prognoses or to demonstrate the causal connection between change in a bodily organ and its psychological roots before the cure. Therefore, diagnoses must be tentative until after the genesis of the illness has emerged during treatment.

When Karola Brede, a sociologist working with the first and foremost German psychosomaticist, Alexander Mitscherlich, addressed these issues, she found that "imprecise" diagnoses, though understood by psychoanalysts, were often unacceptable to the *Krankenkasse* bureaucrats. These administrators, who have to approve payments to lower-class patients, routinely question medical diagnoses (1980, pp. 9–10), and their questions tend to compound and aggravate the patients' suspiciousness—and symptoms. Because the emotional basis for psychosomatic ailments cannot be proven a priori, the administrators' skepticism perpetuates the popular notion that the sufferers are malingerers. In addition, such patients are likely to have postponed treatment for a particularly long time and thus to have suffered irreversible bodily damage. So even when "cured," their psychosomatic illness may appear no more than arrested. The introduction of third-party payment in Germany, however, induced the psychoanalysts to use more medical terminology, and the ensuing legitimation of psychosomatic diagnoses, in turn, led to more psychosomatic diagnoses of poor patients. And because these patients tend to be relatively unsophisticated, their analysts' reports themselves at times would increase their apprehensions and occasionally their symptoms, and thus slow the treatment.

In 1945, there were only a few psychotherapists in Germany who had not collaborated with or closed their eyes to Nazi practices. But no one any longer denounced psychoanalysis as a "Jewish science," and efforts were made to persuade former members of the DPV to return from England or America. Very few of them did so, although Michael Balint, Paula Heimann, and Kurt Eissler, among others, did return to hold sessions. Still, the German (and Austrian) public was extremely uneasy about what some called psychological "garbage" (*Kram*), namely the exploration of unconscious feelings. For a few educated Germans, however, the atrocities of the Holocaust and the shock of the defeat of the Third Reich created an ideological opening for explanations and reforms.

In the 1940s, Anglo-Saxon psychoanalysts were trying to explain the rise of Hitler and the acquiescence of the Germans in the crimes of fascism in psychoanalytic terms (see chapter 12). But they were unaware of the extent to which German psychoanalysts were denying their previous activities. Some of the German therapists, hoping to contribute to the improvement of the "Aryan race," had tried to discover how the manipulation of psychic factors might influence biology. To some extent, even the physicians Jakob von Uexküll ([1928] 1973) and Victor von Weizsäcker (1947), who did not support the Nazis, were implicated, since their metaphysiological experiments focused on what they considered to be psychological manifestations of genetic qualities: they had expected to find differences between Germans and Jews and other "inferior races." Homosexuality and birth defects as well were thought to have genetic origins. Weizsäcker had assumed that sickness could invade an individual's genes, and in his *Gestaltkreislehre* he had focused on the biological side of psychosomatics (*Körpergeschehen*)—that is, on the organic rather than the psychic manifestations of psychosomatic illness. This approach was expected to bypass the blanket generalizations about categories of people, such as Jews and Gypsies, by introducing differentiations.

But Alexander Mitscherlich, who had worked with Weizsäcker, thought that a "proper" psychosomatic theory ultimately might cure the souls of the Germans along with their bodies. To that end, he rejected the "latent anthropology" which was reducing "human reality to achievements based on biology" and had "excused" the Nazis' mass murders (1984, 2:495). Hitler's doctors had focused on the illness rather than on the patient, stated Mitscherlich, and thus no longer could distinguish humans from the lesser species: medicine had become a technique of body repair, and human experience in general was being cut out along with sick organs (1984, 1:98). His own research was aimed at discovering the psychic roots of somatic illness and thus pointing the way to alter "sick" psyches.

Mitscherlich's ideas appealed to the executives of the Rockefeller Foundation, who funded his psychosomatic inpatient clinic in Heidelberg. By

1956, this clinic was affiliated with the university, and Mitscherlich began implementing his plans to found the Sigmund-Freud-Institut in Frankfurt for outpatients only. (There, as well as in the other psychoanalytic clinics—in Berlin, Munich, and Hamburg—both analysands and psychoanalysts were emphasizing the psychosomatic rather than the neurotic aspects of their symptoms.) In 1967, he was appointed the first Professor of Psychoanalysis and Social Psychology at the Johann-Wolfgang Goethe University in Frankfurt.

Following Freud, Mitscherlich expected to locate the point at which a patient's psychic experience had turned into a bodily illness and to find out why specific patients get physically sick rather than, say, overaggressive or neurotic. Although his explorations were medically oriented, he always traced the patients' symptoms to experiences with powerful parents or the Nazi authorities, who had reduced "subjective reality to a structural and functional science of the human organism" so as to justify mass murder in the name of science (Brede, 1972, p. 113). Although Mitscherlich's impassioned lectures against fascism kept him in the public eye, his main contribution to his field was the creation of a school of German psychosomatics in the tradition of Felix Deutsch, Ernst Simmel, and Otto Fenichel (Kutter, 1984).

Essentially, Mitscherlich's followers continued to assume that sickness is a biphasic (psychic and somatic) defense, based on the displacement (*Verdrängung*) of unmanageable early wishes of love, hate, or revenge. Such a diagnosis implicitly follows Anna Freud's theoretical assumptions (see chapter 11) by focusing on structural ego disturbance. This means that Mitscherlich followed an "actual neurosis" model and that his therapy would be aimed at breaking down defenses rather than at locating the narcissistic wound, the breakdown in early object relations, or (at times) the moment when psychic stress was converted into physical illness. Furthermore, Mitscherlich demonstrated how biphasic defenses (*Abwehr*) get desomatized and resomatized in response to both physical and psychic stimuli. Thus he was responsive to Alexander's views of the impact of neurotic conflict on bodily functions, to the assumption that structural ego disturbances engender bodily symptoms, and to the "operative thinking" postulated by French psychosomatics. Mitscherlich also traced these conceptions back to Freud's 1895 formulations of neurasthenia; by doing so, he implicitly accepted the "prepsychoanalysis."

The psychoanalyst Peter Kutter characterized Mitscherlich's so-called German School as incorporating the following tenets:

1. The role of affects (especially helplessness and hopelessness) is central in the preconditions of psychosomatic illness. Unexpressed (*unabgeführte*) affects are important in the dynamics of psychosomatic disorders; they relate

not only to aggression and flight but to mourning, pain, fury, anger, and other human passions.

2. Object relations are marred by "regressive" cathexis (*Besetzung*) of inner objects. Consequently, the internalization of these infantile objects prevents both the development of the personality and realistic assessment of outer reality. Here, pathological mother-child relations are central, and these subsequently were observed in interactional dynamics, not only between mothers and children, but in entire families. Specific syndromes were linked to specific psychosomatic disturbances of communication between mother and infant (Wirschnig and Stierlin, 1982).

3. One of Mitscherlich's students observed that psychosomatic patients had a vague and diffuse sort of "imagination," lacking "real, personal, total objects," and had difficulties in verbalizing (Kutter, 1981, 1984, p. 552). Primitive fantasies about their bodies (patients with stomach and intestinal illness have fantasies turning around mouth or anus), about breathing, heart, or urinary functions, were found—in line with Freud—to correspond to infantile sexual fantasies. (Medical psychoanalysts, trained to think in medical-anatomical terms, stated Kutter, often have trouble comprehending infantile fantasies about the body. Such a comment in part aims to discredit the proposed medicalization of German psychoanalysis.)

4. A "special type of fear," caused by the threat to a symbiotic relationship, was found to differ from neurosis in that it forebodes a total loss of self.

5. Like Mitscherlich and Brede, the psychoanalyst Helmut Thomä postulated a series of partial causes (conflicts, fears, defense mechanisms, object relations, and ego displacements) of psychosomatic illness. This contradicts the specific causal relation Alexander, French, and Pollock (1968) postulated between individuals' psychodynamic configuration and the onset of their illness. (Actually, the direct relation between a psychic trigger and the onset of physical symptoms could never be pinpointed, and psychosomaticists increasingly investigated factors of organ choice.) Furthermore, if all sorts of neurotic symptoms, narcissistic preoedipal elements, weakness of ego functions, and fragile object relations could cause psychosomatic illness, then Schur's notion that all psychosomatic patients shared certain basic characteristics could not hold up.

More recently, the German analyst Peter Stadler (1982) has linked Freud's psychosomatics to Pavlov's physiological findings and to Selye's notions of reactions to stress. Stadler wanted to explain how symbolic and somatic processes derive from the body-soul dualism that pervades everyday language. And Gerd Overbeck's *Illness and Adaptation* (1984) extended our knowledge of psychological roots and illnesses by demonstrating that such illnesses may well be pseudosolutions of social problems—especially when the psychosomatic patient has become adjusted to the conditions that made him sick in the first place.

Other Germans who do psychosomatic research have been examining how mother-child relations may influence "interactional sequences affecting organ systems": reactions to feeding were found to affect the upper intestinal tract and the stomach, and overemphasis on cleanliness was noted to act on the lower intestines. "Pathogenic object relations," such as isolating the child, intruding on or neglecting its psychic needs, were noted to cause specific psychosomatic disorders; and "psychosomatic triangulation"—psychic splitting into subject, object, and the body—may occur when "a weak and threatened self is opposed by a powerful archaic introject which has separated from the body" (Overbeck, 1984, pp. 552–54).

All these investigations, however, indicate that the psychosomatic riddle has not been solved. But postwar German psychosomatics also addressed the social and ethical ends of democracy that Americans were taking for granted. Since American analysts had never tried to invent techniques that would "improve" human organs, they had never worried about following Nazi ideology, which "equates humans with subhumans" and uses medicine as a tool for "politicized slaughter." (In America, physiobiology and psychoanalysis function in separate realms.) Consequently, the Americans never expected, as Mitscherlich did, that a psychoanalytically informed medicine might serve as the basis of a new anthropology or might become an "alternative medicine." Nor did they risk relapsing into the German idealist assumptions inherent in much of Marx and Hegel.

French Psychosomatics

In France, Freud remarked, psychoanalysis was introduced by men of letters. He thought this had happened because *The Interpretation of Dreams* addressed issued beyond medicine. But he noted only vaguely that French medicine was a closed group that brooked no interference from outsiders. When Eugenie Sokolnicka, a Pole who had been analyzed by Jung and Freud and had studied with Ferenczi, offered her services to the Clinic for Mental Illness at the Hospital of Ste.-Anne in 1922, she was rejected because she did not have a medical degree; only physicians were thought to be competent (Jaccard, 1982, p. 22). Psychoanalysis appeared to threaten established means of dealing with psychosomatic ailments, which were based on French views about the connections between biological and mental factors. Teaching hospitals already were being financed by the state, and the acceptable discourse had been established: doctors were to deal with the body and philosophers and theologians with the soul. In the universities, however, intellectual traditions made for fairly fluid discussions of the mind-body problem: the very strength of Cartesianism had encouraged anti-Cartesian queries.

Therefore, psychoanalysis was kept out of French psychosomatic medicine until after the war. But by 1960, a few French psychoanalysts—Michel Fain, Pierre Marty, and Michel de M'Uzan—had made original contributions, postulating that psychosomatic patients had a different personality structure from that of neurotics, psychotics, and "perverts." Instead of trying to diagnose them as neurotic or physically ill, they looked for three types of pathogenic phenomena that they believed were indicative of the psychosomatic structure:

1. Operative thinking (*pensée opératoire*), characterized by a personal and illogical type of logic, causality, and continuity and oriented to immediate, concrete reality. Although such thinking may be abstract and intellectual, these psychosomaticists found it to remain goal-oriented and yet separate from psychic object representations. The psychosomatic patient, they noted, tends to report on persons, events, and things in "devitalized language," as if they do not affect himself but someone else.

2. Reduplication projective, which describes how the psychosomatic patient "projects" his own undifferentiated self-image onto others. (Fain and Marty did not talk of "projection" per se because this psychic defense assumes a certain amount of structuring, which such patients lack.)

3. Inhibited fantasies of the unconscious (*inhibition fantasmatique de base*) are more or less connected to "operative thinking." When such patients have fantasies, these may draw on id or ego as well as superego structures and reproduce actual conditions. (Some authors, such as Joyce McDougall, also noted social "overadaptation"—see the discussion of perversion and psychosis in chapter 11.)

All these syndromes were said to have been drawn from work with patients. Marty, for instance, described patients with such diverse symptoms as spastic colon, hay fever, edema, migraine, rashes, and urinary infections; he found that they all had had similar early object relations. ("Allergic object relations," however, could also be observed in patients without somatic symptoms.) Such people, Marty noticed, kept trying to get exceedingly close to the analyst, to the point of "undifferentiated fusion"; that is, they overprojected or overidentified. One asthmatic patient, for instance, said he "chose his analyst because he thought that the analyst also suffered from asthma," and another patient announced to Marty that he knew he was "expected to speak about his mother" (Brede, 1980, pp. 400–45). In the psychoanalytic situation, it was noted, such persons could not keep their distance but instead identified by projection. Statements such as "you are wearing a beautiful suit today, I too feel better" or "this means you are exactly my age" were common. By projecting their own feelings onto the analyst, these patients identified with him in order to fuse. This made them seem overly loyal and childishly naive—"an impression allergic patients frequently create" (p. 426). Inevitably, in order to deny the patient's dependency on the now reactivated mother object, allergies surfaced when there were no possibilities of identification—during the analyst's vacations or when sessions were abbreviated or canceled. The psychosomatic allergy, therefore, it was maintained, defended against the loss of the primary object (usually the mother), which in turn was found to imply fixation at an archaic, prenatal level (p. 432). Although patients with "allergic object relations" also might suffer from obsession or hysteria, Marty noticed that their need to merge was dominant. Fixated at a pregenital level, these individuals could not deal with aggressive emotions, which contradicted their deep-seated wish to become one with the object. Marty's descriptions of their behavior upon entering analysis were an entertaining attempt to warn psychoanalysts against analytic passivity and against a laissez-faire attitude in the transference.

When Marty wrote his ground-breaking article in 1957, he wanted to know exactly how specific allergies arise from "pregenital fusion." But by stressing pregenital phenomena and postulating that the roots of fixation may be prenatal, he also spoke to the theoretical conflict between Anna Freud and Melanie Klein and their followers, and thus to one of the central questions of allegiance among all Freudians. (Since American classical psychoanalysts were loyal to Anna Freud, they did not take to Marty's work.)

By 1969, Marty was no longer focusing on allergies. Now he thought that "global, psychosomatic regression (of somatic reaction, character and conduct) was determined by an earlier fixation, and was stabilizing around it" (Brede, 1980, p. 446). He quoted Michel Fain's work on primary fixations during the first years of life and then examined the special dynamics of behavior and thought in allergic patients to find out how they deal with secondary trauma. At the same time, Marty kept looking for "a prenatal mechanism of fixation . . . and [for] a relationship between the allergy and some quality of unconscious empathy" (p. 400), which entailed a return to Ferenczi's notions of intrauterine causality.

Such a search directly contradicted Anna Freud (1977), who held that symptoms result from early nondifferentiation and from subsequently acquired defenses. She maintained that at the beginning of life, before somatic and psychological processes are separated from each other, bodily excitations such as hunger, cold, or pain are discharged as easily via mental pathways in the form of displeasure, anxiety, or rage as mental upsets are discharged via disturbances of the body (intake, digestion, elimination, breathing). Such psychosomatic reactions, she asserted, are developmentally determined at this early time of life (p. 36). Individual development, she continued, depends on the "sensitivity" of particular bodily parts, and once a specific organ system—such as the skin, the respiratory system, or the intestinal system—is "chosen" for psychic discharge it becomes more and more vulnerable and sensitive. Marty did not address this issue directly because he attributed allergic fixation to specific types of regression. Indeed, he suggested that the proper use of the countertransference rather than a direct "attack" on somatic symptomatology can lead the patient to psychic reorganization. Here Marty accepted the Freudian concept of libidinal fixation, but he conceptualized it on the most "archaic psychosomatic level" and argued that extreme cases of disorganization that are due to "the early formation of the internalized psychosomatic symptom" exclude libido.

Ultimately, Marty accepted the basic premises of object relations theory—that is, regression to the earliest involvement with the environment—for he thought that allergy formation takes place prior to ego formation. But Marty's search for psychosomatic origins was couched in metapsychological language, and his views of libido theory coincided more with those of the Germans than with the Americans'. Still, Marty and Fain were close to the Lacanians and the Kleinians insofar as they believed that object relations exist from the moment of birth, whereas Mitscherlich and his group, like the American ego psychologists, thought that "reaction formations and defense mechanisms were . . . the preconditions for the transition of alloplastic into autoplastic happening of behavior" (Brede, 1980, p. 398). Mitscherlich had set out to strengthen ego functions, to integrate ego performance, so as to relieve individuals from repetition compulsions that make them relive their early trauma in social situations. According to him, the choice of the organism is a compromise between accepting reality and fulfilling a reckless wish to satisfy "aggressive and libidinal drives" (p. 399). But when Mitscherlich argued that defenses originate in early childhood and in the immature and weak ego, he also came out against those ego psychologists who argue that new defenses may be set up in later years. In this respect he mediated between French and American psychosomatics (pp. 400–01).

Psychosomatics in Austria

Although Austrians and Germans had similar institutional experiences in the Third Reich, almost none of the Austrians went into psychosomatics after the war. Probably because of the extremely small number of psychoanalysts and the traditional emphasis on applied pedagogy most Freudians continued to cooperate with Adlerians, behavior therapists, Rogerians, "neoanalysts," and others in the Institut für Tiefenpsychologie. But none of those therapies dwells on or accepts unconscious motivation.

Wolfgang Wesiak, for example, addressing the Viennese Freudians in 1976, spoke of Freud's focus on the "individual man" and of his own "integration" into the psychoanalytic process. He differentiated psychosomatic medicine from other medical practices as "more than merely an object of natural science," because the patient becomes "a partner endowed with a soul, a person who not only presents the physical and chemical but also the psychodynamic and psychosocial aspects" of his illness (1978, pp. 30–38). In order to downplay the physical aspects of illness, he quoted Freud's letter of October 16, 1932, to Viktor von Weizsäcker:

The explanation of a functional disturbance, in this case, of miction, through the erotization imposed upon the organs of the urinary tract, fully corresponds to the analytic theory I have tried to illustrate with a commonplace parable: it is as if the master of the house had entered into a *liaison d'amour* with the cook, certainly not to the disadvantage of the cooking. You go on to demonstrate the subtle [physical] mechanism of the disturbance by pointing to opposing innervations which necessarily undo or disturb each other. For educational reasons, it was my task to keep analysts away from such investigations, because innervations, vasal dilation, nerve tracts, would have been dangerously seductive to them. They had to learn to restrict their way of thinking to psychology. But to the specialist in internal medicine we may be grateful for broadening our understanding. (1978, p. 31; my translation)

Clearly, Wesiak wanted to effect a radical separation of psychoanalysis and physiology. Just as Ferenczi had divided the history of psychoanalysis, he now divided the history of psychoanalytic psychosomatics into several stages: (1) the speculative period, which lasted until about 1920, when organic symptoms were exposed to psychological interpretation; (2) the fertile period, which was based on the later work of Franz Alexander, who found that both the so-called somatic X-factor and conflict are prerequisite to psychosomatic disease; and (3) the recent period, in which psychosomatic diseases are differentiated from neuroses. Wesiak drew on Mitscherlich's distinction between the phases before and after the breakdown of neurotic defense mechanisms, Flanders Dunbar's typification of personality, and the French view of the "psychosomatic phenomenon," which he described as loss of imagination, inability to integrate psychic functions, and low capacity for identification with others. These tendencies in psychosomatic research, he concluded, link "neuroses, psychosomatic disorders and organic diseases to form a chain." But now physicians tend to specialize, Wesiak continued, so that they no longer learn how to deal with patients who suffer from psychic and somatic symptoms.

Austrian psychoanalysts, of course, are familiar with other psychoanalytic theories and practices, but they tend to remain "Austrian" by stressing the contributions of the past. Wesiak, for instance, mentioned Alexander's and Balint's Austrian background (they were Hungarian) as well as Dunbar's training in Vienna as if these facts were relevant to psychoanalysis itself. He also urged that every Austrian general practitioner learn how to "enter the patient's system of object relations . . . [to] gain insight into her pathology and her individual reality" (p. 35). Wesiak never questioned the focus on application and the absence of psychosomatic and any other psychoanalytic research since the *Anschluss*.

To some extent, the fact that most Austrian Freudians work primarily within hospitals assumes their acceptance of the soma-psyche connection. But it is a connection to psychiatry. Thus even more than elsewhere the psychoanalysts are pitted against those who favor shock and drug treatments, on the one hand, and against the psychologists and social workers, who practice more simplistic therapies, on the other. In such a climate, research is impossible. Furthermore, there is a scarcity of trained individuals able to do such research and of funds to support it. Clearly, the Viennese ambience and the restrictive milieu, which originally induced Freud to look abroad and focus on wider human concerns, have remained rather inhospitable to the pursuits of American, French, and German psychosomatics.

Tentative Conclusions

Psychosomatic medicine, with its stronghold within medicine, to some extent remains the backbone of psychoanalysis in every country. But the United States was the first to encourage large-scale psychosomatic research. Ever since Alexander (1962) had postulated seven psychodynamic patterns correlated to seven diseases (duodenal ulcers, ulcerative colitis, asthma, essential hypertension, rheumatoid arthritis, thyrotoxicoses, and neurodermatitis), other physiological reactions such as heart activity, muscle tone, respiration, galvanic skin resistance, blood pressure, and changes in thyroid functions were being electronically charted. A number of psychoanalysts and psychiatrists have been experimenting with all sorts of physiological interventions, gradually deemphasizing the "adaptive balance between a person and his environment," on which Alexander had focused (p. 21). Alexander questioned whether neurosis was an entirely psychic condition and looked more closely at factors of stress. Psychoanalysts also examined stress as the trigger for emotional and hormonal disruption, but they did not pursue a physical means of cure and were more likely to branch out into family dynamics and to try to attribute an individual's maladaption to the effect of family pathology (Meissner, 1966).

Alexander's core assumption, that neurosis arises as a reaction to the field in which the person operates and that changes in the environment are helpful, contradicted those "orthodox" ego psychologists who held that intrapsychic mechanisms needed to be altered (Meissner, 1966, p. 22). But this turned out to be more difficult than had been expected, for psychosomatic medicine had raised unwarranted hopes (Lipowski, 1977, p. 235). Everywhere, the entry of psychoanalysis into the medical establishment was accompanied by high expectations. And everywhere, it lost prestige when the awaited cures did not fully materialize or when it became clear that they would be extremely costly. So, when not enough patients were cured, more and more psychiatrists joined the biochemical, neurophysiological, and pharmaceutical researchers, accelerating the decline in the demand for classical psychoanalysis. And as one-on-one analytic treatment came to be thought too inefficient and expensive, it was gradually phased out in the clinics.

By the 1970s, as David Mechanic (1980, p. 29) has noted, American psychiatric training had become "more eclectic, with growing concern for scientific rigor, more precise classification, and the investigation of biological hypotheses. . . . Clinical psychology had become more behaviorally oriented." Psychoanalysis now no longer influences the dominant views and approaches to psychological disorder and modes of handling it, as it did in the America of the 1950s. Physiological approaches have won out, although many of the psychoanalysts' formulations of psychosomatics continue to be retained. Thus "pure" psychosomatic medicine was short-lived.[6] In Germany, however, physiological approaches are reminiscent of Nazi experimentation. Yet, psychosomatic medicine remains strong there precisely because it stresses the influence of the psyche on the body. In England, where there is little differentiation between medical and nonmedical analysts, the link to neurological and physiological research always was negligible.

Recent American research on mental illness, such as that by I. Arthur Mirsky (1966), is based on "psychosomatic medicine as a hybrid stemming from the psychophysiological studies of Cannon and the monumental work of Freud," as well as on data from research on animal behavior. But such an inclusive approach remains anathema to most classical Freudians in America and to many of their German and French colleagues. Marty, for example, picks up Alexander's environmental notions in *Les mouvements individuels de vie et de la mort* (1975) by maintaining that attitudes about life and death influence the course of illness (p. 81), although he ignores Alexander's physiological thrust and emphasizes the importance of the ego-ideal in psychosomatic disturbance (Marty, 1968). Marty's broad sweep is in the French rhetorical tradition, even though substantively he did not go much beyond the Viennese Felix Deutsch, who, as early as 1922, described the etiology of organic conversion symptoms in similar fashion.

Approaches to psychosomatics in the various countries differ more in style than in substance. And government policies on reimbursement, diagnostic guidelines, suggestions as to what should be investigated, by whom, and how much to spend for specific projects ultimately determine the direction of psychosomatic research everywhere. The Americans George L. Engel and Arthur H. Schmale, Jr. (1966), for example, attempted to integrate "a group of disorders in which primary biological factors influence both psychic development and somatic vulnerability." A number of German analysts elaborated on their work after having obtained detailed data from new (including working-class) populations in order to satisfy *their* mandated priorities. Similar inquiries were started in America when the 1975 Task Force of the National Institute of Mental Health recommended that collaborative psychosomatic research be fostered in clinical settings dealing with different somatic illnesses, and when research into the link between psychosomatic illness and familial conflicts began to be funded (Meissner, 1966).

No doubt, the decline of classical psychoanalysis influenced American decision makers, but so did the pervasive belief that both more money and "harder" science would generate more knowledge and, eventually, more successful cures. Paradoxically, the promoters of these "hard" studies never failed to go back to the early Freudians, even when concluding (with the psychoanalyst George H. Pollock) that both psychosocial and psychobiological characteristics are increasingly relevant in our understanding of the uniqueness of man (Engel and Schmale, 1966).

All in all, the concerns of the psychosomaticists have not been fully welcomed anywhere. In France, when their research is being funded at all, psychoanalysts are treated as intellectuals: what support they receive—and French intellectuals, unlike their American peers, have much prestige—goes for theoretical rather than empirical investigation. Consequently, the French lack the financial requisites for empirical research even when they have not been viscerally opposed to it. Still, if Robert M. Rose, the 1983 president of the American Psychosomatic Society, was correct in stating that practices have not really changed and the problems have not yet been solved, then we must conclude that the task of psychosomatics, at least so far, might have been insuperable. For neither German reimbursement policies nor massive American research projects have brought us better answers than Freud offered in 1915. Somatization of psychic events, it appears, is universal. And even though approaches to treatment differ, no concrete results have been derived from the French "return to Freud," the American scientific inquiries, or the German socially oriented psychosomatics. Chances are that the German attempts to synthesize Weizsäcker's physiological contributions and Freud's "Studies of Aphasia" and the French efforts to penetrate "prenatal object relations" via new associations through the use of linguistic theory will not prove more fruitful than American psychosomatic research. Hindsight points to the fact that psychosomatic patients get better after they have established a working analytic relationship, but since this is not "objectifiable," we should not be surprised that in America Freudian psychosomatics have been declared dead and that the "new age of psychosomatic psychiatry" has descended upon us (Maxmen, 1985).

Chapter 6

Education

In a speech about psychoanalysis and education at the First International Psycho-Analytical Congress in 1908, Sándor Ferenczi denounced the prevalent teaching methods as leading to faulty character development and serious illness; schools, he said, were hothouses fostering neurosis.[1] Psychoanalysis, he promised, by doing away with excessive repression would transform pedagogy and society (Ferenczi [1908] 1949). Ever since then, educators have applied and misapplied psychoanalysis. Freud himself at first urged teachers and nursery school workers to monitor childrens' emotional behavior since they were more detached than parents. But before long, he decided that they needed an analysis in order to handle the children properly. Since few teachers heeded this advice, they could not go far beyond observing their pupils, although they learned to use psychoanalytic language better. At the same time, some of the teachers' observations of children were paralleled by anthropologists' tales of fairly uninhibited practices in tribal cultures. Flooded by so much new information, many teachers began to confuse notions of education, culture, and therapy.

Until the 1930s, the term *applied psychoanalysis* referred primarily to pedagogy, although it soon came to be used in all sorts of contexts, from popular to clinical. By 1980, the Swiss Freudian Paul Parin, for instance, had "applied" psychoanalysis to Ivory Coast natives (Parin et al., 1971), French feminists had "applied" it to the dialogue "between femininity and Freud's theory of sexuality" (Rose, 1985, p. 128), and the Austrian Elizabeth Brainin together with the Frankfurt analyst Isidor J. Kaminer had "applied" it to smoke out forms of hidden anti-Semitism (1982). In American universities, literary and art works, the lives of their creators, and culture as a whole had been reinterpreted in line with the newest views on narcissism, object relations, and psychopathology. The ubiquity of psychoanalytic language induced a casual use of clinical terms which has increased the confusion even further: teachers borrow the philosophical and clinical idioms of psychoanalysis and use them interchangeably, thereby altering their original meanings and often, in the process, transforming clinical terms into psychobabble (Solnit, 1975, p. 4). The Freudians, however, have had as much disdain for the teachers' simplifications as for those of the insufficiently trained "wild analysts" and the various crackpot therapists. Thus the émigrés never tried to influence the classroom: they stayed in their consulting rooms where it was possible to maintain theoretical purity.

At first, only the German-speaking countries, where philosophic traditions facilitated broader conceptions of Freudian doctrine, allowed psychoanalytic ideas to enter the classroom. Particularly in Austria, where the mixture of nationalities and ethnic populations speaking different languages had made for a variety of disciplinary problems, a watered-down psychoanalysis was enlisted to counter existing authoritarian principles. American pragmatism, on the other hand, had always responded to educational innovations, so that psychoanalysis was just one in a succession of fads. But in France, where educational curricula and methods, in line with the Napoleonic Code, were centralized, even minor reforms needed bureaucratic approval. Thus *la psychanalyse* was kept out of education. (After the rise of Lacan, however, it became an adjunct to the study of linguistics.) In the early 1960s the French philosopher Paul Ricoeur, defining "education" as the moment the child turns into an adult, would take Freudian doctrine for granted in his understanding of modern self-consciousness (1970, pp. 523–24). And by the 1970s, Freud's ideas had filtered into French thinking, and children entering school had been reared in line with his progressive ideas. In this climate, people already knew that repression can be harmful to psychic development and that a child was not a tabula rasa, nor was he innocent and pure.

Freud's Appeal to Educators

In the early days, educational philosophies based on psychoanalytic gospel were becoming increasingly legitimate through scientific psychiatry. Educators who hoped to turn child rearing into a science kept in touch with *all* emerging psychologies—those focusing on the connections between body and mind, on nurture, on nature, on Wundt's "nonanalytic" Völkerpsychologie, on Köhler's Gestalt psychology, and on Pavlovian conditioning. Psychoanalysis, however, was also linked to the humanists and writers the teachers were in touch with. They were affected by such novels as Italo Svevo's *Confessions of Zeno* and Arthur Schnitzler's *Der Reigen*, popular books that blatantly displayed their characters' unconsciously motivated actions, and by the introspection of the modernists, which often followed the psychoanalysts' bent in speculating about the vagaries of the unconscious.

Teachers were attracted to psychoanalysis in a period of rapid professionalization; its scientific cast promised to raise their own status. They went to Freud's public lectures (which were often geared to audiences of educators), and many were converted. Ferenczi had initially addressed pediatricians (since they are the first to handle infants) but soon gave talks to larger audiences, where he blamed adult neuroses on poor early social experiences. By 1909, he was saying that by diverting mental energy to defensive strategies people may turn into emotional cripples. Since educators had been criticized for their inability to maintain discipline and were held responsible for their students' intellectual deficiencies, it is not surprising that they were sympathetic to psychoanalysis, for it appeared to put the blame on the family.

The teachers listened to Ferenczi (later to Adler) and to Freud. But Freud was personally distant and ambivalent: although skeptical of the educators' immediate enterprise, he needed to take them seriously for the sake of his movement. Rather cleverly, he excused his relative distance by stating that he was unfit for applied psychoanalysis, that for him, "education, healing, and ruling were three impossible professions." But he encouraged his daughter Anna to become a "psycho-pedagogue." Later on, he was delighted with her experimental kindergarten.

Teachers, of course, could not force psychoanalysis on an unwilling public, and Adler's "individual psychology" was more palatable to them. But as psychoanalytic concepts became acceptable, they would increasingly influence those attending to the psychological and social development of children. So, as psychoanalysis revolutionized ideas about infants—their sexuality, its relation to feeding, and so on—it challenged educational philosophies.

As early as 1909, the feisty Protestant minister Oskar Pfister wrote to Freud from Switzerland:

The [ethical] difference between your understanding and mine is probably less than you would expect from my professional position. The Protestant ethic had already removed the odium of uncleanliness from sexuality. After all, the Reformation, basically, is no more than an analysis of the [unnecessary] Catholic repression of sexuality, and therefore the anxiety of the Catholic church and its side effects, the witch hunts, political absolutisms, etc. We Protestant ministers . . . feel entirely Protestant and are certain of being insufficiently reformed. We are searching for a new land. (E. L. Freud and Meng, 1963, p. 14)

Pfister was drawn to psychoanalysis because it combined a scientific aura with liberal and humanist concerns and to a lesser extent because it elevated Protestantism over Catholicism. For years, however, he was the only European clergyman "friendly" to psychoanalysis; he shared more of the educational premises of Americans in the Emmanuel movement (a religious group that claimed to combine religion and modern medicine in meeting the psychological, physical, and spiritual needs of parishioners) than those of his fellow pastors, who warned against unleashing unconscious forces. Pfister, however, rejected the idea of childhood sexuality. And unlike Americans who could proselytize from their pulpits, this was difficult for Pfister in the less free-wheeling European religious milieu.

Applied Psychoanalysis before World War II

The application of psychoanalysis to education, stated Freud in the introduction to August Aichhorn's *Wayward Youth* ([1925] 1951), awakened more hopes and interest, attracted more collaborators, and sparked more research than did the work with neurotics (p. 7). Freud strongly supported Aichhorn's work with delinquents from lower-class families at his clinic in Hollabrunn, which not only provided material for new theories but proved that psychoanalysis would not remain confined to the middle class. In contrast to his break with Adler, who wanted to introduce a watered-down psychoanalysis into the school system, Freud was eager to present Aichhorn's suggestions to Viennese educators; Aichhorn, he added, "demonstrated perfectly how useful a personal analysis could be to every educator." Here, Freud was walking a thin line: in order to win converts he had to make psychoanalysis sound simpler than it was, and in order to retain its focus on unconscious content he had to avoid popularizations. Freud warned Aichhorn against the subversion of psychoanalysis by lumping work with "derailed and delinquent children" with the analysis of neurotics, and against the confusion of the "reeducation of the former with treatment of the latter" (p. 8). Actually, Aichhorn was arguing that a strong, socially directed superego depended upon strong early identifications and object relations, which orphans and illegitimate children could not achieve at home. Therefore he used the psychoanalytic transference to induce a "corrective experience" in delinquent adolescents (pp. 51–57).

At the time, the utopian promises of psychoanalysis still loomed so large that broad speculation about its application was de rigueur. Inventing a new pedagogy thus appeared to be an adjunct to democracy. In this spirit, Pfister, among other things, proposed an alternative method of education, *"Paedana-lyse."* It used direct psychoanalytic explanations to motivate students to achieve and to discourage bad behavior. Like Aichhorn, Pfister underplayed his own extraordinary intuition and empathy and assumed that any teacher in any classroom could successfully practice this "art of education" (1913, p. 507). Although a number of teachers followed his lead, few of them could approach his pedagogic results.

In August 1919, after the First World War, Siegfried Bernfeld, whom Helene Deutsch remembered as an enigmatic and fascinating Don Quixote type, founded his "Kinderheim Baumgarten," a commune for approximately three hundred homeless Jewish, delinquent, and working-class orphans. Inspired by Marxist and Zionist ideals, he blended psychoanalysis with other permissive educational concepts in an attempt to heal his charges' emotional scars. Essentially, Bernfeld assumed that "unconditional love and respect" for the children, coupled with nonauthoritarian methods, would turn their asocial impulses into social ones (Peters, [1979] 1985, p. 61). Owing to outside pressures and to mismanagement, the experiment foundered in less than a year. So did Wera Schmidt's "children's laboratory," established in Moscow between 1921 and 1923 to take care of one- to five-year-old children: Schmidt expected to provide "perfect" conditions during the oedipal period to ensure her charges' healthy sexual organization, with the help of an intensive psychoanalytic transference, which, in turn, was expected to engender optimal sublimation (Körner, 1980, p. 771).

Around that time, the German educator Hans Zulliger evolved yet another psychoanalytic pedagogy. By examining the spoken and written statements of his pupils, he presumed to understand their intrapsychic conflicts. He had a very personal style of interpretation and a great deal of intuition and is reported to have helped some of these youngsters. Beyond that, he developed a "structural theory" of the teacher-student relationship, modeled on Freud's "Psychopathology of Everyday Life" (1921). But it did not catch on.

In Vienna, Hermine Hug-Hellmuth explicitly designed an educational therapy based on extrapolations from Freud's case of "Little Hans" (Hug-Hellmuth, 1921, p. 21). Because she was among the first to use toys and games as therapeutic tools, Anna Freud later declared her a forerunner of child analysis. She also influenced child-rearing methods by lecturing on Freud's ideas to parents, teachers, school physicians, and social workers (Peters, 1985,

p. 60). Paradoxically, she may have been a direct victim of psychoanalysis, for she was killed by her nephew and ward, whom, in line with her understanding of psychoanalytic principles, she had overindulged.[2] We know little about her nephew's personality and character, and we can only surmise that her fate put a damper on notions of "unconditional love and acceptance" of child behavior. Since Hug-Hellmuth stipulated in her will that none of her writing be published, we know little as yet about her or her work, although by all accounts she was an educator rather than a psychoanalyst, one who enthusiastically applied Freud's methods.

The famous Maria Montessori tends to be linked to psychoanalysis, although she was influenced more by the psychologist Wilhelm Wundt and the philosopher Johann Friedrich Herbart than by Freud. But her insistence that young children need freedom to explore, to give vent to their "natural inclinations"—which she implemented through her methods of teaching and the physical settings of her schools—paralleled Freud's ideas of viable discipline. He admired her work and told her that his daughter Anna, "an analytical pedagogue, consider[ed] herself one of [Montessori's] disciples" (E. Freud, 1960, pp. 319–20). In 1976, in her introduction to Rita Kramer's biography of Montessori, Anna Freud praised the educator for allowing children to express themselves freely and to feel successful at doing work "in freedom within carefully defined limits" (Kramer, 1988, p. 7; such conditions, of course, are prerequisite for psychoanalytic treatment). By then, Anna Freud had become the doyenne of child analysis; she taught only occasionally in her role as participant observer in the Hampstead nurseries. The first child of psychoanalysis, Anna Freud knew more than others, so that her classroom performances were less rigid than those of her contemporaries.

Anna Freud's pedagogy was coupled to her theoretical concerns. Like her father, she relied on case histories (and firsthand experiences) to illustrate her larger conclusions. We know that she was a gifted analyst and that she had an uncanny ability to gain her young patients' confidence and tap into their psyches. Her ascendance in the psychoanalytic hierarchy certainly transformed applied psychoanalysis and encouraged research on children. Thus Anna Freud's cases were cited frequently because they seemed particularly suggestive. And her contributions were respected not because she was Freud's daughter but because she had been engaged so early in what would become the central issues of the profession.

Melanie Klein also based her theories of object relations on the analysis of children. She had pursued a path similar to Anna Freud's, first in Berlin and then in London. But Klein argued that an analysis should be part of every child's education, whereas Anna Freud believed it was advisable only for cases of infantile neurosis. Klein thought every aspect of the child's play needed to be interpreted as a symbolic manifestation of aggression or libido and that sexual content ought to be verbalized. Anna Freud, however, was more intent on winning the child's confidence—by making dolls' clothes, playing along with suggestions, and entering the child's world—and on pursuing the "educational purposes of psychoanalysis." Hence she focused on uncovering her patients' psychic reality; Klein primarily wanted to reduce their anxiety. For Anna Freud, there could be no viable psychoanalytic transference so long as the child was dependent upon its parents—that is, until the superego was internalized enough to deal with actual parental authority, around the age of five. Klein, however, found that the child's ego emerges from the earliest projections and introjections, which she linked to feeding—that is, around the first oral experiences. Thus, Klein analyzed children Anna Freud deemed too young. (Only later was it clear that Klein's first patient was her own son.) According to Klein's biographer, Phyllis Grosskurth, Anna Freud was an expositor of her father's ideas, but only of those ideas that could be scrutinized in clearly lit, well-ventilated places. She shunned sin, cruelty, suffering. Grosskurth quotes John Bowlby on the difference between Klein and Freud: "Anna Freud worshipped at the shrine of St. Sigmund and Klein at the shrine of St. Melanie" (1986, p. 325). Their analytic differences stood out as both Anna Freud and Klein rose to intellectual leadership in the 1950s, when the Freudians' focus shifted from the education of children to that of infants, and from schools to nurseries.

By about 1926, psychoanalytic education had become a new academic specialty in the German-speaking countries. In the journal *Zeitschrift für psychoanalytische Pädagogik*, in addition to theoretical debates, one could find articles on the psychoanalysis of children and adolescents and case reports and studies by psychoanalytically oriented educators. But this journal ceased publication in 1937 and was not revived after the war because interests had changed. In England, work at the Tavistock clinic, founded in 1920, and the Hampstead clinic, started by Anna Freud and Dorothy Burlingham in 1940, dealt with birth traumas and the effects of war on children rather than with pedagogy. In America the psychoanalytic study of children eventually became a mainstay of the Freudian establishment.

Both Anna Freud and Melanie Klein had noted young children's shorter attention span, their lesser (or not-yet-existing) ability to abstract, and their undeveloped and volatile superegos; and a number of educators had applied some of their findings. Later, when Melanie Klein spoke of "education with analytic impact" on schools, she claimed to be following Freud's differentiation between applying psychoanalysis to the culture at large and to the therapy of disturbed children (Körner, 1980, p. 771). Concentrating on the earliest period of development, she held that the education of a child in therapy must begin before its personality and superego are formed. Anna Freud, on the other hand, for whom the formation of the superego during the oedipal period was crucial, was more concerned with the role of the child analyst as a later reeducating force. Klein and Anna Freud also could not agree on the stage when the superego is completely formed, and this question would be addressed again and again in the annual *The Psychoanalytic Study of the Child*.

This series, started in 1946, and originally edited by Anna Freud, Heinz Hartmann, and Ernst Kris, "replaced" the earlier publications on pedagogy. Around the same time American analysts, in cooperation with philosophers, educators, and anthropologists throughout the world, also began to address what was called the international interests of the child, thus lifting psychoanalytic pedagogy to new heights of generalization.

Within their institutes, the Freudians increasingly examined special areas of child development and problems of adolescence. In the process, they perceived the treatment of neuroses in adults as reeducation, and studies of children as the means to learn about the formation of both healthy and neurotic personalities. And as anthropology, political science, psychology, and the other behavioral sciences came explicitly or implicitly to accept the Freudian unconscious, psychoanalytic concepts began to invade the classrooms of the Western world.

Psychoanalysis in the Service of the Nazis

In Germany applied psychoanalysis took another path when the Nazis tried to exploit it. After most of the Jewish analysts had been expelled, Mattias Heinrich Göring, the field marshal's cousin, co-opted the few remaining Freudians into his institute, which consisted of assorted Adlerians, Jungians, and Seifians.[3] They applied these sundry therapies so boldly that in 1940 Göring could brag to the Führer that the therapists, including the psychoanalysts, were serving the Fatherland by "increasing militance and valiancy, and by strengthening the will and pleasure in work" (Grunert, 1984, p. 869).[4]

What the Nazi therapists practiced was a caricature of psychoanalysis, of course. They aimed to "perfect" the Aryan superrace, to relieve the symptoms and thus lift the morale of workers in munitions plants, and to cure "sexual disorders" and alcoholism. As G. C. Cocks described their program, "The Nazis tried to preempt wartime rebelliousness by workers over wages, working hours or trade union autonomy by using a fusion of terror, racial rhetoric, and the sop of plenty of consumer goods. . . . [They] emphasized 'adjustment' over 'struggle'" (1985, pp. 197–98). Although perverting the liberating components of psychoanalysis, these practices did get some neurotic patients back on the job. In fact, Göring and his crew were successful enough to convince officials in the German Ministry of Medicine, the Labor Front (DAF), the Reich Research Council, the Luftwaffe, the Reich's Health Office, and its recreational branch, Kraft durch Freude, to support them financially.

Whether or not the program saved some individuals from being punished as malingerers, homosexuals, or cowards, at least they were being "protected": a diagnosis of mental instability or retardation, for instance, could mean imprisonment instead of execution. These therapists, for example, secretly took care of a case for Heinrich Himmler: when the seventeen-year-old daughter of an SS commander who had been killed was in danger of being charged with "hereditary degeneracy"—a reason for extermination—Göring saved her (Cocks, 1985, pp. 203–05). The research commission on homosexuality and psychogenic sterility "cured" a number of high-ranking Nazis of homosexuality and thus kept them alive.

On the other hand, the therapists also gave counsel and medical advice to the Nazi youth organizations and to the project *Lebensborn*, which had been set up to "improve" the German race by impregnating its "best" female specimens (Cocks, 1985, pp. 207–08).[5] And the training of industrial psychologists for the Office for Vocational Training and Works Management did not constitute psychoanalysis; nor were the study groups that developed characterological tests for the Labor Front's institute or those that investigated *Ahnenerben* (genetic inheritance) more than boondoggles and theoretical distortions (pp. 200–03).

In any event, the "Freudians" among the Nazi therapists were deeply involved in Nazi projects. Even if they had misgivings, they nevertheless must have subscribed to a good dose of Nazi ideology. But they were saved from punishment by the Allies when the Göring institute was destroyed by Allied bombers in April 1945 and its incriminating records disappeared. Many of its erstwhile members could thus claim innocence and build new practices upon the ashes of the old. In fact, the close links the "psychic educators" had established with government agencies facilitated their postwar activities.

The victors, eager to reeducate and denazify all Germans, immediately accepted the services of the Berlin contingent. As early as July 1945, Dr. Ludwig Zeise, a Munich psychotherapist, told his colleagues that he had been asked by the American authorities to submit a plan for reeducating the German people. Now German therapists were revising their own recent histories, stressing their former "ambivalence" about the Nazis and the hardships they had suffered and trying to contact Jewish analysts in America and England with whom they formerly had been friendly. In sum, German therapists wanted to continue plying their trade, and they peddled the expertise they had acquired as a tool for denazification.

German analysts today report that their postwar compatriots could not have supported in-depth analysis rather than short-term therapy. Not so soon after the war could they have faced all their guilt—of omission if not commission (Kurzweil, 1985). At the time, however, none of them had been analyzed, and thus consciously as well as unconsciously they "conspired" to forget the past.

Psychoanalysis and Postwar Pedagogy

As an adjunct to psychotherapy, the Nazis had created a new profession, "psychagogy." The members of the five Göring institutes had been entrusted with the mental health of the country and with investigating what the Nazis perceived as "hereditary biology." Since the Nazis had not had enough doctors to spare, they had licensed these psychagogues, who had not been required to undergo an analysis to act as guidance counselors and family therapists. Mostly, they told patients what to do and did not pretend to achieve more than quick fixes. So, even though they knew little or nothing about free-association methods or about the transference, they had become regular members of the profession. When after the war former codes on professional access remained in force, this proved to be a problem, for the psychagogues could legitimately claim their previous experience as clinical or experimental psychologists (see Chapter 9).

Eventually, the training of psychagogues would become more stringent. But right after the war they outnumbered other therapists within the Deutsche Gesellschaft für Psychotherapie und Tiefenpsychologie (depth psychology; DGPT), so that the other members tended to cater to them in order to persuade the German government to underwrite mental health insurance. But unlike the Freudians, the psychagogues continued to foster "adjustment" by trying to prevent children's difficulties and neuroses with the help of "sound educational practices and environmental standards in families and schools"

(Cocks, 1985, pp. 207–08). Knowing that the fate of psychoanalysts was intertwined with their own, the psychagogues retained their hold long after the DPV was founded. Actually, theirs was a marriage of convenience. Theoretically, the psychoanalysts' stress on the unconscious and the psychagogues' pragmatic approach were irreconcilable, but together, they fathered German postwar psychoanalysis. Their collusion probably made possible the forty years of silence about Third Reich activities (Kurzweil, 1985).

Although the approach of the psychagogues violated psychoanalytic principles, it seemed to offer the most efficacious means for indoctrination of the Germans into democracy. Thus, by the late 1940s, Freud's teachings, when remembered at all, had become distorted. Margarete Mitscherlich-Nielsen recently recalled that she told the handful of "honest" German Freudians in 1949 that what they were practicing was not psychoanalysis. (Having dual citizenship—German and Danish—she had been allowed to go to London for analysis and training.) German psychoanalysts did not yet understand or recognize the transference. An adept student of psychoanalysis, the anti-Nazi Alexander Mitscherlich, soon advocated the application of psychoanalysis as the road to a new consciousness: his appeals within the DGPT were as eloquent as those to the public and the government.[6]

The government, however, enacted laws that incorporated the psychagogues' vague amalgam of Freudian, Jungian, Adlerian, Seifian, and ad hoc therapies. Thus Göring's psychagogues could go on doing their jobs in schools and in their private practices. By the mid-1950s, however, their reports sounded more psychoanalytic. And although their analytic colleagues objected to being associated with the psychagogues, professional self-interest won out: the analysts needed all the support they could get to pass favorable legislation. Hence they played down internal struggles and did not air them at IPA meetings.

Currently, as some German Freudians address the history of these struggles for the first time, they are expecting again to use psychoanalytic knowledge in the schools, but they plan to do so in a more sophisticated and nonadaptive fashion. Some hope to improve students' mental health by devising progressive teaching techniques (Körner, 1980, p. 781). If teachers were able to allow for transference and then refuse to play the parts of surrogate fathers or mothers, they argue, students might be able to relive early experiences more felicitously and thus gain "corrected" insights. Or they might learn that "reality is not always properly perceived" (p. 782). But Körner pointed also to the problems teachers face when allowing themselves to become stand-ins for primary objects, thus encouraging a type of transference inappropriate in a school setting and open to dangerous manipulation. Nonetheless, it has been argued that such applications might disseminate more recent psychoanalytic knowledge and open up students' minds to the early Freudians' romantic and revolutionary ideals.

What Germans and Austrians call psychoanalytic pedagogy, however, resembles educational psychology, or what is referred to as communication in American classrooms, where teachers and social workers have for years used a popularized psychoanalytic lingo and where guidance counselors have been accustomed to referring severely disturbed children to psychoanalysts and psychiatrists, similar to what the German psychagogues have been doing. In America the popularizations of psychoanalysis contain a blend of behavior, Gestalt, transaction, and ad hoc therapies. In Germany, however, there is less talk of mixing the diverse notions. Though the German psychagogues are keen on exerting maximal influence in the schools, they are not as busily discussing the immediate role of the educator as their American counterparts. Instead, most German therapists, from the classic Freudians to the educators, are afraid that being in authority might lead to authoritarianism. Within the laissez-faire and progressive American educational system—fraught with anarchic tendencies—authoritarianism is one of the lesser dangers, whereas in Germany it is strongly feared.

In France, after 1968, Jacques Lacan proclaimed that transference is everywhere and can even be "transmitted" over television. But this announcement belonged to his provocative technique and his love of overstatement: it had as little to do with the German teachers' use of "transference" as with the privileged dialogue between analyst and analysand. Actually, neither French nor Anglo-Saxon classical Freudians ever considered pedagogy comparable to psychoanalysis. For them, the unconscious is reached in the analytic hour alone and is totally different from other types of interaction. In sum, neither Lacanian nor classical psychoanalysts would deal directly with pedagogy. Thus, most applied psychoanalysis became marginal, and Anglo-Saxon Freudians gradually came to reserve the term for case studies that support their theories or for discussions of literature, art, film, and other such cultural products.

Anglo-Saxon Child Studies

Anna Freud and Melanie Klein had differed about the nature of children's psychic development and the means of improving their mental health long before they confronted each other in the British Psycho-Analytical Society. Essentially, Anna Freud regarded preoedipal children (before their Oedipus complex emerges in the third to fifth year and in relation to the real parents) as different beings from adults. Klein, however, was convinced that the earliest experiences contribute to the Oedipus complex and that the psychoanalyst primarily must help relieve the anxieties caused by the birth trauma and early object relations. Moreover, by accepting suffering as a necessary part of analysis, she denied Anna Freud's assumption that the child might go mad if the deeper layers of the unconscious were touched (Grosskurth, 1986, p. 169).

By the time the Freuds came to London in 1938, Klein had established her position among British analysts and among the immigrants who had come from Germany. She had embarked on rather concrete ways of guiding mother-child relations. Since the mother's breast is not always available, the infant up to the age of six to nine months was perceived as being in a constant state of weaning. Mothers were advised not to try to prevent thumb sucking or masturbation, not to enforce early toilet training, and not to stimulate sexual feelings. Klein also had been supervising Donald Winnicott, a renowned pediatrician who became a leading child analyst; she was treating the children of several psychoanalysts; and she was initiating a number of candidates into her techniques. By the late 1930s, Klein had already begun to speak of the unavoidable psychic damage caused by the birth trauma and of "restitution" and "reparation." But after the Freuds' arrival, Klein's followers—Joan Riviere, Susan Isaaks, Eva Rosenfeld, Paula Heimann—became outnumbered by Anna Freud's contingent, which included, among others, her friend Dorothy Burlingham, Klein's daughter Melitta Schmiedeberg, Edward Glover, and Princess Marie Bonaparte. It was not long before Anna Freud was holding meetings in her home and declaring that candidates for child training who had been analyzed by Kleinians could not benefit from her own teaching (Grosskurth, 1986, p. 243).

Sigmund Freud died on September 23, 1939, twenty days after England declared war on Germany. Upon his death, Anna Freud became the driving force in the psychoanalytic movement. Although Klein held on to her position within the British society (see chapter 9), Anna Freud's theories of child therapy would prevail nearly everywhere. After 1940, she modeled the Hampstead Wartime Nurseries she ran together with Dorothy Burlingham after Siegfried Bernfeld's Kinderheim Baumgarten for children who had been separated from their parents by the war. Their clinical methods for many years were to dominate the child studies of Freudians around the world. By implication, they dominated pedagogic views as well.

American Child Studies

By the time the émigrés arrived in the United States, psychoanalytic ideas were gaining ground in American schools. New mothers soon raised their children according to Dr. Spock's permissive guidelines, which were heavily indebted to the philosophies of Freud, William James, and John Dewey. But the Freudians supplied the major theoretical underpinnings for American child psychology. As psychologists came to focus on the impact of mothering and of separation and on the child's developing ego structure, family dynamics increasingly replaced pedagogy as their main concern. This shift occurred no more consciously than did the psychoanalysts' lessening of interest in questions of culture in general or their increasing concern with childhood trauma caused by war, accidents, or family situations. The Freudians concentrated more and more on children's behavior and closely observed the differences among healthy, neurotic, and perverse children. Analogous to those anthropologists who assumed that simpler societies were nearer to nature and thus easier to comprehend, analysts looked at ever younger children in order better to understand the influence of emotional experience.

In the 1950s, the American Freudians were extrapolating for the most part from psychoanalytic studies of infants (many went to London to learn from English analysts). To improve their techniques for coping with the child's relatively fluid personality, its lack of insight, its inability to free-associate, its idiosyncratic transference, and its low tolerance of anxiety and frustration, they studied particularly with the "Independent Group," whose theories mediated between the Freudians and Kleinians and often questioned both (see chapter 11).

Eager to refine therapeutic techniques, the Freudians went back to Freud's case of "Little Hans" (1909), who had been cured of a phobia about horses. Now, child analysts experimented with the use of building blocks, cards, cars, horses, and dolls as props that might help induce a positive transference and enable children to act out their fantasies. They weighed Melanie Klein's preference for small toys over large ones. They looked at how Winnicott encouraged his young patients to produce simple free-flowing drawings of people. He noted, as Freud had, that young children could deal better with the anxiety connected to mother's absence after they learned to relinquish and retrieve a favorite toy with the help of a string. Lawrence Kubie, at Columbia

University, relied on children's drawings, whereas Erik Erikson looked at toy block constructions to explain children's conflicts in terms of their spatial configurations. But whether the analysts generalized from the therapeutic dyad, played games with groups of children, or observed them through one-way mirrors, they assumed that their aggregate efforts would "cure" enough individuals' neuroses ultimately to change society. Unlike the early Freudians, they no longer thought that psychoanalysis could revolutionize society directly.

Psychoanalysts now concentrated on the interrelations between child and adult analysis. They collected fascinating case histories to generalize about behavior patterns, the effect of mothers' idiosyncracies and habits, parental personalities, and birth order. Dozens of research projects monitoring early experiences were initiated in order to prove or refute assumptions about adult personality. Expecting to locate the onset of mental or even physical ills, Freudians analyzed conditions prior to the phallic-oedipal phase, and they learned more and more about shorter and shorter age spans. Still, as they investigated ever narrower topics, they made fewer generalizations to the society at large.

As the classical Freudians became more professionalized, they started to explore the pain of the birth process and to monitor mother-infant communication down to the most fleeting words, gestures, and glances. Interest in observing infants in the early months of life was sparked by theories on the transition from primary narcissism (the infant is aware only of itself) to object-directed interests (it distinguishes itself from others). Margaret Mahler, an Austro-Hungarian American, stressed the second year of life, when separation-individuation becomes the crucial factor impinging on the child's future independence and its sense of identity. As nurseries were being invaded and mother-child nurturing patterns examined in relation to the child's emerging ego development, oedipal themes were found in children's words, deeds, and paintings (Kris, 1955). Learning philosophies (such as those of Francis Bacon, John Dewey, and Christian pedagogic doctrine) were examined, and it was found profitable to link "the best in medicine, education and the knowledge gained through the techniques applied in psychodynamic therapy" (Liss, 1955). As thousands of lively case studies were written up, presented, and discussed, Freud's ideas were reinforced. His genuis, however, was lacking.

The best case studies resembled Freud's "Wolf-Man" or "Little Hans" in that they read like fairy tales. The worst of them described the unfolding of oedipal entanglements in too predictable a fashion. But on the whole, case histories tended to corroborate the locally acceptable brands of ego psychology. Since only clinical successes were presented and failures were either ignored or explained away, comparisons of therapeutic results were totally inconclusive.

When Margaret Mahler (1955), for instance, began to talk of children whose egos were "constitutionally vulnerable and symbiotically fixated" at an early stage[7] and when Phyllis Greenacre (1955) examined fetishes as "stabilizers for the patient's genital functioning," they established the acceptable methods of psychoanalysis and metapsychology for a new generation of American Freudians. So did René Spitz (1955) when, partly to play down Melanie Klein's emphasis on the mother's breast, he observed that nursing infants perceive the mother's face and breast as one.

After American Freudians had reached consensus on the superiority of ego psychology they supported one another's theses. They may have disagreed with Isakower, for example, that sensations of the mouth or skin surface were reminiscent of the mother's breast, or with Spitz's formulations of the "experiential world of the primal (oral) cavity," but they agreed that convergent results by different psychoanalytic approaches themselves can be considered as theoretical validation and complimented each contribution as a boon to their "science." Yet each national movement guarded its own turf, so to speak.

As the hegemony of the ego psychologists became more firmly established, the sheer bulk of their research crowded out what was being done elsewhere. Nevertheless, German Freudians would manage to bend these findings to their own interests in psychosocial formation; the French would investigate their metaphorical and psychosomatic meanings; and the Kleinians would go their own way, often angry that their explanations were being sidestepped.

But no matter how much the Freudians learned about the stages of children's development—from libidinal dependence to self-reliance, from egocentricity to peer relationships, from the inability to manage bodily functions to controlling them, and from play to work—they could not agree on whether interaction with the environment begins when the id is able to defer gratification and when the ego learns to remember objects, such as the absent mother (A. Freud, 1980, p. 4). Anna Freud, who emphasized the structural relationships and the conflicts between id, ego, and superego, traced the source of secret fantasies and the causes of immature development, confusion, disharmony, and pathology (pp. 5–6) and related the separation-individuation process to physical motility, to the lessening of libidinal dependence, and to the mother's role in encouraging or hampering her child's attempts at independence. The Kleinians addressed these issues in terms of early object relations; the cognitive psychologists, who focus on conscious materials alone, were more interested in the interactions themselves than in their unconscious sources.

The Freudians now spoke of the child's inner and outer worlds (prestages to the adult's sense of reality), of lapses and advances in learning to talk (as primary process replaces secondary process), or of impulse control and (perceived) success. They frequently pointed out that in the first year of life interaction is restricted to infant and mother; that this is when soma and psyche, the child's and the mother's body, as well as self and object are being differentiated; and that failing to learn to separate them spells disaster. The "deviants"—Frommians, Jungians, and Adlerians—were more sanguine about later malleability, and their applications of psychoanalysis remained focused on the larger society. Still, they did not deny the importance of preoedipal stages or the concomitant development of motility, impulse control, secondary process functioning, and object constancy, although they kept emphasizing the impact of the environment.

A number of American child analysts, such as John Sours, Manuel Furer, and Samuel Ritvo, kept in touch with the child study people in London. Those who were in contact with the followers of Klein came to accept her earlier indicators of adult behavior and her emphasis on the primitive fantasy world of earliest (even prenatal) experiences. But until the early 1970s American classical Freudians shunned the Kleinians. Finally, they let them in through the "back door"—that is, in the controversies surrounding Kohut's explanations of the narcissistic self and Kernberg's object relations theory (see chapter 11).

Winnicott had listened to newborn infants' sounds—during, for example, fist-in-mouth, thumb-sucking, babbling, cloth-holding stages—long before he published *Playing and Reality* (1971). He had noted that "transitional objects," as he called all emotional props, were often retained into childhood and would continue to be "absolutely necessary at bed time, [and] when loneliness or depressed moods threatened" (p. 4). Also the paradoxical uses of the baby's teddy bear or security blanket, argued Winnicott, should not be analyzed: the transitional object "belongs" to the infant (to be cuddled, loved, or mutilated) and must never be removed. When he postulated this object as "both standing and not standing for the mother's breast" (p. 6), some American Freudians found him too Kleinian.

Yet even the most dyed-in-the-wool ego psychologists concurred with many of Winnicott's conclusions, though they objected to, first, his saying that he had learned as much from doing psychotherapy as psychoanalysis; second, his praising Klein's concepts and criticizing Mahler's use of the word "symbiosis" as "too rooted in biology" (1971, p. 130); and third, his mentioning that he had been influenced by Lacan's "Stade du Miroir" (1949; see chapter 11), although, he said, he had found Lacan to have replaced the actual mirror with its "precursor . . . the mother's face" and with the child's perceptions of its parent's view (p. 111).

In the 1970s, however, Kohut's and Kernberg's views of object relations started to penetrate Freudian metapsychology and clinical practice (see chapter 11), and Klein's and Winnicott's ideas thereby entered the American mainstream. Twenty years after some of its essays were printed in England (1951), *Playing and Reality* (1971) was published in America. Now, some of the ego psychologists welcomed the notion that the warmth and vitality of a transitional object could connect the child to its external world—through play, art, religious feeling, dreams, fetishes, and even lying, stealing, and so on. And those child analysts who already thought that play was the best means of integrating inner and outer reality picked up Winnicott's objects as the locus of later fantasies and symbols and the child's eventual sense of trust.

The Americans' increasing preoccupation with theoretical minutiae imperceptibly had induced a certain amount of tunnel vision. But the discussions surrounding the transitional object and its acceptance provided an opening that signaled an impending theoretical shift within the IPA. In the meantime, as American Freudians gradually lost some of their influence overseas, they started to realize that they should address the impact on society of the children who had grown up under the influence of psychoanalysis. They did so by "rediscovering" the adolescents most of them had been ignoring—theorizing about them and treating them.

Anglo-Saxon Adolescence

Most American Freudians neglected adolescence. Until some time in the 1960s, they held that little psychic development occurred during the latency period because of "lowered" sexuality and that adolescents' volatile emotions made them unanalyzable. Hence they had few adolescents as patients. But some of the classical analysts did work with disturbed teenagers. By 1960, they were describing the complexities of adolescents' problems and the resurgence of earlier, unresolved sexual and aggressive conflicts and of oedipal wishes. Some maintained that the "family romance" is reactivated in puberty to "protect" the individual from having to face the competitive world. Others believed that this happens because the adolescent is suspended between childhood and adulthood in a transitional phase fraught with insecurity, turmoil, and conflict between instinctual drives and external demands (Lorand and Schneer, 1961, p. x). Peter Blos (1962) spoke of adolescence as a "second individuation" involving the reconciliation of genitality with morality. And Erik Erikson (1968) perceived the roots of "core virtues" in the evolution of adolescent ego strength (p. 235). Essentially, the Freudians agreed that adolescence interrupts peaceful growth and is fraught with neurotic, psychotic, or asocial symptoms that may verge on borderline states or even mental illness (Lorand and Schneer, 1961, p. 221). Such "biological" formulations, however, put the onus on the individual teenager and thus militated against Aichhorn's (1935) or Bernfeld's (1931) assumption, for example, that new role models and group interaction may induce psychic restructuring. In other words, the Freudians were living up to their "conservative" image.

Just as these analysts became more or less aware that they were not keeping up with the society around them, they began to think of adolescents as potential patients (Lorand and Schneer, 1961, p. 241). Now, Sándor Lorand suggested strengthening their egos and offering a better ego ideal for identification; and David Beres (quoting E. Glover) thought that precisely because the adolescent's character was so responsive to its environment, it might be open to influences by the psychoanalysts (Beres, 1971, pp. 1–9).

Thus American Freudians began to look at the growing delinquency around them and to shoulder a certain amount of social responsibility. They could not replicate Aichhorn's and Bernfeld's rather crude experiments with delinquents (Alexander and Staub, 1929), nor did they agree with Franz Alexander's or Theodor Reik's (1925) parallels between neurosis and delinquency. But Werner Muensterberger compared rites of initiation in primitive and modern societies in terms of pressures to conform, to separate from the mother, or to express genital interests (Lorand and Schneer, 1961). And Leo Spiegel (1974) described campus unrest as a repercussion of the unconscious collective atmosphere of depression and meaninglessness, regression, and unstable psychic structure. He blamed disturbances of the self for teenagers' aberrant actions and suggested that psychoanalysis could help them overcome such "deviant" behavior as homosexuality, delinquency, exhibitionism, truancy, pilfering, and suicide attempts, as well as learning disabilities. Although these "problems" generally were perceived as reflections of and responses to larger social concerns, the Freudians tended to insist that intrapsychic phenomena were more influential than social conditions. But their clinical approaches were changing, to judge from their diagnoses: some adolescents now were found to suffer from "temporary psychosis," others proved to be good subjects for research, and yet others became amenable to "limited treatment."

Hyman Spotnitz (1961) pointed to studies that indicated there were no children in psychotherapy between 1936 and 1946 but that in the subsequent decade 40 percent of disturbed children who had been treated had received psychotherapy and nearly half of them psychoanalysis. Spotnitz intimated that the fruitful investigations of young children had set the stage for Freudians to tackle the previously neglected adolescents.[8] Given to self-doubts and with a tendency toward delinquency, adolescents now were to afford the analysts a unique look at the re-eruption of primary narcissism. Since the baby boom generation, which reached the teens in the early 1960s, had become a self-indulgent lot, sociologists and psychologists were constructing their own theories of narcissism. But whereas these social and behavioral scientists used the term descriptively or cognitively, the psychoanalysts addressed the internal dynamics of the adolescent ego. By better understanding the ego's weaknesses and defenses they expected to learn how to strengthen it and thus improve their patients' grip on reality. And as the Freudians noticed new identifications within the ego ideal, they attributed these to the "reprojection of the narcissistic libido to new objects" (Staples and Smarr, 1980, p. 481).

By 1984, the Freudian psychologist Louise Kaplan had synthesized all these studies, tracing adolescence from ancient Greece through Darwin's and Rousseau's views to Freud's in order to unravel the connections among psychological, sociological, and social transformations that affect adolescents (Kaplan, 1984, p. 185). Placing teenagers in history, she talked of their age-old and pervasive longing for intimacy and for restoring commitments to the family life they must reject while growing up (p. 331). She generalized to humanity and to the human instinct of aggressiveness and self-destruction. Kaplan's tour de force was a return to the larger issues Freud and his disciples had addressed in the early days as well as a rapprochement with the cultural issues that concern some of the European Freudians.

Clinical psychologist Katherine Dalsimer provided another such approach (1986). She looked at female adolescence as depicted in five works of literature—*Member of the Wedding*, *The Prime of Miss Jean Brodie*, *Romeo and Juliet*, *Emma*, and the *Diary of Anne Frank*. Stressing the adolescent's search for new relationships at the moment when both rivalrous and sexual oedipal passions threaten to be reawakened, Dalsimer investigated how these new experiences bring individuals into synchrony with wider segments of their society. But as Margaret Mead discovered, for instance, to come of age in Samoa meant that children were initiated into a structured situation, whereas in America they are offered a *choice* among all sorts of conflicting possibilities (Dalsimer, 1986, p. 10). Puberty, therefore, for Dalsimer, stirs different fantasies, based on earlier identifications with the mother as an inner presence that is being redefined throughout life. According to Dalsimer, all young girls learn about femininity "from [their] own experience of life, or the poets" (1986, p. 12).

Delinquency in Germany

German psychoanalysts did not deal with "narcissistic" adolescents but with the children of former Nazis. Therefore, they were interested in reviving Aichhorn's and Bernfeld's experiments with delinquents and neglected adolescents. A number of them thought that their own adolescent behavior during the Nazi period had been a manifestation of delinquency, but a delinquency sanctioned by the authorities (de Boor, 1981, p. 2). They attributed their personal "cures" to the postwar push for reeducation, in which teenagers, as the future leaders of the country, had been the primary targets. Since they had been in the Hitler Youth, the Bund Deutscher Mädchen, and the armed forces, they were helped by psychoanalysis to face their complicity. These circumstances led a few German Freudians to link psychotherapy to sociotherapy.[9] Sometimes they were referring to denazification, at other times to the countering of authoritarian attitudes or even the reform of thieves or murderers. In other words, they expected psychoanalytic miracles as the means of individual and collective redemption.

Consequently, German psychoanalysts had to reformulate educational philosophies and social policy, and implement and apply them. They were asked, for instance, to lend their psychoanalytic competence to an insecure judiciary, as if they were expert on every aspect of criminology. Only then, recalls de Boor (1981), did they discover the gray areas between innocence and criminal guilt and the complexities of competing rights. The Germans, who had been preoccupied while shedding the Nazi past, had been unaware that these are problems endemic to all democratic societies. In addition, they started to address moral questions: when are psychic disturbances due to social conditions that ought to exonerate criminal actions? Where does individual guilt begin to differentiate itself from collective guilt? At what point does deviant behavior become a mental or somatic sickness—a sickness amenable to psychoanalytic cure?

The German psychoanalyst Tilman Moser (1974), for example, is representative of those who investigated the social causes of psychopathology and who advocated that criminals be judged on the basis of their backgrounds rather than "objectively." But because the psychiatrist-criminologist's excessive empathy with criminals easily turns into a doctor-patient relation, he also was against cooperation between lawyers and doctors. Instead, criminals were to be observed in a psychoanalytically oriented clinic, with possible treatment by experienced analysts.

This was what Clemens de Boor (1982), director of Frankfurt's Sigmund-Freud-Institut from 1979 to 1985, managed to do in his rehabilitation center. But he found that ultimately he and his team had not eliminated the "asocial rigidity" of recidivists. Emotional and pedagogic neglect in early life, de Boor argued, had led to the inmates' psychic malfunctioning, which first made them fail in school and at work and then kept them from adapting to prison routines. Even a full-time staff of more than twenty professionals did not change the psychic makeup of ten hardened criminals. Nor did anyone learn much about recidivism. Describing the theoretical underpinnings of this project, Ellen Reinke (1987) was more optimistic. "Psychoanalytic sociotherapy with delinquents is operable," she stated, by applying Lorenzer's notion of "scenic material" (the mix of internalized personal and parental [Nazi] experiences) to the sociotherapeutic process (p. 902). Therapists established corrective emotional relationships with inmates, she reported; they met intensively with colleagues when changing shifts; and they had daily conferences, which included much reflection and self-reflection. Ultimately, however, Reinke too found that the project was relatively unsuccessful, but blamed this on the lack of funds.

Knut Engelhardt (1976), on the other hand, looked to Durkheim for the solution to crime. He elaborated on the important, although irrational, function fulfilled by the criminal in "regulating collective affects" and furthering conformity and legal peace (*Rechtsfrieden*) (p. 11). Unlike Durkheim, however, Engelhardt came up with a model based on practical (psychoanalytic) discourse. He thought the "irrationality of the production and reproduction of criminality" might be stopped by enlightenment linked to emancipation and by cooperation among authorities, prison guards, and prisoners (p. 316). Similar models used in Anglo-Saxon countries, however, have relied on implementing various labeling theories rather than what the Germans called psychoanalytic reflex dialogues—whether in Balint groups (see below) or by resident psychoanalysts.

Another reformer, Julia Schwartzmann, emphasized efforts at prevention. She worked in a home for moderately delinquent girls and followed Aichhorn's and Zulliger's tenets, hoping to cure delinquency by alleviating emotional deprivation at an early age and thus saving her charges from becoming criminals later (Schwartzmann, 1971).

In America, such liberal stances, if not their application, are part of tradition and thus could be taken for granted. But German history and the fact that all these projects were officially funded suggest that by the 1970s at least a semblance of democratic measures had been accepted.

In Hamburg, a specific type of group therapy was started as early as 1950—mostly for doctors who were being instructed in psychoanalytic techniques. They were recruited by being told they would learn to do better what they already were empathically doing with their patients. These groups were named after Michael Balint, who had initiated such pedagogic interventions in order to reach the maximum number of patients. Later, Balint groups of social workers, prison guards and members of other helping professions were initiated as well, and these helped diffuse Freud's ideas in Germany. In 1973 the German Balint Society was created in order to spread "patient-centered" therapy.

In Austria, psychoanalytic pedagogy continued to be dominated by the Adlerians, who regained their hold on the Social Democrats, the majority party, soon after the Russians departed in 1955. Their simpler therapy has remained marginal to Freudian analysis; however, it does enrich the ad hoc practices of a number of teachers who would probably not take to psychoanalysis or libido psychology. At the same time, the adaptive components of ego psychology brought the Adlerians closer to the Freudians.

French Contributions to Pedagogy

The French did not talk directly of psychoanalytic pedagogy until recently. When they did, they stressed Freud's ambivalence about it and then pushed it into questions of language. In that vein, Claude Schauder (1982), following Lacan, argued that psychoanalysis should not adapt the child to its environment (see chapter 11) as American ego psychology does and exaggerated Freud's opposition to pedagogic applications. Forgetting that American Freudians tend to be critical of transactional analysis ("I'm O.K., you're O.K.") and of Rogerian and other simplifications, he went on to contrast this mixed bag of popular American educational projects to Balint groups—"the only psychoanalysis that may bring 'the analytic order' to education" (p. 180). René Gelly, on the other hand, complimented Balint for putting psychoanalysis at the service of medicine. He thought Balint's major strength consisted in juxtaposing the "biological current of official psychoanalysis" to "rational practice" and accepting individuals as part of their environment, without relinquishing the Freudian developmental stages—oral, anal, phallic, and genital (Gelly, 1982). Each of these stages, dominated by the corresponding erogeneous zone (mouth, anus, genitals), is said to make for psychoaffective integration. Therefore, Balint (like Melanie Klein and unlike the American ego psychologists), argued Gelly, rejected the theoretical centrality of primary narcissism. Gelly praised Balint for discrediting American Freudians, for his contributions to pedagogy, and for having invented a psychoanalytically informed bedside manner that helped doctors heal ordinary patients.

The reeducation of drug addicts and alcoholics and the psychoanalysis of delinquents have become nearly as acceptable in France as in England or America, although this tends to take place in clinical settings (Olivienstein, 1982). But, as I note in chapters 4 and 10, Freudian thought took hold in schools and hospitals in much the way it did in the culture at large. Hence *la psychanalyse*, though late in coming, now reaches deep into society. In France it does not claim to be pedagogy. I would maintain, however, that in the post-Lacanian era psychoanalytic pedagogy has become part of mainstream thinking. And because it has, parents send their five-year-olds to school having already reared them on Freudian ideas; that is why teachers no longer need to proselytize.

How Widespread Is Psychoanalytic Pedagogy?

While theoretical elaborations in each country were taking their own turns, specific configurations were influenced by the number of followers such researchers as Anna Freud, Melanie Klein, Margaret Mahler, Donald Winnicott, and René Spitz could attract, and how good they were at getting research funds. By working in small homogeneous groups these analysts often were unaware that like-minded Freudians—that is, those on their own research teams—would automatically support them. Hence local groups either would give positive feedback or would criticize details (of conceptualization, research, and reports) rather than major theoretical ideas. At international meetings, the responses to research reports were exceedingly mixed. But since none of the findings, after 1945, dealt directly with psychagogy, and research itself, until recently, remained Anglo-Saxon, everyone talked of infants' early perceptual capabilities, motor reflexes, strength of internal stimuli, or abilities to organize a matrix of tendencies, energies, drives, and survival instincts.

These concerns strengthened American hegemony even more than their majority membership in the IPA. Conversely, the lack of interest in applied psychoanalysis and the Freudians' (justified) contention that applications so readily renounce the intrapsychic world kept most of the German discussions off the program at IPA meetings.

Some of the ego psychologists, in their scientific language, did go beyond their disciplinary interests. Mortimer Ostow, Judith Kestenberg, and Leo Spiegel, among others, addressed philosophical and pedagogical research as well as physiological and perceptual studies of responses and perceptions. But their knowledge in these fields tended to be limited to specific areas. And most of the time the analysts would approach the issues raised by underlining the implied oedipal themes. Nevertheless, the resulting psychoanalytic hermeneutics would seem to impress intellectuals. The German-speaking analysts, however, tried to generalize from the psychology they practiced in their clinical settings to specific social issues, especially to the authoritarianism they so feared. Given that this is a specific post-Nazi phenomenon, many of their English-speaking colleagues were not too interested.[10] But because in Germany psychoanalysis was to reeducate the masses, the rehabilitation of criminals in a permissive analytic situation was to serve as a model. Still, the Germans ultimately concluded that the rate of success was very low, that this therapy was an even greater luxury than personal analysis five times per week. So, just as in America, psychoanalysis in institutional settings for other than severe neurotics proved too costly; and a sort of "preventive" psychoanalysis of children and adolescents was being advocated. Finally, this turned out to be the subject that would replace pedagogy, and almost the only psychoanalytic activity around which the Freudians of the world would be able to rally.

Chapter 7

The Psychology of Women

Everywhere, both Freud's followers and his critics have agreed that Freud never found out "what woman wants." In the Anglo-Saxon countries there are those who argue that the concept of penis envy is a product of fin-de-siècle Vienna and those who dismiss all of psychoanalysis as a Victorian fossil. In France the debate tends to center on questions of sexuality, on acceptable beliefs about heterosexual and homosexual practices. And detractors in all countries often have blamed Freud for the existence of patriarchy instead of casting him as one of its most enlightened products.

In a letter of August 12, 1925, Freud expressed interest in Abraham's notion of early female libido. And he confessed that "the female side of the problem is extraordinarily obscure to me. If your ideas and observations on the subject already permit communication, I should very much like to hear about them, but I can wait" (Abraham and Freud, 1965, p. 350). When Freud wrote his paper on "Some Psychical Consequences of the Anatomical Distinction between the Sexes," also in August 1925, he expressed doubts about his theory of "sexual equivalence" for the first time and questioned his assumption that the Oedipus complex in boys and girls develops in the same way. Instead, he began by stating that both boys and girls come equipped with specific sexual organs, yield specific biological products (spermatozoa and ova), and display various (and varying quantities of) secondary sexual characteristics. He continued by maintaining that this indicates *bisexuality* to be a universal phenomenon, as though an individual is not a man or a woman but always both—which becomes problematic only when the secondary characteristic is not secondary enough. He concluded that anatomy alone does not define masculinity or femininity, because "the determinants of women's choice of an object are often made unrecognizable by social conditions. [That] women are regarded as weaker . . . is no doubt derived from the dissocial quality which unquestionably characterizes all sexual relations" (*S. E.*, 22 : 114–16).

Freud held that "masculinity" and "femininity" are physical as well as psychological attributes. And when the notion of bisexuality is applied to mental life, both males and females are found to behave in masculine or feminine ways (1933a). This distinction, however, is descriptive of "activity" and "passivity," not of innate traits. Still, the ensuing behavior does correlate with the activity of the male sex-cell, which searches out the (passive) female ovum, and with the male pursuit of the female. Thus masculinity is equated with aggressiveness; and feminine *activity*—in lower species, child rearing and lactation—does seem to "achieve a passive aim." Moreover, "the suppression of women's aggressiveness, which is prescribed for them constitutionally and imposed on them socially, favors the development of powerful masochistic impulses" (*S. E.*, 22 : 116). Masochism, Freud went on, is an outcome of early erotic experience, in which destructive impulses have been diverted inward. He also assumed that incidents and episodes during very early socialization are incorporated into personality structure—one of his central tenets. This formulation would be a major focus of attack by generations of feminists. But the rest of the essay, which deals with the successive phases of libidinal development, was to provide even more food for controversy. For observation of children at play had shown that little girls can be as aggressive as little boys and that they use the clitoris for masturbation, as the penis-equivalent, when entering the phallic phase. The particular timing of this habit proved to Freud that the development of femininity occurred during the oedipal period and coincided with a shift of erotic sensitivity from the clitoris to the vagina. This shift was "one of the two tasks which a woman has to perform in the course of her development" (p. 118). The second consists in the transfer of object-cathexes from the mother to the father.

According to Freud, the normal boy passes through the Oedipus complex "naturally"; to avoid the threat of castration he renounces incestuous, infantile claims on his mother, identifies with his father, and in the process sets up a strong sexual identity as well as a strong superego. The normal girl, however, must give up her early erotic attachment to her mother and must deal with her envy of the penis. Whereas the boy is able to hold onto his love for his mother, the girl must do the opposite by embracing what she now perceives as her mother's inferiority. Unafraid of castration, Freud continued, she tends to remain in the Oedipus complex for an indeterminate period and often does not completely overcome it. As a result, girls never develop as strong a superego as boys do—a factor he thought determined the average feminine character.

Even before writing this seminal paper, Freud had held that there was no direct correlation between biology and psychology and that neither sex was totally "active" or totally "passive." Here he did not concentrate explicitly on female sexuality. But many of his disciples were women, and from the very beginning they had paid attention to the different responses of male and female patients. With few exceptions, such as Aichhorn and Bernfeld, the women analysts were the only ones to do empirical research with children, and several of them, including Helene Deutsch, Karen Horney, Edith Jacobson, and Melanie Klein, were exploring the formation of feminine identity.

Freud, first of all, had wanted to respond to Abraham's speculations about the two successive stages of female sexuality—the shift from clitoral to vaginal. Abraham had introduced the notion that little girls might have vaginal feelings and that these might lead to psychic fusion between the vaginal and anal areas. He had also suggested that psychic events during infancy and puberty were similar, and that the adolescent girl, when replacing the wish for clitoral stimulation with the wish for vaginal penetration, was inversely repeating her early experiences. This implied that (vaginal) psychological femininity is present to begin with and that it is the opposite of (penile) masculinity. Were Freud to accept such a formulation, the clitoris as the locus of masturbation and the resulting feelings of guilt would no longer be as important as he was convinced they were. Furthermore, without such guilt girls would no longer have as much of a burden to repress as he thought, which, in turn, would mean that the less stringent psychoanalytic therapies he opposed might do.

Abraham died the following year, in 1926, and never developed his ideas. But subsequently a number of feminists speculated about them. One of the most influential deviants from Freudian theory was Karen Horney. She argued that the girl's so-called masculine (oedipal) phase is a defense against anxiety about her prospective violation by her father, anxiety resulting from the "biological principle" of her own sexual attraction to him. Another woman analyst, Melanie Klein, maintained that the girl is anxious because she has unconscious knowledge of her primordial infantile feminine sexuality.

These and other pioneer women analysts, although they did not belong to a feminist movement, nevertheless were eager to explore how psychoanalysis might bring about equality of the sexes. Hence their ideas would be accepted, or rejected, by different temporal interests in the culture at large. But there was no overt gender discrimination because psychoanalysis was as accessible to women as it was to men, and because it attracted women of the highest and most impressive caliber (Coleman, 1985).[1] In Vienna, Anna Freud defended her father's ideas in contrast to Austrian feminists who were also ardent socialists and thus had left the fold in 1913, along with Adler. In France, psychoanalysis might not have gotten started without the efforts of Marie Bonaparte and Eugenie Sokolnicka. Later, when Anna Freud and Melanie Klein fought for domination of psychoanalysis in England, even Jones did not object to the fact that the battle of succession was between women rather than men. In America, Karen Horney, who had emigrated in 1932, had parted from the Freudians, but Deutsch, Jacobson, Phyllis Greenacre, and other women more or less followed the traditional Freudian path. These women were training analysts and thus had a larger leadership role and contributed more to theory than did women in other medical specialties. Many of them held influential positions in psychoanalytic institutes: Helene Deutsch in Vienna and Boston, Phyllis Greenacre in New York, Helen McLean and Therese Benedeck in Chicago, Irene Josselyn in Phoenix, Joan Fleming in Denver.

In the late 1960s and early 1970s, Jean Strouse, Juliet Mitchell, Jean Baker Miller, and other women writers began to construct a feminist theory based on Freudian psychoanalysis. And some of the French too began to expand on Lacan's theories, which supported feminist principles. In Germany, Margarete Mitscherlich-Nielsen introduced her own views of "Freudian feminism," based on those of Jacobson, among others. And since the mid-1970s, feminists have been cooperating across the Atlantic, so that the theories of the French feminists have reached into American departments of literature and of French as well as women's studies programs at such universities as Yale, Johns Hopkins, Cornell, and Northwestern.

Horney, Deutsch, Klein, and Jacobson

Three of the women to whom issues of femininity were central—Deutsch, Horney, and Klein—were analyzed by Karl Abraham. Their theories continue to be debated by feminists everywhere. Horney challenged Abraham's theory that the preoedipal girl, upon realizing that she will never have a penis but will be able to have a child, starts to envy her mother and wish for a child by her father. Instead, she concluded from her own observations, the lack of a penis puts the oedipal girl at a "practical" disadvantage, for the possession of a penis is socially valued. The girl identifies with her mother and then is pushed back into the preoedipal phase by her father's inevitable rejection. This experience colors all her future relationships with men: she may react with vengefulness and disappointment, become rebellious rather than passive and submissive (as both Abraham and Freud claimed), or tend to seek refuge in a "fictitious male role."

Helene Deutsch, however, wholeheartedly agreed with Freud that the girl's Oedipus complex is related to castration anxiety. But she emphasized that the clitoris could not be equated with the penis. Horney chided her for not recognizing the male counterpart of penis envy in women—womb envy in boys. She soon concluded that social factors might be as important as biological ones in the perception and subsequent development of all children.

Melanie Klein thought that the girl defends against the feminine attitudes she is bound to internalize through the relationship with her mother not so much because she has masculine tendencies but because she fears and resents her mother, who has thwarted her true feminine needs (her wishes for her father) and threatens to destroy her if she persists in them. And "she shudders at the thought of congess with her father" (Grosskurth, 1986, p. 204). Jones agreed that penis envy was the girl's basic defense. By denying her femininity she hopes to protect herself from attack by her mother and from the man's dangerous penis. According to Phyllis Grosskurth, Jones (1933) considered this to be the girl's only possible response to her anxiety in the first years of life and therefore backed Klein's view that the girl's hatred of her mother does not stem from resentment because of her lack of a penis, as Freud maintained, but from rivalry with the mother for the father's penis.

These were not the only explorations of femininity, although they exemplify the major thrusts. Marie Bonaparte, for instance, focused on the unequal roles of men and women in sex and reproduction—the man's pleasurable coitus, the woman's unpleasurable menstruation and shedding of blood at defloration and childbirth. She contrasted what she saw as women's lack of sexual pleasure to men's pleasure, ultimately concluding that women had to rid themselves of their infantile fears lest they remain masochistic. Helene Deutsch maintained that these fears ultimately would be conquered upon a woman's bearing her own child. Anna Freud discussed differences between boys and girls by relating specific emotional makeup and defense mechanisms to the resolution of the Oedipus complex. In sum, the women analysts took a variety of approaches but shared an interest in whether, how, and to what extent biology was destiny.

Explanations of male and female sexuality, of course, were to expand psychoanalytic theory as well and at the same time were to pave the way toward psychic liberation of both men and women. Not even Horney, however, envisaged a feminist agenda. Like their male colleagues, the women analysts were expanding Freud's "science" at a time when "science" meant progress. But after Klein had left for England in 1926, Horney had moved to Chicago in 1932 (and to New York in 1936), Deutsch had settled in Boston in 1934, and Jacobson had come to New York in 1936, their theories diverged more and more in response to their new surroundings and their deductions from case material, as well as to literary works and anthropological and sociological data

Helene Deutsch, for instance, introduced the second volume of her *Psychology of Women* ([1945] 1973)—on motherhood—by speculating about the differing socialization of European and American women. The Americans, in helping their mates settle the new continent, she thought, had become more emancipated than the Europeans. She assumed, however, that during colonial times they no longer were such rare sexual objects, so that their value decreased—although they increasingly dominated their families.[2] After buttressing this statement with anthropological findings by Briffault and Malinowski and with animal studies, Deutsch stated the obvious: maternal emotion differs in animals and in humans because animal instincts are determined physiologically, whereas human ones are subject to psychological factors. Deutsch talked of the sublimation of motherly instincts and differentiated between the feminine woman, whose narcissistic tendencies and masochistic readiness for painful giving and loving harmonize, and the motherly one, whose narcissistic wish to be loved is transferred from the ego to the child or his substitute (p. 19).

Motherliness, however, may induce maternal love and tenderness or excessive and aberrant motherly feelings; it may harmonize with other psychic tendencies or disturb them; and the conflict between sexuality and motherliness lends depth and richness to the psychology of motherhood (pp. 22–23). But when Deutsch stated that "a psychically integrated woman can gratify both sexuality and motherhood through the mediation of one man," she introduced a moral component. She illustrated her point by psychoanalyzing the characters in Balzac's *Two Women*—one the courtesan and devotee of love, the other the essence of motherhood (p. 26). Like Freud, Deutsch used psychoanalysis to illuminate the fiction but neglected the fact that the work itself was based on psychological conditions that might have had their origin in social customs, mores, and laws—the outcome of outer forces influencing the two women's psyches and behaviors—as well as in Balzac himself. And like Freud, she showed the similarities between the fantasies of Balzac's women and those of her patients. Thus Deutsch Americanized Freud's view of femininity:

Woman overcomes the genital trauma and the penis wish and begins to want a child in the course of a complicated process that has often been misunderstood. . . . The transformation of the penis wish into the wish for a child is often considered a substitute formation instead of a biologically determined dynamic process . . . [for] in the girl's fantasy life there arise analogies that have various motives. In the process of transferring her interest from the outside to the inside of the body, the little girl may include the penis conceived as an internal organ and for some time hold to this concept; thus the penis and the child may be identified with each other in that both are considered parts of the girl's body. (p. 65)

Deutsch, of course, was talking of unconscious mechanisms, not of conscious fantasies alone. Nevertheless, her views of motherhood mirrored the ideals of the 1940s, and the girls she saw were growing up at a time when motherhood was thought to be the only road to female fulfillment. Since this also assumed an acceptance of male superiority and paternalism, it followed that Deutsch would consider women to be naturally masochistic, narcissistic, and passive.[3]

Even before she came to America, Karen Horney had chided Deutsch for concentrating on the presumably inhibiting effects of the phallic phase (when clitoris and penis are equated) instead of recognizing that this notion incorporates the biases of a masculine civilization (Horney, 1926, p. 325), in which envy of masculinity—a driving force in the setting up of cultural values—may be sublimated more successfully than penis envy (p. 331). By 1935 she had gone further, stating that psychoanalysis had supported the assumed connections between masochism and female biology without considering social conditioning (1935, p. 241). She questioned the existence of the girl's "masochistic drive" on the basis of her analyses of literary characters, anthropological observations of tribal women, and her own observation of women patients. Together with Clara Thompson ([1943] 1973), she held that clinical diagnoses also were reflections of the culture. Because the American tendency to be competitive stimulates envy in both men and women, and because women are considered inferior to men, said Thompson, cultural underprivilege appears to validate women's feelings of inadequacy (p. 11). Character development, therefore, may fit the clinical picture of penis envy without having to assume childhood trauma based on the comparison of sexual organs (p. 57).

In *The Neurotic Personality of Our Time* (1937), Horney maintained that neurotic attempts to solicit affection by bribery are more frequently used by women than by men because women are taught to consider love their special domain—the only means to get whatever they may want emotionally or materially. "While men grew up with the conviction that they had to achieve something in life if they wanted to get somewhere, women realized that through love, and through love alone, could they attain happiness, security and prestige" (p. 140). In her later works, Horney no longer seemed to address the psychology of women specifically: she spoke of the inner conflicts of *all* neurotics in modern society. Although her interactions with patients did not differ substantially from those of the classical Freudians, these larger concerns would have estranged her from them even if she had not felt compelled to form her own training institute (see chapter 2). In fact, her own life seemed to prove that women could overcome their "innate" handicap (see Quinn, 1987).

While Deutsch became preoccupied with the Oedipus complex and Horney pursued the sociological roots of fantasies and neuroses, Melanie Klein became more and more immersed in earliest infancy—in the unconscious mechanisms of the interactions between mother and infant subsequent to the birth trauma. She agreed with Freud and Deutsch that the woman's sexual development is complete only after her libido has moved from the oral to the genital, but she thought that this process begins with "the first stirrings of the genital impulses and that the oral, receptive aim of the genitals exercises a determining influence in the *girl's turning to her father*" (Grosskurth, 1986, p. 177).

Klein believed with Horney that masturbation is far less gratifying to a girl than a boy and is yet another frustation in female development. But because the oedipal girl also becomes aware of her mother's "lack," she blames everything on her and thereby aggravates the fear engendered by her impulses to rob and destroy the mother (p. 177). She turns to the father because she has been deprived of the breast and because she inevitably must continue to be frustrated by the mother she fears. Only when she herself becomes a mother will she be able to overcome the anxiety generated at this time. According to Klein, the girl's anxiety about motherhood parallels the boy's fears of castration. Furthermore, Klein's oedipal phases are more flexible than Freud's, since they are determined by what happens during the pregenital period; and she postulated that the boy passes through a feminine (oral) stage of development (see chapter 11). Furthermore, "Kleinian 'space' is [conceptualized] differently from the Freudian topographic and structural models of the mind. . . . There is a phenomenological awareness of a 'translocation' of an aspect of experience," which enables the infant to "place" painful stimulation (inner objects) "into" the mother for modification and containment (Ashbach and Schermer, 1987, pp. 60–61). In other words, a bad object, or experience, is projected into the mother.

Edith Jacobson (1937) found that the superegos of her women patients appeared to be formed through more complex interactions than her colleagues were assuming. Neither "masochism" nor "masculinization," as Hanns Sachs (1928) had stated, nor "outwardly projected castration fears," as Radó (1934) had maintained, could account for the anxiety generated during infantile drive development. The little girl's realization that she has been castrated, Jacobson argued, is much more differentiated than Freudians thought—it includes hate and wishes for revenge and restitution long *before* the onset of depression, the devaluation of the mother, and the move toward the father. And how she experiences this period is *socially* determined. Thus Jacobson argued with Klein about the importance of early sexuality in girls and placed it around the age of three. Jacobson backed Horney's emphasis on social roots, but she held that in girls "social fear" tended to develop out of a "female masochistic and oral disposition toward objects," which engenders superego defenses that later on make for excessive dependency on love objects. Therefore, she concluded, the construction of the superego is helped when the girl believes that her vagina is as important as the boy's penis: fear of castration and fear of hurting one's own genitals serve the same purpose in the development of sexuality (p. 409). (Jacobson, in 1950, analyzed pregnancy fantasies and wishes for babies in boys [pp. 139–52].)

Clearly, Deutsch, Horney, Klein, and Jacobson, following Freud, addressed questions of femininity in terms of female sexuality. Horney and Jacobson, however, were explicit in their exposés of culturally determined masculine biases; Deutsch demonstrated the inhibiting effects of biological differences on female identity; and Klein discussed girls' greater anxiety owing to (oedipal) fantasies of cutting, rubbing, and burning the mother's body with feces and urine. But all of them addressed the inequality between the sexes, and all approached the topic of femininity primarily as an issue in psychoanalytic research.[4] (The focus on motherhood, however conservative it may have been, became the basis of object relations theory—a major theoretical cornerstone—in America, England, and to some extent in France.)

The efforts by early women analysts would be appreciated much later, when feminists began to investigate all sorts of theories to advance their movement. So, even though these analysts did not have an explicitly feminist program, and not all of them spoke of socially induced inequalities, some of their investigations have been mined extensively by contemporary feminists.

What More Do Women Want?

The first Anglo-Saxon feminist to use psychoanalysis as an explicit tool to liberate women was Juliet Mitchell. Indignant that her Marxist friends agreed with Frantz Fanon—who argued that women (in the third world) should be emancipated only after a revolution—she began by investigating the Marxist philosopher Louis Althusser's critique of ideology, which led her to psychoanalysis (1966, pp. 17–18). In particular, she argued that women had been kept out of the labor force not because they were physically weak but because they were needed in the family to please men sexually, to bear children, and to socialize them. Soon she went on to examine a number of Freud-Marx syntheses. But unlike other feminists, who frequently maligned psychoanalysis as the rationale for the bourgeois and patriarchal status quo, she maintained that by rejecting Freud feminists were handicapping themselves.

Mitchell criticized feminists for automatically denouncing Freud without putting his ideas within a broader theoretical and ideological context. She enlarged on Freud's basic theories about sexuality but pointed out that anti-Freudian feminists take Freud's texts too literally, tending to ignore the fact that he spoke of unconscious mental processes when he introduced his concept of penis envy. Instead they transpose it to the realm of conscious decisions and perceptions. Furthermore, Mitchell argued, they erroneously assume that Freud was prescribing what was "normal" and fail to recognize that to him this was always a relative term—in contrast to "neurotic," "pathogenic," or "psychotic." To prove her point, Mitchell quoted from Freud's "Case of Dora," where he said that "so-called sexual perversions are very widely diffused among the whole population." And she reminded us that Freud did not have an inflexible idea of abnormality; he wrote to the mother of a homosexual that "it is a great injustice to persecute homosexuality as a crime—and a cruelty too" (1974, pp. 8, 11).

Only when she tried to explain narcissism did Mitchell betray her influence by the French psychoanalytic discussions: she pointed to Octave Mannoni's distinction between Freud's *Three Essays*, "the book of the drive," and *Interpretation of Dreams*, "the book of desire." She further emphasized that Freud had explicitly denounced the total inadequacy of biologically based instinct theories (1974, p. 3) just as the feminists do. She also went into the infant's "megalomanic moment" of narcissism, its search for itself in the mother's expressions, and the beginnings of the self. Here, Mitchell relied on D. W. Winnicott (see chapter 6) as she blamed current confusions on the inadequate language available to Freud and echoed Lacan's criticism of the neglect of language in psychoanalysis. In fact, she maintained that the paucity of vocabulary has led to the muddled meanings of such words as *masculinity*, *femininity*, and *bisexuality*. By expanding Freud's meaning and providing the context for his interpretations, Mitchell succeeded in making psychoanalysis palatable to many feminists.

After discussing preoedipal sexuality and the Oedipus complex, castration anxieties and penis envy, the preoedipal mother and the oedipal father, Mitchell dissected the prevalent applications of psychoanalysis to the liberation of the family. She retraced Wilhelm Reich's intellectual path. Because he believed that mass neurosis was due to sexual repression, he advocated sexual liberation as the road to socialism. To this end, he constructed his orgone box—the mechanical device that was to achieve it. But Reich had not examined the intricate dynamics of family life; instead he had extrapolated from whatever he found useful in psychoanalytic theory for political ends. This focus, continued Mitchell, led him to a number of extraordinary conclusions: he branded jealousy as pathological and said it was due to the economic dependence of women who are treated as possessions; he found that parental love of children compensated for other deprivations; and he postulated the superiority of the vagina. His sexual revolution failed, stated Mitchell, because the so-called dialectical unity of the sexes was unachievable (p. 223).

R. D. Laing's radical psychoanalysis, Mitchell noted, also had failed in its attempt to eradicate the social causes of schizophrenia by treating "people as people." Tracing his intellectual trajectory, Mitchell showed how in Laing's view of the family he became increasingly hostile to the mother. And she argued that "if psychosis is of pre-Oedipal formation, it is *bound* to have a great deal to do with the pre-Oedipal mother and with the absence of the Oedipal father" (p. 290).

Finally, Mitchell investigated the relation of psychoanalysis to "the second wave of feminism," as represented by Simone de Beauvoir, Betty Friedan, Eva Figes, Germaine Greer, Shulamith Firestone, and Kate Millett. She located women's problems in patriarchy and in "our specific ideology of a natural, biological family [which] re-expresses as a repressed Oedipal saga the kinship structure to which it is in contradiction" (p. 416).

After publishing *Psychoanalysis and Women* (1974) Mitchell herself became a psychoanalyst, always with the aim of exploring feminist issues. Her familiarity with the various psychoanalytic schools lent depth to her work. Originally she had been taken with Lacan's ideas because he "emphasized the uncertain, the illusory, delusive nature of the subject (ego or I), in stressing that this 'I' is a construction that disappears in the unconscious," and because to him women "were nothing other than the different social and economic structures in which they were created" (1984, p. 249).

By 1982, after she had become a psychoanalyst, Mitchell was addressing the intimate relationship between psychoanalysis and femininity in their shifting orientations. This, she pointed out, had *not* been Freud's task, as he had other conceptual purposes. In response to Fliess's biological bent, for instance, Freud explained libido as the masculine factor and repression as the feminine one, as "part of the pursuit of the internal logic of what he needed to describe." And he repudiated both Fliess's biological and Adler's sociological approach to these questions (1984, p. 305). As befits a member of the Middle Group of the British Psycho-Analytical Society, Mitchell mediated between Freud and Klein (see chapter 11), and contrasted their views on femininity:

The boy and the girl have both the same and different drives: where their biology is different, their urges must differ. For Klein the instinct is biological; for Freud it is "our main mythology." The boy and girl have the same objects. In Klein's theory, the object they first take in is predominantly part of the mother, then the whole mother. . . . For Freud it is the attachment to what you have had to abandon that you take in. (1984, p. 310)

Mitchell provided a bridge not only between Freudian and Kleinian views on feminism and between feminism and psychoanalysis but between French and Anglo-Saxon feminists.

What Do French Women Want?

In many ways, Mitchell's career is similar to Julia Kristeva's: both women began as literary critics, became political activists, were drawn to Lacan's ideas, and then became Freudian psychoanalysts. But because Kristeva had come to Paris from Bulgaria, her assumptions differed to some extent from Mitchell's. She belonged to a group of feminists who argued that "feminism exists because women are, and have been, everywhere oppressed at every level of existence, from the simplest social intercourse to the most elaborate discourse" (Marks and Courtivron, 1980, p. 4). Like her teacher Roland Barthes, she was sensitive to the sounds of language, and she went to listen to Lacan, who insisted that only through *mis*understanding—that is, through interpreting what is said along with what is left unsaid—can we ever understand anything. Yet, when she became a psychoanalyst, Kristeva joined the classical Société Psychanalytique de Paris.

The French, of course, are accustomed to Lacan's philosophical allusions. But these helped widen the gap between French and Anglo-Saxon psychoanalysis and between feminists in the two countries. In the *International Journal of Psychoanalysis*, most of the articles are by Anglo-Saxon analysts. Except for an occasional contribution in *Signs* and in deconstructionist publications such as *SubStance*, few French feminist works have reached the United States (Marks and Courtivron, 1980, p. ix). A number of French women, however, had raised feminist questions after the student uprisings in 1968: but they grounded their arguments, more than the Americans did, in theory and in history. And because they found Lacan's ideas useful, they also took to psychoanalysis.

One of the most effective of these feminists was Helene Cixous ([1975] 1980). She developed Lacan's criticism of Jones's differences with Freud (in "Early Feminine Sexuality") and maintained that "sexual difference is not determined merely by the fantasized relationship to anatomy . . . [and thus] to exteriority and to the specular in the elaboration of sexuality—a voyeur's theory" (p. 95). Cixous argued that woman must be asked what *she* wants, how her experience of sexual pleasure (*jouissance*) differs from that of men, and how this pleasure is inscribed at the levels of her body and of her unconscious. For Cixous, there are no such things as destiny, nature, or essence, only structural conditions that must be fought at every level, especially the unconscious one (see also Cixous and Clement, 1986).

Cixous's colleague Luce Irigaray was even more militant. She held that sexuality has always been placed within masculine parameters, whether "virile" clitoral activity is contrasted to "feminine" vaginal passivity or the clitoris is perceived as a little penis. Because her pleasures are never considered, Irigaray maintained, woman has to find them however she can: "by her somewhat servile love of the father-husband capable of giving it to her; by her desire of a penis-child, preferably male; [and] by gaining access to those cultural values which are still 'by right' reserved for males alone" ([1977] 1980, p. 99). For this reason, woman's autoerotism had become more central than man's. In addition, Irigaray stated, the woman's pleasure of the vaginal caress does not have to substitute itself for the clitoral caress; she may even experience the sex act as an intrusion, especially when the man takes her only as the object of *his* pleasure. Still, because the *"women has sex organs just about everywhere . . .* the geography of her pleasure is much more diversified, more multiple in its differences, more complex, more subtle, than [men may] imagine" (pp. 102–03).

Both Cixous and Irigaray, by adapting the Lacanian discourse to feminist ends, provided a sweeping social critique. (To address it here would lead me too far afield.) In one of the American deconstructions of their feminist texts (and those of others), the American feminist critic Jane Gallop (1982) went even further in her "Lacanian" reading of sex differences (see chapter 8). But she paid little attention to the importance of the unconscious in clinical theory. (This problem is compounded when psychoanalysts address politics.) Kristeva, however, faced this dilemma: because every practicing psychoanalyst must be careful not to impose her ideas on her patients, she cannot afford to take public stands. And, Kristeva continued, if an analyst's politics were known, this might be a hindrance in the transference. Since becoming an analyst, she says, her engagement consists of working with individual patients and replaces her former political engagement, but not her politics (Kurzweil, 1986, p. 222).

In introducing their translation of Lacan (in *Feminine Sexuality: Jacques Lacan and the École Freudienne* [1982]), Mitchell and Jacqueline Rose approached feminist questions in the context of psychoanalytic ones.[5] In commenting on Freud's theories of sexuality, they stated that feminists often make the mistake of picking out one idea and then developing it. It might be useful, they suggested, to explore the contradictions in Freud's work (p. 1), as Lacan had done, and not only Freud's work but that of nearly every important analyst.

Mitchell and Rose maintained that Lacan's focus on *desire* and on the *process* of the drive (the subject's specific means of relating to others) was central to feminine sexuality (p. 34). They cited Lacan's reading of Melanie Klein, who "describes the relationship to the mother as a mirrored relationship: the maternal body becomes the receptacle of the drives which the child projects onto it, drives motivated by aggression born of a fundamental disappointment. This is to neglect the fact that the outside . . . is the place where he or she will encounter the third [person], the father" (p. 37). Since the father is synonymous with the law and therefore with the concept of castration, Lacan had addressed the symbolic meaning of castration in the family triangle rather than in the mythic past—in the phallus (as the symbol of unity and fertility belonging to and joining both sexes), which also doubles as the paternal metaphor. Woman was found to be excluded from this phallic definition because she is *not* man (p. 49). But because to Lacan there was no feminine outside language, and the "feminine" in language was produced as a negative term, Mitchell and Rose concluded that Lacan too "was implicated in the phallocentrism he described, just as his own utterance constantly rejoined the mastery which he sought to undermine" (p. 56).

The women in the Société Psychanalytique de Paris did not proclaim their feminism, and none of them joined the feminist movement. Nevertheless, many of them have defended feminist principles and have followed in the footsteps of Bonaparte or Klein by trying to better comprehend feminine sexuality. The most prominent among them are Janine Chasseguet-Smirgel and Joyce McDougall.

In 1964, Chasseguet-Smirgel published a collection of essays on femininity. In her introduction she reviewed the literature and explored the father-daughter relationship, along with problems linked to the basically feminine propensity to incorporate anal-sadistic components together with the paternal penis. She connected female masochism to guilt and to the revolt against an omnipotent mother rather than to the wish to become a man. She tied the "basic feminine wish to be free of the mother" to the work of Jeanne Lampl-de Groot (for whom the castration complex is a secondary formation), Ruth Mack Brunswick (who believed that desire for a child precedes penis envy), and Josine Mueller (who thought the vagina is central early on). She also cited contributions by Carl Müller-Braunschweig, Annie Reich, Hanns Sachs, and Phyllis Greenacre (Chasseguet-Smirgel, 1970).[6] The clinical case she presented at the Montreal Congress in 1987, "Une tentative de solution perverse chez une femme et son échec," related the dreams and fantasies of her patient to her own theoretical premises about female sexuality. In a somewhat different vein, Maria Torok suggested that the envied penis becomes idealized; Catherine Luquet-Parat thought that a "masochistic feminine move" defends against sadistic drives directed toward the father's penis; and Joyce McDougall found that some measure of female homosexuality must be part of every woman's psyche.

Later Chasseguet-Smirgel reexamined the classical conceptions of psychoanalysis in her investigation of perversions and in some of the Lacanians' metaphoric formulations. She maintained, for example, that the child's relinquishing the oedipal object may be tied to his painful recognition of his smallness and the inadequacy of his sexual organ (similar to Lacan's *petit a*)— the tragedy of lost illusions (1985, p. 52). She invoked reality not only as the differences between the sexes but as generational: "The mother has a vagina that the little boy's penis cannot satisfy. . . . If the sight of the female genital organs is so 'traumatic,' it is because it confronts the young male with his inadequacy" (1984, pp. 15–16). Lacan's influence on McDougall was even stronger than on Chasseguet-Smirgel, as McDougall (1985) maintained that the phallus—namely, the symbolic function taken on by the penis in its intra- and intersubjective dialectic rather than the penis detached from its symbolic significance—is truly significant (p. 44). She also stated that the phallus is the basis for determining how the female genitals will be represented in an individual's unconscious. In an earlier essay on female homosexuality, she had stated that the (Lacanian) phallus is taken as the symbol of narcissistic integrity, or as the fundamental signifier of desire (1980, p. 118).

These are only a few examples to indicate that "what women wanted" was an intrinsic element of the theoretical questions the women Freudians of Paris addressed. Since Lacan's more flamboyant activities are usually stressed, his influence on the theories of female sexuality by French Freudians is often overlooked.

The German Feminists

Chasseguet-Smirgel's German counterpart was Margarete Mitscherlich-Nielsen. The first German analyst to study psychoanalysis in London after the Second World War, she was also the first to address directly questions of sexuality. Because of her generally radical views, it was not surprising that in the 1970s she tried to apply psychoanalysis to the liberation of women (Mitscherlich-Nielsen, 1975). By then, feminism had become widespread, and women analysts outside Germany had begun to investigate female sexuality. Mitscherlich-Nielsen herself had been attracted to American feminism during her stay at Palo Alto in 1972–73 and not long after had become a friend of the radical German feminist Alice Schwarzer. Mitscherlich-Nielsen's psychoanalytic feminism can be distinguished from that of her counterparts in other countries in that it is explicitly political. In this respect, she upsets those of her colleagues for whom neutrality is the most essential ingredient of psychoanalytic technique.

In the introduction to *Die friedfertige Frau* (*The Peace-loving Woman;* 1985) Mitscherlich-Nielsen wondered why men go to war and women seem to accept men's destructive drives more or less willingly—as victims, forced accomplices, or servants. Long before this, she recalled, she had been interested in the social determinants of psychic reality (1985, p. viii). Now she went back to some of the major contributions by Freudians (including Freud) in an attempt to prove that women are better equipped than men to combat the irrationalities of modern society. But this was only part of a larger aim: she wanted to find the means of saving the "fatherless society" her late husband, Alexander Mitscherlich, had brilliantly described. Along with him, she had exposed the psychic legacies of the Hitler regime in order to further democracy in the Federal Republic. Her younger feminist friends now were denouncing the inadequacies of this democracy: she agreed with them that prevalent practices in the economy and in politics were based on moral double standards. "Everywhere," she noted, "men's associations, fraternities, and manliness are self-idealizing; and they militate against true fatherliness—which stands for humanity, civic duty and integrity" (p. 172).

Mitscherlich-Nielsen always explained the psychic processes of her patients in the context of their lives, which in turn she related to postwar German realities. She maintained that her compatriots' hatred of Turks and other "guest-workers" was comparable to the anti-Semitism of the Nazis and that this was related to the prevailing socialization of (unconscious) male and female ways of expressing aggression, which in turn was institutionalized in the division of labor. Even among German psychoanalysts, she stated, writings on female psychology—by Chasseguet-Smirgel's group in 1964, by neo-Kleinians, and by the contributors to the special 1976 issue of the *Journal of the American Psychoanalytic Association*—had gone more or less unnoticed (p. 22). Had her colleagues paid attention, she said, they might have been more aware of women's unconscious hatred of their mothers, which is rooted in (or at least aggravated by) patriarchal family relations. Where fathers did not assist in the child's upbringing, Mitscherlich-Nielsen often repeated, disturbances of early mother-child relations tend to be played out in later sexual disturbances or in alcohol or drug abuse. Citing Freudian and neo-Freudian discussions of object relations theory, narcissism, womb envy, and drive theory, Mitscherlich-Nielsen held that most psychoanalysts, though continuing to dispute the content and roots of women's superego, no longer question Freud's tentative speculations about femininity but mistakenly assume them to be indisputable facts (p. 47).

Still, Mitscherlich-Nielsen did not think that abstract discussions of the emancipation of women were useful. Instead, she advocated addressing such concrete issues as abortion and overpopulation. She agreed with Annie Reich's observation that women tend to overvalue everything "manly" and that the girl's early socialization toward the consideration of others limits her later freedom of choice (p. 145). Constantly mediating between unconscious drives and political realities, Mitscherlich-Nielsen ultimately came down against those who dominate the affairs of the world, who decide upon war and peace: for they are the same men who exert their power over women.

Here Mitscherlich-Nielsen was joined by Marxists, particularly by the male Marxists around *Psyche*, her own journal (see chapter 10). She became an idol to German-speaking feminists, whose research she heavily influenced. One of the Swiss feminists, Maya Nadig (1986), in her ethnoanalysis of Mexican peasant women, which bridged both culture and class, uncovered the sort of unconscious meanings and psychic dynamics of the socialization of women

Mitscherlich-Nielsen had addressed. Another, Waltraud Gölter (1983), who examined the "problematic socialization of female identity" in the works of Marguerite Duras, Christa Wolf, Anaïs Nin, Simone de Beauvoir, and others, was influenced by Mitscherlich-Nielsen when she showed how an inevitably "open" identity formation may bring about freedom from compulsive habits of thinking as well as a utopian consciousness that may induce great creativity. Another feminist disciple of Mitscherlich-Nielsen, Ellen K. Reinke-Köberer (1978), took issue with the theses of Chasseguet-Smirgel's group, arguing that the analysts' views themselves influence their drives (and drive theories) and that cultural and long-standing individual and family-specific role models lead them to conclude (erroneously) that "culture is destiny."[7] Carol Hagemann-White (1978) arrived at a similar conclusion, maintaining that psychoanalytic practice and particularly the difficulties of female patients in analysis—along with definitions of mental illness and health in patriarchy—can be influenced by feminist protest.

But Mitscherlich-Nielsen also had followers among more conservative women analysts. These were the women who, like Chasseguet-Smirgel, expected to apply psychoanalysis to the liberation of women's psyches without meddling in politics. In fact, Chasseguet-Smirgel and Mitscherlich-Nielsen ultimately clashed over mixing psychoanalysis with politics: Chasseguet-Smirgel insisted that psychoanalysis primarily should stick to its own mission, whereas Mitscherlich-Nielsen endorsed antinuclear resolutions and other leftist proclamations (see chapter 12).

The Fate of Femininity

If Anglo-Saxon feminists were more familiar with Mitscherlich-Nielsen's views, many of them might go along with her politicalization of psychoanalysis. But both male and female Anglo-Saxon Freudians tend to be more attached to "scientific" arguments and thus started to examine the issues the feminists raised in terms of traditional psychoanalytic theories. In 1976, for instance, William Grossman and Walter Stewart distinguished between the early phase of penis envy, which occurs in the first two years of life and is registered as a narcissistic injury, and a later phase, which represents an effort to resolve oedipal conflicts. They suggested (with illustrations from cases) that penis envy ought to be considered "the manifest content of a symptom rather than 'bedrock'" (1976). Eleanor Galenson and Herman Roiphe (1976) examined early genital-zone experiences as influences on subsequent sexual identity and ego functions. On the basis of observational research, they concluded that Freud was only partially correct about the connections between penis envy, the female castration complex, and feminine development; these occur earlier than Freud thought and are related to fears of object and anal loss as well as to affective experiences with parents. Earlier, Robert Stoller (1964), when addressing ambiguous male core-gender identity, hypothesized the intrusion of an unknown "biological force" as a determinant of sexual identity. And Roy Schafer (1974) proposed that "psychoanalysts who genuinely appreciate ego psychology" ought to deal with issues connected to the exploitation of women. He concluded that Freud, in his thinking on women, had been applying a nineteenth-century biological-medical framework, which inevitably flawed his clinical and theoretical insights. These are only a few examples indicating that classical American Freudians were taking the feminist ideas seriously.[8]

Ethel Person (1980), in an overview of these issues, challenged the popular assumptions that sexuality is an innate force that achieves its ideal expression when free of cultural repression and that female sexuality is inhibited (hyposexual) while male sexuality represents the norm (p. 36). She differentiated between biological sex, gender, sexual behavior, and reproduction, and between theories about the nature of sexuality and about sexual motivation. All these theories, she went on, are expected to explain too much: the motor force behind the desire for sexual behavior; the strength of the sexual impulse as subjectively experienced; the absence, avoidance, or inhibition of sexuality and the variable intensity of sexual desire; the diversity of erotic stimuli and situations that may trigger them; and the existence of a "sex print"—that is, an individual's restrictions of erotic responses, the confluence of sexual and nonsexual meanings in both sexual and nonsexual behavior, and the cultural preoccupation with sexuality (pp. 37–38). In addition, Person pointed out, two major paradigms explain the source of sexual motivation: a biological (libido) theory postulating a fixed sexual drive, and a (conditioned) "appetitional" one acknowledging a neural reflex for orgasmic release. Whereas the former assumes that tension will be discharged via sublimation, neurosis, or perversion, the latter considers the pursuit of pleasure to be the motive behind sexuality. But neither of them, Person stated, is as satisfactory as the "amalgam of Freud's psychological theory and object relations theory, which places the appetitional component in a developmental motivational context" (p. 38). After explaining the pros and cons of the first two paradigms and summarizing the arguments of their major proponents and opponents, Person came out for an object relations approach—even though it too is limited by specific problems of internalization, such as affect, perception, maturational stages, conflict, and so on. In other words, she maintained that object relations theory could account for cultural influences on sexuality. Still, she conceded that "culture" can explain neither how sexuality influences the development of the autonomous personality nor the variations of individual personality structure within each culture (p. 46). Person then pointed to the problems associated with the issues she had enumerated and their manifestations in adolescents of both sexes—in behavior and sexual fantasies reflecting both sexual and nonsexual motives. She asserted that sexual liberation and female liberation are separate, but that structures of gender and sex print do mediate between sexuality and identity formation. Therefore, she concluded, it may be difficult to "liberate" sexuality from the contaminants of power, but she hoped that female liberation might act as midwife in the struggle (p. 61).

Inevitably, Person's (1983) reevaluation of female sexuality led her to consider how views of male sexuality might be incomplete or skewed, since these too suffer from cultural biases. In her review of Alan P. Bell and Martin S. Weinberg's report, *Homosexualities* (1978), she examined their views on sexual experience, their typologies, and the relation between homosexual lifestyles and psychological adjustment. And even though she accused these authors of bypassing many difficult questions, of drawing larger conclusions than their methods warrant, and of relying on a behaviorist conception, she commended them for drawing attention to the fact that male and female homosexuals construct different psychodynamics, symbolic universes, and gender organization. In *The Psychology of Men* (Fogel, Lane, and Liebert, 1986), Person addressed the fact that not only the conceptualizations of female sexuality but those of male sexuality as well are incomplete if not skewed because they fail to recognize that boys' "fundamental sexual problem is the struggle to achieve phallic strength and power vis-à-vis other men" and that the fantasies accompanying the mother-son relationship have their own impact (p. 72). To learn more about these dynamics, Person explored the widespread male fantasies of "the omniavailable woman and lesbian sex," which might parallel homosexual and transvestite solutions of the oedipal conflict (p. 73).

One of the most plausible theses connecting psychoanalysis and feminism is that proposed by sociologist Nancy Chodorow (1978). She maintained, among other things, that Mitchell had placed too much emphasis on women under patriarchy and too little on Freud's own "unexamined patriarchal cultural assumptions, . . . [his] blindness, contempt for women, mysogyny, [and unsubstantiated] claims about biology" (p. 142). Chodorow wanted to find out why women take on *all* mothering functions, not just birth. After rejecting physiological, biological, hormonal, and even sociological theories on the subject as unconvincing, she settled on object relations theory as the best means to understand "the reproduction of mothering as a central and constituting element in the social organization and reproduction of gender" (p. 7). Chodorow traced the consequences of gender differences in preoedipal, oedipal, and postoedipal configurations; she demonstrated how male-female sexual differences are reinforced in the individual's psyche at every step of socialization; and she pointed to the consequences of these practices for *all* women. In her view, Freud's account of superego formation was plausible. But by focusing on the psychological consequences of women's mothering, she noted asymmetries in the experiences of girls and boys. These experiences, Chodorow maintained, have their repercussions in role learning that is replayed in the family (p. 169). Thus "women mother daughters who, when they become women, mother" (p. 209). This argument, however, as the psychoanalyst and historian Peter Loewenberg observed, "left out the body." He and other critics chided Chodorow for ignoring biological reality, such as gestation and early bonding.

Chodorow, even more than Mitchell or the French feminists, helped convince American nonpsychoanalytic feminists that psychoanalysis was not analogous to the plague. But she could not have drawn on object relations theory had Freudian analysts like Otto Kernberg (see chapter 11) and Person not supplied the theoretical tools. On the other hand, the feminist movement itself helped legitimate such an extension of psychoanalysis. The urge to know more about homosexuality, for instance, to stop perceiving it as a sickness or as arrested development, sparked heated debates among analysts; also such questions as the source of women's psychic mechanisms in early penis envy once more became of interest to analysts. This probably would not have happened without the investigations of the feminists.

And without the feminists and the deconstructionists (literary critics who were influenced by Lacan; see chapter 8) psychoanalysis could not have moved into the universities—into departments of English and French literature—as a legitimate subject. And as psychoanalytic feminism sparked by the women's liberation movement inadvertently brought psychoanalysis into academic establishments, conversely, in countries that had not accepted psychoanalysis, or in those like Austria or Hungary which paid it only lip service, feminism did not tend to flourish.

Chapter 8

Literature
and Criticism

On October 15, 1897, Freud wrote to Fliess that all male children are in love with their mothers and jealous of their fathers, and that this was why *Oedipus Rex* was so gripping: "The Greek legend seizes upon a compulsion which everyone recognizes because he has felt traces of it within himself. Everyone in the audience was once a budding Oedipus in fantasy, and each recoils in horror from the dream fulfillment here transplanted into reality, with the full quantity of repression which separates his infantile state from his present one" (Masson, 1985, p. 272). Ever since then, Oedipus, the wayward son, has been the inspiration for countless psychoanalytic studies of literature; and the relation of literature to psychoanalysis has reflected a large variety of interests and approaches by individuals in both disciplines.

Art and Neurosis: The Early Links

On Wednesday evenings, the circle around Freud was absorbed in enlarging on the connections among creativity, society, and neurosis. According to Nunberg, it was difficult at first for the members to find patients and thus to obtain case material, whereas literary works, as nonclinical sources, were ready at hand. And unlike Freud, the disciples, in response also to their extraordinarily creative ambience, were more interested in penetrating the artistic expression of the unconscious than in its meaning for psychoanalytical theory (Nunberg and Federn, 1962, 1:xxviii). In effect, in thirty-five of the fifty-three meetings held between October 10, 1906, and June 3, 1908—almost two-thirds of the gatherings—artists and their works were either mentioned or made the central topic of discussion.

By the time Freud wrote *The Interpretation of Dreams*, in 1899, he was convinced of his hypothesis that we are moved by the fate of Oedipus because it might have been our own, because we all are born with the same curse. (Freud actually was explaining male behavior, but he thought it had a universal component.) Even if we doubt that men are destined to direct their first sexual impulses toward their mothers and their first hateful ones toward their fathers, he stated, their dreams say otherwise.[1] According to Freud, King Oedipus, who slew his father, Laius, and wed his mother, Jocasta, fulfilled his wish—a wish every male child has. But most boys learn to withdraw their sexual impulses from their mother and forget their jealousy of their father. Hence, Freud said, we now recoil from the person to whom this primitive childhood wish has been granted, with the revulsion the repression of these wishes has engendered in our minds.

Freud realized that the death of his father figured prominently in his own dreams and that the dreams were full of his reactions to earlier sexual fantasies connected to his father. These preoccupations, in turn, led him to elaborate on the Oedipus legend, whose source Freud located in the "dream material of immemorial antiquity." Shakespeare's *Hamlet* also intrigued him because Hamlet was

able to do anything but take vengeance upon the man who did away with his father and has taken his father's place with his mother. . . . The loathing which should have driven him to revenge is thus replaced by self-reproach, by conscientious scruples, which tell him that he himself is no better than the murderer whom he is required to punish. (Brill, 1938, p. 310)

Interspersing the narrative with his own speculations and conclusions, Freud went on to state that Hamlet was

translating into consciousness what had to remain unconscious in the mind of the hero. . . . The sexual aversion which Hamlet expressed in conversation with Ophelia is perfectly consistent with this deduction—the same sexual aversion which during the next few years was increasingly to take possession of the poet's soul, until it found its supreme utterance in *Timon of Athens*. It can, of course, be only the poet's own psychology with which we are confronted in *Hamlet*. (Brill, 1938 p. 310)

This is the first time Freud was to link a literary work with its author's life and unconscious motives. More like a literary critic than a physician, he explained that differences between Greek and modern drama manifest the various ways in which societies handle the inevitable sexual repression: the ancient Greeks enacted and realized their wish-fantasies, whereas modern society is more circumspect. But immediately after making this literary judgment Freud appended a medical diagnosis: in *Oedipus Rex* the basic wish fantasy of the child is realized in dreams; in *Hamlet* it remains repressed, and we learn of its existence—as we discover the relevant facts in a neurosis—only through the inhibitory effects it produces.

Freud further proclaimed that poets had always known about the unconscious. Moreover, quoting Friedrich Schiller, who realized that intellect may inhibit imagination and creativity, and Goethe, who believed that creativity entailed searching for "the good and the true," Freud observed that unconscious drives and fantasies were the wellsprings of imagination and artistic creation as well as of neurosis. Freud was also reflecting the literary spirit of fin-de-siècle Vienna. The two leading romantics (in Vienna only the statues of a few Hapsburg rulers are more prominent than those of Goethe and Schiller) were being lionized at the same time that modernism was replacing romanticism. And Freud greatly admired the leading contemporary writers: he corresponded with, among others, Lion Feuchtwanger, Thomas Mann, Romain Rolland, and Arnold and Stefan Zweig.[2]

Freud thought poets incorporate the essence of creativity because, like dreamers, they give free rein to their imagination, allow themselves to make wild associations, and condense a maximum of meanings into a minimum of words. Less organized than prose, poetry nevertheless dramatizes both the dreams and the preoccupations of ordinary men and women. But all literary works, Freud believed, even forms less compressed than poetry, are rooted in writers' dreams as well as in their lives. In response to Jung's particular concern with the connections between the historical-cultural and the individual unconscious, Freud wrote "Delusions and Dreams," a study of *Gradiva*, a popular novella by Wilhelm Jensen. *Gradiva* (1907a) is about a neurotic archaeologist daydreamer who falls in love with the statue of a young woman, goes to Pompei where he believes the model for the statue lives, and there meets a woman he is convinced is Gradiva in the flesh, thus experiencing her presence in both reality and fantasy. Freud explained the protagonist's "delusional" experience, his preoccupation with the young woman's stride, her feet and her sandals, as manifestations of repressed childhood wishes and expressions of erotic fantasies meant to enact preoedipal bliss.

Freud's analysis of *Gradiva*, which has often been cited as an example of psychoanalytic criticism (for example, by Wyatt 1981), provided him with the raw material for *Creative Writers and Daydreaming* (1908e). Here, he laid the groundwork for countless studies of artistic works in relation to their authors' lives and psychological drives. Because both artists and children are serious about their fantasy worlds and nevertheless distinguish them clearly from reality, their imaginary activities and behavior can be compared: both originate works of their own and rearrange the things of the world in their own fashion. But when the writer draws on his imagination and transforms it partly through formal means, Freud maintained, he transcends his own person. His product, therefore, becomes "a source of pleasure for the hearers and spectators at the performance of a writer's work" (*S.E.*, 9:142).

Creativity and Neurosis

Otto Rank was the first disciple who set out to prove the existence of the (artistic) unconscious: "Every genuine poetical creation . . . proceed[s] from more than one motive, more than one impulse in the mind of the poet, and . . . admit[s] of more than one interpretation." Rank's paper "The Artist" was his original passport into the Wednesday Society. Freud helped get it published two years later, and it remained central to most subsequent psychoanalyses of literature. According to Rank's biographer, J. D. Lieberman (1985), he and Freud complemented each other: Freud was the scientist-artist, Rank the artist-scientist. Freud credited Rank for his original insights in updated versions of *The Interpretation of Dreams*.

Rank ([1907] 1932) emphasized the relationships among the artist's conscious will-to-art, his process of self-forming and self-training, his personality, and his productivity. The creative impulse, he held, lies equally at the root of artistic production and of live experience and manifests itself in the whole personality, which, in turn, is perpetually re-created and thus produces artwork and experience in the same way. Rank further argued that the creative impulse, "which attempts to turn ephemeral life into personal immortality," expresses the artist's wish to transform death into life (Kurzweil and Phillips, 1983, p. 41). Although he first thought this impulse was rooted in sexuality, he gradually changed his mind and perceived it as an expression of *anti*sexual tendencies—"the life impulse made to serve the individual will," or sublimation (p. 41). And he insisted that the dynamics among impulse, fear, and will determine productivity and that through these dynamics the artist remolds himself. The neurotic, on the other hand, is unable to put this creative process to use, to detach it from his person. In much more detail than Freud, Rank discussed primitive art (expressing collective ideology linked to religion), classical art (a social concept of art perpetuated by idealization), and modern art (based on genius, concretization, and artistic individuality), and then went into the effect of the interplay among these variables on specific artists. Both artists and neurotics suffer from ego conflicts, stated Rank, but the artist may sublimate them through his work.

While Rank was trying to figure out how and by whom art is created, most of the other disciples were analyzing specific works or the psychic makeup of specific artists. Postmortem psychoanalyses of Leonardo, Shakespeare, Kleist, Dostoevsky, Swift, Poe, and others were taken as seriously as the cases of analytic patients. Ernest Jones (1949), for instance, noted that although Shakespeare drew on earlier versions of the story he immortalized in *Hamlet*, his own version, properly apprehended, provides new insight into the poet's personality. According to Jones, Shakespeare changed the public murder of the Saxo-Belleforest saga into a secret one and then "intensified the plot by the previous incestuous adultery of the Queen." By calling attention to these and other alterations, Jones could interpret Claudius's attack on his brother as both a murderous aggression and a homosexual assault (he claimed that readiness to interchange the sexes was a prominent theme in all Shakespeare's plays). And he could conclude that "Shakespeare wrote *Hamlet* as a more or less successful abreaction of the intolerable emotions aroused by the painful situation he depicts in his Sonnets," his betrayal by both his beloved young noble and his mistress. Shakespeare, states Jones, had smothered his resentment and had become "reconciled" to his betrayers. Though many subsequent analyses of Shakespeare's primal conflicts dispute Jones's diagnosis, his view of Hamlet has become a classic of psychoanalytic interpretation. By now, *Hamlet* is no longer the melancholy gentleman of the eighteenth-century view or the delicate poet of the nineteenth but a man with an Oedipus complex that prevents him from acting (Holland, 1964, p. 158). Norman Holland has also reminded us that Freud's thoughts about *Hamlet* helped lead him to the Oedipus complex. But, he cautions, it does not make sense to "lift Hamlet out of the play and treat him as a living person" (pp. 158, 159), and to identify with his feelings of fragmentation, splitting, and decomposition.

Marie Bonaparte expanded the use of psychoanalysis in literary criticism when she examined the mental processes and their accompanying effects during literary creation. Edgar Allan Poe, for instance, was "sinking into the unconscious" and while passing from the unconscious to the preconscious was subject to rather illogical thought processess (Phillips, 1957, p. 58). She cautioned against examining "localized regions"—that is, components of the psyche—rather than concentrating on its dynamics, its changing conditions. Bonaparte also traced Poe's increasing displacement of psychic intensity chronologically through his works—the representation of woman as a building in *The Fall of the House of Usher*, the presentation of Mother in *Metzengerstein*, the indirect confession of impotence in *Loss of Breath*—and thereby demonstrated that Poe's talent was feeding on his defensive mechanisms. Simultaneously, her insights into Poe as a person supported Freud's theses that "the child, ontogenetically similar to our remote ancestors, passes through an animistic stage whose symbols still rule our soul, whether we be primitives or highly civilized," and that "Poe's sado-necrophilist genius was destined to awake, in other countries and hearts, the same mighty and eternal instincts of those who recognized themselves in him" (Phillips, 1957, pp. 64, 87).

As Freud became increasingly busy with the spread of the movement and with reworking the central concepts (around 1915), he seemed to be less inclined to try to legitimate psychoanalysis via literature. So, when the Freudians no longer needed literature to prove the validity of psychoanalysis, psychoanalysis was used to enrich the study of literature.

Soon writers and artists were ready to apply Freudian principles in their own creative fashion. In America, the heyday of these activities occurred during the 1940s and 1950s, when writers who had had a Freudian analysis incorporated what they were learning into their work. Over the years, such studies have become part of the psychoanalytic enterprise. The best of them apply new concepts and subtle critical tools to comprehend both the concerns and the unconscious intentions of an artist.

In England, neither Anna Freud nor Melanie Klein was concerned with literature, and few of their followers dealt with it (see chapter 7). In the 1970s, some German analysts, such as Johannes Cremerius and Peter Dettmering, started to investigate the literature on "literature and psychoanalysis." Many of these inquiries were indebted to Kurt Eissler's (1971) distinction between "exopoetic" (external influences *on* the work) and "endopoetic" (internal *to* the work) interpretations, as well as to Adorno's *Aesthetic Theory* (1970).

In France, Lacan ([1966] 1977) had already introduced a new form of psychoanalytic criticism with his structural-linguistic interpretation of Poe's "The Purloined Letter" (pp. 146–78). Although he stressed Bonaparte's French roots and rejected her "American" approach (he lumped her ideas with those of the Freudian ego-psychologists he detested), Lacan chose this text as the prototype for his new form of psychoanalytic criticism.

As we noted in chapter 7, Lacanian psychoanalysis influenced Marxist disclaimers and feminist literary studies in American universities. Eventually, some of these ideas were exported to the German-speaking countries, where they infiltrated the native psychoanalytic theories of literature. Many classical

American Freudians, who disapproved of Lacan's practices, gradually *did* take an interest in questions of language and thereby addressed some of his original textual questions on the connections of art to neurosis.

Some Classical Approaches

Probably the most impressive of Freud's own contributions to literary psychoanalysis was his work on Dostoevsky (*S.E.*, 21:173–94), though some of his facts have recently been questioned. (Others are on Leonardo [*S.E.*, 11: 59–137], Goethe [*S.E.*, 21:208–12], and Michelangelo [*S.E.*, 13:211–38]). Freud, who considered Dostoevsky the greatest of modern writers, distinguished between his talent and his neurosis, between his moral and his antisocial tendencies. Freud maintained that Dostoevsky's epilepsy was of neurotic origin and assumed that his seizures grew stronger after the age of eighteen, when he witnessed his father's murder. Freud then used this "turning point in his neurosis" to explain Dostoevsky's feelings of guilt as being due to earlier unconscious wishes to see his father dead. These feelings, he claimed, determined Dostoevsky's attitudes toward such authority figures as God and the tsar. Freud illuminated some of Dostoevsky's deeper dreads and conflicts such as obsessive gambling by relating his subject's life to his works and to suggestions of heterosexuality and homosexuality. For Freud, Dostoevsky's basic ambivalence also explained his boundless sympathy for the criminal, whom he almost cast as the Redeemer burdened by the guilt that others ought to have borne—an identification based on Dostoevsky's own murderous impulses (Phillips, 1957, p. 15).

Phyllis Greenacre's study of Jonathan Swift is exemplary among the many contributions by later psychoanalysts. She portrayed Swift as a witty, charming, tortured man who suffered from oedipal problems, hypochondria, fear of death and sexuality, fantasies of masturbation, and homosexuality. In fact, Greenacre's summary of Swift's psychic history demonstrates the typical application of Freudian ego psychology in America during the 1950s:

This study of Swift was stimulated by an interest in fetishism and the part played in its development by sensations of the instability of body size. It is pertinent then to make some brief further references to these questions here. There is no indication that Swift was an overt fetishist, although he shares much in the structure of his personality with those who develop the manifest symptom. The anal fixation was intense and binding, and the genital response so impaired and limited at best, that he was predisposed to later weakness. A retreat from genital sexuality did actually occur in his early adult life, probably beginning with the unhappy relationship to Jane Waring, the first of the goddesses. After this he never again seemed willing to consider marriage, while his expressed demands were that women who were closest to him should be as much like boys as possible. His genital demands were probably partly sublimated through his creative writings, but even these showed the stamp of his strong anal character. He did not need a fetish because he resigned from physical genitality. In a sense, his converting of the women of his choice into boys fulfilled a fetishistic need. Especially Stella was to be the faithful, dependable, unchanging bisexualized object, a cornerstone for his life. With her death he began to go to pieces.

Lemuel Gulliver went a step further than his creator in that he was a married man, who was however continually escaping from his marriage which was so predominantly disgusting to him though his periodic sojourns at home sufficed sometimes for the depositing of a child with his wife. . . . The *Travels* appear as the acting out of Lemuel's masturbatory fantasies which, like the character of Swift, are closely interwoven with anal preoccupations and ambitions rather than with genital ones. (Phillips, 1957, pp. 134)

Another type of approach was exemplified by Henry Lowenfeld, who generalized from one of his cases. By recounting some of her childhood experiences and the traumatic events she kept remembering in her dreams, a woman artist he was treating managed to uncover the roots of her neurosis. Lowenfeld noted that like other artists she was more sensitive to stimulation than ordinary people and therefore apt to provoke traumatic experiences. Artists' oedipal guilt feelings are stronger as well, Lowenfeld believed, but these are alleviated by approval for creative work, to which their narcissistic feelings are transferred. Still, Lowenfeld's patient's fantasies were full of conflict and tension, and she felt only temporary relief after completing a work. Her bisexuality played a large role, he found, and she often equated productive work of art with giving birth. By reproducing unfulfilled experiences, and by alternately identifying with and fearing external stimuli, most artists, he noted, swing between introjection and projection—the process of artistic sublimation.

Other inquiries yielded insights into specific clinical details. Wittels, for instance, analyzed the work of Heinrich von Kleist ([1954] 1957), who after struggling against homosexuality killed himself at the age of thirty-four, and Reik ([1949] 1957) discussed the personal sources of E. T. A Hoffmann's tales of his three loves—the doll, the seductress, and the artist. Yet the myriad of studies did not bring the Freudians any closer to understanding the sources of artistic creation, for they were limited by their own approach. As William Phillips observed:

Any total approach to art that sees the creative gift or process as a form of neurosis is bound to produce a lopsided and absurd theory. If art is considered as a form of sublimation, or a variety of dream or fantasy, or even as a therapeutic activity, then we have no criteria for judging it, nor any way of distinguishing it from other kinds of dream or fantasy, or therapy. And as for the many ingenious exercises revealing art to be oral or anal, sadistic or masochistic, narcissistic, totemic, the best that can be said of them is that they apply equally well to a doodle, a Grandma Moses, or a Jackson Pollock. (1957, p. xvi)

The Literary Critics

After psychoanalytic lore had become ubiquitous, almost mainstream, the analysts wrote primarily "scientific" papers to present at meetings, and the best of the literary critics, such as Lionel Trilling, William Empson, William Phillips, Alfred Kazin, William Barrett, Geoffrey Hartman, and Kenneth Burke, and art critics, such as E. H. Gombrich and Meyer Schapiro, focused on the subtle links between art and neurosis. American literary critics also modified and expanded on Freudian analysts. Some of them psychoanalyzed the protagonists of works of fiction; others went into the texts to discern authors' motives. Many were polemical, disputing the findings of psycho-analysts and other critics. Thus countless books and essays were written starting from a variety of assumptions—*all* of them claiming derivation from the master.

The literary critics not only knew more about literature than the Freudi-ans but had neither to strive for scientific veracity nor to prove a theory. Lionel Trilling (1950), for instance, argued strongly against the idea that the exercise of the imagination resembles insanity. Although Freud himself had modified a number of his early formulations, Trilling found that some of Freud's followers clung to myths about the poet as the *genus irritabile* who finds virtue in illness, genius in neurosis, or inspiration in his "wound" (p. 177). Trilling granted that psychoanalytic insights into family situations and into temperament demonstrated that neurotic or psychotic perceptions of reality tend to be more intense than normal ones and that creative individuals may be closer to their unconscious than others, but he argued that this does not locate the artist's power in his neurosis; it only acknowledges that the writer exhibits his unconscious, that he is more aware of what happens to him and more articulate and truthful than others. An artist's neurosis, Trilling con-ceded, may have a special relationship to what he does, and he may exploit his activity as an *activity of conflict*. Nevertheless, his genius—of perception, real-ization, and representation—is an irreducible gift.

The poet W. H. Auden (1977) agreed with Trilling, adding that the men-tally alert child, by combining fantasy with craftsmanship, may become an artist in order to escape the demands of an unhappy family life. For Auden, creation, like psychoanalysis, is a process of the artist's reliving his selective internalization of the world in a new situation: he uses the artistic medium as his means of communication (Kurzweil and Phillips, 1983, p. 125). But psychoanalysis, Auden went on, has also become part of the environment and influences both the artist and the man in the street: writers such as Thomas Mann and D. H. Lawrence wrote about Freud; Robert Graves and Herbert Read, among others, used his terminology; and surrealism adopted his clinical technique. Freud's ideas have entered the modern mind, but Auden cautioned that neither psychology nor art can tell people how to behave.

Like Trilling and Auden, the critic Erich Heller (1976) pointed out that no one could be untouched by Freud's theories. Nevertheless, he stated, it is irrelevant to keep asking whether or not specific writers had been "influenced" by him or had "learned" from him. Heller located the ubiquity of Freud's ideas in, for example, Thomas Mann's approach to questions of morality in *Death in Venice*: Aschenbach's real will is revealed when, after he has decided to leave Venice, his suitcase is lost and he is "forced" to stay on. His unconscious desire is manifested, Heller writes, when he is "almost convulsed with reckless delight, an unbelievable joy," at delaying his departure. Similarly, in *The Magic Mountain*, Hans Castorp waits seven years for the return of the Russian woman he has secretly fallen in love with, while using his minor illness as a pretext for remaining at the sanatorium. Both of these characters would appear to be acting out some of Mann's fantasies and to confirm notions about the unconscious.

Heller believed that Freud had been naive in expecting to get to the bottom of psychic phenomena, forgetting that he was projecting the morality of his own day onto the primeval murderers (in *Totem and Taboo*) or assuming that these early men were psychically ready to believe in God. Psychoanalysis could not set up a hierarchy of ethics to guide modern consciousness any more than philosophy or religion could, Heller stated, although it could support beliefs in the utmost freedom of expression. Freudian tenets, he went on, gave rise to the stream-of-consciousness novel and other experimental works. It no longer was possible to think of poetry as the "hiding place of truth," as Goethe had done, or to speak of the tension between mythology and psychology, as Kleist had done. (Heller considers Nietzsche, who celebrated the irrational nature of man, the "first psychologist of Europe.") According to Heller, that was how modern consciousness had been conceived before the advent of Freud and the Age of Analysis. Now, psychology included also the reaction against psychology, such as the response by Kafka, who was "against psychology." All in all, Heller was not critical of Freud but of the "flippant" and distorted applications of his ideas.

In yet another vein, the philosopher William Barrett (1947) argued that writers and philosophers, though occupied with the search for truth, cannot escape the warp of their own existence. He cited as an example Swift's narrative of Gulliver's travels into the countries of the mad. The book was a product of Swift's madness, Barrett maintained, of his introverted disposition, deriving from an excessive need for love during the oedipal period—which led to ambivalence engendered by the indirectness of gratification and the inordinate sense of guilt. Swift's mental existence was precarious; his world of impulses and motives was like that of ordinary people, but writ large. Swift, like all writers and philosophers, Barrett concluded, was particularly vulnerable to pressures by the Zeitgeist—pressures that exacerbate internal tensions.

In the America of the 1960s and 1970s Freudian critics were more numerous and their writing more varied; but they theorized less. They had so little in common that one can give only examples of the applications of psychoanalysis to literature. Now, the literary ctitics not only went more directly to Freud's texts but also to specific works. They extended existing explorations of Dostoevsky, Shakespeare, Swift, Kafka, Lewis Carroll, the Bloomsbury circle, and other classical figures. Elizabeth Dalton, Cushing Strout, Jan Ellen Goldstein, and Steven Marcus are among the best of these critics.

Dalton (1978) agreed with Freud that Dostoevsky's epilepsy was "the central expression of the author's neurosis, and thus fundamental to his life and character." Much of Dostoevsky's fiction, according to Dalton, indirectly explored the meaning of the illness. She substantiated this theme by pointing out that Dostoevsky's novels have several epileptics. Dalton suggested that the breaks in the narrative in *The Idiot* were connected to the bouts of epilepsy, which, despite its organic basis, assumed psychological meaning rooted in Doestoevskys's negatively resolved Oedipus complex. She focused on Myshkin's fits, arguing that, overdetermined by his passive experiences of passion, by his lust, hatred, and aggression, epilepsy was Myshkin's (and Dostoevsky's) unique attribute. Myshkin epitomized the "equivocal relationship between the most debased and the most exalted aspects of human experience" which so profoundly shaped and informed the writer's work. He was not only weak and "idiotic" but capable of mystical experiences and of a "sense of ecstatic merging" that allowed him to regress "to the timeless world of the primitive ego . . . [so that] the fit is also the revenge of the superego which can be deposed only temporarily for the release of sexual and aggressive energy" (pp. 607–08).

Cushing Strout (1979) wrote about the James family, noting the mutual influence of the various members, particularly Henry and William. Each of them, interestingly enough, reported a nightmare. Henry James never explicitly connected his early dream about the Louvre to his fiction, but Strout found that it had served as inspiration for "The Jolly Corner." Even though a number of events and ideas in the dream were reversed in the story, Strout pointed out that ideas and themes overlapped and that the story involved Henry's rivalry with his older brother, William. Although Strout conceded that psychoanalyzing a dead author has many drawbacks, he felt that James's stories, with their ambiguities and ambivalences, are "historical documents in the life of the subject" and must be understood in the context of the author's biography. In sum, Strout held that the powerful themes in James's past, when looked at in conjunction with everything we know about his family, the relations among its members, and about psychoanalysis, found ample expression in his works, but that creative activity did not fully exorcise the ghost in his soul (p. 52).

Jan Ellen Goldstein (1974), a historian, attempted to explain why the Bloomsbury writers helped import psychoanalysis to England: they had been influenced by the Cambridge don G. E. Moore, whose value system had encouraged modes of self-examination that anticipated Freud. Nevertheless, some of these writers remained ambivalent: Virginia Woolf shunned psychoanalysis during her numerous breakdowns and was "satisfied" with the diagnosis of "neurasthenia"; yet, as Goldstein pointed out, *Mrs. Dalloway* was "toying with the applicability of a Freudian conception of mental breakdown." And in "The Leaning Tower," Goldstein found, Woolf depicted the self-absorption of the writers of the 1930s as a symptom of a general cultural neurosis, while also crediting psychoanalysis with eventually curing neuroses (p. 463). Leonard Woolf, on the other hand, published Freud out of admiration and intellectual conviction while remaining personally aloof. *His* version of Freud was summed up in his assertion that " 'the sense of sin is universal in human beings,' that it develops inevitably from infantile sexual feelings and oedipal conflict, [and that it] . . . now and then may erupt, unsuspected and 'with devastating results'" (p. 470). Yet, Woolf's "Freudianism" shifts emphasis. Whereas for Freud "civilization" requires controlling aggressive impulses—with their accompanying sense of guilt or sin—Woolf deems such control feasible and thus concludes that "true 'civilization' is without discontents" (p. 474).

One of the younger critics influenced by Trilling, Steven Marcus, has used his extensive knowledge of psychoanalysis in his study of the sexual mores of *The Other Victorians* (1966). More recently, in "Freud and Dora" (1974), he examined this case history as a piece of writing—constructed like a novel that dealt with symptoms and dreams as well as events. Like a fiction writer, Marcus stated, Freud used his Prefatory Remarks to the Dora case as a framing device, rehearsing motives, reasons, intentions, and events while divulging just enough of Dora's and the case's secrets to keep the reader's interest. Freud, who repeatedly disavowed literary intentions, must have been aware, according to Marcus, of how effectively he was "softening up" the reader with his unique expository and narrative authority. Marcus showed how Freud's prose was similar to that of the fully developed nineteenth-century novel as well as to twentieth-century modernist fiction. He then put Freud himself on the analyst's couch, pointing up, for instance, the dialogue of Freud and Dora about the "hidden connections" and indicating how Freud by the end of this case history had become its central character. Freud blamed Dora for the abrupt termination of the analysis rather than his own negative countertransference, Marcus says, but he used the writing of the case history, much as a creative writer does, to neutralize the "cluster of unanalyzed impulses and ambivalences" in himself.

Marcus maintained that Freud had invented a new form of literature, and literary critic Harold Bloom (1986), after "despairing" of psychoanalysis as an isolated and disreputable therapy, spoke of Freud as the greatest modern writer, "the central imagination of our age" (p. 27). Bloom also called Freud the best exponent of the fiction of the self, whose use of the Oedipus complex located modern poets in relation to their ancestors. And Bloom was much more critical of American Freudians than Trilling had been. In addition, Bloom distanced himself from his deconstructionist colleagues at Yale's Department of Literature, who, though sympathetic to Freud, had their own version of psychoanalytic criticism. The many discussions among them all may have led Bloom to announce that "Freud's importance to our own culture continues to increase almost in direct proportion to the waning of psychoanalysis as a therapy" (Bloom, 1986, p. 26).

The French Connection

Marcus's "Freud and Dora," which originally appeared in *Partisan Review*, was reprinted in virtually every anthology dealing with literature and psychoanalysis. In one of these collections, the editors, Bernheimer and Kahane, credited Marcus with having done the first and probably the best reading of the case as a work of literature (1985, p. ix). This does not imply that Marcus is an exponent of the deconstruction of texts. On the contrary, he is against the general assumptions of the deconstructionists as well as the way they weld Freud's ideas to Marxist, feminist, and other radical or pseudoradical rereadings. In effect, in Marcus's introduction to a new edition of Freud's *Three Essays on the Theory of Sexuality* (1984, pp. 22–41) and in his pieces on cultural change (pp. 165–208) and on the "Rat Man" (pp. 87–164), he continued to represent what some would call "traditional" literary criticism against that of the deconstructionists.

Lacan's contribution on the Dora case, which among other things contained a strong attack on Freud for neglecting the countertransference, had been presented to the Congress of Romance-Language Psychoanalysts in 1951. It was translated into English by Jacqueline Rose for inclusion in Mitchell and Rose, *Feminine Sexuality: Jacques Lacan and the Ecole Freudienne* (1983), and was reprinted by Bernheimer and Kahane because of its extraordinary impact on subsequent interpreters (1985, p. x).

In "Seminar on 'The Purloined Letter,'" Lacan emphasized the role of language even more (1972, pp. 38–72). Language, represented by the letter, Lacan said, confers power upon whoever possesses it—the minister, the queen, Dupin. According to Lacan, "the creator's unconscious memories . . . with his complexes," *excluded* Poe's person from the text; that is, he was "replaced" as the *signifier*.[3] By heuristically separating the narration of the drama from the conditions of its narration, he was reconstructing and reinterpreting the scenes, the protagonists' motives for action, the maneuvers, the guile, and so on, on separate levels. He divided the drama itself into the first scene, in the queen's boudoir, where she receives the compromising letter she must hide from the king. Minister D., noticing the queen's distress, replaces this letter with one of similar appearance—a maneuver the queen watches but cannot prevent. In the second scene, which takes place in the minister's office, the minister succeeds in fooling the police but not the deceitful and mysterious Dupin, who ultimately steals the letter—which also is the object of deceit and counterdeceit.

This interpretation helped Lacan make his mark in the French structuralist movement of the 1950s and 1960s. As he got more and more involved in plays on words, as he invented new metaphors and metonyms, inserted new meanings and discarded old ones, his new psychoanalytic language was taking shape. Now, as he mediated between *signifiers* and *signifieds*, he referred to the purloined letter, among other things, as refuse handled by the police; and he moved from the seal on this letter to the meaning of seals in general, to that of stamps, and of handwriting. He also free-associated to opposers and possessors of letters, to treason and translation. His imaginative and speculative free associations, alternately metonymic and metaphoric, ended up by affirming the "circularity" of the connections among the post office, Baudelairisms, social phenomena, emotions, and motivations. And he concluded that ultimately "the sender receives from the receiver his own message in reverse form . . . [since] a letter always arrives at its destination" (1972, p. 72).

Intercontinental Transferences

In America, Lacan's example opened the floodgates for the most varied inquiries. After his method of association started to catch on in Yale's French department, it migrated to such literary strongholds as Cornell, Johns Hopkins, and Northwestern. In 1977, Shoshana Felman stated in her introduction to the double issue of *Yale French Studies* that the deconstructionists were "reinventing the seemingly self-evident questions of the mutual relationship between literature and psychoanalysis" (p. 5).[4] The "French" critics certainly reinvented this marriage—by "attempting to disrupt the monolithic, master-slave structure," and by "submitting psychoanalysis to the literary perspective." According to Felman they were examining the unconscious components of texts in the way "a psychoanalyst views his patient." Since literature and psychoanalysis *traverse* each other, argued Felman, each "contains the other in its *otherness to itself*, in its *unconscious*," so that the "self-subversive blind spot of psychoanalytical *thought*" would be revealed (pp. 9–10).

Lacan's contribution to Felman's project was the translation of his 1959 presentation to his seminar, "Desire and the Interpretation of Desire in *Hamlet*" (1977, pp. 11–52). His rereading of this drama, not surprisingly, is focused on the relationship between Hamlet and "the Other"—alternately represented by Ophelia and Claudius, occasionally by Laertes and Polonius, and always by the *phallus*, the unconscious narcissistic attachment. Going beyond Freud, who tended to oppose neurosis to health, to art, or to psychosis, Lacan expected to "articulate the true opposition between neurosis and perversion" (p. 16). In perversion, he stated, the "accent is on the object *a*"—the fantasy which represents the substrata of desire; in neurosis the accent is "on the other term of the fantasy, the $." With the help of a complicated formula, Lacan explains the ongoing psychoanalytic experience and the relationship between desire and fantasy (p. 28). This formulation alone was bound to start a flurry of (academic) psychoanalytic deconstructions. But whereas the French enjoyed the provocative aspects of Lacan's playfulness without taking him too seriously, and celebrated him as another intellectual superstar, American literary critics introduced his ideas in the university—on a par with Jacques Derrida, his counterpart in philosophy and his intellectual opponent.[5]

In the 1980s, an increasing number of English departments in American universities were being split between "conventional" and "deconstructionist" Freudian critics. (The psychoanalysts paid little attention to the deconstructionists.)[6] French classical Freudians, however, felt compelled to deal with some of the issues Lacan had raised.[7] When Janine Chasseguet-Smirgel started to focus on the relation between creativity and perversion, and on the ego ideal, she found she had to deal with questions of literature and artistic creation (see chapter 11). But Chasseguet-Smirgel was less concerned with the analysis of literary texts, either traditionally or through deconstruction, than with establishing certain theoretical principles. Nor did she analyze specific authors, as her colleagues Gilles Deleuze ([1969] 1979) and Haidee Faimberg (1977) had done. Instead, she found, for instance, that "regression to the anal-sadistic phase brings about the erosion of the double difference between the sexes and the generations, . . . and [she considered] this regression to be substantially the same as perversion" (Chasseguet-Smirgel, 1984, p. 2). Referring to her previous studies of the Marquis de Sade as the essence of perversion, she now went on to show how Sade's fantasies of transsexuality, adultery, and interchangeable erotogenic zones were related to his pleasure in transgression (p. 3). Sade wanted to break down the barriers separating man from woman, child from adult, mother from son, daughter from father, brother from sister, and the erotogenic zones from each other; he set out to create an undifferentiated *anal* universe, full of endless and repetitive taboos, and of sacrilege. This "anal-sadistic universe of confusion and homogenization, according to Chasseguet-Smirgel, constitutes an imitation or parody of the genital universe of the father" (p. 11). (This theme had been central in Barthes's *Sade Fourier Loyola* and had become a Lacanian preoccupation, and thus a popular topic among French intellectuals.)

Defining perversion as more pathological than sexual deviance, Chasseguet-Smirgel also argued that Caligula, for instance, by having been brought up among the troops and having witnessed tortures and executions, gluttony and adultery, had been conditioned to cruelty in early life. She reinterpreted the original *clinical* narratives of Freud's case of "Little Hans" by comparing them to those of adult perverts, while adding to the analysis of Freud's "Wolf Man"—who remained unable to relinquish his infantile (father) oedipal object—by interpreting the case from the perspective of recent theories of narcissism. She concluded that "phallic monism is a means of healing a part of the narcissistic injury, . . . [stemming from] the child's helplessness" (p. 53). Applying these concepts to "Aestheticism, Creation and Perversion" Chasseguet-Smirgel went to Rilke, Oscar Wilde, and Shakespeare, to show how the fear of having his anality exposed is a necessary component of the pervert's existence. Basically, Chasseguet-Smirgel reexamined a vast body of literature from Sophocles to Hans Christian Andersen in a provocative and idiosyncratic manner.

During this same period, the philosopher J. -B. Pontalis, who had been Lacan's disciple, rooted the "Freudian saga" in the tradition of Nietzsche, in therapy and in Freud's reading of Michelangelo's Moses (1970, p. 5). In his *Nouvelle Revue de Psychanalyse*, Pontalis printed philosophical and literary symposia on large themes: Ideals, the Archaic, Views on French Psychoanalysis, the Confusion in Thinking. These contributions tended to be in the realm of metapsychology, as their authors rethought the psychoanalytic past and took on specific clinical issues.

The French classical analysts Madelaine and Henri Vermorel (1985) traced Freud's intellectual trajectory "from Oedipus to Moses," from Greek to Germanic culture, especially to Goethe and Schiller. By placing Freud in the tradition of Schlegel, Schleiermacher, Schelling, Spinoza, and Rousseau, as well as in "the Germanic scientific romanticism" (Helmholtz's "unconscious inference," Brücke's "physiological reductionism," von Müller's idealism, Meynert's "mythological anatomo-physiology of the brain") and in Jewish humor, the authors argued that psychoanalysis was a product of the prevalent "romantic *Bildung*" (p. 4).

Maria Torok (1981), though a classical analyst, called the analytic journey a passage through words—words that pass between the patient on the couch and the analyst in the easy chair. She treated psychoanalytic texts as narratives and emphasized especially those by Ferenczi, Melanie Klein, and other Hungarian psychoanalysts in order to show that these pioneers had been unfairly relegated to the sidelines.[8] Torok appealed to deconstructionists because she emphasized verbal residues, the history of names—particularly the father's name, which takes on special meaning because of childhood experiences. What Torok termed the *bizarrerie* of Kleinian theory, for example, could be apprehended only by unraveling the secrets of "Melanie Mell's" (Klein's) own childhood fantasies, and the resulting centrality of the breast (p. 214).

Torok's rather idiosyncratic themes are closely linked to her observations of patients. But she has upset her fellow members in the Société Psychanalytique de Paris by championing what she calls a closer contact and thus "another hearing" and rejects "finding the machinery behind what a patient says," behind oedipal trauma—by concentrating more on the effects of contact and memories of touching (1983, personal communication).

These activities alone would have placed Torok on the periphery of the SPP. But she also contributed to *Confrontation*, the controversial journal started by the Freudian René Major, and flirted with Derrida's brand of deconstruction. Together with her late husband, Nicolas Abraham, she had reread the case of the Wolf-Man and had concluded that Freud, Ruth Mack Brunswick, and Muriel Gardiner, all of whom had written about the case had not understood the Wolf-Man because they did not know Russian—his native (and sometimes dream) language—and did not take account of the fact that his early language had been his nanny's German. Furthermore, Torok (with Abraham, [1976] 1986) was critical of Jones's translations and interpretations of Freud's informal notes because they ignore, for instance, the meaning of Freud's use of various abbreviations of the unconscious as UBw, or conscience-perception as WBs. By *designifying* these abbreviations from their customary semantic use, stated Abraham and Torok, Jones had relegated them to a state of "*anasemie*." Such a state, then, was found to be similar to that of some melancholic patients, in whom an "autonomous *crypte* may have been installed within the self" (this state is the result of early trauma that prevented identification with an Other), which, in turn, may have given rise to a *cryptofantasm*, that is, to a phenomenon that belongs to metapsychology (p. 299).

Confrontation was filled with deconstructionist pieces by such writers as Torok, Derrida, and Felman, as well as with contributions from psychoanalysts like Major and Imre Hermann (Ferenczi's disciple who had gone into internal exile in Hungary). Given the deconstructionist dictum that every text is fair game, a number of proponents set out to work on Balzac, Flaubert, Proust, and Oscar Wilde as well as writing on biblical, political, and ethnic issues. *Confrontation* increasingly attracted classical Freudians as well as Lacanians and analysts of other hues. Only in exceptional cases did it print articles by nonpsychoanalysts.

In sum, French classical analysts, like their American counterparts, wrote about questions of the unconscious in Western literary traditions and in specific works. But because the French language itself is more rhetorical than English or German, French Freudians more often resorted to literary analogies when discussing clinical material. This also led some of them to use

Lacanian formulations, which are quite literary. So, when their texts were translated, they appeared in *Diacritics*, *Yale French Studies*, and other publications read by students of deconstruction rather than in psychoanalytic journals.

Across the Channel

The emigration of Lacanian concepts to England paralleled their voyage to America, but on a much smaller scale. Along with the subversive politics of the heretical *Anti-Oedipus* of Deleuze and Guattari ([1972] 1977; see chapter 12),[9] English literary critics first applied Lacan's notions to issues of feminism. These inevitably were being mixed up with literary exploits, with individual and global political aims, and with the idealistic components of old and new Freud-Marx syntheses. In addition, the issues were aired at academic conferences where the abstract level of discourse allowed for theoretical and intellectual excursions, which practicing psychoanalysts usually did not go in for.

Victoria Hamilton, for instance, who had taken a degree in philosophy at University College, London (with Richard Wollheim, another psychoanalytic critic), and then had started her training at the Tavistock Clinic, "incorporated" the "transition" between psychoanalysis and literature in her inquiry into *Narcissus and Oedipus* (1982). Following object relations and attachment theory, Hamilton recounted and reexplored the Greek myths Freud had used to explain his theories of psychic development—through their adaptations by Shakespeare, Robert Graves, Gregory Bateson, and many others—and then linked these to subsequent psychoanalytic interpretations. She challenged Freud's theory of the unconscious from the perspective of child development, as she interspersed her own observations of children with fragments of the myth of Narcissus (p. 113).

Juliet Mitchell pointed out that Freud's work dealt with the unconscious rather than with child development and that Hamilton was emphasizing behavior in children rather than their unconscious (and as yet unknown) motives (1984, p. 280). Still, Hamilton's reading of the classical myths, I believe, was related to problems of child analysis (most psychoanalytic roads lead to child development) and to the issues sparked by the traumatic "controversies" between Anna Freud and Melanie Klein (see chapter 11). Mitchell, however, defended the tragic nature of Freud's vision, while Hamilton, in a more Kleinian vein, thought that the "good-enough mother" would facilitate adaptation. Clearly, Mitchell's radicalism, which put the roots of neurosis as much in society as in the family, could not accept such a view.

There also were "traditional" English literary critics, such as Richard Ellman, who thought that psychoanalysis had disrupted the literary biographers' pretensions and that "writers [who] fancied they were eagles are only clams" (1984, p. 466). Drawing on a wide range of literature, Ellman described how the word *Freudian* unfortunately got to mean *sexual*. He also criticized some post-Freudian biographers for distorting facts in order to stay within Freudian theory; but he concluded that Freud nevertheless remains a model—albeit "a tricky one" (p. 478).

The German Scenario

In postwar Germany the relation between literature and psychoanalysis was not examined until the 1970s. By then, the enormous need for therapists was beginning to be filled, and German psychoanalysts could allow themselves to give their energies to literary exploration and, as Goethe had admonished, make their fathers' tradition their own. Before then, the interpretation of literary texts by *any* German psychoanalyst, I believe, would have appeared frivolous and self-indulgent.

Psyche was the first publication to print such essays; and Margarete Mitscherlich-Nielsen contributed early on. In 1976, she interpreted Kafka's fiction as she would a psychoanalytic case. By "using understanding and intuition," the analyst is able "to penetrate to the unconscious meanings of literary or biographic texts," she maintained, as she tried to explain why Kafka deemed *Metamorphosis* an indiscretion and why he called writing both "the most important thing in the world" and "a form of prayer." She explored Kafka's feelings of loneliness, his lifelong friendship with Max Brod, his closeness to his sister Ottla, the influence of Prague anti-Semitism and of his parents, and the roots of his self-destructiveness in early object relations. In sum, her treatment leaned on ego psychology in its implication that Kafka's art "protected" him from his neurosis and in her conclusion that "the nature of the description protects the conscious mind of the reader" ([1976] 1983, p. 287).

Johannes Cremerius (1979) described Musil's *Man without Qualities* as "psychoanalytic fiction *par excellence*." He noted how Musil had oscillated between accepting, rejecting, and denying psychoanalysis, while at the same time trying to find his own psychological solutions. Typical of his time, he chose to "forget" this knowledge, even though he was in touch with Alfred Döblin, who had written on psychoanalysis and whose work he admired.

Cremerius concluded that Musil's writings "displayed the paradoxes, crises and needs of the time, as well as a mirror for us." This essay also used the methods of the more traditional Anglo-Saxon psychoanalysts, at a time when much of Musil's work was unavailable in English. These methods continue to be applied to works by Austrian and German authors such as Raimund, Nestroy, and Eichendorff, who probably will never be translated, as well as to Rilke whose reputation is global. But as German psychoanalytic critics increasingly "analyzed" local writers they turned to essentially German themes exploring the Hitler period and its aftermath.[10]

Most of the German psychoanalysts who applied analysis to literature were more interested than Cremerius in the "adaptive" themes of literary and Freudian exegeses, which had become the code word for conservatism, anti-Marxism, imperialism, and "American hegemony"—whether imputed to psychoanalytic associations or to the forces of occupation. Others, particularly Freudians around the Kassel Institute for Psychoanalysis, explored "the three relatives"—psychoanalysis, literature, and *Literaturwissenschaft* (science of literature)—from current perspectives such as the divided consciousness of psychoanalysis, the tension between individual and society, the consequences of "medicalization," the split between theoretical and clinical pursuits, and the impact of the environment on psychoanalytic thought. In order to comprehend such intricate subjects, these psychoanalytic critics added cultural history and mythology to their topics of investigation. In their publication *Fragmente*, they addressed the importance of forgetting—which in Germany *always* refers also to the Nazi period, whether in general discussion, in fiction generally, or in analyses of the reception of movies about Hitler and television programs about the Holocaust (Perner and Tholen, 1983, p. 10).

Because the "psychoanalysis and literature enterprise" came so late, the German contingent had the many Anglo-Saxon studies and approaches to choose from. Students of American studies would analyze specific and often minor American writers in a variety of psychoanalytic fashions.[11] More frequently, however, they turned to German authors whose works also demanded a thorough grounding in philosophy. These German analysts examined events, for example, through the terror-ridden dreams of Jewish protagonists, or they focused on the defense mechanisms of Nazis. Such psychoanalytic criticism, for instance, viewed Kant's critique of pure reason as a literary text, compared German and French interpretations of it, and then concluded that Germans ultimately had limited the public use of reason to proclamations by intellectual and political authorities. Thus they had learned to be "critical of themselves, yet obedient to the state" (Perner and Tholen, 1983, p. 11). In France, however, critiques of king and country, these analysts found, had encouraged the emancipation of citizens, thus furthering individualism.

As the Germans were catching up on what Anglo-Saxon Freudians had been doing for years, some of them looked to the French and commented on Barthes's "u-topic location" of language—as a possible means of encouraging social change. Literature may be employed as the means to self-examination, argued Peter Dettmering (1983), who analyzed Jean Paul's 1803 political romance, *Titan*, in terms of the author's motivations.[12]

By the 1980s, regular meetings of psychoanalysts and literary critics were held in Freiburg on such themes as "Methods of Dream Interpretation in Literary Texts," "Sartre's Notion of 'Neurosis-Art,'" and "Ideas on the Writing of Women" (Krauss and Wolff, 1982). Now, the psychoanalysts addressed questions of "Fascist Socialization and Social Criticism in Such Works as Bernhard Vesper's Autobiography, *Die Reise*," and "Social-Psychological Thoughts on Rousseau's Autobiography," and "The Fantasy World of Karl May" (Cremerius et al., 1981). In 1984, at the third meeting of the Freiburg group, they looked into such issues as "Brother Hitler, Faustus and the Doctor in Vienna," "The Subjectivity of the Biographer," and "The Resurrection of Gottfried Benn from the Spirit of Fascism" (Cremerius et al., 1983). And the series on "The Psychology of the Twentieth Century" led to a volume on "Transcendence, Imagination and Creativity," in which Heinrich Mettler, Claus D. Eck, Sebastian Goeppert, and Peter Dettmering wrote on the influence of psychoanalysis on modern literature.[13]

Dettmering, who was most prolific, also wrote psychoanalytic film criticism (1984), as did a number of other psychoanalysts. Margarete Mitscherlich-Nielsen and Mechthild Krüger-Zeul dealt with specific movies and applied the various psychoanalytic methods for literary works to *Holocaust* (1979) and *Maria Braun* (1986). Historians such as Barbara Eppensteiner, Karl Fallend, and Johannes Reichmayr (1987) reminded us that when psychoanalysis got public attention in the 1920s moviemakers started to apply it: although Freud refused to get involved, Karl Abraham and Hanns Sachs, in 1925 and 1926, cooperated with G. W. Pabst in producing *Secrets of the Soul*, which was intended to familiarize the public with psychoanalysis.[14]

Fragmente attests to the seriousness of literary psychoanalysts' efforts to construct a "metadisciplinary method of literary analysis" as Tholen and Wetzel, among others, maintained, for instance, in the November 1985 issue. The methods of these German scholars and analysts were similar to those used elsewhere, but the themes and conclusions always kept coming back to

German issues, and this indicates once more the protean qualities of psychoanalytic concerns. Thomas Mann and Robert Musil, Goethe and Frisch,
Horkheimer and Adorno, and other Germans appear consistently in German
contributions. And nowhere but in Germany does one find anything on
Wilhelm Busch, the popular writer of adult and children's stories (Pietzcker,
1984). Nor is there as strong an interest in "art and neurosis" in Germany as
there was at the turn of the century.[15]

In an entirely different vein, the German Lacanians who had established
themselves in 1978 in Berlin reprinted a number of Lacan's lectures in *Der
Wunderblock* with their own elaborations.[16] Like Lacan, they juxtaposed the
imaginary, the real, and the symbolic, and they emphasized the importance of
the phallus in every conceivable connection. But they sometimes addressed
new topics, from Leonardo to Habermas, and from Samuel Weber's reading
of Lacan (1982) to Genet's views of sexuality.[17]

Literature and Psychoanalysis: A Proliferation of Tongues

Everywhere, psychoanalysts, writers, and literary critics had their own versions of psychoanalytic studies. In America, not even the contributors could
agree on what their activities ultimately were proving or what they amounted
to; they all had their own prejudices. Thus psychoanalysts no longer produced such monumental essays as Joseph Coltrera did in 1965, when he drew
on much of Western writing and the Freudians' elaborations on it to suggest
a psychoanalytic aesthetic based on ego psychology. In 1978, Alan Roland,
for example, edited an overview of the French discussions by such psychoanalysts as Serge Leclaire, André Green, and J. -B. Pontalis, including papers
comparing the French and American sociocultural milieus, American inquiries into creativity and the creative process, and Lacanian discussions of works
by Proust, Sartre, and Pirandello. In the same year, Geoffrey Hartman (1978)
maintained that literary case studies and interpretations that reveal the author's hidden motives (be it love or hate) have become dated and that the
emphasis now must be on "understanding from within the institutional development of psychoanalysis, and from the inner development of Freud's
writing." By including an examination of the psychoanalyst's profession and
status, Hartman cast psychoanalysis as both written and social text (p. vii).

In France, Julia Kristeva applied psychoanalysis to expose the illusions of
fascism and Stalinism (1982a). Fantasies and beliefs, she held, may serve as an
antidote to a writer's political discourse. Thus she perceived Céline's anti-
Semitism, for example, as a manifestation of the crisis of modern interpretive

systems inherent in the symbolic function. And in a book published the same year ([1980] 1982b), she psychoanalytically examined literary works dealing with revulsion and horror from the unclean, self-disgust at contamination, and the "undoing" rituals we often take for granted. In Germany, Frederick Wyatt, a native Viennese analyst who after practicing in the United States returned to teach and practice in Freiburg, concentrated on the narrative aspects of psychoanalysis by comparing the entire process, much as Freud had done, to story-telling, listening, and interpreting (1986a, pp. 193–210).

In our own collection, my coeditor and I set out to provide a general overview of *Literature and Psychoanalysis* (Kurzweil and Phillips, 1983) by assembling some of the best work that had been done—from Freud to the recent "French connection." Since then, the multitude of studies by literary critics and analysts and the psychoanalytic interpretations of artists' psyches and creations has grown geometrically.

The psychoanalysts' habit of using literary works to illustrate their theories or construct a new hermeneutics has been perpetuated in attempts to hold external critics at bay, as well as to sway colleagues to their own views and methods of analysis. Stanley Leavy, a Freudian who in 1970 wrote on Keats, ten years later published a book about Lacan and was arguing for a variety of linguistic approaches to psychoanalysis (for example, Leavy, 1980, 1983a, 1983b). In fact, Leavy, whose scholarship is wide-ranging, was not the only analyst who now started to adapt some of the ideas of literary critics and philosophers and try to convince his colleagues that their own ego-psychological approach was too narrow.

As cross-disciplinary gatherings of Freudians and literary critics proliferated in America, literary scholars learned more and more about the contingencies and repercussions of clinical theory and practice, and some of them extended the sympathies they previously had had only for Freud to his "sons." Furthermore, when American Freudians began to lose patients to nonmedical therapists, they demedicalized, however unofficially, by training a number of literary critics, historians, and philosophers. Some of the new trainees became nonmedical psychoanalysts. One of these, Gail Reed (1983), explored Voltaire's *Candide* in connection with the readers' "defensive and characterological responses," with their identifications and countertransferences to the "infantile openness" of Candide. She noted that the reader keeps oscillating between participating in the dangers of Candide's world and the safer one of the omniscient, objective narrator, while the plot contributes to his identification with wishes for safety and security. In a later contribution, Reed (1985) "defended" the psychoanalysts' approach to criticism against those literary critics who stick too closely to their texts and thereby tend to overlook the unconscious elements psychoanalysts deal with. This happens, she held, because listening to a patient differs drastically from reading clinical theory—even though Freud's study of Leonardo did *resemble* a clinical investigation (p. 257). Reed, who is a classical Freudian, also used the language of literary critics as she commented on the two polarities of interpretation (in the comments on Leonardo) each corresponding to one set of assumptions toward language. And she cautioned Freudians against glibly affirming their dogma as well as against taking "a holiday from the clinical stance" (1985).

Surely, analysts such as Leavy and Reed are the best public relations emissaries the Freudians could wish for. Louise Kaplan (1987), whose special expertise derived from work with perverse patients, is another in her analysis of the artistic creations, falsehoods, and perversions of the eighteenth-century "impostor-poet" Thomas Chatterton. Having been exposed to deconstruction—whether they liked or dismissed it—these psychoanalysts addressed the linguistic questions in all their ramifications. And because they had the proper credentials, even the doctrinaire ego psychologists could not dismiss them as unable to deal with unconscious material or as superficial. So, as Freudians and neo-Freudians, deconstructionist and "straight" critics, psychoanalytic historians and biographers, entered more and more into dialogues with one another, Oedipus began to be mediated by anti-Oedipus, and the "traditional" approach by its deconstructionist foe.[18] Everywhere, these transfusions themselves have enlivened the debates about literature and psychoanalysis, although there seems to be no way to bring coherence to the many psychoanalytic readings and reinterpretations. In effect, both literature and psychoanalysis continue to pursue the endless search for the roots of the unconscious and have come no closer to the answers than Oedipus was at the end of his life. But, like Oedipus, they cannot give up.

Part Three

PSYCHOANALYSIS
SINCE 1945

Chapter 9

The Organizational Network

Freud wanted his movement to be carried by the momentum of its discoveries, and he expected his faithful followers to disseminate them. To that end, he developed a strong international organization, with Karl Abraham, Sándor Ferenczi, Ernest Jones, Otto Rank, Hanns Sachs, and later on Max Eitingon as his executive committee. But Freud tended to overestimate the talents of his followers because he underestimated his own charisma and the competition among his heirs.

The personalities of the leading disciples were bound to dominate both organizational and theoretical directions of the movement. Were Ferenczi to have his way, the relationship between analyst and analysand would overshadow the theory; were Rank to succeed, therapy would become as important as analysis. As it happened, the team of Abraham and Eitingon won out, and scientific theory soon started to rule the roost. We can only speculate about whether this would have occurred had they been less energetic and gifted administrators or had Jones been at the helm earlier on. Still, Abraham's and Eitingon's organizational talents were enhanced by institutional conditions in Berlin and by the fact that Eitingon had a wealthy and generous father.

As long as Freud was alive, the disciples had cooperated. He had managed to keep rivalries within bounds, by praise or simple control. But Freud died as Europe was falling apart, as 90 percent of psychoanalysis was moving to Anglo Saxon territory, and just after the IPA had lost official control over the APA. At that time, many Berliners came to America, where their theoretical and organizational models were soon adopted. In fact, the German contingent was central in transplanting the movement, along with the requirements for professional access they had developed. Anna Freud had anticipated such an understanding between the Germans and the Americans. Since she did not have a medical degree and would not be a second-class member of an analytic community that was certain to question her intellectual leadership, she and Freud chose to accept Jones's invitation and go to England in 1938.

In England, however, Anna Freud found that the ideas of Melanie Klein, who had been in London since 1926, had begun to dominate the British Psycho-Analytical Society. So when Jones did not unconditionally back Anna Freud's interpretations as the only valid ones, theoretical differences divided the Freudians. Jones mediated between the two "prima donnas" in order to preserve unity—alas not harmony—within the London institute.[1]

The English Controversy

The struggle between Anna Freud and Melanie Klein was based on theoretical and personal rivalries antedating the so-called Controversial Discussions of 1943 and 1944. Both women knew that how psychoanalysis was conceptualized would determine its intellectual future, what candidates would be trained, for how long they would need to be analyzed, and by whom. Therefore, the victor in these discussions could expect to control Freud's heritage. That was why the London analysts—even while under siege by German bombers and working with children displaced and disturbed by the war—were so involved in their own battles. Jones was attracted to Melanie Klein's views but at the same time did not want to cross Anna Freud. As president of both the London institute and the IPA, he wished above all to hold the movement together, to do whatever was necessary to avoid a split that would weaken it. In typical English fashion, he expected to "muddle through" by imprecision and flexibility. In a country long noted for not pushing things to the extreme and where inclusiveness is considered a supreme virtue, it was possible and probably easier than elsewhere to prevail upon warring psychoanalysts not to let acrimony get the upper hand.

Scientific disagreements and struggles for power could not be avoided, particularly in setting up training standards for candidates. Jones, in order to preserve his society, began by praising Freud's genius and playing down his own attraction to Klein's focus on anxiety as the root of neuroses, while assuring Anna Freud of his loyalty. He stayed above the fray by officially stating that both Anna Freud and Melanie Klein were perpetuating Freud's ideas. Thus Jones managed an uneasy truce, even though he could not prevent their personal animosity from growing or their followers from clearly taking sides (Segal, 1979, p. 93).

In order for both Klein and Anna Freud to pursue their own intellectual paths and train students within the institute, the British analysts agreed that the society would accommodate three distinct schools: the followers of Melanie Klein (Group A), those of Anna Freud (Group B, and the Middle or Independent Group, which initially accepted some of the ideas of each. (According to Kohon [1986], it was the Middle Group that would turn out to be both independent and innovative by developing the theory of object relations.) All three groups were to be equally represented on administrative bodies. New candidates would be allowed to follow their own inclinations: they were to have their instruction in one of the schools for two years and then were to attend a combined seminar for a year taught by analysts of different orientations (p. 110). Ultimately, this gentlemen's agreement would provide the English psychoanalysts with a broader range of options than did the narrower "American" ego psychology. As Joseph Sandler (1984a) was to state many years later, "psychoanalytic taste corresponded to the training one had, but one learned to listen to others, and this allowed for eclecticism." But this was an unexpected and unforeseen boon.

During World War II, these internal struggles separated the English analysts from their American colleagues even more than did the mine-ridden Atlantic. The situation of the Londoners, whose theoretical differences seemed to provide a favorable climate for the animated debates by such third-generation Freudians as Michael Balint, Wilfred Bion, and Donald Winnicott, militated against the increasingly hierarchical conditions the Americans were creating. In any event, the Londoners' institutional accommodation allowed for theoretical differences: no one in England ever would have suggested, as some Americans were to do in 1975, that Kleinians be disqualified as training analysts (*IPA Bulletin*, 1976, p. 187). For the intrainstitutional diversity of the Londoners encouraged organizational flexibility. Much later, whenever ideological factors threatened to divide the members of a psychoanalytic organization, this institute would be held up as exemplary.

In fact, similar issues surround every split and near-split. Implicitly, the problems center on theoretical ascendancy, which, in turn, influences policies of referrals and potential income. The Freudians themselves often explain the opinions of colleagues with whom they disagree as transference to the theory or to the clinical approach of their own analysts, or as the longing for or identification with a father. But, whether they sooner or later consider their "analyst-fathers" sterile, or talk of generational and oedipal revolts, they do so in psychoanalytic terms—always stressing the unconscious motives of individuals over institutional priorities. The latter, I believe, are equally at stake.

The IPA Is Reconstituted

The meeting of the IPA in Zurich in August 1949 was a watershed: the first one in eleven years, the first one after the war, and the last one to have an original disciple at the helm. Jones, the only surviving member of Freud's committee, was about to step down as president. It had been decided to meet in Switzerland, he informed the assembled members, in part to "reward" the Swiss for their neutrality during the war and in part to recall their early support of the IPA. Jones used this "historic occasion" to stress the need for unity and restate the IPA's functions. The prewar disagreements between the American and European contingents, he claimed, had been settled, and they now were ready to reestablish international cooperation.

Jones began by reporting on the composition of the organization. Of the approximately 800 members, about 450 were American (180 from New York, 50 from Chicago, 52 from Boston, 43 from Washington/Baltimore, and the others from Detroit, Los Angeles, Philadelphia, and San Francisco); 122 were British. This meant that whereas twenty years earlier 90 percent of the membership spoke German, now over 70 percent spoke English (*IPA Bulletin*, 1949, p. 181). Outside the "English" realm, only the Dutch had a functioning training institute, with 3 certified training analysts and 39 members, although societies in Italy, Israel, and Sweden expected to grow and establish institutes soon. Jones announced that twenty societies had asked for admission to the IPA; some of these had been recognized provisionally, and others had been told to wait. He went on to describe the inordinate difficulties psychoanalytic institutions had faced during the Nazi era and to commemorate Freud along with eighty-two other members who had died, fifteen of them in concentration camps. He asked the membership to resolve various problems which had divided the committees, such as the acceptability of two Brazilian societies and the reconstitution of the German association. Both issues hinged on the viability of psychoanalysis in repressive societies. Indeed, the members of the executive committee had not managed to agree on just how much political freedom is required for patients to talk freely and how far removed analysts must be from the ruling politicians. Although they upheld Freud's view that persons who must keep military or political secrets cannot free-associate, they did not agree on whether they themselves could function as analysts in a police state.[2]

Now that Freud was no longer there to adjudicate, these knotty problems had to be settled by new statutes. The analysts voted to publish all statutes in the *Bulletin* of the association and in the *International Journal of Psychoanalysis*, to which English-speaking members had to subscribe. To accommodate analysts in places that did not have a psychoanalytic society, they created a category for direct members. Finally, they agreed that local statutes could not contradict those of the IPA. All in all, the proceedings were quite formal: the revised rules, though seemingly simple and objective, incorporated complicated compromises. No one seemed to realize how soon these rules would have to be circumvented.

Essentially, the revival of the IPA was to facilitate international cooperation and growth. The Freudians realized that they needed to remain flexible to allow for the diverse conditions psychoanalysis was facing in specific countries and that intellectual unity was increasingly hard to come by. But they did not yet fathom how very differently their member organizations would develop in response to national and local conditions.

By vesting a great deal of authority in committees pledged to confidentiality, particularly in the committee on admissions, the Freudians expected to solve the basic problems about whom to admit to candidacy. Such committees, it was hoped, might be able to mediate between ideological differences and to dissipate the heat before an issue would be put before the membership. Elected officials had a great deal of discretionary power and were expected to defuse potential eruptions. Thus the minutes of IPA meetings give the impression of much more harmony than ever existed.

After 1949, elected functionaries would prepare major decisions at precongress meetings: they would suggest members for committees and agree on future congress locations and on topics and keynote speakers. Basically, they were to hammer out the mechanics of international cooperation and alignments. The Freudians decided also that members of the local society where a congress was to be held would automatically become the organizers of that congress. These persons would have a good deal to say about the program, and their newly acquired visibility would lead to other powerful positions later.

Eventually, the democratization of the IPA and demographic shifts in membership required that new countries and geographical areas be represented on the executive committee. This meant that leadership would not always be in the hands of the most experienced psychoanalysts. Quite often, congenial compromise candidates would be voted in. In this the IPA was like other international bodies. But whatever their qualities, the officers of the IPA constituted an elite that functioned more or less like the earlier committee. This similarity led some of them to ignore the fact that their leadership position was based to some extent on shifting alliances related to committee work rather than on talent or charisma alone.

Holding IPA office ensured the analysts' future international standing and provided a forum for their own theoretical preferences. Further, IPA officials, as members of enabling committees passing on new societies and institutes, had access to privileged knowledge about their colleagues' professional and personal lives. Although they were sworn to secrecy, the information they gathered provided a source of power, both within the IPA and in the profession at large. So even if they did not use this power, committee members, being privy to secrets, were sometimes accused of being devious or highhanded or authoritarian when they did not welcome a new society or accept a regular member as training analyst.

This remains a crucial and yet insoluble dilemma of all psyshoanalytic bodies. Secrecy *is* mandatory. Otherwise potential members could not be subjected to the necessary scrutiny in evaluating them: their colleagues would not report their doubts, and predicting how they might interact with patients would be even more difficult. Yet this degree of confidentiality does go against all principles of democracy.

Only rarely does the membership find out exactly what goes on during closed committee meetings, and then long after the fact. Indeed, IPA committees have enormous discretionary power. In Portugal in 1967, for instance, the Visiting Enabling Committee rejected two of the four candidates they had been asked to approve. Four full-fledged analysts had proposed them in order to form an affiliated study group in preparation for starting a society. The visitors judged that one of the four candidates was too rigid and that another suffered from paranoid schizophrenic symptoms (Parin, 1984, p. 631). It soon turned out that their Portuguese colleagues were aware of these individuals' personality problems but found their acceptance expedient because they were well connected to the ruling dictator; the admission of the candidates, their sponsors hoped, would help legitimate psychoanalysis in Portugal; their rejection, it was feared, would brand psychoanalysis a subversive activity. Faced with this choice, three members of the IPA committee decided to close their eyes; the fourth member, Paul Parin, resigned. Later, Parin (1984) accused his colleagues of "adaptation" in order to gain influence and maintained that by "caving in" they were depriving psychoanalysis of its necessary critical bite.

The German psychoanalyst Hans Füchtner reported a somewhat similar crisis within the Brazilian Psychoanalytic Society of Rio de Janeiro during the mid-1970s. A candidate had allegedly helped a torturer by watching over the psychic and physical state of the victim (Füchtner, 1984). Füchtner had relied on his own observations at the Brazilian analysts' meetings and on the information from those who were closely involved in the dispute. But, given the need for secrecy imposed by the conditions of the dictatorship, it is unclear whether Füchtner was too harsh, or Galina Schneider (1985), a former president of the Brazilian institute who backed the accused was too forgiving. Still, there is no doubt that something objectionable did occur. According to Füchtner, the Brazilian analysts often treated representatives of the dictatorship and guerrillas, whereas according to Schneider "members of neither of these groups were looking for insight but were acting out their conflicts in their daily lives." Füchtner accused specific analysts of being authoritarian, while Schneider pointed out that the Brazilian analysts had tried successfully to tighten and clarify their statutes to cope with the situation. What she held against Füchtner most of all was his judgmental stance and the resulting polarization of the protagonists. Like Parin, she stated, he was arguing "against all forms of political repression" without fully understanding the specific context. The most recent comment, however, by Helena Celinia Besserman Vianna (1988), points out that the accused (his name "Lobo" means "Wolf," he used the pseudonym "Lamb," and he was defended by a lawyer named "Lion") was denounced by a former victim after the regime became somewhat democratized, and thus he is unfit to be a psychoanalyst.

At the time, the IPA had sent a fact-finding committee to investigate the Brazilian crisis. Schneider concluded that the committee's fairness had helped avert a split in the Brazilian organization and that the dispute had democratized her institute. But the IPA had its own interests as well, insofar as it wanted to retain its members and attract new ones and to enforce its benign rule. In fact, to judge by the importance given the reports on membership, the IPA tends to measure its success at least in part by the growth in membership.

The figures, however, are not reliable. Institutes in Brazil, Argentina, Italy, and Finland as a rule do not report membership numbers. Individuals who fail to pay dues may or may not be counted. Persons accepted in one country may move to another without advising the IPA office. True, attendance at IPA meetings is routinely reported in the *Bulletin* (categorized in terms of members, guests, and candidates), but attendance may be indicative of financial status or of the number of vacationing analysts rather than of institutional viability. In 1982, for instance, IPA president Adam Limentani, a Londoner of Italian origin, announced that membership was around 5,000, that there are approximately 350 new members every year, and that there had been a demographic shift into formerly less developed areas, so that North America now had 45 percent of the total membership, Europe, Asia, and Australia 37 percent, and Latin America 18 percent. (Five or six years earlier these figures had been North America 51 percent, Europe, Asia, and Australia 36 percent, and Latin America 13 percent; *Bulletin*, 1982, p. 102). But if these figures and rates were constant and there were 800 members in 1949, the IPA ought to have had 12,350 members (minus those who died) in 1982.

The American Psychoanalytic Association

The IPA's interregnum during the Second World War had moved the APA to the center, and the APA postwar statutes had enlarged the American group's sphere. Between 1946 and 1960, thirteen psychoanalytic societies, eight institutes, and four teaching centers were officially recognized in the United States. So were a number of institutes connected to universities, which were not directly linked with their local psychoanalytic societies. By the end of the 1960s, the APA reported that its membership included 1,302 individuals, twenty-nine local societies, and twenty-one approved training institutes. Apparently, the growth in institutional bases did not bring with it a corresponding number of members.

As more and more psychiatrists and intellectuals were won over to psychoanalysis—some of them attracted by Erik Erikson's notions of development and identity or by anthropologists' and sociologists' popularizations—more and more prospective candidates applied for training. In response, the APA tightened its training requirements. In fact, this success was taken by some as proof that medicalization had not hurt them. So they continued to ignore the existence of the nonmedical Freudians as well as all other therapies.[3]

Not every Freudian was sanguine about the situation. When Siegfried Bernfeld spoke to the San Francisco Psychoanalytic Society in 1953, he pointed to the contradictions inherent in psychoanalytic training. He maintained that teachers of reading and of psychoanalysis, as members of professions controlled by specific rules and statutes, both incorporate some sort of authoritarianism: but only psychoanalysis, which deals with unconscious mechanisms, allows this authoritarian attitude to become part of the learner's ego-ideal. When this happens, Bernfeld went on, the analytic pair is no longer able to interact freely. And this danger is heightened when medical education is imposed: doctors are expected to exude authority. Hence inherent contradictions of psychoanalytic and medical training cannot be analyzed, and candidates tend to become servile, thus perpetuating their infantile traits.

In 1960, Kurt Lewin and Helen Ross addressed these issues by focusing on the didactic shortcomings of supervising analysts and on the fact that clinical teaching is often done at the expense of theory. They found that the inordinate length of the training contributes to the high dropout rate of candidates. Like Bernfeld, they criticized the candidates' dependence on their teachers—an issue that would not get onto the official agenda until the Vienna meetings of 1971 (Kurzweil, 1971).

Bernfeld's talk was not printed until 1962, nine years after his death, and the issue was not taken seriously until a few APA presidents began to address it—Bandler in 1960, Rangell in 1962 and 1967, Ritvo in 1971, Astley in 1974. In their official capacity, presidents realized that fewer requests for new organizations were reaching the APA, fewer candidates were applying, analysts were turning away fewer patients, and the average age of members was rising sharply. Presumably, the most prestigious Freudians, who were in demand as training analysts, were less aware of the declining general demand.

Some of their colleagues blamed the lack of new members on a dearth of ideas rather than on organizational stagnation. Anna Freud, for example, thought that psychoanalysis was not in a "creative era." This led Charles K. Hofling and Robert W. Meyers (1972) to ask American Freudians what "discoveries" they thought had been made in the thirty years since Freud's death. A third of the respondents were uneasy with the term *discovery*; another third mentioned elaborations on Freud's ideas (narcissism, object relations theory, separation-individuation); others cited investigations into "society" and "behavior." Because "no single technical advance received a majority of votes, although ego analysis approached it," the authors concluded that the major discoveries had been made by Freud (p. 520). But how, we must ask, can a movement that had flourished on discoveries continue to thrive without adding new ones?

An ever increasing theoretical narrowness apparently debilitated the APA. But this narrowness was induced primarily by the tightening and perfecting of the organization, which imposed more and more rules upon its members.

Ironically, as some of the Europeans were accusing American ego psychologists of being too adaptive to their milieu, the organization was becoming more rigid: the more entrenched psychoanalysis became, the more sectarian habits—reinforced by organizational requirements—separated classical Freudians from the larger society. Even liberalizing their stance against lay analysis at the end of the 1950s (to accept a few research psychoanalysts) and again in 1972 did not change the situation: this belated bow to lay analysis was opening the gate at a time when fewer prospective candidates were trying to enter. And when, in 1985, the clinical section of the American Psychological Association sued the APA for having denied its members access, the Freudians would be forced to liberalize their policies. The Freudians' general isolationism, often bordering on arrogance, also had not endeared them to the public at large. So by the time they became less critical of lay analysts their prestige was declining.

Essentially, the Americans had imported the Berliners' curriculum. But they imposed it on young doctors, whereas the Berliners had recruited laymen as well. And in the 1920s, when psychoanalysts were a heterogeneous group, it made sense that a candidate be admitted or refused after three interviews by members of the executive committee, that the executive committee appoint a training analyst before deciding when the candidate could proceed to further training, that the training would last at least six months, and that the supervisor would determine when the analysis was completed (Bernfeld, 1962). Furthermore, in Berlin, where doctors, laymen, social workers, and teachers had attended seminars together, they had learned from each other and had expanded their horizons.

In America, these rules were being applied by a group of medical specialists. Hence the give and take in didactic seminars was among homogeneous groups of aspiring doctors, and discussions increasingly revolved around medical rather than cultural issues. Instead of instituting minimal professional standards as the Berliners had done, the Americans now were concerned with establishing their credentials, with integrating themselves into hospitals, and with other "objective" circumstances. Also, the Berliners' "at least six months" of training had turned into "at least four years." This not only added to the Freudians' isolation but inevitably attracted only those who could afford the expense. As the ever longer period of study grew financially burdensome, the dropout rate rose. Some of the dropouts, in turn, supplied the easier and cheaper therapies the public wanted. Here, the impact of the larger social forces converged with that of APA policies: as the demand for shorter therapies increased, more of these were offered, and fewer classical analysts were entering the profession. (Recently, when the New York Psycho-analytic Society started to admit "selected nonmedical" persons to analytic training, they had few applicants.)

Psychoanalysis after the Third Reich

At first, APA and IPA policies were being interpreted rigidly outside the Anglo-Saxon countries. The Europeans, who did not understand American condi-tions, confused American institutional priorities, often formulated in re-sponse to governmental requirements, with clinical and theoretical issues. Nevertheless, the few Freudians who had stayed on in Germany had every reason to court their former Jewish colleagues: they exaggerated the extent to which they had secretly practiced psychoanalysis during the Hitler years, and they downplayed the fact that this had been done under Nazi auspices (Schwidder, 1950–51; Cocks, 1985).

In order to be readmitted by the IPA, Felix Boehm, Harald Schultz-Hencke, Karl Müller-Braunschweig, and Werner Kemper founded the Ber-liner Psychoanalytische Gesellschaft in October 1945. In 1946, they renamed it Deutsche Psychoanalytische Gesellschaft (DPG). And in March of that year, Kemper and Schultz-Hencke organized a polyclinic—the Central Institute for Psychogenic Illness (Zentralinstitut für psychogene Erkrankungen). They stressed that this had become possible only "after a year of self-sacrificing and selfless actions by all co-workers" (Schwidder, 1950–51, p. 383). Soon, the got the Versicherungsanstalt Berlin (the Insurance Company of Berlin), itself backed by the government, to underwrite them. This apparently was the first time in German history that public authorities acknowledged neu-rosis as an illness covered by national health insurance. By arguing that pre-ventive psychotherapy would be two to ten times cheaper than shock, drug, or other interventions for advanced disturbances, these analysts had sold the authorities on the idea. (They predicted that the sudden defeat of the Nazis would engender enormous psychic distress in most of the population.)

In May 1947, the Berliners founded the Institut für Psychotherapie, which represented Freudians, Jungians, Adlerians, and "neo-psychoanalysts." In fact, by accommodating these diverse orientations, the structure of the insti-tute was a replica of Göring's establishment. And in 1949, they set up the Deutsche Gesellschaft für Psychotherapie und Tiefenpsychologie (DGPT) as the umbrella organization that would represent the interests of all therapists.

It was easier to cooperate for the sake of professional acceptance than to agree on how to practice psychoanalysis, however. So, when Jones reported to the IPA that the German situation was difficult, he did not know how much deceit and anxiety lay behind these difficulties, for the German analysts carefully restricted their public disagreements to theory. Müller-Braunschweig attacked Schultz-Hencke for systematizing at the expense of resistances, for reducing the libidinal stages to preanalytic notions, and for replacing Freud's concepts with "fundamental antithetic drives" (ego and sex instincts, Eros and death instincts). He found Schultz-Hencke's notions of possessive strivings ("captive" and retentive) and of striving for self-assertion and sexuality (including aggression and "autochthonous" tenderness) to be conventional formulations that bypassed dealing with the psychoanalytic unconscious. Müller-Braunschweig accused Schultz-Hencke of being imprecise, dogmatic, and preoccupied with terminology (*IPA Bulletin*, 1949, p. 204). Yet, in spite of his sharp attacks on the theories of his colleague, even Müller-Braunschweig remained as silent about the recent Nazi past as everyone else.

Ironically, the Berliners were refused admission to the IPA because they did not have a sufficiently clear Freudian orientation and because their training facilities were not adequate. Although Boehm had stated publicly that the moneys for an institute would not be available "for the next ten years," Müller-Braunschweig managed to create the Deutsche Psychoanalytische Vereinigung (DPV) the following year. Essentially, this step led the IPA to accept the Berliners in 1951.

Soon societies were being started in other cities—in Freiburg, Kassel, Ulm, Tübingen, Düsseldorf, Bremen, and Munich. When a society was large enough, it would form an institute and ask for its acceptance by the DPV. At first, Berlin was central; financial support by the Berlin Insurance Company had allowed them to train child therapists and educational psychologists. And the more Anglo-Saxon visitors came over to instruct them, the more removed they seemed from their Nazi past. In any event, the German psychoanalysts did manage to exclude from their journals and from organizational life those therapists who had been dedicated Nazis. The Munich group, for instance, turned down Erna Göring as a member in 1947, and they pushed the older Nazi therapists into relative obscurity (Cocks, 1985, p. 235).

In 1951, Walter Seitz, head of the outpatient clinic at the University of Munich and director of the Institute for Psychological Research and Psychotherapy, surveyed the existing psychotherapeutic community and found that it could be divided into four groups: (1) those who espoused "classical depth psychology," (2) lay psychotherapists with degrees in psychology, (3) "wild" psychotherapists who had been admitted by the so called Health Practitioners Law of 1939 and thus were neither psychologists nor physicians, and

(4) psychiatrists belonging to the General Medical Society for Psychotherapy, which had been reestablished in 1948 (Cocks, 1985, pp. 236–37). Seitz also pointed out that the psychiatrists alone, under the leadership of Ernst Kretschmer, were pushing for medicalization. These discussions between psychiatrists and psychoanalysts, although they superficially resembled those that had led Freud to write "On the Question of Lay Analysis," took place now not among Freudians but among individuals, some of whom had practiced more or less dubious therapy and research in the Third Reich. The psychotherapists, however, to some extent helped keep theoretical conflicts within boundaries in order to achieve their overall aim: to persuade the authorities to accept neurosis as a reimbursable illness.

Psychoanalysis Becomes Reimbursable

In 1967, the German psychoanalysts' cooperation paid off: new mental health insurance laws covered psychoanalytic therapy. (The German state does not pay directly for health services, but the *Reichversicherungsordnung* [state insurance laws] mandate that everyone contribute to a general sickness fund—*Krankenkasse*.) These laws are complex; they are governed by agreements among employers' associations, unions, and state authorities and depend upon accommodation between conflicting political *Länder* (regions) and the interests of the professions (Brede, private communication, 1984). Their implementation was due to the psychoanalysts' concerted efforts after 1945, when they had agitated for the social rights of patients and had set up therapeutic centers and clinics for those who could not afford even the minimum charge of DM 15, then under four dollars (Haarstrich, 1977, p. 10).

In order to exert the appropriate pressure on the government, psychotherapists of all denominations had strengthened their organizations and set up new liaisons. Each victory would spur them on to cooperate further and to maneuver behind the scenes. When the 1967 law was revised in 1976, clause number 386 of this financial ruling covered "acute neurotic illness" and "neurotic disturbances with psychic and somatic symptomatology."

Twenty-seven items legally define ailments treatable by psychotherapy—including neurotic symptoms, phobias, depression, and psychically impaired personality functioning—and the conditions under which psychoanalytic psychotherapy may be applied. Since the psychoanalysts (after much disagreement among themselves) had pushed this law through, they also had had to sound more sanguine about potential cures than they may have felt. And they had had to hammer out just how many analytic sessions would be needed to achieve the expected cures. Eventually, they agreed that it would be best to begin by providing 40 to 50 hours of one-on-one psychotherapeutic one-hour sessions or two-hour group sessions. But soon they found that more is better and that most individuals need 160 hours of individual therapy or 80 to 120 two-hour sessions. Finally, a ceiling of 300 hours was approved, except for the most serious cases.

But the analysts had not bargained for the various formalities required for reimbursement, in particular for the official requests before treatment could begin. Indeed, analysts have to present their patients' histories in a way that will convince the authorities that treatment is badly needed, that it will change the patients' work and life, and that this can be achieved only with the help of psychoanalysis (*Deutsches Ärzteblatt*, 1976). Under these conditions, they must justify, at least to themselves, abrogating the absolute privacy of the analytic relationship.

Soon the issue of medicalization cropped up once again. At the instigation of Mitscherlich, in particular, German psychoanalysts had insisted that a one-to-one ratio between medical and lay analysts was optimal. About half of the German analysts were psychologists. But because neuroses were legally classified as illnesses, a bona fide physician was "needed" to cure them. The Freudians surmounted this obstacle by requiring that a psychologist's official forms be signed by a medically trained psychoanalyst before being submitted to the relevant bureaucrat for approval (the bureaucrat had to be a psychoanalyst). Thereby, they introduced yet another breach of privacy. So, as the paperwork multiplied, the psychoanalysts became increasingly perturbed about confidentiality. A number of them began to wonder whether the involvement of the authorities did not corrupt the psychoanalyst's integrity. Some leftists among them went further and warned against the danger of political co-optation, which ultimately might invade the psychoanalytic dyad. And a few classical analysts opposed reimbursement because they feared interference.

When every citizen became entitled to therapy, the financial security of every psychotherapist was assured. After 1967, fees were doubled, the status of nonmedical psychotherapists (who were to receive 90 percent of the stipulated remuneration) and of educational psychologists, or *Psychagogen* (who were to receive 80 percent) was clarified, and guidelines for child therapy were codified. One notes when reading their bulletins that psychoanalysts spoke more and more of dealing with "patients" rather than with "clients" or "analysands," and that they were more likely now to polarize notions of sickness and health. In addition, issues of patients' rights seemed to recede, and psychoanalytic politics gradually moved to the center. This was bound to happen, of course, when the functionaries' power increased and the analysts had to defend themselves against inequities as well as against paperwork.

As the demand for psychoanalytic therapy spread, costs rose. Hence the government tried to cut back on the number of allowable sessions and to evaluate results more strictly, thus boosting the functionaries' authority again. Keeping patients' files remained the knottiest issue. Although assured that these would remain locked forever, the psychoanalysts wondered how this would be feasible in case of changes in bureaucratic personnel or a fire or other calamitous circumstance. Some Freudians thought it was worth risking the possible breach of privacy for the sake of patients who otherwise would not be treated at all, whereas left-leaning colleagues pointed to the potentially repressive uses of these files and cited the onus some employers still attach to persons who seek psychological help.

When scanning the yearly reports of Frankfurt's Sigmund-Freud-Institut, one is struck by the increasing references to "contributions to the mental health of the population." Comparing these to reports from other countries, one notices that German candidates, among other things, are being taught how to deal with administrative-technical requirements; that more short-term therapists, educational psychologists, theologians, and teachers are being trained in response to the availability of resources from the sickness fund—*Kassenleistung* (de Boor, 1974, 1975); and that there is a concerted effort to recruit patients from the lower classes by proselytizing them about psychoanalysis and informing them that treatment and initial interviews are reimbursable.

All in all, therapy appears to have gained momentum at the expense of research—despite studies of sterility, of the mid-life crisis in women, and of interventions in hospitals and the criminal justice system—as cooperation with the bureaucracies became more and more important (de Boor, 1975, 1976). When in 1977 Clemens de Boor, director of the Sigmund-Freud-Institut, reported on the number of patients who were treated (as is necessary to ensure further funding), he pleaded that more resources be made available for psychoanalytic training.[4] Some of his colleagues who advocated more of the sociopsychological research Mitscherlich had initiated were certain that de Boor had sold out to the state for the sake of money. They were afraid of tightening the bond with the authorities, of capitulating to the increasing requests for reports of therapeutic "results."

Whether psychoanalysts deal with neurotic or psychosomatic symptoms, their official reports must indicate that all other sources of disease have been ruled out. At this point it seems in the patient's interest to exaggerate the chances of his cure. And the credibility of the analyst is questionable if the patient is found to be well just at the time when benefits are about to run out. To avoid this situation, some psychoanalysts said they would tell their patients during the first session that they expected to cure their illness after at most three hundred visits, but that because the patient might want additional help in order to "feel better," it might be a good idea to start saving money right away. Needless to say, questions have arisen about these practices.

Ironically, as the authorities required more and more stringent credentials, the issues surrounding reimbursement once more brought home the distinctions between physicians and lay analysts. A number of doctors started to push for excluding psychologists. Some of the medical analysts proposed psychoanalysis as a medical specialty (*Facharzt für Psychoanalyse*); thus it might be possible for them to earn as much as their colleagues in radiology, urology, or surgery. But psychoanalysis as a medical specialty would necessitate university examination and the choice and promotion of candidates by nonanalysts, which would introduce unreliable and unprofessional criteria (Loch, 1977, p. 50). Furthermore, some thought they then would be following the American example of medicalization that so many of them had been criticizing for years.

The impact of reimbursement policies continues to dominate professional meetings. Some have been advocating broader social policies that might prevent mental illness and have argued against reimbursement as a threat to personal privacy. But it often is unclear whether these "radicals" are against state interference on principle, whether they equate such interference with Nazi practices, or whether they object to the changes the laws have imposed on psychoanalysis itself. Still, most psychoanalysts recognize how beneficial the policies have been to them—even though 80 percent of the members of the DPV thought, in 1977, that it would be useful to have patients pay something so as not to put the analyst "into the role of the giving or withholding mother" (Rosenkötter and von Schweinichen, 1981).

In a report on these questions, the psychoanalyst Johannes Cremerius maintained that "self-payment" versus reimbursement, limitless versus limited treatment, two people versus the presence of a third, and psychoanalysis versus psychotherapy are false issues—or at least not central. What counted, he said, was the meaning of the psychoanalytic process, its functions and consequences, and its techniques. Cremerius diagnosed his colleagues as suffering from "unreflective countertransference that demonstrates the consensus within the professional community." He suggested that *all* questions of payment—as a means of expressing seduction, resistance, disdain, and "narcissistic hurt"—be dealt with analytically (Cremerius, 1981a), that social consciousness mandates third-party payment, and that psychoanalysts "practice what best suits each patient" (p. 22).

Realistically, psychoanalytic insights and techniques cannot be divorced from their professional context. This was pointed out by one of the evaluators of the sick funds, Ulrich Ehebald, who accused his colleagues in the DPV of claiming to adhere to IPA rules while unreflectingly going along with some of them and ignoring others (1977, p. 18). Paradoxically, the decision to accept insurance money had reinforced the analysts' links to the DPV at the same time the quarrels within this organization were growing more intense. Thus the professional autonomy the psychoanalysts cherish was eroded even further and was increasingly confined to their analytic hours. Even relationships with patients, warned the educator and psychoanalyst Horst-Eberhard Richter, are increasingly influenced by involvements with medical insurance systems (for third-party payment for treatment as well as for didactic analyses) and by the analysts' preoccupations with these matters.

Clearly, the enormous German "psychoboom" was fueled by the organized efforts of the entire therapeutic community, and they extended their influence at the expense of a certain amount of autonomy. Furthermore, their integration into the public health services also strengthened the psychoanalysts' ties with the DGPT, the lobbying organization for all therapists. By the early 1980s, the German analysts had become the second largest contingent within the IPA—right after the Americans.

Psychoanalysis in Postwar Austria

After 1945, psychoanalysis in Austria was in as much disarray as in Germany. But whereas the Germans were eager to rebuild, the Austrians simply wanted to ignore it. Whether this was due to the Russian presence until 1955, to the small size of the country, or to the reluctance of the Viennese to face up to their Nazi past is immaterial: the general disinterest in psychoanalysis was palpable. The psychoanalyst Wilhelm Solms-Rödelheim recalled being told by a leading physician that there was not much sense in trying to "do anything" for the psychoanalysts (1959, p. 1185).

Both inside and outside academia, prominent psychologists were as hostile to analysis as the physicians; thus there were no Viennese to ask their émigrés to return, as the Germans had done. Nor did the émigrés press the issue. But August Aichhorn and Alfred von Winterstein, the only two pre-

1938 analysts still in Vienna, did want to orchestrate a comeback. Aichhorn wanted to resume his work with delinquents but decided that recruiting and training young analysts was more important; he proposed in April 1946 that the Viennese analysts give talks to civic associations to spread their ideas. Although the American occupation forces also welcomed such efforts as a means of denazification, there was little response. Aichhorn died in 1949, and Winterstein, who succeeded him as president of the WPV, reported to Müller-Braunschweig that membership had dropped from thirteen in 1948 to ten in 1950 (Solms-Rödelheim, 1959, p. 1185). That Winterstein had no medical degree and the inflexible authorities insisted on dealing with doctors did not help matters; he had to consult a psychiatrist every time he wanted to take on a patient. When claims are "properly" presented, the Austrian state health insurance system does cover psychoanalysis. But reimbursement procedures are based on reputation, so that prestigious doctors, I was told, have always had an easier time. Futhermore, well-connected patients may arrange for reimbursement as well.

Viennese officials took no notice of psychoanalysis until around 1970, after Anna Freud had agreed that the 1971 IPA congress be held in Vienna. A year later, the number of local analysts was variously estimated between seven and twenty-seven (Kurzweil, 1971). In these circumstances one could hardly talk of a psychoanalytic organization, although formally the WPV had never been dissolved. Even in 1983, it seems, Vienna had only nine training analysts, and candidates had to wait between two and four years; under such circumstances, personal criteria dominated. Disagreements, at times turning into feuds, tended to be between individuals rather than factions and quickly became personal.

Next to the Sigmund Freud Gesellschaft, the Institut für Tiefenpsychologie at the Allgemeinen Krankenhaus is considered *the* center for psychoanalysis. Its long-time director, Hans Strotzka, whose preferred mode of treatment always was short-term therapy, presided over a group of ten Adlerians, Rogerians, behavior therapists, Jungians, and Freudians. Since this institute belongs to the hospital, and its members teach at the University of Vienna, Freudian analysis always had to take a back seat. But in 1982, the young and more malleable Peter Schuster was chosen as Strotzka's successor. In 1983, the institute was run in a committeelike fashion, and by 1984 Schuster was ready to give up this onerous task and was replaced by Wolfgang Berner. Schuster's psychoanalytic orientation favored Otto Kernberg's object relations theory, although he too found that the more cost-effective short-term therapies were advisable for most clinic patients. Undoubtedly this practice derives at least partly from the fact that an institute depending upon the goodwill of hospital officials must watch its finances carefully and that it must respond to the majority of patients who hope their ailments are physical rather than mental. Furthermore, Austrian psychoanalysts must first become full-fledged psychiatrists, which means they must hold a full-time and poorly paid job while spending much time and money for their analytic training. Hence many give up and remain in psychiatry.[5]

Most of the older members of the WPV work in private practice: they prefer not to deal with the Austrian health services. According to them, private practice is the only means of conducting proper psychoanalysis without becoming embroiled in bureaucratic hassles. Also, like Harald Leupold-Löwenthal and Solms-Rödelheim, both former presidents of the association, they tend to be disdainful of cooperation with "lesser" therapies. Thus they were angry when, in 1981, Hedda Eppel, a children's analyst who had spent the war years in England, proposed, as they saw it, to "water down" her psychoanalysis with group therapy.

In spite of their differences, however, the Freudians cooperated to revitalize Viennese psychoanalysis. They pushed the Austrian authorities to back them in forming the Sigmund Freud Gesellschaft. By 1982, reported Leupold-Löwenthal, it had 1,200 members (one third each in Austria, elsewhere in Europe, and in the United States). Without pressure from this organization, the Austrian government might have withdrawn its financial support of the Gesellschaft and of its library. The Viennese analysts also started to sponsor a yearly university lecture (the first one given in 1980 by Anna Freud) to overcome "intellectual sterility and isolation." And, in order to keep in closer touch with IPA colleagues, they now invite them to seminars and work weeks and to international symposia at a resort, Grundlsee. But none of these endeavors is research-oriented, although Leupold-Löwenthal in 1984 thought there might be a few tentative efforts being made in that direction (personal communication).

The Viennese Freudians in the early 1980s appeared to be responding to the demands of their own minor "psychoboom"—a boom originating in the demand for Adlerian or Rogerian therapies, in psychiatry, and in ideologies of "personal growth" (Kommittee für Alternativen, 1980, p. 11). Even though psychoanalytic practice is minimal, many Austrians now believe that therapy will help them to "feel better." Elizabeth Jandl-Jager, a sociologist, behavior therapist, and professor at the University of Vienna, thought in 1984 that there had been a general increase in neuroses and psychosomatic illness among the Viennese and found that long-standing and pervasive prejudices against psychoanalysis had been diminishing. In fact, Catholic organizations have supplied much of the psychological help: they already had their connections with families and *Caritas* and other facilities (Jandl-Jager, personal communication, July 1984). The wpv, however, has not been able to do much more than advocate further acceptance by health insurance systems and by educational and rehabilitational institutions while also trying to attract candidates.

Most recently, there has been an upswing. Since passage of a law regulating training as well as reimbursement policies for help by psychologists (*Psychologengesetz* of 1986), the psychoanalysts' prestige and the number of candidates have been rising steadily. Also, approximately twenty thousand visitors troop through Freud's apartment every year, although this would seem to indicate only that the Freudians have managed to attract tourists.

The Renewal of the Société Psychanalytique de Paris

When the war ended, psychoanalysis was languishing in France as in the rest of Europe. The *Revue Française de Psychanalyse*, which resumed publication in 1948, reported that in 1945 and 1946, those members of the society who had returned to Paris met from time to time. By the end of 1946, the Société Psychanalytique de Paris (spp) was able once again to hold monthly meetings as it had before the war (Mijolla, 1982, pp. 44–45). In 1947 Sacha Nacht was elected president, and a Commission on Training was established in preparation for an institute. Jacques Lacan, a member of this body, was the author of the "règlement et doctrine de la commission de l'enseignement."

At the time, no one had any inkling that Lacan would cause such havoc in the organization or that he soon would dominate French psychoanalysis. It started with his advocacy of short sessions and his challenge to the minimum training requirements for psychoanalysts that the others were ready to agree upon: three quarters of an hour three times per week over a period of twelve months (see chapter 11 for details of Lacan's proposals). Since the training requirements already represented a considerable compromise by the ipa in response to the postwar situation and Nacht wanted ipa affiliation, he vigorously opposed Lacan.

In recent years, Lacanians have described their early history as consisting of major battles (see, for example, J. A. Miller, 1976, 1977; Roudinesco, 1982, 1986). But because the negotiations then were confidential, one can only conjecture about what went on and whether or not the personal tension between Lacan and Nacht was as strong as is claimed. We do know, however, that

French Freudians were eager to prove to the IPA that they were a viable group and wanted to have an approved institute as soon as possible.

In 1953, Serge Lebovici reported to the IPA that the Institut de Psychanalyse, which was set up in 1952, had seventy students and 100 candidates and that it was holding weekly seminars on technique (Nacht), on Freud's texts (Lacan), and on child analysis (Lebovici). Since IPA admittance was crucial, Lebovici did not report publicly that Lacan was supervising about forty of the candidates and therefore was unable to give any of them more than twenty to thirty minutes a week. Lebovici and his colleagues wanted to curb Lacan but did not seem able to do so. Hence Nacht, in his role as president, asked the IPA to appoint an investigative commission. Because Nacht was central in the negotiations around this increasingly bitter controversy, the members of the SPP asked him to stay in office for another year. (He was to have stepped down in 1952).

When the IPA commission ruled against Lacan in 1953, a number of students and colleagues (Lagache, Dolto, Favez-Boutonier, Reverchon-Jouve) backed him publicly and together formed the Société Française de Psychanalyse (SFP). From then on, the members of the SPP officially ignored the Lacanians, although they sometimes felt compelled to respond to Lacan's flamboyant public pronouncements.

The Lacanians had their own disagreements around 1959, between those who chose to follow Lacan through thick and thin and members of the "French Study Group" (Lagache, Anzieu, Granoff), who wanted to accommodate the IPA enough to gain admittance. Some also thought Lacan was going too far in his revisions of Freud. Another IPA commission was formed, and it recommended in 1963 that the SFP be admitted provided that Lacan and Dolto were removed as training analysts and their candidates were supervised by others.

Lacan struck back in public lectures on the "Nom-du-Père," which cleverly denounced authoritarian methods practiced in the name of Freud. He also formed the Ecole Freudienne. As his public appeal grew, he increasingly attacked the classical Freudians, and the SPP could no longer ignore him. Besides claiming to read Freud anew "as he should be read," Lacan denounced the inevitable sterility and conservatism of all organizations, particularly psychoanalytic ones. Innovation, he insisted, could exist only outside formal structures. The unveiling of the unconscious as an ongoing process was likened by Lacan to a permanent revolution, but as such it could be no more than a myth because it was expected to occur within a routinized bureaucratic structure (Jacquot, 1975).

In 1969, some of his collaborators—among them Piera Aulagnier, François Perrier, and Jean-Paul Valbrega—took this antiinstitutionalism to heart and resigned to form the Quatrième Groupe. Although this particular split did not directly affect the SPP, all of psychoanalysis was influenced by the fact that some of Lacan's students had set up a Department of Psychoanalysis at the University of Vincennes. The ensuing ferment was considered revolutionary, and the members of the SPP in contrast were viewed as part of the hated establishment.

Still, many of the classical Freudians had medical degrees and connections to psychiatry, and they could quietly trade on their medical prestige.[6] Some of them advised a number of ministerial commissions on mental health and child psychiatry, and they expanded on whatever footholds in hospitals and clinics they had had before the Lacanians "captured" Vincennes. Nevertheless, almost every psychoanalyst had been influenced by Lacan's stress on language and his free-wheeling style. And even the classical Freudians found they were acquiring more patients: the publicity Lacan had generated boosted public demand for psychoanalysis.

After 1970, when some of Lacan's students decided to take on patients, Lacan invented *la passe*—the practice of presenting a case to two senior analysts whom the treating analyst had not trained with—to counteract malpractice and yet avoid creating a hierarchy among his group. But this allegedly democratic practice soon was found to be as "repressive" as that of the "authoritarian" SPP. Lacan had triggered rising expectations which soon led to total anarchy, for neither he nor the authorities knew how to stop people from declaring themselves bona fide analysts. To regulate matters, Lacan established rules for psychoanalysis at the University of Paris VIII—a theoretical course of studies accompanied by "a personal analysis pursued up to the so-called didactic level," which would lead to the "doctorat du troisième cycle" ("Annonces," 1975, p. 119). Soon, psychoanalysts of the Société Française de Psychanalyse, headed by Jean Laplanche, offered *their* "doctorat du troisième cycle" at the University of Paris VII—complete with theses on psychoanalytic methods, theory, and history. At the time, Serge Lebovici of the SPP, in an open letter to his colleague André Green, argued for the granting of doctorates in mental health, but insisted that health professionals be trained at psychoanalytic institutes attached to the IPA (Lebovici, 1977). Essentially, under the existing system, all Freudians evaluated prospective students' emotional qualities and disabilities, and they wondered how fair or democratic it was to keep out candidates on the basis of an interview or how related emotional makeup is to intellectual achievement; meanwhile, the authorities continued to bar them from the plum of French appointments at the Centre Na-tionale de Recherches (CNRS)—lifetime stipends to do research (Laplanche, 1982). They all agreed that the situation had been triggered by the bureau-crats' resistance to psychoanalysis. Basically, the classical Freudians were try-ing to catch up with the popular Lacanians, without relinquishing their more stringent analytic rules.

Behind the theoretical and ethical questions and those about democracy and political liberation were issues of access to the profession, to potential students, to jobs, and to influence in the booming and constantly expanding mental health field. These concerns occupied analysts despite the fact that a survey of the entire French population indicated that 80 percent did not know Lacan's name and that 65 percent would refuse to enter analysis even if it were offered free of charge (Ouzouf, 1980). By 1984, in fact, demand in Paris had leveled off, and many analysts were looking for patients.

In this respect, French and German problems were similar: in both countries universities and hospitals almost entirely operate under the aegis of governmental bodies, so that the legislative measures initiated after 1968 pitted the psychoanalysts against psychiatrists and paraprofessionals, on the one hand, and against competing psychotherapies, on the other. To protect their livelihood, they felt compelled to push their institutional interests in both countries in unctuous and self-promotional language. To press their case, they frequently cited the practices of other countries—albeit out of context.

Altogether, by the late 1970s both French and German psychoanalysts (personally and through their representative associations) were heavily en-gaged in professional politics to enhance their careers and prestige. (The Austrians had been enmeshed in them all along, but—except for Salzburg—on a minuscule scale.) In addition, involvement with politicians was geared toward the adoption of alternative therapies—an interesting topic which, however, is beyond the scope of this book.

By 1982, titular SPP membership was 62 and associate membership 340. This imbalance, however, does not give the true picture, for it grew out of a dispute about a practice René Major, a member, had initiated: he had decided to stimulate "confrontations"—open discussions with dissident analysts, both in meetings and in his new journal, *Confrontation*. This was in defiance of the senior analysts of the SPP and led them to deny Major titular member-ship. (They did not suspend him even though he stopped paying dues.) To demonstrate their solidarity with him, most of the other associates volun-tarily continued on at the lower, associate status. But this was just one instance of the growing accommodation to the Parisian flair for intellectual drama and the consequent bending of IPA rules.

Among French associations, only the SPP and the SFP (which had eighteen titular and sixteen associated members in 1968) continue to keep close track of their membership. Lacan's aversion to keeping records and his dedication to freedom from organizational constraint had generated chaos long before his death in 1981. Since then, the situation has gotten even more out of hand, and no one has a clear idea of how many people practice la psychanalyse.

In 1983, five individuals were mentioned as possible successors to Lacan. The largest and most organized group, la Cause de l'École Freudienne, was led by Jacques-Alain Miller, Lacan's son-in-law and literary executor. This group set up a Freud library, holds regular seminars, conducts a formal course of study, publishes newsletters and journals, and has established branches around France and overseas. Another contender, Françoise Dolto, who expected to rally people around the memory of Lacan by mourning him as their intellectual father and by encouraging his followers to build on his teachings, attracted about 250 people. (She died in 1988.) Charles Melman, whose allure and style replicate Lacan's, holds seminars at the Salpêtrière—an ingenious way to allude to his descent from Charcot via Freud and Lacan. He attracted between 150 and 200 persons. André Green, who belongs to the SPP but has a lecture style like that of Lacan's (complete with complicated diagrams of how the ear responds to sounds and the meanings of language), has given public talks in a packed lecture hall at the University of Paris–Joussieux. Major's *Confrontation* at first was seen as pushing him to the forefront, but he has had fewer and fewer meetings and, I was told, thought "he had done his job" and now is more interested in seeing patients. Smaller nuclei keep forming and dissolving, but none has ever drawn more than fifty persons. By 1986, there were fourteen Lacanian groups, each claiming to be the "true" successor, and a few of them had started journals.[7]

Critiques of organization have become de rigueur. In response to this general attitude, some new groups expect members to register for each meeting they attend, but some require only annual reregistration. The most anarchic of them, those who expect "total freedom" from organizational restraints—and listeners of all sects—pay registration fees without registering. This practice has made it impossible to ascertain the overlap between groups: some individuals always have followed the lectures of two or more of the mini-gurus, many analysts enjoy the intellectual bravura of psychoanalytic performances, and there are those who attend in order to make professional contacts. In this cacophony of Freudian interest and talk, the SPP remains the one institutional group with solid connection to psychiatry and to the rest of the French mental health establishment, and the only one (next to the smaller SFP and the Quatrième Groupe) adhering to a firmly established training program. On the whole, the SPP is less rigid than the other organizations affiliated with the IPA. Most of its members remain in touch with "deviants." In 1986, for instance, Alain de Mijolla, a member of the SPP, organized a meeting under the auspices of the newly formed International Freudian Society on "Spontaneous Clinical Exchanges," in which three cases were discussed by representatives of six different orientations. And in 1987, he launched his International Association for the History of Psychoanalysis with heterogeneous participants from most European countries and America.

Current Organizational Links

While institutes around the world were flouting IPA rules, its central committees pretended that they were perpetuating the Americans' standards, though they occasionally had to bend them. But in 1979, Edward Joseph, who, as president of the IPA, had been asked to determine exactly what was going on in the affiliated institutes, reported on the differences among them.[8] He noted that psychoanalysis had succumbed to national and institutional pressures and that many of the local rules contravened those of the IPA. Age requirements and other criteria for admission to training, personal analysis, supervision, and clinical experience before and after graduation all covered an enormous range (Joseph, 1979). Joseph, a skillful mediator, declared that the profession was in a state of anarchy, and yet he praised its ubiquity throughout all modern societies. Hoping to bring order out of chaos, he chided his colleagues for their inability to agree even on whether psychoanalysis is a natural science or one of the human sciences. He described the consequences of competing definitions of psychoanalysis for pedagogic and clinical practice and maintained that it is possible to practice therapy *and* to address philosophical issues without losing sight of the fact that psychoanalysis above all is a cure. This restatement of Freud served as a diplomatic reproach to those analysts who, under French influence, had been seduced by philosophy—presumably at the expense of clinical work—and as an indirect boost to the "American mainstream." His presidential role required him to forge unity, to reach consensus. The IPA officials are weary of rocking the boat: aware that dissenters always set up competing organizations, they strive to avoid further splits. Thus Joseph too was soft-pedaling strict ego psychology for the sake of organizational cohesion and harmony. And he dealt gingerly, with the perennial conflict between the principles of confidentiality and institutional democracy.

Disagreements in the early 1980s once more revolved around the scientific questions, which in fact had generated the organizational diversities in the first place. But because these question, at least in part, were determined by specific milieus, not all the analysts were concerned with issues outside their own theoretical sphere. Many of the French, for example, rejected parts of ego psychology as too narrow and accepted a number of Kleinian and Lacanian notions. The Berliners from the DPV, rather close to both the New Yorkers and the Londoners, did not share the sociological bent of their Frankfurt colleagues, some of whom argued that the emphasis on ego defenses had pushed out drive theory. But the Buenos Aires contingent and other South Americans did support the Frankfurters on this issue, though from a Kleinian perspective (according to which the ego is less important because personality formation is thought to begin *before* the ego is structured). And the Viennese kept reminding them all of their debt to Freud's Vienna.

Clearly, local and national societies have evolved in response to their own interests and needs and have been shaped by their dominant figures, who, in turn, have acted in the name of their members. Consequently, training analysts' and supervisors' personalities and beliefs have left indelible imprints on their institutes. Inevitably, there would be increasingly divergent priorities from one institute to another, so that cooperation in the IPA has become more and more problematic. What then holds the IPA together? Is it sentimentality, allegiance to Freud's dreams, the chance to take a tax-deductible vacation, scientific curiosity, or the fact that organizations usually do not dissolve voluntarily? Or are the scientific exchanges at IPA meetings a necessary means for intellectual growth, particularly when revolving around central psychoanalytic themes such as aggression, projective identification, defense mechanisms, or repression?

Ever since 1985, when four members of Section 39 of the American Psychological Association (the Group for the Advancement of Psychotherapy and Psychoanalysis in Psychology, or GAPPP) brought a class action suit against the American Psychoanalytic Association, two of its affiliated institutes (the Columbia University Center for Psychoanalytic Training and Research and the New York Psychoanalytic Institute), and the International Psychoanalytic Association, these questions have become central. The plaintiffs sued because they (and a few thousand other nonmedical psychoanalysts and psychotherapists) had been denied access to training in the two institutes and thus to the APA and the IPA. The lack of access was said to have deprived mental health workers and psychologists of the best available training, of taking part in psychoanalytic research, and of international contact: they sued on grounds of discrimination and restraint of trade in order to join the psychoanalytic elite and to command its higher fees. In November 1988, the president of the APA informed the membership that a settlement had been reached. But, he stated, the plaintiffs did not win their lawsuit as they reported to the press: there was a voluntary agreement in the best interest of both parties. In fact, he went on, the association had been debating how to train and integrate nonmedical candidates since the 1970s; and they had already developed and were voting on a plan around the time the lawsuit was filed. Moreover, since May 1988 fifty-two applications had been approved: and the $650,000 which the plaintiffs were awarded were not for damages but for legal fees—to be paid by the defendants' insurance carriers. The repercussions of the court action, of course, do not bode especially well for cooperation in the future.

In 1987, the IPA, which never did require its members to have a medical degree (although its American members have to be associated with the APA which almost exclusively admitted doctors), voted to admit Freudian institutes and their members whose training was up to their standards. In fact, they started on-site visits to a number of institutes in the spring of 1988. Compromise solutions will undoubtedly be forthcoming, which will depend upon the acceptability of training (within these institutes and often in such places as the Tavistock and Hampstead clinics) of individual members. Inevitably, the 1938 Regional Association agreement between APA and IPA will be altered (Wallerstein, 1987). Chances are that the APA will continue to act as the gatekeeper in America. Still, IPA membership alone will be a boon: to belong is prestigious, and, once accepted, an individual belongs for life, unlike the situation among other doctors or psychologists, who must pass exams when moving from one state or country to another. The selectivity of the training process, as established by international standards, assures psychoanalysts that once they have passed, they may practice anywhere in the world.

Chapter 10

The Cultural
Unconscious in
National Costume

By 1945, every country either had its own psychoanalytic tradition or was aware of the lack of one. And as Freud's ideas were increasingly being adapted to national concerns, they were also being molded in response to institutional needs and to interpretations by dominant figures. In America, many prominent intellectuals and professionals had been analyzed, and some were talking publicly about their psychoanalyses. Entertainers routinely joked about their personal experiences and mimicked the analysts' German accents—at the same time familiarizing the public with the psychoanalytic process. Psychoanalysis had come of age.

The disputes between Freudians and "deviants," mostly the group around Horney and Fromm, actually had bolstered belief in the viability of the psychoanalytic enterprise by the larger public. Moreover, by the late 1940s the Freudians competed with the critical Frankfurt scholars, led by Adorno (1950), in explaining the Holocaust, anti-Semitism, and German aggression. As some psychologists started to adopt Freudian language, and as cooperation with anthropologists expanded, psychoanalysis both entered and legitimated the cultural unconscious. By the early 1950s the prestige of psychoanalysis was at its peak: analysts earned a good deal of money, and their institutes had more applicants for candidacy than they could handle.

We noted in chapter 2 that the arrival of the émigré analysts in America had been a boon. According to Lewis Coser, they "published more books and contributed much more to psychoanalytic journals . . . [than their native colleagues] and transformed not only American psychoanalysis but also psychology and general culture" (Coser, 1984). In analyzing the responses to a questionnaire sent to members of the Boston, New York, and San Francisco institutes, he and Rose Laub Coser found that eight of the ten "most influential" Freudians and over half of the training analysts who were named more than twice as "most memorable" were refugees; all three of the training analysts who received over ten votes had been born in Europe (p. 52). When Hofling and Meyers (1972) asked who had made the most important psychoanalytic discoveries, fifteen of the seventeen analysts who were mentioned more than four times were born in Europe (p. 520); when they asked who was responsible for new discoveries only 10 of the 258 positive responses named native Americans (p. 519). But American Freudians also published more theoretical articles than they had before the émigré analysts became established, and they all extrapolated from their experiences to the culture at large.

In Germany, the more venturesome Freudians took on the cultural psychoanalysts; a few "purists" noted that investigations of German character by sociologists and anthropologists were superficial because they did not deal with the unconscious psychic mechanisms determining character; and a number of analysts, led by the Mitscherlichs, proposed their own theories about the causes of Nazi atrocities.

Most classical American psychoanalysts donated time to work in clinics. Their candidates analyzed clinic patients, and they instructed social workers, medical interns, and general practitioners in the latest discoveries about psychic dynamics and clinical methods. Because they were initiating individuals who would not become psychoanalysts, they inevitably simplified their scientific language. At the time, however, they did not realize that these simplifications were contributing to the split between an increasingly abstruse psychoanalytic theory developed within their institutes and its applications by people who were unaware of the intricacies of this theory.

The widespread dissemination of psychoanalysis raised the psychoanalysts' status: they were thought to possess special insight into *all* people and thus were feared by some and admired by others. Psychoanalysts increasingly were hailed as clairvoyant and were asked to sit on every court dealing with human concerns. They passed judgment—on the sanity of criminals, the motivations of poor students, the viability of family life, the role of mothers—in ever more scientific and abstract language. This impressed those for whom theoretical arguments themselves implied profundity. The Freudians' public services (frequently sponsored by foundations and the government) also helped disseminate psychoanalytic ideas, as did the visibility of psychoanalysts who became hospital administrators.

The spread of psychoanalysis itself and its links to psychiatry and other professions necessitated a certain amount of control against professional misconduct and malpractice. Given the American Freudians' attitudes toward lay analysis, they found it appropriate to scrutinize the émigrés and keep out nonmedical people. Some of the Americans were afraid that the influx of too many Europeans would threaten their own livelihoods. Therefore, they urged the émigrés to start institutes outside New York, Los Angeles, or Boston. The spread of psychoanalysis in places such as Detroit, Philadelphia, and Washington helped bolster the Freudians' impact and status.

The situation in England was not very different, although the scale was much smaller and Londoners did not exclude lay analysts. The Freudians there, who at first had worried that the immigrants would take over the few patients they had, found new ones after Freud arrived in 1938. Although hampered by the blitz, Anna Freud's and Dorothy Burlingham's work at the Hampstead nursery added to the activities and prestige of the analysts.

After the war, many of the Londoners joined American Freudians in "reeducating" the Continentals: Paula Heiman and Michael Balint were as influential as Kurt Eissler and René Spitz. The inevitable "Matthew effect," the halo surrounding them owing to their success in exile,[1] preceded them to a demoralized postwar Europe; they were impatient to rebuild not only psychoanalysis but all its institutions. The Europeans were eager to receive the Freudians, who, in turn, wanted to export their new know-how. And their ambitions coincided with the aims of the Allied advisers who gradually were taking over from the victorious American army.

We noted in chapter 5 that the Anglo-Saxon psychoanalysts helped legitimate German psychosomatic medicine and in chapter 6 that they influenced general education. But their impact on psychology and on the return of psychoanalysis itself, though less direct, was even more decisive: collectively, they succeeded in turning an antipsychoanalytic Europe into a hospitable one. Since they had convinced some of the authorities that psychoanalytic inquiries might help explain the origins of the activities the Nazis had engaged in and supply a means of rehabilitating the entire German population, the psychoanalysts' endeavors received relatively broad support.

In France, such inquiries began much later than in Germany. They were sparked by the "structuralists," after Lévi-Strauss had published his *Structural Anthropology* ([1955] 1963) and Foucault his *Madness and Civilization* ([1961] 1965). Now, psychoanalysis, among other things, became part of the general intellectual discussions centering on existential phenomenology and antipsychiatry. And inquiries into the cultural unconscious from a Freudian perspective began to inspire the best of France's minds and to spark the wholesale introduction of Freudian writing. Even though the anthropologist Lévi-Strauss, the Marxist philosopher Louis Althusser, the philosopher-historian Michel Foucault, and the writer Roland Barthes soon denied being structuralists, none of them ever directly rejected (Lacanian) "structural" psychoanalysis as one of their theoretical tools. Whether Lacan succeeded in popularizing psychoanalysis by reconceptualizing the Oedipus complex or by elevating Freud's language over his ideas is secondary to the fact that psychoanalysis ultimately moved into the place existentialism had occupied.

From Nazi Practice to the New Germany

Alexander Mitscherlich's impact on German psychoanalysis was felt long before Lacan captured Paris. Even before he became a physician, Mitscherlich had been a free-thinking, marginal member of the left. Hence he went off to Zurich to study medicine after Hitler came to power (1939, p. 628). During an illegal trip to Germany he was imprisoned and upon his release remained in Heidelberg. According to psychoanalyst Hermann Argelander, "the lively spirit of Heidelberg" and the presence of Jaspers, Heidegger, and Viktor von Weizsäcker during the Nazi period led him to overlook "the unpleasant everyday circumstances in the University" in order to continue his medical studies (1983, pp. 292–97). In its library, Mitscherlich came upon hidden copies of Freud's banned works. Reading them after 1933, Argelander noted, had been an act of political courage and daring.

Consequently, in 1945 Mitscherlich (1980) could point to his "clean" political past and the Allies could ask him to help investigate the Nazi doctors' crimes. Thus he learned about the unspeakable medical experiments on human beings and about what had gone on in the extermination camps. Outraged at the barbarism, but identified with the reconstruction of the Federal Republic, he gave impassioned public lectures on the need to return Germans to "humanity." He attacked those who thought the country could ever thrive without acknowledging German guilt. His medical peers, however, turned against him for publicizing their former activities (Fetscher, 1983, p. 301). They called him, among other things, a liar and a defamer; they denied complicity in or even knowledge of the atrocities; and they ostracized him. He retorted that the Germans' outcries against him "seemed to defend the apparently 'untouchable' documents of the extermination camps" (p. 302), and he went on to investigate the psychological mechanisms behind their irrational defenses. In the process, Mitscherlich cast himself as the conscience of his country, exploring the connections between individual and collective guilt. "One cannot speak of the collective guilt of *all* Germans, or even of *Germans alone*," he maintained in 1947; yet "it would be a shameful subterfuge if Germans were to deny responsibility for the deeds perpetrated during national socialism" (Mitscherlich and Mielke, 1947, p. 302). Only by facing what German physicians had done in the name of science, he insisted, could Germany rejoin humanity. The road to civilization, Mitscherlich said, was "paved by psychoanalysis."

As a communist during his student years, Mitscherlich had learned to smoke out right-wing and fascist leanings. This experience alerted him to left-wing propaganda as well, and he soon distrusted Stalinism. Naturally attuned to the ideas of the critical sociologists Max Horkheimer and Theodor Adorno, who, in 1950, had returned from New York to lecture at the University of Frankfurt, he soon collaborated with Jürgen Habermas, their star student. Although ultimately Habermas would believe that "communicative competence" was a better means for rehumanization than psychoanalysis, Mitscherlich remained a psychoanalyst. He found that the ideology of a dictatorship locates

morally uncontrollable tendencies of the *individual in the collective person of the masses—in the figure of a devilish, dangerous opponent, full of deathly aggression*. This opponent [then] turns into the archenemy, whose negative qualities upon closer examination unconsciously are being identified with and projected onto his victim. (my translation of Fetscher's quote from Mitscherlich and Mielke, 1947, p. 303)

Basically, both Mitscherlich and Habermas were addressing theoretial questions of political legitimation and were trying to keep Nazi collaborators out of office. But outside Germany, few people truly understood that the young generation was turning toward an exaggerated, idealized Marxism as the bulwark against the authoritarian tendencies they sensed in themselves. Habermas taught them Marxist criticism and Mitscherlich its psychoanalytic counterpart. But by 1968, the students perceived them both as "lib-labs," professors who criticized East and West even-handedly and did not act on their convictions against domination by totalitarianism and consumerism, respectively.

Still, Mitscherlich now reminded his countrymen that they had been stereotyping and maligning Jews and Bolsheviks long before Hitler: by projecting negative qualities onto them they were falling into their former habit of psychic denial. Hoping to block every avenue that might lead to inhuman behavior, he admonished his fellow citizens against using the cold war to further anti-Bolshevism. He even argued that the miraculous reconstruction of Germany was not only a manifestation of the proverbial work ethic but yet another means of proving German superiority, or re-identifying with the grandfathers' generation—and an unconscious justification for authoritarian practices. Later, in *Society without the Father* (1963), he described the repercussions of the "psychological orphanage" Germany's youth was inhabiting.

In essence, Mitscherlich found that German youngsters had been blaming their loneliness on the fact that their fathers had been on the front while they grew up. In fact, they had suffered much more when these fathers returned and "forgot" their conscious and unconscious complicity by totally blocking out the recent past. In other words, Mitscherlich condemned the fathers for refusing to answer their children's questions after they came home. Later, in *Die Unfähigkeit zu trauern* (1967) (written with Margarete Mitscherlich-Nielsen), he attacked the majority of Germans who had managed to rid themselves so easily of their emotional ties to national socialism and to the Führer. The Mitscherlichs maintained that Hitler had not been mourned because the Germans' collective identification with him had been a specifically "German way to love." Because this happened via the ego-ideal, true object relations, they explained, had been bypassed in order to allow the former idol to disappear without a trace. The lack of mourning and the "dreamlike" vanishing of the past, said the Mitscherlichs, had to result in a loss of self-esteem, in melancholia, and in psychic stress. Germans dealt with these emotions, they continued, by identifying with the victors—the Russians in the East and the Americans in the West. They called on Germans to oppose all ideologies and to battle against their emotional "character defects" with the help of psychoanalysis. How else could unconscious guilt and aggression surface and be dealt with?

In 1949, at the first postwar Congress of Internal Medicine, Mitscherlich advocated that psychosomatic knowledge be widely applied and disseminated because its potential powers went beyond curing individuals' bodily and psychological ills. To implement his grandiose plans, he relied on his prestige, his extraordinary will power, the goodwill of American and British (mostly Jewish) analysts, and the reputation of his new psychosomatic clinic at Heidelberg.[2]

Psychoanalysis à la Mitscherlich was being advanced when he staged two huge celebrations, in Frankfurt and Heidelberg, to commemorate Freud's one hundredth birthday, in 1956. Leading foreign psychoanalysts came to lecture, and Mitscherlich, by pointing to the success of these events, managed to convince powerful and influential politicians (who happened to have been opponents of the Nazis) to "raise the status of psychoanalysis." Thus the regional officials of the Land Hessen agreed to create and support Frankfurt's Sigmund-Freud-Institut.

The institute attracted new disciples. Among them, Alfred Lorenzer and Lutz Rosenkötter investigated the long-range effects of trauma and then informed the authorities that the Nazis' victims might be entitled to restitution payments in years to come. Margarete Mitscherlich-Nielsen, Hans-Eberhard Richter, and Johannes Cremerius formed a "Bernfeld circle" to investigate the eventual application of the social-critical elements of psychoanalysis. And in the anniversary volume of the Sigmund-Freud-Institut, Karola Brede reported on an earlier project (1964–70) to investigate the advisability and effect of psychoanalytic interpretation in the course of the psychoanalytic process (1986).

Although some of these postwar collaborators later would criticize the bureaucratic interference government support would encourage, so long as Mitscherlich was there he drew support from prominent figures, among them Heinrich Böll, Jürgen Habermas, Rudolf Augstein, Kurt Bidenkopf, Helmuth Becker, and René König. People still talk of the excitement he created: how he attracted the most promising young people, how he got sociologists and psychologists to lend their theoretical expertise and psychoanalysts their clinical know-how. Ultimately, the psychoanalysts who were learning about unconscious mechanisms that had been operative in their patients during Hitler's regime and the sociologists who were investigating mass psychology would pool their information and extrapolate from it for the future of Germany. Such a way of reaching to the nexus of individual and societal psychic mechanisms, said Mitscherlich, paraphrasing Freud, was "the only reliable means [that could] defend against the inhumanities of civilization [and advance] the search for truth about ourselves."

Mitscherlich's ability to change his views and to take unpopular stands and his insistence that self-motivation was essential helped revive both German psychiatry and psychoanalysis (Loch, 1983, pp. 342–43). His advice to young psychoanalysts, I have been told, was sensitive, kind, and always honest—whether he warned them against imprudent "eclecticism" or against becoming overly philosophical. This sort of critical undercutting of received knowledge was said to perpetuate the Nietzschean tradition of looking to "the truth" beyond truth itself, and to reaffirm the German idealist-humanistic legacy of Hegel. In substance, the sociologists at his institute inquired into the psychosocial roots of aggression and studied the social elements inducing psychosomatic illness from a psychoanalytically oriented perspective; their contributions helped psychologists to investigate symbols, trauma, language, ethnology.[3] These explorations were published in *Psyche*, the journal Mitscherlich founded in 1947 to serve as a forum for psychosomatics as well as for psychoanalytic and neo-Marxist criticism. *Psyche* printed extensive case histories and the work of authors who would not want to be together in the same room.

When Mitscherlich founded *Psyche*, I was told, he had no idea how useful it would become. Not even he had guessed at the extent of the German psychotherapists' complicity with the Nazis (Cocks, 1985). The sudden ending of the war had allowed many German therapists to explain their former collaboration as a life-saving device, to "forget" that between 1933 and 1945 they had become richer and that they had been controlled by the Nazi state (Grunert, 1984, p. 867). After the war, they recalled only what was expedient: they "forgot" that in 1941 John F. Rittmeister, a member of the Reichsinstitut and for a while the director of its polyclinic, had been executed as an enemy of the Reich,[4] or that Mattias Heinrich Göring was in charge of the institute.

Actually, it took nearly forty years before surviving participants could talk openly. Walter Bräutigam recalled that as a young candidate at the institute he had found the Freudian members—Müller-Braunschweig, Schultz-Hencke, Riemann, and Kemper—more trustworthy than their Jungian and Adlerian colleagues (1984, p. 911). But memories are tricky: according to Kaethe Dräger, who had been a member of the so-called (Freudian) Gruppe A, no more than 5 percent of the therapists belonged to the Nazi party. Historian Geoffrey Cocks, who did not directly differentiate between Gruppe A and the others, found that "the percentage of party members among the early spokesmen for psychotherapy in the Third Reich and among the leadership of the German General Medical Society for Psychotherapy and the Göring Institute was much higher than that—37.17 percent had joined the party between 1930 and 1938" (1985, p. 48). Recollections diverged even more when it came to the role of Erna Göring, the wife of the director. She had been accepted as a member although she had had neither a didactic analysis nor case experience. Was she a Nazi or a friendly informer? She is said to have told her analyst of official suspicions about his colleagues, thus permitting him to forewarn them. But for the most part she was feared, so that her presence alone would have sufficed to undermine psychoanalytic confidentiality. In any event, most of the psychoanalysts did go along with Göring by holding that it was patriotic to take care of the Germans' mental health (Brainin and Kaminer, 1982, p. 994).

After 1945, Mitscherlich only suspected collusion. He could not know that the physical destruction of the Reichsinstitut had helped cover up cooperation by many therapists, including those in Gruppe A. But Johannes Grunert accidentally discovered some records of the Berlin institute in the archives of the Munich psychoanalytic society only a few years ago. Grunert concluded from these files that the psychotherapists had been at the Nazis' beck and call and that "medical psychology *as an institutional and professional entity* fared much better under National Socialism than might have been expected" (p. 871). On the one hand, the therapists had become entrenched; on the other, they had managed to elude direct control: the Nazis had been vague about the will of the masses the psychotherapists were to help manipulate, and the chaos among competing bureaucracies led the therapists to believe they were professionally autonomous. Still, a number of psychoanalysts belonged to the Nazi elite. Therefore, Grunert questioned whether, when the Allies took over, they "experienced débacle or liberation . . . [since] there were a number of indications that the loss of advantages and privileges was more painful than the relief from fear, shame and yoke" (p. 875). But in 1950, the Berlin therapist Werner Schwidder, reporting on the Nazi period in *Psyche*, maintained that "therapeutic and scientific work had been *un*influenced by the political aims that then were being promoted" (1950–51, p. 382).

The Allied occupation forces could not know that in April 1945 the Berlin institute's assets had been sent to Munich for safety. Occupation authorities were receptive to cooperation by all professional organizations for they served as channels of contact, and they especially welcomed the psychoanalysts' expertise: the German therapists, however, were exchanging the blessing of the Nazis for that of the Allies. *Psyche* became a bulletin of information on how to reconstruct the past, how to apply ego theories, and how to further antifascist thinking. In addition, it served as a forum for comments on ego psychology, attacks on "conservative" psychoanalysis, and discussions on applied psychosomatics. *Psyche* also printed cultural comparisons between tribal and advanced societies by Paul Parin, Mario Erdheim, Helmut Dahmer, Fritz Morgenthaler, and Klaus Horn. They all adopted an adversary perspective, in line with Mitscherlich's antifascism.

"German" Revisions of the Cultural Unconscious

The Swiss psychoanalyst Paul Parin, hoping to learn about unconscious mechanisms by psychoanalyzing members of a West African tribe, the Agnis, settled among them for about two years. He concluded that Agnis and Europeans have different ways of internalizing traditions and customs (Parin et al., 1971). Bracketing the psychoanalytic way of thinking itself, he expected to avoid so-called cultural errors by mediating between prevalent provincial perspectives and psychoanalytic ideas in a neo-Hegelian manner.[5] Agni men were found to idealize a "happy outlook and state of mind," and to lack Western ideals of accomplishment and "process of becoming." Because neither activity nor passivity was inherently good or bad, Parin maintained, the Agni self emerged without anal aggression, urethral ambition, or "phallic-oedipal centering of the libidinal object" (p. 546). Thus Parin cast the Agni as a modern version of Rousseau's noble savage—a savage partly aware of the industrial civilization he rejects. Parin's ethnopsychoanalysis combined Marxism, moralism, idealism, and the language of *Totem and Taboo;* he attacked "the cultural malaise of Western Civilization: One asks oneself whether somewhere in the world there are no better sociopsychological solutions: an education for freer, happier people, whose aggression will not end in murderous or suicidal wars, who do not sacrifice their children, do not hate their begetters and do not mutilate their love life" (p. 549; my translation).

Following Freud, Mitscherlich and Parin assumed that we could learn about our own society by studying primitive ones. But Parin, in order to point out the evils of class society, also included an analysis of German intellectual traditions. And to evaluate societal norms he revived the *Völkerkunde* (ethnology) of Freud's time.

When Parin left for Africa, he was a classical Freudian and a leading member of the IPA. But soon thereafter he accused his classical colleagues of being too preoccupied with the ego and its object relations and of having adopted bourgeois values.[6] Not wanting to incorporate these values in his theory, Parin expanded on Freud's early conceptualizations of drives and on Bernfeld's insights into adolescents' identity formation. In order to separate Freud's original observations from the idealist humanism of his time and to get a firmer grasp on intrapsychic processes within modern class structure—in the family, the destiny of specific drives, the shaping of class consciousness and of personality—Parin retraced Freud's path. But even accepting Freud's controversial assumptions about ethnology did not allow him to pinpoint when an individual's drives are "merging" with culturally induced psychic processes. Still, along with Mitscherlich and Habermas, Parin expected to prove that psychoanalysis is not simply a stopgap theory or "a floodlight for the indirect enlightenment of a historical-philosophical whole" (Habermas, 1982).

Sociologist Helmuth Dahmer, copublisher of *Psyche* (with Mitscherlich-Nielsen and Rosenkötter), set out to improve on philosopher Herbert Marcuse's Marx-Freud synthesis (1982). He cast both Marx and Freud as critical theorists who had expected to raise the consciousness of those whose fate they wanted to change. What Marx hoped to accomplish by the revolution of the proletariat, Dahmer stated, Freud expected to achieve by augmenting consciousness, through the "experimental acting" that patients were learning in their psychoanalyses. Thus, Dahmer concluded that "the 'objects' of both Freud's and Marx's critical theories have the possibility of becoming subjects, subjects of collective and of individual life histories" (p. 9).

To implement this theory, Dahmer reconstructed the genesis of psychoanalysis through the works of Freud and his leftist disciples (Ferenczi, Bernfeld, Reich, Fromm, and Fenichel). In the process, he argued against the Marxists' customary antipsychologism as well as against what he called American, or "adaptive," psychoanalysis. Since capitalism inevitably had contaminated psychoanalysis and had reduced *Gemeinschaft* to *Gesellschaft*, faulty perspectives and societal blindness, he held, were inevitable. So even Marxists, because they were socialized into capitalist society, were bound to suffer from a false consciousness (p. 377). According to Dahmer, this was why sociology and psychoanalysis could not be integrated. But Marxists such as Bernfeld, who were attuned to psychoanalysis, allegedly had taken the intellectual leap: they were able to use psychoanalysis for their own ends and thus could help modify the fate of their fellow citizens and of history (p. 385). (Ironically, Dahmer's opponents always ended up by dismissing him because he had not had a psychoanalysis.) In sum, Dahmer proposed an expanded critical theory that would cut through the "pseudo-concrete family framework" in order to initiate better societal practices and to enable us all to recognize historical truth (p. 386).

Dahmer's synthesis ran into the same theoretical difficulties as that of such predecessors as Reich, Fromm, and Marcuse, but it has more currency in Frankfurt than a conservative ego psychology, which—rightly or wrongly—is thought to allow for domination by analyst over patient, and thus for authoritarianism. Dahmer seemed to assume that enough psychotherapists could be trained to unravel the psychic "misunderstandings" of potential patients along with the societal ones, apparently not seeing the insuperable obstacle of analyzing nearly every German citizen. He also did away with the couch and thus with the free flow of patients' unconscious material.

Mario Erdheim's "ethnopsychoanalysis" took off from *Totem and Taboo*. He mediated between Freudian concepts and empirical facts while postulating the ethnologist's own self (perceived as analogous to the psychoanalyst's) as the research tool par excellence.[7] Because the participant observer's own cultural role inevitably disintegrates during fieldwork, and unconscious values and props of identity begin to founder when perceptions change, researchers, Erdheim claimed, "routinely" experience something akin to "social death" (1982, pp. 25–38). This state, he said, moved "between the analysis of one's own and the foreign culture . . . [for] to note things 'there' that become knowledge 'here' produces a sort of productive tension . . . [that] may awaken [conscious and unconscious] wishes and institute processes that will be blocked upon returning to one's own culture" (p. 34; my translation).

In essence, Erdheim compared Freud's creative state while discovering psychoanalysis to that of the ethnopsychoanalyst in the field.[8] After recounting how Freud had synthesized the universal components of family relationships with Austrian politics and Jewishness, his own professional hopes and status, and childhood memories and delusions of grandeur, Erdheim concluded that Freud had come to terms with the Nietzschean wish for power—the linchpin of Erdheim's thesis. As a product of his surroundings, Freud had "discovered" the Oedipus complex by "linking the banal fact that every adult once was a child to a theory of culture" (p. 84).

Returning to anthropology (Tylor, Marx, and Lévi-Strauss), Erdheim described the differences in personality formation among people living in "hot" societies (which allow for various rates of change) and "cold" ones (which freeze historical change), and then elaborated on those that evolve into mass culture. In the latter, psychic change is the product of impersonal institutions. But in *Totem and Taboo*, said Erdheim, reinterpreting Marx, the masses were closely related to their leader. Thus they were both his direct product and the basis for domination as perceived by the underclass.[9] When preoedipal identification "moved" from the father to the leader, however, mass psychology turned into individual psychology. Thus individuals in modern societies, Erdheim maintained, must control their sexual and aggressive drives for the sake of other interests (p. 197); and, for the sake of civilization, they transfer the dynamics of family interactions to other institutions. Dominators then benefit from the resulting (unconscious) projection (p. 199), from a social production of the unconscious that parallels the basic socialization process between men and women and the one between dominators and dominated (pp. 301–06).

Moving from sixteenth-century Aztec religion to nineteenth-century Europe, Erdheim found that control is always achieved through identification with the aggressor and that it hinges on the initiation of adolescents into adulthood: in modern societies children are "manipulated" into adult work and sexuality. Thereby, their "creative impulses and communication between id, ego and superego" (p. 307) are being stunted so that they suffer from ever more inflexible "crippled" egos, feelings of guilt, and compliance with social obligations. These factors, in turn, play into the hands of powerful rulers who "regulate" the unconscious and thereby help produce the "fantasma of the good ruler" (p. 319), who allegedly exploits narcissism and needs to be loved and admired by a group that minimally "controls" his needs for admiration. Because domination induces narcissism, psychoanalysis is the only way out.

This was how Erdheim accounted for the rise of Hitler. Erdheim's talents and broad background predisposed him to extend psychoanalysis into power relations: a Swiss whose early years had been spent in South America, he became a schoolteacher and was exposed to the French structuralist debates before being trained in psychoanalysis and ethnology. Erdheim's work is as unknown outside German territory as are the contributions of Dahmer, Brede, Lorenzer, or Morgenthaler. But this is only partly due to the cost of translations: the Marxist "connection" has less currency in countries with other traditions, and even in Germany it remains confined to a fairly small circle of vociferous "critical" psychoanalysts. In fact, many practicing psychoanalysts, I found, try to stay out of the political debates. In addition, theoretical examinations of the Nazi era (except for sensationalist media treatment) are less immediate and therefore less urgent outside Germany, except when applied to general questions of prejudice.

The Cultural Unconscious in France

The French unconscious has been conceived broadly, freely, and imaginatively, and it has been rooted in philosophy rather than in psychiatry or ethnology. Hence, the French conceptualized the etiologies of the unconscious at the highest level of abstraction. Psychoanalytic ideas had been peripheral in France because they did not support the tenets of the leading intellectuals or of the psychiatric establishment.

Immediately after the war, in 1945, the discussions between those intellectuals who had collaborated with the Nazis and those who had joined the resistance catapulted them all into the limelight. Sartre, at the center, soon maintained that psyche coexists with consciousness rather than preceding it and thereby closed off fruitful debates about psychoanalysis. The success of existentialism in both serious and pop incarnations kept psychoanalysis at bay until 1956, when Khrushchev's denunciations of Stalin proved Sartre's support of the Communists to have been ill-advised. Now, Sartre's politics started to fall into disrepute, and his philosophy was questioned.[10] In 1960, the philosopher Henri Ey organized a conference about "the unconscious" (1966, pp. 14–15), which he described as "the depth of being, as the opposite of nothingness, as absent from the field of consciousness, yet other than negation"—in a most Sartrean fashion. Thus, psychoanalysis entered the cultural conscious by a back door, not in the form of therapy, but as a component of yet another political philosophy. This was due largely to the proliferation of what some have termed the poetics of Freud's thought.[11]

Serge Moscovici, in his extensive sociological survey (1961), noted that the French knew little about psychoanalysis during the 1950s, that it was hardly mentioned by the media, and that books on the subjects did not sell. He also observed that many thought of psychoanalysis as an American import, like Coca-Cola and supermarkets. But Lacan put it on the cultural map. He challenged the classical Freudians, couched his attacks in political rhetoric, and thereby excited the public imagination.

Lacan's earlier indictments of the IPA as dominated by the Americans and the sharp disagreements these had triggered had been in the professional realm. Now, he called attention to the liberalizing potential of psychoanalysis. Within a few years, Parisian bookstores would devote entire sections to books on la psychanalyse: the subject was considered sexy, and it sold. By 1980, over three million copies of Freud's works and 110,000 copies of Lacan's *Ecrits* (a work totally unintelligible to the larger public) had been sold (Castel, 1980). One hundred and fifty new titles appear yearly, and virtually every publisher has a series on psychoanalysis. Even classical Freudians "benefited" from Lacan's frequent appearances on television and other popular media (Clément, [1981] 1983, p. 8). But this was after 1968, when Lacan had touched a chord among radical students and others on the left. So whereas psychoanalysis had previously been vaguely associated with conservatism, it suddenly began to be perceived as revolutionary and moved to the center of the culture (Kurzweil, 1980; Turkle, 1978).

After 1945, classical Freudians had revived the IPA: they had argued about the optimal length of training analyses and of individual sessions and had vied with one another for influence on the organization in the name of Freud. But Lacan opposed these "Americans" in typically French fashion: at the congress in Rome in 1953, he insisted that American analysts had been co-opted by the empiricists, had adopted some aspects of behaviorism, and not only had medicalized the discipline but had engendered a false scientism. Hence Lacan wanted the French association to break away from the IPA. But since the Americans held the majority of IPA votes, and many of his French colleagues objected to *his* practices, Lacan's suggestions were doomed. After his expulsion, he was free to vent his anger against the "establishment" and to take his version of Freud "into the street"—that is, to the culture at large. In fact, he converted and amalgamated his anti-IPA and anti-American sentiments into catchy slogans about the language of psychoanalysis and soon became a culture hero.

When Lacan acted as godfather, midwife, and public relations man to the structuralist movement, the movement reciprocated. Foucault's investigations into the history of medicine and of sexuality, for instance, touched on Lacanian observations, as did Barthes's explorations of the unexpressed erotic and emotional contents of written texts. Althusser's attempt to adopt Lacan's notion of the mirror-stage (see chapter 11) in order to comprehend better the earliest socialization process (he expected to learn how to counteract the infant's identification with adults whose unconscious had been indoctrinated by capitalist modes of thought and action) helped legitimate Lacanian psychoanalysis among the left. The idea that it might be possible to recast the personalities of future generations by changing the language (including body language and emotional messages) of the Other (usually the mother) held out hopes to French Marxists, who realized that capitalist relations of domination persisted in socialist societies—as Lenin already had observed.

Lacan's timing had been perfect: he had "joined the students" during the 1968 events, although his actions consisted of words and gestures alone. Thus he managed to take over the Department of Psychiatry at the University of Vincennes. The new Department of Psychoanalysis, which had very liberal admissions policies, offered courses in psychoanalysis for university credit—courses primarily centering on Lacan. Disciples aired theoretical controversies and endlessly dissected and free-associated to every one of his pronouncements. Some of these students claimed to have entered politics because they understood Lacan to have equated politics with the pursuit of self-interest. Asking for the accreditation of courses on psychoanalysis, therefore, was perceived as a political act. But later on, Lacan accused these same students of having played a successful game—a game that needed to be analyzed, he declared, lest its players remain "pawns of the government." These polemics themselves established la psychanalyse à la Lacan. According to J.-B. Pontalis, a philosopher-analyst who was close to Lacan between 1953 and 1959, Lacan's seminars with philosophers and writers almost single-handedly swung them over to psychoanalysis.

French classical Freudians have played down Lacan's influence. But one is struck by their own emphasis on language, an emphasis shared with Lacan. Though rejecting Lacan's theories, they remain aware of the use of words and the differentiation of hearing (*écoute*) from one analyst to another. In part, this derives from the fact that patients who previously were with Lacanians inadvertently bring with them Lacan's use of language and mode of thinking. But even more to the point, Lacanisms have spread throughout the culture.

Lacan maintained that transference is everywhere and that it functions predominantly outside the psychoanalytic session—in relation, then, not only to the analyst but also to politicians and other dominant figures. This extension of the transference among other things justified the structuralists' explorations of discourses with and among authority figures—including actors, doctors, and television interviewers. Still, we might question whether this type of "analysis" actually could change individuals' ways of dealing with authorities without some sort of psychotherapy, or whether unconscious responses really do follow from such public discourse, even if and when behavior is being affected. In other words, the cultural impact of Lacanian analysis could not and did not produce a population of psychoanalyzed citizens. On the one hand, Lacanian analysts did elaborate on what Freud had said long ago, in much simpler and more comprehensible language. On the other hand, classical Freudians were quick to recognize that they had to enter the Lacanian dialogue in response to some patients. Some of their colleagues in the IPA, however, became convinced that they had been "contaminated."

Lacan's death in 1981 created a vacuum, and the fight for succession enlarged the Lacanian polemics. His ideas continued to be explored, although the outrageous pronouncements and the excitement were missing. And many of the leaders of rival groups who touted one or another of Lacan's slogans as their leitmotiv seemed boring and inauthentic. Some groups started their own publications. Others invited psychoanalysts of different orientations to confront each other at their meetings and in their journal. Yet others, through *L'Âne* (edited by Lacan's daughter, Judith Miller) the Ecole de la cause freudienne, the unofficial successor to the Ecole freudienne, continued to venerate Lacan by expanding upon his contributions—what he had said in his public seminars, and in such *Ecrits* as "*Intervention sur le transfert*" (1952), "*Position de l'inconscient"* (1966), *"La chose freudienne"* (1956), and *"La science et la vérité"* (1966). But Lacan's style and charisma were missing.

By the 1960s a wide layer of the Parisian intellectual public had begun to accept and argue about notions of symbolism and the unconscious meaning of dreams, jokes, and rites. People were reading Freud in a popularized Lacanian version. This rereading itself reinforced notions of psychoanalysis *à la française.* Thus it does not matter whether one considers Lacan a genius and an intellectual hero or an impostor and a fraud. His presence and, as he might have said, his absence as well were responsible for the fact that psychoanalysis became a broad topic of discussion, gradually replacing the earlier knee-jerk Marxism, without fully relinquishing anti-Americanism.

In both America and France, psychoanalysis helped promulgate notions of individual self-realization, and in both countries classical psychoanalysis was being maligned as conservative, as too respectable. But that is where the parallel stops. For the popularizations of Freud in America, where Marxism was unpopular, came mostly from Freudo-Marxists like Fromm, Reich, and Marcuse, whereas in France, where Marxism was at home, they derived from the intellectuals' applications of structural linguistics. So in both countries the radical claims for psychoanalysis were based on the opposition to familiar and accepted theoretical discourses and to existing biases.

Classical Freudians could not accept the primacy of sociocultural and linguistic symbolisms over those of individual experience. If, as Lacan said, structures impose themselves on the infant as a matter of course and before awareness sets in, and the infant "absorbs" the symbolic order as a corollary to its language and its linguistic order, then Freud's id-ego-superego theory would be overshadowed or discarded. And by illustrating how language interprets intimate lived experience through immersion in a symbolic order rather than in the immediately lived truth, Lacan postulated language as a "trap" for the self and for lived experience. Such a revision of psychoanalytic theory and of immediate cultural variables (social origin and class) was meant to undercut the class-specific use of language and "elitism."

Even if Lacan had not been pleased to be "misunderstood," the fact that he superimposed linguistic theory on psychoanalysis made his pronouncements less and less intelligible to the uninitiated. In the mid-1960s, Lacan joined Althusser, Lévi-Strauss, and Barthes in publishing *Les Cahiers pour l'analyse,* thus turning their critical endeavors into an intellectual movement (Barthes, 1967, p. 7). In this climate, the propositions of "linguistic" psychoanalysis became assumptions. Soon, no one any longer questioned whether a self-assured disposition really could hide a vulnerable unconscious structure or whether unconscious signifiers, governed by metaphoric and metonymic associations over time, produce an ever more complex network: most French intellectuals accepted that both conscious and unconscious thought were organized in accordance with linguistic structures.

The superimposing of structural linguistics onto psychoanalysis posed countless intellectual problems. First of all, it is easier to state that incest is prohibited and that the Oedipus complex is rooted in unconscious social structures than it is to prove exactly how an individual becomes aware of his autonomy in society while growing into the symbolic order. Second, though most intellectuals will agree that symbols mediate relationships between man and man or self and other, and that such mediation inserts the child into its family with the help of encoded language, Lacan's emphasis on flux and mediation has been foreign to Anglo-Saxon empiricism. (Traditional societies, in fact, draw larger conclusions from family than more modern ones.) Although they might take seriously Lacan's central thesis of *le nom du père* in relation to *le non du père*,[12] they tend to consider many of his alliterations and play on words as exercises in frivolity. Given the complex jargon, people had trouble thinking of neurotics, for instance, as "having lost the symbolic reference of the signifiers constituting the central points of the structure of their personality" or of having "repressed the symptom's signified" (Lemaire, 1977)—formulations that flow from the distinctions between the Real, the Imaginary, and the Symbolic.

According to Anika Lemaire, one of Lacan's disciples, Lacan's "genius consist[ed] in having turned to his advantage the elaboration of the most recent and the most fashionable thought" (1977, p. 227). In fact, she believed that this loner had enlivened and rejuvenated Freudian psychoanalysis (p. 247). But whether we overestimate or deny Lacan's clinical contributions, he did move psychoanalysis into the center of French intellectual life. This alone would have made him legendary after his death had he not already been a living legend.

Austrian Psychoanalysis after the Second World War

Once more, Austria's lagging interest in psychoanalysis becomes apparent. Freud's ideas still have not permeated Austrian culture, even though many schoolchildren now are taken on visits to the Freud Museum. In fact, Austrian psychoanalysts continue to talk of a general resistance, although they note that simpler therapies like transaction analysis or Gestalt therapy are increasingly acceptable. Only in 1971, after Anna Freud had agreed to hold the

27th ipa congress in Vienna, did Freud's home become a historic site—in a city that otherwise lives off its history. And the Sigmund Freud Gesellschaft, which, together with the museum, is housed at Berggasse 19, is financed only partially by the Austrian government. The ipa contributes the balance.

The Viennese have been as ambivalent about the Freudians as they were about other intellectuals such as Wittgenstein or Karl Popper, and as they had been about Freud himself. Thus in 1971 it was reported by the press that most Viennese still did not know that outside of Austria Freud's reputation exceeded that of Mozart or Johann Strauss and that many Austrians had not even heard of him. This situation has recently improved, partly because the seven Viennese analysts accepted by the ipa in the meantime have trained a number of candidates, and also because of the attention psychoanalysis got from some of the radical students of 1968. But most Viennese psychoanalysts practice on a part-time basis, and very few of them do research. Psychoanalyst Hans Strotzka has said that the Austrian climate was counterproductive to scholarship because "the Jews are missing from the life of the mind" and because there had been "brain drains" for political reasons in 1934, 1938, and 1945. Strotzka himself is a prolific writer and, according to the American analyst Leopold Bellak, a first-rate short-term therapist. But, given the close cooperation among Freudians, Adlerians, Rogerians, and behavior therapists, theoretical boundaries are blurred. The more orthodox Freudians, who disapprove of this situation, prefer to keep to themselves and exchange ideas with their peers in the ipa. Those who work together at the Allgemeines Krankenhaus mostly do so in order to procure government funds and to settle issues of certification and reimbursement. They meet in case conferences to decide on the type of treatment best suited for specific patients: their personal and theoretical disagreements rarely reach outside professional or hospital walls.

Psychoanalysis or psychoanalytic therapy in a hospital setting can be problematic: patients must walk through other wards to see their analysts; doctors wear white coats; and formal admitting procedures underline the fact that the patients are mentally ill. True, treatment in such an environment also indicates that psychoanalysis is available to all, as a democratic right. The least sophisticated patients, however, tend to be the most frightened and therefore often do not come.

I was informed that in spite of the egalitarian ethos, final diagnoses tend to follow class lines: those who can pay also tend to be more educated and thus more verbal, so that they often are found to need psychoanalysis or psychoanalytic therapy; the poor are more often assigned to behavior modification. This appears to result in part from the fact that psychiatrists dominate mental health treatment and have ultimate authority over patients in hospital settings. In any event, these conditions together with the requirement that psychoanalysts must practice psychiatry for a number of years before being admitted to candidacy and that Adlerian therapy is more established, have helped perpetuate the low status of Freudian psychoanalysis.

No wonder, then, that psychoanalysis in Austria is in a weak position. In 1985, however, the situation was changing and demand was growing. And by 1987, the wpv had at least forty young candidates, all of them eager to practice analysis rather than therapy alone. General interest has also been rising, at least judging by the fact that the Freud Museum has many more Austrian visitors than before and that psychoanalysis is featured as part of the fin-de-siècle which is being revived all around, most recently with a mammoth exhibition.

There is also a young and growing contingent in Salzburg, an offshoot of the radical Munich analytic group started by the late Igor Caruso. Caruso trained in Buenos Aires, was first with the Institut für Tiefenpsychologie, and then held the chair in psychoanalysis at the University of Salzburg. His political ideas inspired Marxist students—students attuned to the German radical tradition and to the works of the Zurich analysts Erdheim, Morgenthaler, and Parin. These origins made the Salzburg candidates more "Swiss" in spirit than Austrian.

The Anglo-Saxons Reevaluate

In 1958, the philosopher Sidney Hook, at a symposium organized by philosophers, sociologists, and psychoanalysts, addressed the state of psychoanalysis "as a scientific theory, mostly from a metapsychological perspective." They could not agree on whether psychoanalysis was science or philosophy, metapsychology or therapy. Robert Waelder (1962), a Viennese who had settled in Philadelphia, insisted that psychoanalytic assumptions would one day be testable and pointed out that precisely because it was all of these things, and because people talked about them without drawing distinctions, or even knew that they were talking on different levels, animosities were bound to mushroom. For many years Waelder's pyramid of distinctions—clinical observation, interpretation, generalization, theory, metapsychology, and philosophy—was accepted.

Apart from the philosophical evaluations, Erik Erikson had started a new genre of historical analysis—psychohistory. In his book on Martin Luther

(1958), Erikson had treated him as the product of his social and economic class, of northern European consciousness, and of his early excremental experiences and language, which had led to an uncompromising certainty and rectitude (Loewenberg, 1983, p. 25). Thus Erikson had interwoven Luther's personal history and his social milieu to explain how his identity had been formed.

Peter Loewenberg, a Los Angeles historian and psychoanalyst, later refined the psychohistorical method. Loewenberg held that psychohistory, though thought of by some as value-free, can be used to serve both radical and conservative cultural positions. He suggested that it provides a tool for historians—a tool that needs perfecting. He used it in his excellent portrayals of such leftists as Otto Bauer and Victor and Friedrich Adler, as well as of the Nazi Heinrich Himmler (pp. 33–34).

In a different vein, the intellectual historian Christopher Lasch (1978) wrote about narcissism "as a defense against aggressive impulses rather than self-love" and pathological narcissism as a critical tool to comprehend cultural change. The use of these complex concepts in what became a popular book itself indicates how widely accepted psychoanalysis had become in the America of the 1980s. That this book has been extensively translated appears to attest to the American Freudians' "intellectual hegemony."

The ubiquity of psychoanalysis also engendered an interest in biographical reinterpretations. Historian William J. McGrath (1986), for example, reconstructed Freud's student days (drawing on Freud's previously unavailable letters to his friend Eduard Silberstein) in relation to the rise of anti-Semitism and nationalism. Like the historian Carl Schorske, he located Freud in the turbulent philosophical and literary maelstrom of the disintegrating Hapsburg Empire, which helped shape his ideas—ideas themselves nurtured by early dreams, fantasies, and aspirations. And Ronald Clark's (1980) competent biography has been superseded by Peter Gay's (1988), whose thoughtful use of previously unavailable materials is a distinctive contribution.

The majority of American sociologists have shunned psychoanalysis, although Talcott Parsons made it the cornerstone of his personality system (Kurzweil, 1987a). His student Gerald Platt, together with Fred Weinstein (1973), aware of the problems inherent in fusing psychoanalysis and structural-functionalism, rethought the theoretical problems and found that an object relations approach was the most congenial for such a sociological project. Since any network of object relations lends psychic support and meaning to everyday situations, they argued, its loss also tends to bring about psychic and social instability. Robert Endleman (1981), trained in sociology, anthropology, and psychoanalysis, maintained that relevant aspects of all three disciplines have been applied successfully to issues of human evolution, sex differences, homosexuality, and the relationship between deviance and psychopathology. After surveying and integrating the enormous literature on these subjects, Endleman concluded that even though psychoanalysis is far from complete or perfect, it is still the best psychology we have (p. 4).

In recent years, though less popular than the denigrations of psychoanalysis, the reevaluations of the history, and the publication of Freudians' letters and biographies, there has been an upsurge of philosophical contributions. These picked up the issues the 1958 philosophical symposium had reviewed and explored them more systematically. These contributions, however, no longer address Waelder's "levels" but deal with specific criticisms.[13] One of the most interesting and stimulating of these approaches was by the "hermeneuticists"—philosophers Jürgen Habermas and Paul Ricoeur and psychoanalysts George Klein and Roy Schafer. Basically, they all argued, or assumed, that causal validations need not be tested by scientific standards—as the followers of Karl Popper and the empiricists demanded—because psychoanalysis has its own scientific method of arriving at interpretive insights.

Adolph Grünbaum (1984), however, offered the most serious objections to these hermeneutic positions. He began by questioning the status of psychoanalysis as a natural science by way of Freud's own contradictory statements. Freud had originally rebuffed the methodological separatism of the *Geisteswissenschaften*, then had considered "psychoanalysis a part of the mental science of psychology" (*S.E.*, 22:158), and nevertheless had gone on to maintain that "no new sources of knowledge or methods of research have come into being" (*S.E.*, 22:159). This led Grünbaum to conclude that Freud had applied the neurological terminology of the 1895 "Project" in an increasingly "mentalistic" sense, so that the empirical basis of the central concept of repression could not be proven—even if one accepts its basis in the (universal) sexual striving of infants, in dreams, slips of the tongue, remembering and forgetting. By separating the "metapsychology" from the clinical theory of repression, Grünbaum went on, "Freud's criterion of scientificity [became] methodologically [though] not ontologically reductive" (1983, p. 7).

Thus Grünbaum refuted the hermeneuticians' "philosophical reconstruction of the clinical theory . . . [as] a mythic exegesis of Freud's own perennial notion of scientificity" (p. 93). But he also denied the Popperian claim that psychoanalytic theory was *not* testable by demonstrating that some of Freud's predictions, particularly the connection between repressed homosexuality and paranoia, *could* be tested. He then argued that clinical material—as the product of free association—is more contaminated than Freud had assumed, citing the psychoanalyst Judd Marmor, who had found that patients, by responding to their therapists' expressions, glances, "uh-huhs," and so on (p. 211), tend to validate whatever theory their analyst happens to adhere to. This allegedly supported Freud's clinical observations but "proved" that his edifice—because it was based on observations of data patients "produced"—was flawed (Grünbaum, 1983, p. 13). Ultimately, Grünbaum concluded that the psychoanalytic method suffers from epistemic defects but that extra-clinical studies may yet prove Freud's cardinal hypothesis (p. 27).

Grünbaum's complex argument was criticized not only by the philosophers he was refuting but by many of those who wanted to bury psychoanalysis. The literary critic and former "Freudian" Frederick Crews (1985), for instance, wrote of the demise of psychoanalysis and pitied the analysts who had been "caught up in a medical and intellectual charade." He denounced Ernest Jones as a hagiographer and Freud as having provided insights only into his own mind.

One of the humanists, Ilham Dilman (1984), argued that Freud made an original and lasting contribution to psychology by demonstrating that his was a "*noncausal conception of the mind . . . [and that his] determinism was a vision of man's slavery to a part of himself and the possibility of the individual's liberation from such bondage*" (p. 3). Dilman elaborated on Freud's distinctive way of thinking and on the value of his road to self-knowledge. Grünbaum, of course, dismissed such an argument as too steeped in idealism—claiming he did not want to demonstrate the conditions that shackle individuals. Nor was Grünbaum addressing questions of freedom and autonomy, for Dilman spoke to Freud the moralist—from a moral (rather than a scientific) philosophical perspective.

Judith Van Herik (1982), on the other hand, addressed Phillip Rieff's *Freud: The Mind of the Moralist* (1959), which saw Freud's "pejorative image of women" as part of the "general critical component of Western philosophies" (p. 3). Reading Freud's ideas on religion in tandem with those on gender, she discovered that Freud had discerned similar mental structures in femininity and Christian "illusion," in masculinity and "Jewish renunciation of wish," and in the human (masculine) ideal and postreligious psychoanalytic "scientific attitude" (p. 2). The primacy and importance of the father, the dangers of wish-fulfilling illusions, and the differing perceptions of feminine and masculine development, she demonstrated, were all rooted in his psychology of religion. She did not dismiss Freud's achievements.

W. W. Meissner (1984a), a Boston Jesuit and a psychoanalyst, pointed to the dynamics between religion and psychoanalysis. Because psychoanalysis arose in a culture antithetical to religion, he argued, Freud used a scientistic model of mind, so that anything that smacked of the spiritual or "supernatural" was anathema to him (pp. 3–4). Yet throughout his life religion surfaced in the dreams he reported, in his correspondence, and in his works on religion itself. Hence, Meissner noted, Freud had explained the evolution of Jewish monotheism in relation to psychic and religious dynamisms and to the interplay between communal forces and intrapsychic ones—the roots of religious phenomena (p. 133). Still, even Meissner thought that the tension between psychoanalysis and religious experience may not be entirely resolvable, because it includes a number of dialectics: the relative emphasis on conscious versus unconscious; on freedom versus determinism; on understanding experience in epigenetic or reductionist terms; on behavior as teleological or casual, as moral or instinctually motivated; and on the theologian's belief in the supernatural the psychoanalyst rejects (p. 205). All these handicaps, however, according to Meissner, might be overcome by exploring the connections between compatibility and incompatibility in order to gain insight into human conditions of freedom (pp. 239–50).

In the 1960s, leading sociologists suggested some interesting explanations of sociological behavior. There was, for example, David Riesman's (1950) theory of "other-directedness." Peter Berger (1963) talked of "lack of character" owing to the multiple roles individuals must play in modern society, and Erving Goffman (1959) noted a corresponding need for "impression management."

In the 1970s, there was a large shift in sociological conceptions of self, which, tacitly accepting the focus on narcissism, started to converge with the Freudian conception. These studies were directed at explaining the increasing preoccupation of the "me-generation" with themselves. Furthermore, the psychoanalysts' diagnoses seemed to bear out what the sociologists were saying, for patients who came to the analysts displayed fewer symptoms of structural neuroses, and analysts no longer saw the hysterical types Freud had described. Now, patients suffered from difficulties in working, loving, and relating. Hans Morgenthau and Ethel Person (1978) noted that the shift in symptomatology corresponded to a shift in theoretical emphasis—a shift to the explanations and findings by Mahler, Jacobson, Kohut, and Kernberg. They noted that "the formation and maintenance of both ego ideal or ideal self and superego in personality structure reflect the historical process and changing cultural values, . . . [and that] the current cultural crisis was manifested through the many faces of narcissism [and] reflected the loss of a con-sensually validated value scheme." Now, these authors pointed out, the nar-cissistic personality may arise in response to cultural dilemmas and not just out of disordered individual development. Freud, of course, had maintained this all along.

When Morris Eagle (1984), a professor of psychology in Canada, sum-marized *Recent Developments in Psychoanalysis* he emphasized that disorders of the self may arise not only as a result of culturally accepted child-rearing practices but in response to other social factors (p. 73). However, he argued primarily that the many reformulations and alterations are more than exten-sions of Freud's theses.[14] By demonstrating (with comparisons to sophisti-cated studies on monkeys) that maternal care (object relations) is a crucial and independent factor in determining the child's affective and cognitive links, Eagle supported Balint's "primary object love" and Fairbairn's "object-seeking" libido—in opposition to Freud's "pleasure-seeking" one and to "primary narcissism." Eagle's conceptualization ultimately led him to con-clude that biological imperatives, as the sources of our desires, must find their way into our psychological and experiential world: self-organization is a bio-logically evolved adaptive hierarchical structure coordinating all sorts of functions (p. 207). Such a theory, or synthesis of diverging "classical" theo-ries, I believe, is itself a response to the Babel of psychoanalytic practices and languages and might be a fulcrum around which the factions within the vari-ous psychoanalytic associations could unite.

American Freudians also have been facing a number of concrete battles. In his push for consumers' rights in the late 1960s and early 1970s, Ralph Nader, for instance, argued for the accountability of all professionals, includ-ing psychoanalysts. This meant, among other things, that Freudians were pushed to "prove" their professionalism by providing evidence of the efficacy of their therapy. A few of them, such as Otto Kernberg, Margaret Mahler, and Robert Wallerstein, set up control groups to measure the progress of psychoanalytic patients in the way other psychologists do; other psycho-analysts fell back on their medical credentials.[15] By 1980, governmental agen-cies had cut mental health benefits in hospitals and outpatient clinics as well as money for basic research. But the heaviest blow was dealt by the American Psychiatric Association when, in the third edition of the Diagnostic Manual (DSM III; 1980), psychoneurosis was eliminated as a distinct category of ill-ness, thereby disallowing much of the available insurance reimbursement. This produced an emphasis on the physical manifestations of psychic ailments—the final blow in reducing the "art" of Freudian therapy and "returning" it to medicine.

Comparisons of Freud's Cultural Influence in the Various Countries

Seventeen years after treatment for psychic disturbances became legally reimbursable, the German sociologist-journalist Hans-Martin Lohmann argued that "battalions of doctors were marching on the paved roads of psychoanalysis toward social prestige" (1984a, p. 11). He wondered how much corruption of consciousness this entailed. Such "conventionalization through self-castration," he stated, had been noted by Adorno (1951) (and by Kurt Eissler), who had predicted that psychoanalysis eventually would die of conformity and self-satisfaction—"a beauty no longer able to disturb the sleep of humanity." But Adorno and Eissler were talking about America, where, according to Lohmann, Freudian lay analysis, which presumably could be less rigid, had been slain long before, around 1928.

In every country, however, professionalization could occur only after a certain sector of the public had accepted psychoanalytic premises and after leading psychoanalysts had cooperated with the legal authorities to regulate access to practice. (It has been argued, however, that the fact that the Americans, for instance, closed their gates early and that the Germans began to train lay analysts and then licensed only those who had completed "classical" training reflected the interests of established groups.) In any event, psychoanalysis in America was appealing to broad segments of the population, and its survival in one form or another was being assured through governmental policies. In Germany, however, psychoanalysis also was thought to further social criticism. But when the success of Mitscherlich's enterprise converted psychoanalysis into a therapeutic profession, it gradually turned into a sinecure for some of these therapists. Individual therapy alone no longer incorporated the early social criticism—the critical edge of psychoanalysis.

Mitscherlich's intellectual successors, however, attacked this "new malaise." They depicted German psychoanalysts as money grubbers who, like their American counterparts, sit behind their couches and plot to limit access to the profession in order to maintain their elite status. Remembering Mitscherlich's insistence that psychoanalysis also be a tool for research and that psychologists and sociologists work with analysts, they strongly opposed the proposed medicalization of German psychoanalysis. They argued against setting up a situation, similar to the American one, where poorly trained therapists practice on a "black market" and attack the "authorized" practitioners as "elitist." In Germany, of course, these "black marketeers" also compete for patients who have already spent their permissible reimbursement hours. There has been a good deal of criticism of the psychoanalysts' short-range view in their moment of triumph, on the ground that it was turning them, once again, into a caste courting defeat—unless "critical psychoanalysis" were to prevail.

In France, this sort of criticism came from Lacan and from countermovements such as anti-Oedipus (see chapter 12)—which diligently questioned the legitimation processes of every movement. But there too, after psychoanalysis had become acceptable, simpler and more cost-effective therapies gained ground. Elsewhere this process was fairly slow, but in France psychoanalysis made a rather sudden quantitative jump.

In England psychoanalysis never really took hold outside London, and it retained its upper-class aura. Still, the fact that the theoretical innovations emanated from the Tavistock and Hampstead clinics' child studies and from the object relations elaborated by the Middle Group established English psychoanalysis firmly.

In Austria, Alderians had paved the way for the Freudians with the public, but according to the Freudians the Adlerians had allowed individuals' defenses against unconscious knowledge to remain intact, so that their patients had not had a real psychoanalysis. This seems to have held true, however, for most Catholic-dominated and Communist countries—in the former because of religiosity, and in the latter, repression.

But everywhere, generational differences were observable. While older people continued to shun psychoanalysis except as a last resort, rebelling students in many countries, I was told, employed it to criticize their elders. After having accepted American ideals, at least those of their own generation, German youths, mostly as an antidote to fascism, were being encouraged to examine Freud in conjunction with Marx. Yet, when they started to become anti-American (allegedly in response to the Vietnam War), their inquiries into American history—however superficial—also led them to look into their own past. This activity, in turn, pushed them to take note of their ambivalences and to examine them in psychoanalytic terms. There were fewer radical students in Austria and no figures comparable to Horkheimer and Adorno (after having spread critical thought they were being attacked as too uncritical), who had returned to teach in Vienna. Thus German intellectuals had been pushed to confront their complicity with the Nazis and their own anti-Semitism, whereas Austrian intellectuals had managed to obfuscate or "forget" it: they behaved as if they had been Hitler's victims rather than his hosts.

America, with its 250 "official" therapies—from Wilhelm Stekel's "Active Analytic Psychotherapy" to "Zaraleya Psychoenergetic Technique"—has become the foremost "therapeutic society." Few of these therapies would be acceptable to Freud, although they all have a certain relation to psychoanalysis: some, when not referring to work with the unconscious, deny its existence; others speak of the self or the ego but deny all relation to classical analysis in affirming the uniqueness or efficacy of *their* practices; and others (though "officially deviant") do affirm their descent from Freud. (More of these "easier" therapies are being transplanted to Europe, where they are recast to fit specific conditions.) Even though the classical Freudians have been reduced to an ever smaller caste, psychoanalytic ideas—if not directly then indirectly—have penetrated every American hamlet and intellectual endeavor. And like Coca-Cola, Ivory soap, and blue jeans, they have been marketed and accepted throughout the rest of the world.

Chapter 11

Theoretical Innovations

By the end of the Second World War the theoretical lines had been drawn. Adlerians and Jungians, in spite of having made common cause with the Freudians under the Nazis, remained persona non grata with Freudians nearly everywhere. The followers of Otto Rank were supporting short-term therapies and developing techniques for themselves and other "imitators." The "culturalists" had left the fold, so that the "scientists" could elaborate their theories without disruptive interference. And they all had their own associations. Most of the followers of Abraham and Eitingon were attuned to Anna Freud's focus on defenses and most of Ferenczi's to the techniques of Melanie Klein. Meanwhile, the more eclectic analysts of the Middle Group were investigating the ramifications of object relations. But as more and more of the Freudians as well as their imitators, mediators, and innovators tried to solve the psychological riddles Freud had left behind, they developed a veritable Babel of theories.

The forced exodus from Central Europe had not only scattered the early analysts all over the world but opened their minds to new situations—situations they promptly analyzed.[1] In the process, they reformulated a number of Freud's concepts and added new ones. Given that Freud no longer could synthesize their contributions and that Anna Freud did not command enough authority to do so, the Freudians lacked a true, or single, intellectual center.

256

In England institutional conditions encouraged "many flowers to bloom," whereas in America the so-called ego psychologists prevailed. Because the analysis of defenses is ego-oriented, Anna Freud and the Americans tended to see eye to eye, whereas Melanie Klein's ideas appealed to a number of South Americans, were praised by Lacan, and inspired such Londoners as D. W. Winnicott, Joan Riviere, and Paula Heimann. Since some of Klein's and her followers' ideas, and those of such French analysts as Béla Grunberger and Maria Torok (who came from Hungary), can be traced to Ferenzci, some have argued that they perpetuated the Budapest School. (Its revival in Budapest itself is yet another phenomenon.)

But wherever the Freudians located their origins, they would link themselves to Freud, not just out of loyalty but out of a desire to promote their own concepts; they all wanted to win converts and to transcend their immediate milieu. By presenting papers at IPA meetings, the best, or at least the most convincing, theorists would be celebrated. Thus the globe-trotting psychoanalysts carried new ideas from one setting to another and perpetuated the movement.

The Rise of Anglo-Saxon Ego Theory

We have noted why Anna Freud and Melanie Klein could not get along and how Jones helped "resolve" their differences. But cleavage among the Londoners alone could not explain why ego psychology was so inordinately successful in America, or why American Freudians so readily went along with the former Viennese Freudian Heinz Hartmann. In fact, Hartmann's "Ego Psychology and the Problem of Adaptation" (1958) was originally presented to the WPV in 1937, a year after Anna Freud (1936) had demonstrated that the ego, because of its link to perceived reality, tended to dominate id mechanisms. This was also after Ives Hendrick (1936) had shown that individuals dominate reality by using their competence and ego strength, and after Siegfried Bernfeld (1931) had inferred that people tend to project their own ways of interaction onto others.

But theories themselves are projected and adapted in specific fashion. For example, Hartmann's statement that "adaptation to social structure and co-operation is essential to humanity" was being heeded only after his arrival in America ([1939] 1958, p. 31). Indeed, it converged with the popular melting-pot ideology and provided a theory for common beliefs. Furthermore, it could explain how and why some groups of immigrants got along better than others, and why in Europe whole populations were adapting to fascism. During World War II, the Freudians explored the relevant mechanisms of intra-psychic conflict by focusing on the integration and coordination of contra-dictory drives, as Freud had suggested in "The Ego and the Id" (1923).

By the time the war ended, Hartmann, Ernst Kris, and Rudolph Loewen-stein (1946) could state with confidence:

Psychoanalysis has developed under social conditions rare in science. . . . The situa-tion of the 1940s is hardly reminiscent of the period of early teamwork; large groups of psychoanalysts work in ever looser contact with each other and the diffusion of psychoanalytic concepts in psychiatry, their extension into psychosomatic medicine, social work and various educational and psychological techniques, opens up new vistas of development. (p. 11)

These authors, eager to bring all the modifications and reformulations of Freud's theories under one roof, set out to integrate early hypotheses and later shifts and emphases and to address "problems of ego development and superego formation" (1946, p. 13). They expected to clarify psychoanalytic terms from a structural perspective by separating them from and subordinat-ing them to questions of libidinal development. They also maintained that the concepts of id, ego, and superego were already *in incubo* in some of the formulations of the 1890s. And by demonstrating that recently accumulated empirical data *did* fit into Freud's "three centers of psychic functioning (char-acterized by their developmental level, their amount of energy, and their in-terdependence at a given time)," they further justified their claims (p. 14). Their relation to Freudian orthodoxy was to be the subject of many subse-quent controversies. But Freud himself had not been clear: in *Beyond the Plea-sure Principle* (1920), he had concluded that "the ego is the true reservoir of the libido," but two years later he reversed himself and "recognized the id as the great reservoir of the libido." According to Strachey, Freud had envisaged two processes: (1) original object cathexes go out from the id to the ego indi-rectly, and (2) the whole libido goes from id to ego and reaches objects only indirectly (*S.E.*, 19 : 63 – 66).[2] In any event, Hartmann, Kris, and Loewenstein chose to read Freud in the following way:

1. They stayed away from biological correlations, because Freud had once said that he preferred using psychological terminology until an ade-quate physiological vocabulary was available (1946, p. 15).[3] Since the time was not yet ripe for such substitution, they decided to stay away from Freud's par-allels between the psychic and the central nervous systems. (This opened them to attacks by some psychosomaticists, especially in France, who insisted that psychoanalysis has to connect biological, psychic, *and* linguistic features.)

2. They objected to the use of metaphoric language as nonscientific, because "metaphor infringes on meaning and anthropomorphizes the structural concepts." Thus they also argued against Franz Alexander, for whom "the id, ego and superego had become exalted actors on the psychic stage" (p. 15). (Rejecting metaphoric formulations *also* goes against the French grain.)

3. They decided to "replace the word 'ego' in Freud's text by the word 'self,'" because Freud had used the term ambiguously, sometimes referring to the whole person, sometimes to his psychic organization. (This differentiation, it has been argued, was to make psychoanalysis sound more scientific.)

4. Instead of speaking of superego approval and disapproval, they concentrated on degrees of tension between psychic mechanisms. Such an approach was to lead toward a developmental model of ego control. Child studies had yielded much empirical information on the effects of toilet training—of stimuli influencing conflicts between elimination and retention, the child's attempts to control, and the mother's requests—and they expected to systematize these data. Because Freud's own metaphors had led them to understand the part anthropomorphism plays in introspective thinking, the authors decided to employ his structural concepts and to separate them from the drives (pp. 17–21).

5. They held that the defense mechanisms controlling instinctual drives take root toward the end of the first year and found that by then the child's lasting object relations (to mother) were in place. Because of this "newfound security," they noted, anxiety was taking on new shapes (p. 27).

6. After establishing that defenses were central, they concentrated on specific ego defenses—to cope with id impulses, with the outer world, and later with the superego. Now, repression was thought to demarcate sharply the boundaries between id and ego (pp. 28–29). (This was why in the 1950s and 1960s American candidates were taught that the analytic focus *must* be on defense mechanisms.)

7. They described the replacement of the pleasure principle by the reality principle as a learning process that transforms libidinal energy into aim-inhibited libidinal energy. And this process, they noted, enriched the child's inner world (p. 30).

8. Summarizing Freud's ideas on superego formation during the oedipal period, the authors wanted to explain how early (and rigid) moral conduct becomes differentiated. hence they distinguished the child's identification with the idealized parent (his perception was altering along with maturation) from the psychic energy that gets sublimated and used in idealization and

from the internalized aggressive attitudes, which were found to be the energy behind superego demands.

9. Unlike Freud, who thought that personality development was more or less complete at this point, Hartmann, Kris, and Loewenstein expected existing psychological structures to be modified by development itself. (This supported Piaget's theory of children's moral development—from moral absolutism to differentiation—via a gradual adjustment of superego functions during latency.)

10. As adolescents look for support outside the family, the authors continued, they may choose a new set of ideals. In this process, the condition that had accompanied superego formation in the first place—rebellion—was said to be reactivated. And this situation was found to trigger changes in identification.

11. But the superego also takes its clues from cultural forces, which impinge on its functions. Instead of pursuing this point, however, they simply said that when social values change rapidly and new ones do not replace them, or when "new ideals of conduct do not supplement the older structure of the superego," individuals become compliant (pp. 34–35).[4]

12. In conclusion, they repeated that dynamic and genetic variables are responsible for the formation of psychic structure and proposed to prove their hypotheses by means of psychoanalytic observation of infants and children (p. 36).

Hartmann, Kris, and Loewenstein's basic propositions became the American Freudians' bible for the next two decades. They encouraged and bolstered scientific research in education, developmental psychology, and social psychology. At the IPA congress in 1949, the flowers they planted were still in full bloom. The Freudians' most prestigious publications, the *International Journal of Psychoanalysis*, the *Psychoanalytic Quarterly*, and the *Psychoanalytic Study of the Child*, increasingly printed articles on concerns of the ego and the superego and techniques of breaking down defenses. Ego psychology started to crowd out most other tentative approaches. And even though the Freudians had their near-heretics, the discussions they engendered themselves boosted and legitimated ego psychology.

Jeanne Lampl-de Groot (1947), for example, maintained that the focus on ego and superego tends to deny the significance of the id drives in shaping them. She agreed with Hartmann that the ego develops out of an inborn core but put more weight on the id (as reservoir of mental powers and determinant of drive development) than he did. Thereby, she questioned whether there really exists an undifferentiated phase from which both ego and id are said to emerge. Instead, she maintained, intelligence grows out of an inborn ego-core, out of Freud's "instinctual trends," which, like Piaget's "réflexe hereditaire," stay in touch with the environment—at first with the id and later with the superego. Thus Lampl-de Groot backed Hartmann, Kris, and Loewenstein in holding that "when ego ideal and judging functions form a unity" self-respect is strengthened (p. 10). But she was more free-wheeling. She even borrowed from Adler's ideas on power and approved of some of the observations by the psychologists Karl and Charlotte Bühler and Wilhelm Stern. And like Anna Freud, she postulated the superego as an heir to the Oedipus complex—internalized by means of identification and thus depending on parental influence.

The more radical theoretical views which were being debated at the first postwar meeting of the IPA soon fell away. In 1949 Lacan presented his new version of "The Mirror Stage, Source of the I-Function as shown by Psychoanalytic Experience"; Daniel Lagache of the SPP offered "From Homosexuality to Jealousy"; Henri Flournoy of Switzerland spoke of "Poetry and Childhood Memory"; and Karl Müller-Braunschweig and Harald Schultz-Hencke argued about whether or not Schultz-Hencke's neo-analysis was psychoanalysis or had been Hitler's handmaiden (*Bulletin*, pp. 178–208). But a much larger array of articles pointed to the coming predominance of ego theory: the Londoner Edward Glover spoke on "Functional Aspects of the Mental Apparatus"; his colleague Willy Hoffer on "Oral Aggressiveness and Ego Development"; René Spitz on "Anxiety in Infancy: A Study of Its Phenomenology"; Gustav Bychowski, of the New York Psychoanalytic Institute, on "Therapy of the Weak Ego." Anna Freud presented "Some Clinical Remarks concerning the Treatment of Cases of Male Homosexuality"; the Freudians debated the merits of Michael Balint's "Changes in Therapeutical Aims and Techniques" and Herbert Rosenfeld's "A Note on the Psychopathology of Confusional States in Chronic Schizophrenia." All in all, the American ego psychologists' scientific formulations, supported by a number of Londoners, impressed their colleagues enough that they tried adopting them. In any event, the "Americans" Hartmann, Kris, and Loewenstein had already started to dominate the theoretical drift.

Anna Freud versus Melanie Klein

Melanie Klein's contribution at the 1949 congress was "On the Criteria for the Termination of a Psychoanalysis" (1950, pp. 78–80). She spoke of the conflicts and anxieties during the first year of life, focusing on what she saw as the two main processes of development—the "paranoid-schizoid position," when anxiety is maximal, and the "depressive position," when the baby begins to differentiate itself from the mother and realizes that it both loves and hates her. By postulating that the child's ego emerges from the earliest mechanisms of projection and introjection, she talked of "putting things outside" and "taking them inside." And by maintaining that the child's first oral experiences, its perceptions, gratifications, and responses to feeding, influence all the later developmental stages, it follows that the earliest somatic experiences inevitably revolve around feeding. But for Anna Freud disturbances in children stem from the unsuccessful negotiation of the Oedipus complex—a stage that comes long after the first year of life. In her heuristic scheme, the child's ego is constructed primarily by the way it represses its instincts and handles the integration of these instincts during the oedipal period. Thus she accounted for her father's oedipal theory as well as for her own emphasis on defensive mechanisms.

In *The Psychoanalysis of Children* (1932), Klein elaborated on Freud's juxtaposition of the love and death instincts; she found that mourning reactivates the most terrifying anxieties of earliest infancy. By observing how these panics are handled, she evolved her theory of depressive and paranoid positions as well as her ideas of restitutive and reparative mechanisms—based on the infant's perceptions and subsequent internalization of love, hate, and sadism, of good and bad objects. Freud, however, had talked more of how the mourner tests reality, whereas Klein's concern was with how and why separation reawakens the earliest unconscious fantasies that induced the paranoid feelings and manic defenses in the first place. She noticed that each separation from a loved one induces mourning and thereby revives these traumatic events, along with the infant's "terror of disintegration and total annihilation [which] is the deepest fear stirred by the operation of the death instinct within" (Segal, 1979, p. 115).[5] That was why Klein regarded the struggle between life and death instincts as central to survival from the moment of birth. Freud, however, had assumed that the handling of this conflict was being resolved along with the oedipal trauma and was also an expression of the castration fear.

In her later works, Klein (1957) added envy as one of the fundamental and most primitive emotions arising in infancy. She considered the (successful or unsuccessful) initial feeding experiences to be the linchpin of future psychic life and therefore concentrated on the infant's responses to its mother's breast:

The love, care and food received from the mother stir in the infant two opposite reactions: one of gratification leading to love, a primitive form of gratitude, the other of hostility and envy, based on the realization that the source of food, love and comfort lies outside one's self. Those feelings are not related to the physical feeding only. For the gratified infant . . . idealizes the breast and experiences it as a fount of love, understanding, wisdom and creativity. . . . Envy of the breast is stirred by gratification . . . but can also, paradoxically, be stirred by frustration and deprivation. (Segal, 1979, pp. 139–40).

When Klein began to draw detailed distinctions among envy, jealousy, and greed, she advised her fellow psychoanalysts on how to help integrate their patients' split-off envy. She expected them to learn the "proper" technique for overcoming the inevitably "negative therapeutic reactions" caused by the child's initial response to the therapist. Still, she also realized that in the severely disturbed envy was constitutional and thus could be neither altered nor integrated. Constitution, however, once more invoked "nature" as well as the metaphoric and biologic connections the ego psychologists preferred to bracket.

Inevitably, the theoretical controversies between the followers of Anna Freud and Melanie Klein became intense not only because their ideas diverged more and more but also because their differences were embedded in child therapy—the empirical core of their work and the center of their professional being. Anna Freud, for example, taught her students to form an alliance with their young patients' own ego capacities. For her, as long as the child was dependent on its parents, there could be no viable psychoanalytic transference; child therapy was thus not possible before the superego was strong enough to deal with actual parental authority—that is, not until around the age of five. Melanie Klein, however, assuming that general anxiety and dependence allow very young children to develop a strong and early transference, argued that no matter how difficult it might be to reach them, their analysts ought to ferret out their disturbances at once and to speak about them at what they deemed the proper moment. In fact, precisely because she believed that early interplay between loving and aggressive impulses determines the course of the oedipal conflict, she expected to address these earliest experiences directly. The sooner this happened, she insisted, the "easier" it might be for the child to recall them, and the less the child would suffer.

This theoretical conflict was exemplified, for instance, at the Hamburg congress in 1985, when Edna O'Shaugnessy, a London Kleinian, described how she had helped a three-and-a-half-year-old boy. She depicted his terrifying anxieties, his excessive clinging to his mother, and his defiance of her, and went on to recount how she had gained his confidence by playing, talking, and interpreting. The analysis, she maintained, helped him through a specific crisis and at the same time revealed underlying problems owing to his early development. Almost before she had finished, Serge Lebovici, a French colleague and former IPA president, attacked her for having intervened too much and having relied on the sort of suggestive interpretations the ego psychologists avoid. He doubted that she could have had the impact she claimed or that she had dealt with any of the child's deeper disturbances. On the surface, his comments seemed to relate to questions of therapeutic method alone. But they also involved the validity of his own more classical theories and methods.

Still, at least one of Klein's concepts—projective identification as the mechanism structuring the functions of the mind—has now been adapted by a number of mainstream Freudians. In essence, this concept refers to primitive projection and postulates that a partial or an entire self may in fantasy be projected into (rather than onto) an object. The therapy accompanying this particular view of psychic construction was found to be especially useful for the treatment of patients with psychotic delusions and for borderline personalities. (In America such patients for a long time had been handed over to the psychiatrists.) When Joseph Sandler, the London Freudian and for some years the director of the Sigmund Freud Center in Jerusalem, set out to show why projective identification is such a useful concept, he explained that Anna Freud had anticipated it in her notion of "altruistic surrender" when she described "living through another person" and emphasized the importance of vicarious gratification of unconscious and forbidden wishes (1984b, p. 8). But Klein had gone beyond such "superficial" projection:

Projective identification has manifold aims [insofar as] it may be directed towards the ideal object to avoid separation, . . . toward the bad object to gain control of the source of danger . . . [for] bad parts of the self may be projected in order to get rid of them as well as to attack and destroy the object [whereas] good parts may be projected to avoid separation or to keep them safe from bad things inside or to improve the external object through a kind of primitive projective reparation. (Sandler, 1984b, p. 9)

Sandler thought that individuals elicit the projected behavior in others through subtle unconscious pressures in normal life and that they do so even more in the transference-countertransference—allowing for a sort of vicarious gratification. The London child psychologists, of course, had been dealing all along with projective identification as they mediated between Klein's "infant's capacities and overtures for 'primitive relationships' in the earliest phase of life [and]

Anna Freud's . . . instinctual drives [that are] 'object-relating' rather than 'object-seeking'" (Daws and Boston, 1977, p. 264).

But American ego psychologists not only agreed with Anna Freud (and Freud) on the centrality of defenses but held to a genetic metapsychology that differed from Klein's. Nor did they take to Klein's reliance on ever more metapsychological phenomena in ever younger children, as her descriptions were becoming either too metaphoric or too physiological.

When Hartmann addressed these issues in "The Technical Implications of Ego Psychology" (1951), he had assumed that psychoanalysis had come of age and that "the interdependent role of technique and theory" had become more important than clinical discoveries; he had asserted that ego psychology's theories had advanced beyond its techniques. Therefore, he had suggested that efforts be directed toward understanding the dynamic and economic properties of mental life and their intrasystemic functions (that is, whether or not autonomous ego functions are interfered with or otherwise hampered by defensive ones). And he had emphasized again that the only way to improve psychoanalytic techniques would be by learning more about the unconscious mechanisms of resistance—that is, by engaging in research.

The Americans certainly tried to do so, to judge by the proliferation of empirical studies, commentaries, and case reports. In the process, they revived and reexplored every one of Freud's ideas. They questioned the extent to which the psychological constitution of the ego and the outer world go hand in hand; they examined how the unlimited narcissism of the newborn gets socialized; and they wondered about the conditions of transition from primary to secondary narcissism. Some held that the transformation of the ego—from its primitive beginnings to its full development—helps transform the ego's libido into object relationships. Others, such as the Viennese émigré Hans Loewald, thought that this happens when "earlier and deeper levels of ego-reality are penetrated and integrated as dynamic sources of higher organization" (1951, p. 18). Now, the Freudians moved toward a more fluid view than Hartmann's, as the less "scientifically" oriented among them considered his concept of the ego to be "fixated at its full development."

In general, the ambience of the Londoners lent itself to more flexibility. Members of all three groups were likely to note the implications of projective identification or to question whether or not superego formation might begin in infancy rather than during the oedipal phase. Thus Paula Heimann could maintain that the techniques of the Freudians and Kleinians actually did converge (1950, p. 81), and Margaret Little (1951, pp. 32–40) could talk of "a synthetic kind of defense mechanism produced by the combined unconscious work of patient and analyst." This judgment seemed to be echoed by Annie Reich (1951, pp. 25–31) in America when she held that all patients aim to turn the analyst into a "screen onto which they can project their infantile objects, to whom they can react with infantile emotions and impulses, or with defenses against them."

Signs of Theoretical Restlessness

Until the early 1960s, variations on these themes set the theoretical tone among American ego psychologists and the members of London's Hampstead and Tavistock clinics. By then, many American and British analysts had instructed potential colleagues on the Continent, and others had established societies in South America. Now, all these younger psychoanalysts did their own research, based not only on what they had learned from their analysts and supervisors but also on what they considered useful to the particular situations they were encountering. Their adaptations and the Londoners' influence eventually succeeded in threatening the supremacy of the American ego psychologists, who felt increasingly defensive. But for some time, they all more or less cooperated in research on children and adolescents, or at least in discussions of their findings in numerous symposia. The global themes at large congresses, such as "sublimation" (APA, 1954), "aggression" (IPA, 1971), "affects" (IPA, 1977), and "research and practice" (IPA, 1975), always featured analysts who were working with children. Furthermore, many of the American and Continental Freudians also went to seminars in London. So in spite of growing theoretical divergences they continued to present the world with a united—though less and less popular—front and to accept Anna Freud as their symbolic leader.

By the mid-1960s, a number of criticisms had shaken the American analysts' complacency. Kurt Eissler (1965), much like Bernfeld before him, had assaulted medical orthodoxy and pointed to the dangers inherent in a "respectable psychoanalysis tied to universities." But this sort of self-criticism was mild compared to the disapproval by some of the leading Londoners such as Wilfred R. Bion (1970), John Bowlby (1970), and those whose theories routinely had been rejected by the classical ego psychologists.

No doubt, this was what motivated Bion's scathing attack on American control (1970). According to him, Freud had taught ordinary people to illuminate the mind (just as Faraday had shown them how to illuminate a room by touching a switch); but the American Freudians were ordinary people who had taken on Freud's airs yet lacked his talents: they went in for scientifica-tion, vulgarization, and simplification (p. 74). By institutionalizing psycho-analysis, Bion concluded, they had institutionalized their own establishment and control by their group (p. 82).

Bion was anathema to the ego psychologists for a number of reasons. First, he did group therapy and observed the formation and resistance of sub-groups (see, for example, Pines, 1985). Noting that groups behave just like individuals in that they rely on fight or flight, pairing, and dependence, he analyzed the expectations and resistances of members of subgroups regarding their leaders as he would analyze the manifestations of individuals' trans-ference phenomena. Second, he treated psychotics and borderline patients. Assuming that every psychotic has a normal as well as a psychotic personality, he "examined the schizophrenic experience of attacking thoughts by attack-ing the links between objects and between object and self, the precursers of thought" (Grotstein, 1985, p. 302). Third, this led him to deduce that the psychotic experience resulted from the mother's failure to contain her in-fant's fear of dying, an explicitly Kleinian position. In fact, James S. Grotstein maintained that Bion's concepts of the *container and the contained* influenced Klein's metapsychology (in her formulation of the adaptive principle which explains how internal psychic reality accedes to the external one) as well as the rest of Freudian metapsychology. Fourth, he supplemented language (the vehicle of desire) with mathematical symbolization, in line with Lacanian and deconstructionist views holding that Language (L) and Knowledge (K) can no more than approximate Truth (T) (pp. 298–99). Fifth, his theories of transformations and of an infantile mental catastrophe as the basis for the development of a psychotic personality once more supported and relied on Melanie Klein's paranoid-schizoid and depressive positions (p. 304).

Inevitably, Bion's views did not support the Oedipus complex as the linchpin of psychic development. And he argued, for example, against the analyst's recording of dreams, associations, gestures, or any other data, be-cause this would prevent him from properly experiencing a session. Patience alone, he maintained, could allow unconscious materials to surface, although the process would be helped by interpretation to reduce anxiety and en-gender feelings of security (1970, p. 124).

Bion accused American ego psychologists of being false Messiahs, of being greedy and envious, and of simplifying and schematizing. Although the Americans for a while reciprocated not through confrontation but through silence, ultimately Bion's attacks led them to talk *about* psychoanalysis in ad-dition simply to practicing it—as Bion had admonished. And like Lacan, he kept accusing them of not facing their wishes for validation, popular repute, and approval in their own analyses and reanalyses (p. 66).

Understandably, most of the Americans were no more eager to discuss Bion's contributions than those of other dissenters, such as Melanie Klein or John Bowlby. Bowlby ([1969] 1980) essentially differentiated among behavior that initiates interactions (touching, embracing, reaching, calling), behavior that occurs in response to the mother's initiatives, attempts to avoid separation (clinging, crying, following), and exploration owing to fear or withdrawal. He found that every child's most traumatic experience of attachment and loss was rooted in separation anxiety and subsequent mourning (for the mother rather than her breast). Now, orality became central. Analyzed by the Kleinian Joan Riviere, Bowlby became an independent when he began to interpret Anna Freud's and Dorothy Burlingham's work with orphans and displaced children. Soon, he addressed the ideas of René Spitz (1946, 1955), Winnicott (1960), Fairbairn ([1952] 1954), Freud, Karl Abraham, and Melanie Klein. He also took a more ethological view of instinctual life than Freud had done when he postulated that it follows a predictable pattern (based on a sequence of behavior) in order to preserve both individual and species. Yet Bowlby's notions of *social releasers* (human faces and voices tend to bring about babbling) and *social suppressors* (rocking or rapidly walking with the infant tends to end its crying from loneliness) assumed a rather relaxed (Kleinian) therapeutic setting (including the use of imagination) rather than the personal detachment and "rigorous and objective scientism" advocated by most ego psychologists. He also paid more attention to the social context than Freud had done. Differentiating between stimuli and responses to them, he argued that infants' friendly responses such as smiling and babbling are easily elicited and reinforced by human stimuli; picking them up and holding them most rapidly end crying caused by nakedness but not that caused by pain, cold, or hunger.

Anna Freud first criticized Bowlby for assuming that an inborn urge ties the infant to its mother and later for arguing that this tie was being disrupted. She asserted that Bowlby dealt with the activities of drives rather than with their mental representation, ignoring the fact that "the pleasure principle . . . governs all mental activity and processes, including the tie to the mother" (A. Freud, 1960, p. 64). By discussing Bowlby's ideas in ego-psychological terms, she could chide him for having understood infantile narcissism descriptively rather than metapsychologically and for having perceived the child's attachment to the mother not because she had nurtured it but because she had given birth. And she could talk of children's *withdrawal* rather than their *de-*

spair: since she had observed children who upon separation had lost such ego functions as speech or bowel or bladder control, she noted that pathology resulted from what happened during the time libido was being withdrawn from the mother (p. 61).

Max Schur (1960) took another approach. Focusing on Bowlby's comparisons of the child's behavior to the instinctive and phylogenetive behavior of animals, he felt that Bowlby ignored interspecies differences and "assumed [that] the fully innate, unlearned character of most complex behavior patterns [belonged to] . . . an instinctual response system," such as sucking, crying, smiling, or clinging (p. 64). Schur held that Bowlby's theories were "reversing" Freud's sequence by moving from a psychological concept of instinctual drive to a biophysical one (p. 67), thus confusing drive behavior with its characterization and primary with secondary drives. Consequently, Bowlby was unable to account properly for complex interactions central to "primary anxiety" (p. 78).

René Spitz (1960) could not agree with Bowlby's Kleinian cast, because he held that loss of the mother figure and loss of the breast are both undynamic formulations: object relations depend upon perceptual and emotional maturation, and the meaning of behavior in interchanges between libidinal and aggressive drives counts more than its manifestations. That the classical Freudians finally took note of these dissidents indicated that their former self-satisfaction had given way and that they were ready for reformulations—as the discussions around Heinz Kohut's conceptions of the self and Otto Kernberg's object relations were to prove (see below).

By the late 1970s, Freudians felt beleaguered, not least because the media kept reporting that shorter therapies were found to be as effective as four to five weekly sessions over at least four years. Although these claims could be dismissed when they were made by outsiders, when made by individuals such as Eissler, Bion, or Winnicott they posed a threat within the IPA. By now, the growing South American contingent also supported the forces opposing the ego psychologists. Led by one of the Argentina society's founding fathers, Angel Garma (1971), they advocated expanding and elaborating on Freud's death instinct. Soon, the Argentinians traced both Kleinian practices and metapsychology to Freud's metapsychology and by 1984 were arguing for the superiority and legitimacy of the Kleinian School (Bianchedi et al., 1984).

The ensuing discussions ultimately paralleled the disagreements between Freud and Ferenczi, with the Freudians taking sides as they revived and exaggerated this old conflict. Now, the ego psychologists appeared more conservative than they actually were. In fact, they were doing psychotherapy and were treating fewer and fewer analytic patients. But it took them a long time to admit that they were diluting their psychoanalysis with psychotherapy.

Listening to Lacan

Since the early 1970s, Lacan's theories to some extent had filtered back into the IPA, in part via the South Americans, and in part via the younger members among the French. Lacan's ouster, of course, had slowed his influence. But his growing importance in French culture at large nearly paralleled the waning hegemony of the American ego psychologists. Their radically antagonistic premises did not allow for cohabitation. First of all, Lacan had maintained that language was the intervening structure in the psychoanalytic relationship and that its neglect falsified all of Freud. His often-repeated idea that "the unconscious is structured like a language," which assumed a dialectical relationship between words and meaning, between specific discourse and personal relations, as well as between all the possible associations and reciprocal connections between them, challenged accepted Freudian methods. Second, Lacan's patients did not have neuroses (or psychoses) in need of cure but had bodies whose symptoms presented themselves in metaphoric forms— symptoms whose roots were to be discovered (and eliminated) with the help of structuralist language analysis. Third, he attacked the ego psychologists' analysis of resistances as "reinforcing the objectifying position in the subject," thereby distorting or missing what still remained unconscious ([1966] 1977, pp. 30–39).

Lacan proceeded to reread Freud's texts with the help of Saussurean dialectical relationships—between *langue* and *parole*, and between levels of speech and systems of signs, which also were said to account for the dual aspects of concept and sound image. This approach led him to conceive of the ego as the locus of misapprehensions, "the site of the subject's imaginary identifications" derived from "outside"—that is, from the child's first apprehension of itself in the mirror, and from what he called the "specular reflections" in its parents. Basically, Lacan stated, this original self-perception (at between six and eighteen months of age) is of fundamental psychological importance, especially since it occurs in the preverbal stage:

The *mirror image* situates the agency of the ego, before its social determination, in a fictional direction, which will always remain irreducible for the individual alone, or rather, which will only rejoin the coming into being of the subject asymptomatically, whatever the success of the dialectical syntheses by which he must resolve as *I* his discordance with his own reality (Lacan, [1966] 1977, p. 2).

Lacan proposed that therefore the ego originated in the "dialectic of narcissistic identifications with external Imagos" and during secondary identification searched for a moral, conformist ideal. Thus it was constructed around self-perception and was "composed of layers of structures . . . corresponding to Freud's topographical distinctions between conscious, preconscious and unconscious," each with its own meanings, concepts, and ideas in discourses (pp. 3–4). Since every word has overlapping significations, and every utterance has roots and reverberations in yet other utterances, he attacked the ego psychologists' focus on defenses as inadequate. Their interpretations, he maintained, are counterproductive and worthless because psychoanalysts' words cannot nail down meaning any more than words by ordinary mortals can.

So far as I know, no American Freudian ever claimed to have found the "final meaning" of a patient's associations. Many of them, in fact, agreed with the Los Angeles Freudians Robert Stoller and Ralph Greenson and with their colleague from Yale, Stanley Leavy, in that they wanted psychoanalysts to be simple, clear, concrete, and direct and to use words that could not be misunderstood. In practice, of course, this view clashed with those of Lacan's followers who explored chains of signifiers in order to get to the origins of desire.

Freud had held that "something in the nature of the sexual instinct itself is unfavorable to the realization of complete satisfaction." Lacan said that ego psychologists, a term that gradually came to signify *all* American Freudians, had not grasped the full implications of this statement and had reduced sexuality to a need ([1966] 1977, pp. 281–91). Instead of simply reiterating that the child's oedipal wishes *had* to leave the id ungratified and forever dissatisfied, he spoke of desire as being before and beyond demand: through endless sublimations, multiple displacements from one signifier to another, the primal unconscious desire becomes alienated in demand, "whose proper characteristics are eluded in the notion of frustration" (p. 286). He went on to elaborate that "if the desire for the mother *is* the phallus, the child wishes to be the phallus in order to satisfy that desire . . . because that demand requires that he be the pallus" (p. 289). (How this inspired feminist theory is discussed in chapter 7.)

Because such articulation can never be taken at face value, Lacan contended that plays on words, parapraxes, slips of the tongue, and other sorts of double meanings tell more than words alone. His own free associations to this truism and the play on words often were turned into theory. One of these theories derived from the relationship between the father's name and his authority. It was used as a weapon against opponents, against the Freudians' invocations of Freud. Thus Lacan's *nom du père* and its association to the *non du père*—as carrier of the law as well as of the phallus—not only put down his colleagues in the IPA but also elaborated on the signifier of the unconscious— that is, of the *imaginaire*. Lacan linked this concept, on the one hand, to the *symbolic* order and to death (the symbolic father who signified this law through the incest taboo was said to be the dead father), and on the other hand, to the *real*—that is, the order that corresponds to the birth of the triadic (oedi- pal) situation. This situation once more was discussed in terms of the ana- lytic dyad, where the patient makes *regressive* demands in the transference- countertransference relationship.

When Lacan proposed to improve this type of interaction by having the patient analyze the analyst, most of his classical peers were aghast. Yet Stanley Leavy, a leading American Freudian, thought that Lacan offered "a newer and keener insight into the minds of patients, and freed . . . [psychoanalysts] of the pseudobiological dependencies of the traditional libido theory or the occult tautologies that constitute much of ego psychology" (1983a, p. 6). In other words, Leavy suggested that American Freudians reexamine their views of therapy. In intent though not in method, Lacan seemed to be echoing the idea of the psychoanalyst Leo Stone, who divided the therapeutic relation- ship into "three types of coexisting patterns: the real and actual integrated one; . . . the transference-countertransference; and the . . . routinized activi- ties, deprivations and prohibitions originating in . . . analytic technique . . . [that] must be *lived out*" (Stone, 1961, p. 55).

Neither Leavy nor Stone supported Lacan's methods of exploiting the insecurity of the analysand—for instance, by allowing the analyst to read his mail and receive phone calls during the analytic hour, and to end a session within five to twenty-five minutes. Lacan justified this flexibility by recalling how unstructured Freud's early analyses had been and by insisting that in- sights come between rather than during sessions. He created even more havoc by decreeing that candidates instinctively know when they are ready to function as analysts and should not be held back by organizational rules. To overcome this obstacle, he instituted *la passe*—the step that was to "free" the candidate from his or her supervisor. The candidate was to present a "com- pleted" case to a group of "impartial" analysts—that is, to Lacanians with whom he had had little or no contact and who were unfamiliar with the case.

Many Lacanians, however, ended up practicing without having *passed*. Even those who did pass lacked their master's charisma. Some turned to imi- tating his style of dress, speech and manner. Others adopted his habit of equivocation, and yet others followed his advice by prolonging their silences to the point of not saying anything at all. Theoretically weak, they all were on the alert for the emergence of the "language of the unconscious."

After this unconscious language became the talk of the town, it filtered back to the SPP. Soon, some of its members began to speculate about verbal expressions of the transference. They questioned how the return of the repressed was being articulated, how children's dream symbols were manifested in contrast to written and/or adult symbols, and how such symbols were being expressed in the analytic situation. André Green, for example, though never breaking with the SPP, contrasted discourse and language by postulating the bodily presence in the imaginaire. Later, Green (1973) attacked Lacan for neglecting affect: if it derived from representation in language, how could it be displaced outside language? His colleague J. A. Gendrot (1968) delineated the differences between phonetic and semantic language. And Guy Rosolato said he was rejecting Jones's view of symbolism as a negative and regressive aspect of defense mechanisms, as he went on to conceptualize symbol formation in linguistic terms—via metonymic coherence and metaphoric symbols being expressed through sexuality and according to laws of language determined by the symbolic father (1978, pp. 303–13).

But for many years most members of the SPP had toed the classical line. According to Ilse and Robert Barande, they had been discussing object relations in more or less classical fashion. Béla Grunberger, a native Hungarian, found in 1954 that Freud's and Ferenczi's ideas still prevailed over Melanie Klein's, that regression rather than early fixation ultimately weighed most heavily in infantile neurosis—even though he implicitly accepted "passive introjection" as part of identification (Barande and Barande, 1975, p. 85). Yet he rejected the idea of a therapeutic working alliance between analyst and patient, which American Freudians take for granted, on the ground that the ego works in the direction of resistance rather than health (Oliner, 1988). Serge Viderman came out for constructive interpretation at the most opportune moment (p. 87) and later on elaborated on the spontaneity of the transference, whose "past is deformed by projection and whose present is brought on by the defense" (p. 89). Serge Lebovici, the Barandes noted, tried to unite his colleagues by denouncing the French fondness for abstract interpretation as well as blindly following a specific (American) theoretical model that did not sufficiently account for the patient's associations. Like Freud, he suggested, psychoanalysts ought to speak of constructions rather than of reconstructions (pp. 87–88). Conrad Stein (1971) noted that clinical techniques had improved; and F. Pasche (1969) accused the Kleinians of atemporal interpretations.

All these rejections of Kleinian formulations—which to some extent had been called forth by the Lacanians—indicate that object relations theory nevertheless was gaining in currency among the Parisians. At that time, American Freudians had no such preoccupations. Nor did they write books against Lacan. By 1970, Didier Anzieu (a member of the SPF and an early disciple of Lacan) was even talking of the "introjection of the mother's speaking mouth"—a formulation no American Freudian could have dreamed up. By 1986, Anzieu had rejected Lacan's therapy, particularly his refusal to work through the negative transference and his expectation to remain forever the *maître penseur* of his "students" (1986, pp. 41–69).

In 1979, Serge Lebovici, then president of the IPA, boasted of the classical training offered by the SPP, whereas four years later he was upset by the pervasive Lacanian influence (personal communications). But many Freudians outside France remained unaware of this impact. At the first congress of the Sigmund Freud Center in Jerusalem (May 1984), for instance, a French participant, when commenting on a case from the floor, elaborated on the real, the imaginary, and the symbolic orders. But no one in the audience seemed to take note that this was a Lacanian sequence, as the discussions moved into questions of symbolism. Nor did any of the French classical Freudians consider themselves in any way heretical.

German Theoretical Trends

Postwar Freudians in Germany followed two different theoretical paths. This was not very noticeable at first, when those who took their lead from the Berliners did all they could to catch up with the Anglo-Saxons. But soon, Mitscherlich also would be informing psychologists, judges, and physicians that psychoanalysts are not pulling doves out of hats like magicians but, rather, are applying a complex clinical method; and he set out to legitimate them as scientists (1967, p. 9). At the same time, he wanted to improve this method to help reclaim the German psyche—the task of the Frankfurt School.

Those who were eager only to emulate the Anglo-Saxons did not make any specific theoretical contributions. They set up societies and later on institutes in order to train candidates who would see private or clinic patients. But Mitscherlich, as was noted in chapters 5 and 6, intended to mold psychoanalysis into a tool to explore further Freud's dialectic between the ego and the id. Strictly speaking, he did not add to clinical psychoanalytic theory. Yet, by extending it to apply to social and political factors in Germany (1970), he expected to undercut identification with Nazi fathers and leaders and to change traditional relations to authority. The Germans were unable to mourn (either for Hitler or for the atrocities they had committed or had not prevented), argued Mitscherlich, because in their "fatherless society" their egos had remained underdeveloped: psychoanalysis alone *might* redeem them. Essentially, Mitscherlich maintained that ambivalent wishes, demands by the id and the superego, and their social manifestations had to be brought into consciousness before the members of "deindividualized masses" could develop a viable ego ideal and could "destroy" their former idols. But each German had to face this past individually via a more or less "pragmatic" Freudian analysis.

Although Mitscherlich's own early theoretical interest was in psychosomatics, he encouraged his followers to reach further. The most theoretical among them was Alfred Lorenzer. He tried, for instance, to extend Viktor von Weizsäcker's (1947) experimental research on the influence of the *Umwelt* (outer world) on nervous substances to understand how and why physical reflexes are triggered by moving objects and how and why some automatic responses to speed and light are accompanied by optical illusions and others are not in order to locate the subjective determinants of these and other events (p. 9). He drew especially on the German physiobiologist and anthropologist Jakob von Uexküll, who had conceptualized the Umwelt as coherent with our "planned corporeality." Like von Uexküll, Lorenzer began by pointing to the differences between animal and human behavior (owing to language) and tried to get to the nexus of individual-social subjectivity by reviewing what had been said about it by everyone from Kant to Marx and Piaget. Among the plethora of theories, he found that Freud's libido theory came closest to an "understanding praxis."

Since socialization is rooted in the mother-child dyad, as well as in the specific interaction between preverbal and language development and in the child's "biological/instrumental equipment," Lorenzer postulated that "impulses are related to ongoing changes in object relations and biological maturation" (1981, p. 97). He went on to compare the formation of language signals and symbols in psychotics and neurotics and concluded that the unconscious of *all* children internalizes class-specific language. (The lower-class mother, for instance, was found to react more readily to nonverbal gestures and stereotypes than her middle-class counterpart.) Lorenzer expected to redress this inequality by reconstructing the early trauma with the help of psychoanalysis (focusing on and working with the patient's alternation between libidinal closeness and distancing [1981, pp. 154–55]).

At the same time, Lorenzer criticized ego psychology as adaptive to the status quo and tried to construct psychoanalysis as it might have been had it not fragmented into various factions. Hence he adopted Lacan's use of language to mediate among psychological, societal, and biological data—though he was careful not to subordinate any one of them to any other (1973, pp. 48–49). But he did not pursue Lacan's objections to psychoanalytic organization or his penchant for free association. Instead, Lorenzer expected to "find the roots of mental disturbance . . . [to] explain its patterns, [to] discover the drive [that is] defined biologically," and to liken this drive to "the organismic synthesis of social discourse with nature" (1984, p. 212).

Moreover, Lorenzer returned to the 1895 *Project*, which he examined as "a network of metaphors based on a non-mystifying hermeneutic of the body [that] reaches beyond 'physiology' and 'social analysis'" (1984, p. 214). This return to the theoretical womb—with the help of the most sophisticated methods of French language analysis—ultimately connected him to his German idealist past. And, like the Mitscherlichs, Lorenzer found that regressive psychic mechanisms and the wish to avoid risks while being protected were mirrored in the social structures of dictatorships. In fact, Lorenzer too wanted to find out how the search for a "super-father" might interfere with good parent-child relations and how discussing real conflicts might reduce aggression and "grotesquely inflated narcissism" (Mitscherlich and Mitscherlich-Nielsen, 1967, p. 39). Since the Nazi past was found to have damaged the development of "productive narcissism" in puberty by interfering with the dissolution of early object relations and the creation of new ego ideals and identifications, the vast majority of German (unanalyzed) parents and children still were found to be retreating into themselves.

New Links among Object Relations, Perversion, and Narcissism

While the Germans were looking to Freud's theories of narcissism to help them understand the side effects of extreme authoritarianism, French analysts were increasingly examining the consequences of the narcissistic desire for the penis as the symbol of omnipotence or power. Their American peers hoped that a greater focus on the narcissistic aspects of the ego might help explain—and undo—the unexpected consequences of permissive upbringing. So although they were addressing very different issues, the psychoanalysts in these countries nevertheless counted on finding their answers in Freud's formulations of 1914 and 1915. In "On Narcissism" (1914c) Freud had argued that the infant at first is indifferent to the external world, so that pleasure and satisfaction are primarily autoerotic. In "Instincts and Their Vicissitudes" (1915c) he had held that the infant acquires unpleasurable objects from contact with this world. Thus by taking in (introjecting) pleasurable environmental stimuli and casting out (projecting) unpleasurable ones "the *original* 'reality-ego'" was said to change "into a purified pleasure-ego" (*S.E.*, 14: 136). But this was a hypothesis rather than scientific evidence: both the mechanisms of Freud's formulations and the role and fate of early narcissism were yet to be revealed by infant research. Among the profusion of American investigations on this subject, Margaret Mahler's contributions stand out.

Mahler, trained as a pediatrician, at first worked with autistic children at a baby clinic in Vienna. Drawing on psychoanalytic observations of these children and normal ones, she concluded that autism and symbiotic childhood psychosis develops in children who have not experienced their mothers emotionally and thus suffer from ego deficiencies. In 1959, she headed a team of researchers observing the intimate interactions between normal mothers and their infants. They analyzed unfolding mother-child relations in tandem with the children's emerging sense of self and thereby started to differentiate between the subphases of the separation-individuation process. Soon this focus on development led Mahler's associate Manuel Furer (1967) to perceive "identification with the comforter" as indicative of future superego formation. He found also that such identification "increases the child's capacity to bind its aggression and helps bring about the required reaction formation" (pp. 277–80). Together with John B. McDevitt, Mahler looked at the connections between adaptation and defense and learned that a child's character traits are determined by its adaptive style and its defensive behavior, which "gradually become internalized as more or less successful defense mechanisms" (1979, p. 100). Stressing the child's sensitivity to separation from birth to about three years, Mahler conceptualized loneliness, vulnerability, and helplessness from the perspective of the "reality-ego." Hence she was observing phenomena that Melanie Klein had located at an even earlier unconscious level and that Piaget had ascribed to cognition. Her coworkers Anni Bergman and Steven Ellman maintained that Mahler, like Freud, observed "cognitive structures that develop in relation to the self (selves) and important object representations," and they noted that Mahler's "developmental lines . . . [and] cognitive structures" were not Piaget's (1985, p. 251). Indeed, Mahler's concern with separation and individuation belonged to American ego psychology.

So did the work of Heinz Kohut. But whereas Mahler's "self" was rooted primarily in Freud's 1914–15 contributions, Kohut, a Vienna-born neurologist who graduated from the Chicago Institute of Psychoanalysis after the Second World War, basically took Freud's 1917 works as his theoretical point of departure. This meant that like Melanie Klein he took Freud's death instinct seriously and that *his* "self" developed from a more unconscious—or metapsychological—level than Mahler's. What to her was individuation to Kohut was the establishment of an autonomous self.

Kohut had noted that children tend to make up for the "unavoidable shortcomings" of maternal care and the concomitant primary narcissism either by evolving a grandiose and exhibitionist self-image or by creating an idealized parental imago. As the gleam in the mother's eye mirrors the child's exhibitionist display, he found, the child's self-esteem and grandiosity get inflated. For Kohut narcissistic disorders may begin as soon as the baby is born. Depending upon the severity of his or her misperceptions, the child might start to suffer from temporary or permanent self-fragmentation or from self/ self-object failures (unsuccessful integration of early experiences) that engender feelings of emptiness and loneliness. Hyman L. Muslin (1985) summarized these exceedingly complex psychodynamics:

When the cohesive self breaks down or becomes fragmented, in response to a self-object rupture, it may . . . maintain a state of *chronic frustration* (protracted fragmentation disorders, borderline personalities), . . . may repair itself, . . . (episodic fragmentation), may reequilibrate itself with newly developed defenses against self-object bonds (narcissistic personality disorders), . . . or may focus on drives that are salient in the current developmental phase . . . as a manifestation of a regressive reaction (neurotic syndromes). (p. 213)

Because these narcissistic structures are bound to show up in the transference neuroses, Kohut now reconceptualized the psychoanalytic method of curing them. He had noticed that earlier experiences of both grandiose self and idealized parental imago are mobilized during the *idealizing transference* and that the vicissitudes of narcissism could be alleviated by strengthening ego functions (1971, p. 28). But this meant that the analyst had to break through his patients' extraordinarily resistant walls of defenses against infantile (oedipal) wishes by providing large doses of approval during the working-through process. Such patients, however, continue to be particularly fearful of regression to early traumatic events and of reexperiencing their accompanying rejection, Kohut maintained, and therefore construct many obstacles within the "mirror transference"—which alone can handle the nearly insurmountable frustrations and discomforts brought on by the analysis itself. Even the most skilled analyst, Kohut continued, may have difficulty in dealing with a patient who suddenly idealizes him and just as suddenly turns on him. The analyst, he cautioned, may overlook his own intolerance to the release of narcissistic tensions, but he will be compensated when watching such a patient's "growing self-esteem and realistic enjoyment, and the unfolding of moderate achievement, humor, empathy, wisdom and creativity" (1971, p. 199).

Kohut's conceptualization of the self was useful to the social scientists and philosophers with whom he cooperated in Chicago and to others who wanted to explain the "loose morals" and glorification of the self by what came to be known as the "me-generation." But his theories and methods of dealing with narcissistic disorders, psychoses, and borderline states challenged those of other analysts, like Otto Kernberg, the rising star on the psychoanalytic horizon.

Unlike Kohut, who did not believe that narcissistic personalities were seriously threatened with massive disintegration, Kernberg saw them as suffering from a combination of pathological condensation of real self, ideal self, and object structures; of repression and dissociations; of devaluation of object representations and blurred superego boundaries. Although I am here oversimplifying one aspect of a five-stage developmental model, essentially Kernberg locates the grandiose self in the relationship of the self to object representations and external objects as well as in the struggle between love and aggression (Kernberg, 1976, p. 116).

Kernberg disagreed primarily with Kohut's notion that narcissistic investment and object investment have the same origin and then evolve independently. Instead, he maintained, both normal and pathological narcissism are rooted in the relationship of the self to object representations and external objects, as well as in the struggle between love and aggression. Basically, Kernberg held that individuals continue to expand their intrapsychic structures from the moment they are born. Insofar as these derive from the interactions between mother and child, psychoanalysis can uncover their social roots; but this does not equate object relations and interactive behavior. Like Freud in "The Ego and the Id," Kernberg linked the origins of ego and superego *and* those of the id to the very earliest object relations. Reminding his colleagues of the biological determinants of psychic phenomena, he suggested that they account for such distinctions as the anthropologist Niko Tinbergen (1951) had made between consummatory and appetitive behavior,[6] as Konrad Lorenz (1963) had noted in the "instinct movements" of animals responding to temporal needs, and as Bowlby had shown in his "planned hierarchy" of flexible responses (Kernberg, 1976, p. 89).

Kernberg for the most part retained Freud's tripartite structure of ego, id, and superego for analyzing the oedipal period and applied object relations theory to describe infant development (Carsky and Ellman, 1985, pp. 259–60). Thus he used the Kleinian theories of splitting and projective identification for the so-called low-level defenses and derived repression and isolation for the so-called high-level defenses from ego psychology. In order not to relativize the various concepts, Kernberg (1976) postulated "units of internalized object relations as subsystems . . . [that] integrate both drives and psychic structures" and placed instincts at the level of a "suprasystem of the personality at large" (p. 86). He could thereby account for neurophysiological and neuropsychological factors and could "integrate" the Kleinians' schizoid and depressive phases as well as Mahler's developmental theories.

Kernberg himself specialized in borderline adults—individuals who manifest rapidly fluctuating, and contradictory, ego states and whose transference reactions quickly move from idealization and love to rage and hatred. But whereas Kohut traced such behavior to its narcissistic roots, Kernberg located it in the process of splitting during early infancy and in the reenactment of primary-process behavior. This diagnosis, in turn, led Kernberg to differentiate three types of internalization—object-images or object-representations, self-images or self-representations, and drive derivatives or particular affective dispositions. He then constructed a detailed model of developmental stages—normal autism (first month of life), normal "symbiosis" (third or fourth to between sixth and ninth month), differentiation between self and other (six to nine months to eighteen to thirty-six months), and integration of contradictory representations (from the end of the third year through the oedipal period). Narcissistic disorders were rooted in the latter stage, and the formation of a healthy personality in the next one. Furthermore, Kernberg distinguished between high-level and low-level character pathology and explained why the borderline personality organization as such was stable, though characterized as ego pathology. He suggested that analysts focus on prospective patients' self-understanding, their relations with others, and their grasp of reality and recommended that most narcissistic disorders be treated by psychoanalysis, with modifications and supportive treatment when indicated. Some patients, he found, may be protected against irreparable damage by a period of hospitalization.

By integrating the Kleinians' bad and good objects and the depressive position, Kernberg broke American taboos; and by accusing the Kleinians of imprecision and of having neglected Freud's structural concepts, he bridged the ever widening theoretical gaps. But Kernberg was equipped to do so. Born in Vienna, he grew up and became a psychoanalyst in Chile and now is a member of the Columbia University Center for Psychoanalytic Training and Research. Hence he became one of a handful of Freudians conversant with other psychoanalytic schools and is able to translate the meanings of analytic terms by taking account of their users' background.[7] This ability, as well as his preoccupations with pathology rather than neurosis, struck a chord among a number of French psychoanalysts. Furthermore, Kernberg indicated his familiarity with the French discussions of perversions in his introduction to the English translation of Janine Chasseguet-Smirgel's *Creativity and Perversion* (1984).

In this book, Chasseguet-Smirgel offers a very illuminating view of the many psychoanalytic explanations of femininity and their links to sociopolitical reality. According to Christopher Lasch, Chasseguet-Smirgel's most important contribution was in casting Freud's "ego ideal" as the heir to primary narcissism—the heir to the infantile illusion of omnipotence (1985; introduction by Lasch, p. ix). By separating the ego ideal from the superego, Chasseguet-Smirgel had been able to trace how idealized erotic passion, religion, and art in some individuals may take the place of the original wish to fuse with the mother and how in others narcissistic illusion may turn into perversions. To Lasch (1982), whose theory of the "narcissistic personality" had been extrapolated from both Kohut's and Kernberg's work, this division helped explain "emotional shallowness, fear of intimacy, hypochondria, pseudoself-insight and promiscuous pansexuality."

But Chasseguet-Smirgel's ideas proved most useful to Nancy Chodorow's thesis that mothering is structurally reproduced. Chasseguet-Smirgel had described how the omnipotent preoedipal mother always inflicts a "narcissistic wound," so that she "causes feeling of incompleteness . . . in children of both sexes" (Chodorow, 1978, p. 122).

Chasseguet-Smirgel's (1985) discussion of "phallic power" went further in examining the links between perversion, anal-sadistic regression, anomie, and hubris. She found, for example, that "the pervert's aim is to disavow the father's [genital] capacities and to accomplish a [magic] transmutation of reality by delving into the undifferentiated and anal-sadistic dimension. Having idealized it, he proclaims its superiority over the father's genital universe" (p. 78). This metaphoric version of the Oedipus complex led Chasseguet-Smirgel to equate the denial of castration and denial of the differences between the sexes. She described how some of her patients exemplified and paralleled Freudian principles and then moved on to talk of fetishism and of the plurality of meaning Lacan had been hammering home. She stated that "the fetish means at once the affirmation and the disavowal of the so-called castration of women" (p. 78). To prove the point, she quoted Joyce McDougall, who in "Primal Scene and Sexual Perversion," went further in the resolution of the enigma by stressing that the construction of the fetish is not only linked with the need to disavow the absence of the penis, supporting the castration fears, but is also linked with the need to disavow the maternal orifice which is proof of sexual relations between the parents—proof of the primal scene. [And she cited] Béla Grunberger who [had argued] . . . that the fetish is the commemorative monument of intense anal exchanges between mother and son, . . . [for whom] the exclusion of the genital penis and of the genital father is signified and maintained through the very presence of the fetish. (1985, p. 81)

In France, perversion was a special object of attention, sparked probably by the Parisian intellectuals' revival of Sade. American analysts, who had dealt with perversions years before (see Greenacre, 1950; Rangell, 1953; Bak, 1968), were less interested in Chasseguet-Smirgel's views on perversion than were the French, for whom it had become a popular subject.

Joyce McDougall's work, among other things, distinguishes between homosexual and virile women: both fail to identify with their mothers, but the homosexual woman is said primarily to "castrate" the father of his penis and his rights over the mother, while the virile one is found to idealize a desexualized masculinity. McDougall's presentation and interpretation of her work with psychotics are brilliant; she has maintained that many of her patients are more interesting than the protagonists in most modern fiction.

In spite of their unorthodox stances, Chasseguet-Smirgel, Grunberger, and McDougall are counted among the conservatives within the SPP. However, many of their younger colleagues, particularly those who interpret the psychoanalytic texts even more broadly and who have been flirting with the eclectic approaches of those who met around *Confrontation*, are more open to free-wheeling interpretations and therefore closer to the Lacanians. (From what they say, their clinical techniques nevertheless are consonant with the criteria prescribed by the IPA.)

The Current State of Theory

The fact that Freud constantly added to and reformulated his theories not only gave rise to many theoretical tongues but encouraged his followers to continue expanding his ideas. At international meetings the older Freudians predictably tend to stick to the more classical themes and the younger ones to introduce new twists. In the ensuing theoretical bedlam, someone like Kernberg stands out intellectually, particularly for his grasp of the many competing theories. He traces his own formulations of ego splitting to Freud's observations of "love turning to hate" (1984) and defines object relations more broadly than Anna Freud (1936) and thus is closer to Melanie Klein. (Sometimes he seems perilously close to Lacan's dialogue between the self and the Other.) He finds that the objects of both Kohutians and Sullivanians are stuck within the psychic apparatus—where psychic structures so readily get fixed and replayed; he maintains that the ego psychologists' structures are conceived at too high a level of abstraction and thereby "cause" conflict between drives and libido; he traces his own theory from Mahler, Fairbairn, Klein, and Edith Jacobson. In essence, Kernberg is a kind of ubiquitous presence, on the highest level of abstraction, while contributing to clinical techniques for dealing with narcissistic and borderline patients.

Ultimately, in the metapsychological discussions it is difficult to say which theories are more valid, but there are better or worse clinicians and psychoanalysts with greater or lesser appeal to potential patients. Popularity, however, whether in the culture at large or within the profession, is not the same as theoretical validity. Nor is the fact that psychoanalysts, any more than psychologists, economists, or sociologists, do not have an overall explanatory or unifying theory an indictment: it simply makes them normal children of the Zeitgeist. For while this confirms that current psychoanalytic theories do not exhibit the dramatic originality of Freud, still it appears that so far they are better than others in explaining issues of the self. Nevertheless, the fragmentation of psychoanalytic theory proves also that the Freudians primarily are united by their profession rather than by their ideas.

Chapter 12

Psychoanalysis
and Politics

According to Freud's "rule of abstinence," psychoanalysts must not impose their personal beliefs on their patients. But Freud and the early followers supported radical, sometimes Marxist, goals, and from the very beginning, the possibility that these political views would intrude into clinical practice was questioned. To what extent therapy and politics can be kept separate has been debated ever since, and the tension between them has plagued every Freudian.

Paradoxically, during each of the two world wars the psychoanalytic movement made quantum leaps, because political officials asked the Freudians for assistance. By the end of the First World War, their prestige was high, for they had helped to rehabilitate thousands of neurotic soldiers. According to Bernfeld (1930), "psychic and sexual suffering, physical and love disturbances that eluded all of the medical arts [had become] curable." At the start of the Second World War, U.S. Colonel William J. "Wild Bill" Donovan, director of a new agency, which became the Office of Strategic Services, commissioned the psychoanalyst Walter Langer (1972) to furnish a psychological portrait of Hitler (p. 3). Donovan was not alone in believing that psychoanalysis might be helpful for psychological warfare and that it could explain the appeal as well as the behavior of authoritarian politicians and predict their future public actions (Loewenberg, 1983, p. 31).

In England, too, the psychoanalyst Pearl King (1988) reported, the Freudians cooperated with the armed forces and by 1944 controlled their psychiatric division. Together with the rest of the public, they recognized that Hitler had to be opposed by force, and they offered their services to cure soldiers suffering from battle fatigue and depression and generally to keep up the morale of those on the front and those being bombed at home. Hence, on both sides of the Atlantic, the Freudians received legitimation from their governments. This led them to redouble both theoretical and clinical efforts. In the process, they expected to get to the origins of human aggression in order to reduce its negative impact—to eliminate the combativeness of individuals and nations.

Viennese Politics

Freud was plagued by the contradiction between scientific and political aims. He dealt with it, for the most part, by separating the two realms. But many of his early followers had been drawn to psychoanalysis in order to exploit its democratizing potential (Nunberg and Federn, 1962; Reichmayr and Wiesbauer, 1979). Adler and Stekel in particular insisted on more or less immediately applying therapeutic insights to politics. Most Anglo-Saxon Freudians' reminiscences tend to overlook this fact. Recently, however, a few young, radical Austrians have reviewed the records and have reminded us that the leading disciples were ardent Social Democrats: Josef K. Friedjung; Ludwig Jekels; Karl Furtmüller; David Ernst Oppenheim; Hugo Heller, Freud's publisher; Wilhelm Stekel; and Margarete Hilferding, wife of the prominent Social Democrat Rudolf Hilferding and first woman member of the WPV (Reichmayr and Wiesbauer, 1979, p. 29).

Many of the early Freudians' theoretical disagreements were intricately linked to political differences although they were attributed to neuroses or character traits (see chapter 2). This confusion between politics and neurosis, of course, obfuscated the fact that the disciples had their own personal and political agendas and priorities—in addition to their character traits. When Wittels, for instance, presented a lengthy and rather questionable thesis about the unconscious meaning of menstruation, he went on to conclude that all feminists would have wanted to have been born as men. Adler responded in Marxist terms, by arguing that women's fate arose from patriarchal and property relations. Wittels retorted that "one cannot be a Freudian and a Social Democrat at the same time" (Nunberg and Federn, 1962, 1:352–53). This statement polarized the issue and bolstered the accusations of generations of feminists and leftists—whether they were out to prove the Freudians' conservatism or the absurdity of speculations about the female unconscious. Although Hitschmann soon charged that Wittels's research was inspired by his interest in pregnancy, chaste female medical students, and syphilis because all of them were thwarting him, the real disagreements were about implementing socialist ideals.

At another time, when Adler spoke on "The Psychology of Marxism (March 10, 1909), Freud, Paul Federn, Eduard Hitschmann, Albert Joachim, Rank, and Maximilian Steiner got into a heated argument. Tempers flared, and personal grudges were aired. Isidor Sadger was upset enough to ask Freud to take a more forceful position in handling disputes, lest personal dislikes lead to permanent ruptures. (Both Freud and Sadger stressed the personal— that is, the unconscious psychological—aspects of the polemics rather than their political content.) Freud, put out, responded that if people could not tolerate scientific disagreements he might as well close up shop. In any event, the line between social amenities and the "scientific" utility of disputes got thinner and thinner.

Although Freud would stress his theoretical differences with Adler, these too had political roots. Adler did not want to wait until psychoanalysis was perfected before applying it in the Vienna school system by training and politicizing teachers, who, in turn, would enlighten their pupils and the pupils' families. And he asserted that neurosis was a manifestation of the larger sociopolitical organization rather than of the family romance and that antisocial behavior was a means to elude social constraints (Sperber, 1972, p. 187). This is not to say that Freud was against socialism, as has been claimed, but only that he put his psychoanalysis above his politics.

Reichmayr and Wiesbauer have insisted that Freud has incorrectly been branded as conservative. By analyzing the Austrians' electoral choices, they discovered that he had been a socialist, though not an active one. And they "proved" that Freud, along with 80 to 90 percent of the members of the Wiener Psychoanalytischer Verein (DPV), must have voted for the Social Democrats until long after the split with Adler (p. 31). Had he been a conservative, these authors held, he would not have figured so prominently in the biographies of such contemporaries as Ludwig Wittgenstein, Arthur Schnitzler, and Hugo von Hoffmansthal; nor would he have been a member of the left-oriented student organization or the left-leaning Leseverein, where he met Victor Adler. Freud idealized Adler to the point of wanting to live in his former apartment when he set up his practice. Furthermore, Freud kept in touch with the Zionist leader Theodor Herzl—whom he perceived as yet another fighter for human rights—at a time when Zionism was a radical idea.

Reichmayr and Wiesbauer blamed Ernest Jones primarily for the prevalent misreading of the early Freudians' politics. They argued that Jones played down their political creed in his single-minded devotion to psychoanalysis, and that today's Freudians, who know their psychoanalytic history almost entirely through Jones's biography of Freud, have remained unaware that this "bible" expresses Jones's Anglo-Saxon perspective and his wish to hold the IPA together. Reichmayr and Wiesbauer attacked Jones's report of the meeting in 1911 at which Adler stepped down as president of the WPV and started the Verein für Individualpsychologie. Jones had reported eight negative votes against five positive ones; but he failed to mention that twenty-one persons had attended this meeting and that eight had abstained, thus making the Freudian victory appear more definitive than it had been. (Adler already had formed the VFPF, and the question was whether or not it would be permissible to belong to both the VFPF and the WPV.) Reichmayr and Wiesbauer, however, concluded that Jones's omission "characterized his entire writing of the history" and proved his antisocialist tendencies as well as his lack of political sophistication. Thus they felt justified in wondering what other aspects of psychoanalytic history Jones had whitewashed.

Humanist Visions

The more the Freudians were convinced that psychoanalysis was a science, the less they entered the political arena. After their far-left had left with Adler, the remaining left did not really try to tamper with accepted psychoanalytic theory—except to attack elitist training criteria. But the Freudians would continue to have their disagreements when searching for the means to improve the social fabric of their communities. At times, they more or less united by addressing global political issues concerned with the future of humanity, such as how to avoid wars and (much later) nuclear destruction. At other times, they took public positions against totalitarianism and atrocities. And in authoritarian societies, such as Argentina, Brazil, and Hungary, they sometimes maintained that the analysis of a few leading individuals eventually would spread to other political figures and thus alleviate repression. They also offered psychoanalytic insights into the personalities of leaders such as Nixon and Reagan or dictators such as Hitler and Stalin. These efforts were justified primarily by pointing to Freud and Bullitt's portrait of *Woodrow*

Wilson (1966)—itself one of Freud's less persuasive works. In principle, however, classical Freudians maintained that their job of analyzing individuals precluded active political stances, insofar as public visibility might interfere with the transference in individual analyses. In America, they tended to avoid direct political involvement.

Both the psychoanalysts' politics and their "psychoanalyses" of politicians were couched in the locally accepted idiom. Thus the French were wont to point to the unconscious meaning of the words, acts, gestures, and leaps of imagination of their leaders and to analyze their use of language; the Americans tended to focus on the pitfalls of idealizing their leaders and especially their presidents; the Germans, fearful of falling for another dictator, tried to find new means of undercutting and exposing unhealthy authority relations; the English sooner or later ended up by examining and blaming child-rearing practices for unwanted outcomes; and the Austrians, for the most part, equivocated. From time to time there were Freud-Marx syntheses, and these reiterated the evils of capitalist relations of production and processes of dehumanization, linking them to the homegrown Freudian discourse. (This holds true, for example, for Americans like Richard Lichtman [1982] and Lauren Langman [1978], who set out to integrate Freud and Marx; for Joel Kovel [1981], who expects to use Marx in order to reconstruct psychoanalysis; as well as for the Italian Sebastian Timpanaro's [1974] theoretical propositions about the coming revolution.)

When such agendas were picked up and elaborated by anthropologists, philosophers, sociologists, and psychologists, or by political leaders, the application to political ends, insofar as it dealt with conscious phenomena, would tend to simplify or misconstrue psychoanalytic principles. This problem was even greater when Freudians addressed the general public and attempted to familiarize nonintellectuals with the mechanisms of the collective unconscious. Still, like Freud, his followers periodically left their consulting rooms to try to save the world; and like Freud, they did this by generalizing from the individual patients on their couches to society at large, or to humanity.

Freud's Political Unconscious

The effect of war, Freud stated, may be to produce a regression to the earliest state of human development, in which emotional reactions would be inaccessible to reason (*S.E.*, 22:195–215). Individuals' proximity to death (the unconscious denies the possibility of its own death while also fearing it) and the accompanying possibility of heroism, he went on, make life seem less precious during wartime than are "certain abstract general ideas," and unrealistic illusions are fostered (p. 291). Psychoanalysis could be cast not only as the destroyer of illusions but as a tool for peace. Freud, of course, had said that he did not know how to implement peace because both good and bad instincts are part of so-called human nature. When Albert Einstein asked him to join in his call for pacifism, Freud insisted that he was a pacifist, but he despaired of war's ever being eradicated. Thus, he told Einstein, "We are pacifists because we are obliged to be for organic reasons" (p. 214).

Despite Freud's pessimism about individual human nature and society, his followers retained a streak of idealism about the future. In addition to speculating about the prevention of war they addressed questions of democracy and anti-Semitism. Whenever psychoanalysts were mobilized to support peace movements, antinuclear protests, antiapartheid and anti-Nazi groups, they would routinely quote Freud to support the cause. It would seem that they had come to believe in the efficacy of what Nathan Leites (1948) called "psycho-cultural analyses of social events."

The Americans' Political Excursions

As we have noted, the anthropological and sociological investigations of tribal societies and later of advanced industrial ones nearly always had political overtones. Although not every study drew parallels between the repetition compulsion of neurotic or psychotic primary process thinking and the magic rituals in tribal societies, as Freud had postulated in *Totem and Taboo*, the very collaboration between the disciples of Franz Boas and psychoanalysts such as Kardiner and Radó at Columbia University would indicate a belief in such a parallel.

Furthermore, when Erik Erikson (1950), for instance, noted that the cultural conditioning of the Dakota and Yurok Indians had its own built-in wisdom, with its own type of reactions to the genetic process of psychosexual development, he did so in purely psychoanalytic terms and drew his conclusions from purely psychoanalytic assumptions. But the Bureau of Indian Affairs used this study as a basis for overhauling its policies. Erikson, of course, was not alone in assuming that child-rearing practices, which included inculcating children with the whole array of unconscious defenses, interests, and coping mechanisms, were ultimately responsible for the private behavior and political attitudes of leaders and citizens and, therefore, for the fate of nations. Erikson certainly was aware of the complexity of these issues. Nevertheless, when a number of German Freudians examined his book in 1978, they were "shocked" by Erikson's "subtly ethnocentric depiction of Indians, . . . and . . . his *systematic* blindness toward domination (Elrod, Heinz, and Dahmer, 1978, pp. 7–8).

Robert Waelder, who had left Vienna to practice in Philadelphia, took another tack: he discussed the psychological processes underlying political attitudes. The fundamental difference between authoritarianism and totalitarianism, he held, is the impact of these systems on their victims: authoritarianism is "only" oppressive, whereas totalitarianism is also degrading and demoralizing. Whereas in an authoritarian system the subjects often must pay exorbitant taxes, serve in the army, and abstain from overtly criticizing the government, in a totalitarian system *"they may be whipped, and [also] have to kiss the rod"* (Waelder, 1960, p. 12). Unlike Fromm, for whom the solution lay in a reorganization of society, Waelder spoke against those Americans who did not want to take *any* action against totalitarianism "lest we become totalitarian in the process of fighting it" (p. 18). We should not assume, he said, that Americans will never face an emergency serious enough to require enforced discipline. Were this to happen, he held, the temporary curtailment of some personal liberties would be a small price to pay for the preservation of democracy (p. 19). Psychologically, he went on, totalitarianism is rooted in paranoia—as either the product of an ideology or a result of extreme danger. But rational paranoia deals with temporary emergencies, whereas its irrational (ideological) form never ends. And the paranoid personality (monistic ideologist), unaware of complexity and inaccessible to influence by reason, is able to explain away facts. In such people (Lenin was given as an example), Waelder argued, paranoid ideology convinces its devotees of the eternal righteousness of their cause and thereby allows them to be ruthless without suffering from pangs of conscience (p. 23). Essentially, Waelder was attacking Marxism-Leninism for its intellectual dogmatism and describing its relation to the paranoid syndrome. He was not alone, however, in demonstrating the similarities between Soviet communism and fascism.[1]

During this period, the political scientist Harold Lasswell, the foremost authority investigating the connections between personality and politics, agreed with the psychoanalysts that private motives may be displaced onto public objects and rationalized away as public interest. Just as research on children was pointing to the consequences of early and traumatic separation from the mother, to the hostility and unbearable anxiety deriving from such separations, and to unconscious hostility and regression to primal anxiety and rage, Lasswell connected these mechanisms to those that had fueled Nazism:

German youth between the two wars had grown up hungry and had suffered from inadequate mothering and family disruptions. They had joined Hitler's movement in order to compensate for earlier deprivation of mothering and family life and to identify with fathers who had been in uniform (Loewenberg, 1983, p. 264).

Norbert Bromberg (1960), a psychoanalyst, maintained that individuals in all repressive societies tend either to identify with the dominant totalitarian ideology or to adopt it as an expedient for survival. He explored the evolution of his patients' defensive mechanisms, showing how involvement in a totalitarian movement had helped one of them cope with anxieties that were due to conflictual identifications. Apparently

the political arena provided an almost tailor-made medium for the exercise of his feelings. He identified himself and the women in his family with the proletariat [in America], according to his lights, a weak and inferior, but noble class in conflict with the powerful, tyrannical, capitalistic class, personified more immediately by his father and more eminently by the President of the United States. In this struggle he saw the workers and himself aided by the Communist movement and by Stalin as its leader. (p. 37)

Another type of political inquiry was exemplified by Kurt Eissler's (1960) psychoanalytic study of eight American soldiers. The army, in order to streamline its organization, had asked him to develop a means of establishing what personality types would make the best officers and soldiers. Eissler chose eight apparently "normal" men whom he then analyzed. But he could not detect a coherent pattern, although he noted that they all had successfully competed against their fathers—fathers who had not been overly concerned with their sons' moral development but had encouraged the boys to go to church. Eissler found that their neuroses did not seem to interfere with their duties as soldiers and that some of them were doing better in the army than they had in civilian life. Their psychopathology apparently did not keep them from "performing society's tasks."

Since both pathological and normal men may make efficient soldiers, Eissler went on to compare the personalities of his eight soldiers with those of other patients he had treated. He concluded (with due reference to Hartmann's concept of mental health) on a broad note:

What present society calls normality, is a balanced mixture of . . . the urge to prove one's omnipotence at all costs; the surrender with or without inner struggle to the exigencies of the moment or the future, enforced by the blotting out of individuality; and the projection of a fear into a sector of reality which becomes the goal of an aggressive impulse without the superego's raising a feeling of guilt. . . . By surrendering to reality the ego enjoys masochistic pleasure and the superego is pacified by submitting to the displeasure of reality. By attaching a paranoid projection to a sector of reality the id is drained of aggression and the superego is placated by rationalization. (p. 88)

The prominent political philosopher Nathan Leites, quoting Hartmann and Kris, had questioned whether analyses of political behavior really grew out of the "genetic conditions . . . [rooted in] an individual's past [which] . . . later on [engender] similar reactions in structurally analogous political situations" (1948, pp. 102–03). At best, Leites found such assumptions imprecise. He wondered, for instance, whether Americans were not overgeneralizing from the "will to achieve," which clearly was less important elsewhere in the world, and whether it was possible to construct a valid scale on which a highly effort-oriented individual could even be compared to members of his own culture, much less to those of others. He criticized the vagueness of such terms as *intentions, acts,* and *emotional weights.* Comparative data about Romanian and American (or Japanese and Chinese) effort orientation were less than valid, he stated, for reward systems differ from one culture to another; and so does acceptable behavior during the process of socialization; and their accompanying emotions, in turn, are internalized (and expressed) in line with accepted means of communication—which differ from culture to culture. The adult models children aspire to differ as well, and so do social, economic, and political aspects of the adult environment children learn to internalize. All these scientific investigations thus assumed a nonexistent typicality and did not account for class differences, for idiosyncratic aspects of fantasy life, or for the fact that different children may react positively or negatively to the same emotional environment.

Upon reading these studies of psychoanalytic politics now, one marvels at the nonpolitical politics they *all* share. The least daring of the investigators explicitly adhere to Freud's structural theory; they frequently pull in random medical knowledge, philosophy, and literature. Rarely do they question the assumption that psychoanalytic insight will induce more moral political behavior by leaders and followers. Furthermore, the scientific and somewhat antiseptic stance of these studies takes it for granted that social scientists and politicians will heed the analysts.

The Freudian émigrés (they now were the establishment) very quickly had become successful and identified with America. They had been accepted by a society where anti-Semitism was kept under wraps. (Any guilt they might feel at having been saved while less fortunate European Jews had ended up in the Nazi death camps would be the subject of later inquiries.) In the

1940s and the 1950s the leading Freudians were full of praise for America and offered the psychological prescriptions that would save its democratic institutions. Even the "Marxists" among them, such as Fromm, Bernfeld, and Fenichel, though critical of psychoanalytic organizations, of many leading political figures, and of consumption-oriented life-styles and antiintellectualism, primarily were busy with their patients. To some extent, of course, the psychoanalysts inspired the social scientists' cross-cultural studies, the accumulation of data in area files, and the construction of profiles of personalities typical of specific societies. And it was the psychoanalysts' theories that helped sociologists nail down the "relatively enduring personality characteristics and patterns shared by the adult members of a society"—what Inkeles and Levinson (1954) called "national character" (p. 983). All that, along with the analysts' roles as consultants to government agencies, as heads of psychiatric hospitals and clinics, and as gurus at large justified their high status.

By the mid-1960s, a few Freudians such as Leo Stone and Charles Fischer had begun to question their own complacency, and by the end of that decade they had started to take note of the criticism directed at them by German and French colleagues who distrusted not only the viability of their organizational politics but the realpolitik American psychoanalysts either professed or took for granted. Now, they were being accused of having adapted and of having sold out, or at least forgotten, Freud's broader cultural and political aims.

Anti-Semitism and Realpolitik in the Unconscious and the Conscious

After Hitler's victory in 1933, anti-Semitism had to be dealt with concretely. Thus, Freud wrote to Arnold Zweig in September 1934 that "in view of the renewed persecutions . . . [he was] asking [himself] again how the Jew came to be what he is and why he has drawn upon himself this undying hatred"; and he sat down to write *The Man Moses, a historical novel* (E. Freud, 1968, p. 102). In the same letter, he informed Zweig that the leading Catholic theologian Father Schmidt was responsible for Vienna's Catholic orthodoxy and Austria's anti-Semitic politics: he was also a confidant of the pope, and abhorred psychoanalysis. Schmidt's Vatican connections were thought to have helped bring about the banning of Edoardo Weiss's *Rivista di Psicoanalisi* in Rome—allegedly countermanding a personal promise by Mussolini. That was why Freud decided not to publish his *Moses* just then: "Were this danger confined to myself it would make little impression on me, but to deprive all our members in Vienna of their livelihood strikes me as too great a responsibility" (E. Freud, 1968, p. 103). In February 1934, he had written to his son Ernst in London that "the future [is] uncertain; either Austrian fascism or the swastika. In the latter event we shall have to leave; native fascism we are willing to take in our stride . . . because it can hardly treat us as badly as its German cousin" (Mitscherlich-Nielsen, 1972, p. 172). Apparently, Freud underestimated the strength of Austrian anti-Semitism.

But most of Freud's disciples had reason to feel less sanguine: they had persisted in their political activism and thus were vulnerable as Jews *and* as Social Democrats. This meant that even before the Anschluss they had had to hide the radical politics everyone knew they were committed to. Edith Jacobson, for instance, was imprisoned in Berlin in 1935. But it was unclear whether this was because she was Jewish or because she belonged to a resistance group, *Neu Beginnen* (Brecht et al., 1985).[2] Those who might have been implicated with her, such as Fenichel and Bernfeld—both of them *Wandervögel*, members of a leftist organization dedicated to saving the ecology from bourgeois development—had to conceal their socialism. In any event, the Freudians were leaving Nazi territory to save themselves from an anti-Semitism that had run amok.

Once these psychoanalysts left the Continent, they poured their energies into theory, expecting to weld it into the ultimate weapon against fascism, anti-Semitism, and every other antiliberal bias. Thus, as noted above, theory got mixed up with realpolitik, and methods of child rearing and mothering with political aggression. After 1945, Anglo-Saxon Freudians, although continuing to search for better solutions, began to export their new knowledge.

The Freudians Relearn German

In 1945, the so-called Freudians of the Göring Institut, we recall, were only too eager to become affiliated with the Freudians in Anglo-Saxon countries. Hence they invested most of their energies in reestablishing contact with former colleagues and in feigning anti-Nazi and philo-Semitic sentiments. Their politics were aimed at survival, at rebuilding their institutes along with their country, at playing down the *Gleichschaltung* (cooperation with non-Freudians) and playing up their "allegiance" to Freud, and at accommodation in general. In other words, German psychotherapists (unselfconsciously) were living up to the image of the "authoritarian personality" by blindly accepting the victors' ideas. But few of the cooperating "Anglo-Saxons" at that time confronted these therapists or took them to task. Those "Anglo-Saxons" who expected to reestablish psychoanalysis quickly and wanted to reclaim the country with the help of their expertise banked on reeducating the Germans rather than on looking for answers about the recent past. And those who refused to forgive or forget, who found it too painful to renew contact with *any* German, were unable to be constructively critical. The émigré analysts, who now considered themselves American or British, tended to identify with the Allies' political aims—first in the war against the Nazis and then in the cold war.

The German psychoanalysts' ensuing organizational maneuvers have been described elsewhere (see chapter 9). Here, I want to recall only that German would-be Freudians used the political impasse and the naïveté of the occupying forces to reestablish themselves in the only manner they knew— by perpetuating the infrastructures of the defeated Nazi system. Their fellow Germans—all of whom were guilty of collaboration by omission if not commission, and who knew about some of the Reichsinstituts' activities—remained silent. How else could it have taken nearly forty years for the world to learn about German Seelenheilkunde and its links to euthanasia and genetic experiments?

Inevitably, those Germans who wanted to be bona fide psychoanalysts had to be analyzed and in the process would have to face the anti-Semitism they had imbibed with their mothers' milk. But even if the Germans had had the necessary personnel, they did not differentiate sufficiently between psychoanalysis and one-on-one treatment by psychotherapists. (In 1950, for example, it was hoped that some of the first batch of psychotherapists to graduate from the Berlin institute in the following year would come to work in the Berlin-Grünewald clinic, which had two "medical-psychological" persons on staff [Wiegman, 1950–51, p. 389].) Furthermore, the discussions then revolved around mental sickness (itself a political designation insofar as "malaise" or "feeling bad" would not be reimbursed), around the profound unease and depression engendered by the nation's defeat, and to a lesser extent around the murders committed in the name of anti-Semitism—a monstrous history they could not address practically because there were no longer any Jews.

The splitting of German psychoanalysis into two groups (Deutsche Psychoanalytische Gesellschaft and Deutsche Psychoanalytische Vereinigung) had led to two apologetic versions of its fate during the Third Reich: those in the DPG claimed to have saved it in order to justify its uninterrupted continuation in 1945; those in the DPV spoke of a new start (Lohmann and Rosenkötter, 1982, pp. 961–62). The Freudians, of course, belonged only to the DPV. But within this organization, there developed yet another split, between the followers of the Mitscherlichs, who insisted that anti-Semitism was just one more manifestation of German infantile authoritarianism, and the "nonpolitical" members of the profession, who took it for granted that their choice of a "Jewish" profession and their inevitable identification with Freud would itself set them above the anti-Semites. They wanted to learn their craft, see their patients, and avoid politics.

Yet all German Freudians sooner or later found that anti-Semitism had been at the core of German inhumanity. Thus they felt that transference and countertransference alone could deal with the analysts' professional-personal identification with both Germanness and Freud. By airing these issues, Freudians thought that psychoanalysis could ultimately save both Jews and anti-Semites. To that end, Mitscherlich sponsored an international symposium in 1962, "The Psychological and Social Assumptions of Anti-Semitism: Analysis of the Psychodynamics of a Prejudice" (Mitscherlich et al., 1966). Mitscherlich, who initiated the discussions, expected to surpass Freud in "reconciling man with his culture" in order to eradicate the boundless aggression and prejudice that had allowed for genocide (p. 256). Educators who expect obedience fuel hostility, he admonished, and then they insist that their charges suppress it. Individuals thereby identify more strongly with the aggressor (as the Germans had done with the Führer) and with the celebration of war. In a survey, Alphons Silbermann, a German sociologist, found that the country's elite, particularly its youth, had become more philo-Semitic but that there was also a "sort of xenophobia in order to repress Jewish influence" (Mitscherlich et al., 1966, p. 258). Why hate Jews rather than others, asked the Parisian analyst Béla Grunberger. Because there is a part of the ego that has been split off from the rest of the subject's personality and which, by taking away a large component of libido, submits to authority, he answered. Because of the split, the fractured ego was full of fear and subject to intensive castration anxiety. Grunberger then traced the anti-Semite's projection to regressive mechanisms originating in the pregenital superego and in the anal components of his sexuality. These lend themselves to deindividualized regressions that allow for the discharge of *all* negative drives and for inner equilibrium. The "successful" anti-Semite's ego, therefore, was said to be in complete harmony with the ego-ideal and thus able to perceive all evil within the Jew and all good within himself. It is very difficult to do justice to this complex argument, or even to indicate how Grunberger, by drawing on Sartre's arguments in *Anti-Semite and Jew* ([1946] 1965) and the history of Judaism and Christianity, concluded that oedipal ambivalence toward the father and anal-sadistic relations in early childhood are the anti-Semite's irrevocable inheritance.

Martin Wangh's analysis of anti-Semitism also focused on regression and on the identification with prejudiced parents, psychoanalytic comparisons between Judaism and Christianity, and the influence of church attendance, familial political tradition, and status as energizers of anti-Semitism. But none of the ordinary explanations, added Wangh, can account for the regression to prehuman behavior, for the lack of inhibition against human sacrifice, slavery, and cannibalism. Instead, Wangh, like Lasswell, blamed conditions between 1917 and 1920, when many of the Nazis had been young hungry children, whose fathers were in the war; thus they were bound to have had "reinforced Oedipus complexes" and fantasies of death and murder that defied psychoanalysis because they were based on reality (Mitscherlich et al., 1966, p. 292). Furthermore, longing for the father, Wangh maintained, had strengthened childish homosexual wishes which later would be transformed into excessive patriotism and submission to authority. The father's absence was interpreted as rejection which then was projected onto the Jews; and identification with his military role was reenacted by marching to the Nazis' tunes. Ultimately, Wangh also laid the greater worldwide crime rate at the doorstep of war.

The educator Wolfgang Hochheimer, essentially in agreement with the other speakers at Mitscherlich's conference, asked how one might dynamically interfere in individuals' psychic processes in order to do away with anti-Semitism. Other discussants, among them the sociologists Horkheimer and René König, brought out differences between anti-Semitism in Germany and that found elsewhere by pointing out that the German love of efficiency and organization had "perfected" it, by discussing the difference between Jewish and non-Jewish mothers, and by emphasizing that anti-Semitism is a social illness.

Mitscherlich's multidisciplinary thrust and his move away from psychosomatics into the sociopolitical realm became evident at this Frankfurt conference. In 1962, he had not yet denounced ego psychology as too adaptive. He also had invited the few French Freudians willing to cross the Rhine. Soon, he would publish *Society without the Father* ([1963] 1969) and *The Inability to Mourn* (1967)—both examining the psychological effects of the Nazi era on every German, the past guilt that continued to plague the present, and the personal and political implications of these factors for German youth. He also continued to sponsor sociological and psychological studies of the national psyche. Thus he and his colleagues, such as Habermas, Adorno, Horkheimer, and Helmuth Becker, set up "cooperation between sociology and psychoanalysis" and supervised a variety of projects by young scholars

(Mitscherlich et al., 1970). Although these Germans' critical inquiries were similar to some by the American left, unlike the latter, they took Talcott Parsons's and Heinz Hartmann's work as seriously as Fromm's, Bernfeld's and Wilhelm Reich's—at a time when their ideas had already peaked in America.

Part of the Mitscherlichs' effort to reeducate the public was rooted in psychosomatic medicine and another part in their cooperation with Horkheimer and Adorno's new Institut für Sozialforschung. As they insisted on bringing Nazi atrocities into the open, they converted a part of German psychoanalysis from a therapy into a politics. Some of this happened with the help of colleagues in the IPA, and some was due to the prevalent leftist thought at Frankfurt's university, which Mitscherlich approved of and which, at first, was almost the only endogenous force to come to terms with the Nazi past. Still, when, in the late 1960s, German students brutally attacked Adorno as a "fascist" and displayed behavior resembling that of the Hitler Youth, Mitscherlich was alarmed.[3] But, at the same time, these confrontations introduced German students to psychoanalysis.

Klaus Menne and Klaus Schröter (1980), for instance, investigated the importance of verbal ability in psychoanalytic patients and its replacement by manual laborers with body language. Lower-class patients, they found, are no more prone to ego deficiencies and disturbances than others. Beneath seeming ego disorders, however, they "hide" rigid defenses connected to unconscious fantasies that cannot be reconciled with lower-class norms: they are more likely to act out their emotions than are their middle class counterparts. *Psyche* reprinted Bernfeld's ([1962] 1984) plea for lay analysis (a talk he had given in 1952 shortly before he died) to warn German psychoanalysts against medicalizing their profession; he thought it would thereby be deprived of its critical and political edge. They published Kurt Eissler's (1986) somewhat tongue-in-cheek suggestion that the United Nations resolve to condemn to death all members of the nation that would drop the first atom bomb (he was drawing a parallel between Moses' curse at Mount Ebal and the threat of nuclear power) in part to demonstrate the Germans' helplessness against atomic warfare because of their geographic location and in part to honor Eissler, who had done so much for German psychoanalysis.

In Austria, we recall, political activities were rare. But in Salzburg, Professor Igor Caruso (1980) had started to teach clinical psychology based on psychoanalytic principles but entailing "new psychotherapeutic methods [and] psychoanalytic group therapy." It was, he wrote, "geared to research in ethnopsychology, social work, and political psychology" (p. 1). Upon Caruso's early retirement because of illness in 1979, the process of choosing his replacement brought the ideological components of his controversial approach into the open. His students violently protested the sub-rosa negotiations leading to the appointment of a nonpsychoanalyst (their accusations later led the "guilty" senior professor to sue their leader for libel and to win). It is clear, however, that psychoanalysis was being equated with a radicalism that aimed to expose repressive secretive procedures and that, in the process, as it was being applied in conjunction with other therapies, the search for the unconscious was neglected. This "radical" political psychoanalysis gained more adherents than its classical variety, although in Vienna neither the few Freudians practicing at home nor those integrated in the Allgemeines Krankenhaus were politically engaged, at least not openly.

Superficially, the German-speaking Swiss seemed caught between their allegiances to country and language; their French-speaking colleagues in the IPA for the most part went along with the Parisians, while their own sympathies lay with Mitscherlich's ideas, or rather to their left. As we noted in chapters 9 and 10, the Zurichers Paul Parin and Goldy Matthey-Parin had leftist political agendas that finally distanced them from the IPA. Parin, who had fought as a communist and partisan alongside Tito, reportedly had left Yugoslavia when Stalinism took over. According to him (and to other neo-Marxist intellectuals such as Günther Grass), the rampant consumerist values in democracies were nearly as repressive as Stalinism and therefore had to be opposed. So, unlike Fromm, whose Marxism was as wide-ranging as Parin's but who expected "loving" individuals to change society, Parin wanted to bring about change through revolutionary activities. Influenced by German preoccupations with mass rather than individual psychology, Parin now compared Germans' responses to the Nazis to Freud's views in "Group Analysis and the Adaptation of the Ego." Like Freud and Mitscherlich (1970), he frequently maintained that the more individuals adapt to their culture, the more they regress to primitive levels of behavior: aggression would elicit either flight or obedience. But Parin went further, implying that adaptation by American ego psychologists was a form of obedience to American complacency, and thereby justified his own explicit anti-Americanism.

After Mario Erdheim received an appointment at Frankfurt's university, he commuted there from Zurich. Thus "radical psychoanalysis," which exchanged analysts, sympathies, and political information, started to establish its triangular base in Frankfurt, Salzburg, and Zurich, radiating from there to Bremen, Linz, and Hamburg.

During the same period, Mitscherlich and his staff had been training a bevy of clinical analysts who ultimately left politics. They set up private practices and were more or less steeped in the ego psychology they had learned. Inevitably, they clashed over adapting to American Freudians, over interpretations of the Hitler past, and over medicalization and reimbursement policies. These fights, we recall, gained momentum after the reimbursement laws that assured psychoanalysts a high steady income had been enacted in 1967 and 1976. When the psychoanalytic history of the Nazis began to be exhumed, further conflicts erupted. Thus, psychoanalytic and national politics overlapped and diverged.

From Psychoanalysis to la Psychanalyse

Lacan was the motor driving psychoanalysis in France—and sometimes driving it crazy. But even without Lacan, I believe, French Freudians would have rejected as stale some of the ego psychologists' rote applications and elaborations of Freudian formulas. Eager to remain within the IPA, most members of the Société Psychanalytique de Paris did not push their politics so far as to jeopardize their affiliation. They did identify with the native culture as well as with Freud's universalism, but they were too busy reestablishing themselves to profess openly the anti-Americanism that was an ingredient of French patriotism right after the war.

Although around 1969 many neo-Marxists adopted Freudian ideas, they usually did not differentiate between the positions of classical Freudians and those of Lacanians, simply selecting what they thought would further their radicalism. The Lacanians reciprocated when addressing political issues. Thus the (mostly Lacanian) rhetoric became politicized, or pseudopoliticized. François Gantheret (1969), for instance, like some of his German counterparts, noted that Freud's radical vision of civilization had been played down by the Freudians and, paralleling Marx, maintained that sexual function tied to an object puts individuals into a position similar to the one they occupy when dispensing material goods to others (p. 15). He took up the cry against psychoanalytic associations, which echoed Lacan. In fact, along with many of the students, he accepted the idea that psychoanalysis à la Lacan was a leftist critique of society equal to Marxism. This view was bolstered by Louis Althusser, whose attempts to implement his scientific Marxism with the help of Lacanian formulations held the attention of *tout-Paris*. Even the classical Freudians had to take him into account (Kurzweil, 1980, pp. 35–56). Furthermore, they too wanted to stay abreast of the increasingly popular "sexual discourse" and of its critique by, for instance, Jean Baudrillard (1971), who held that all the fuss over this subject only served to mystify and rationalize the existing distribution of power within the political, social, and moral spheres.

Soon, Gilles Deleuze and Felix Guattari's ([1972] 1971) *Anti-Oedipus* would shock all denominations of Parisian Freudians. These authors depicted modern society as schizoid, peopled by human "desiring machines," by "bodies without organs" that are "factories of desire"—but factories whose controls remain elsewhere. Replacing the Freudian id with these machines, they postulated machines driving other machines with all sorts of couplings and connections: the breast is a machine producing milk and the mouth yet another one coupled to it (p. 1). But all the body's machines are subject to social production, to capitalist production, in an economy that is said to encompass all the materials and energies existing within the social field. Thus Deleuze and Guattari postulated a "libidinal economy" as the unconscious or micropolitical level of the political one. The two economies are connected through money, they held, because behind every investment of interest and money there is desire, and behind desire looms money or interest. In their eclectic tour de force, Deleuze and Guattari's Freudo-Marxism drew on the ideas of such writers as Samuel Beckett, Henry Miller, and D. H. Lawrence, as well as such philosophers as Nietzsche, Henry Lefebvre, and Martin Buber.

For the following decade, psychoanalytic politics (including those of the body) became a Parisian preoccupation. No matter how they tried, the Freudians could not avoid entering the fray. They felt chastised, for example, by Robert Castel's *Le psychanalysme* (1973). He noted that psychoanalysis had become ubiquitous—that it was present in psychiatry, parapsychiatry, medicine, paramedicine, education, reeducation of delinquents, public and private industry, and the media; that it produced "non-politics automatically in the way a baker bakes bread" (p. 54); and that it was a personalized service mobilizing "poor students, proletarian intellectuals, fringe academicians" and yet was out to establish itself as an aristocracy (p. 88). In order to keep up its myth of the perpetual revolution of the unconscious, Castels went on, it had to infiltrate all sectors of the mental health field. That was easy, he believed, since analysts were attuned to the origins of their patients' unhappiness and thus could play on them. But Castel was as dubious about the Althusser-Lacan axis as he was about the classical Freudians. For whoever had been either "on the couch or on the easy chair," he maintained, had become aware "of a certain rapport with power, hierarchical formalities, continuation of a sociopolitical equilibrium based on exploitation, and on segregation" (p. 255).

Some of the members of the SPP, of course, had their own critiques of the turn of events, if only because psychoanalysis *had* become mainstream. Moreover, as members of the Parisian intellectual milieu, they had been taught to be self-critical and to distrust official acceptance. In addition, one of the central figures, Michel Foucault, in *Madness and Civilization* ([1961] 1965) in *I, Pierre Rivière . . .* ([1973] 1975), and later in *The History of Sexuality I* ([1976] 1978), demonstrated how all the doctors ever since the French Revolution had "conspired" with those in power to keep the mad in their place. Hence the Freudians felt obliged to examine seriously their own role within the mental health profession and their links to political power in hospitals and health administration. These polemics themselves, while promoting its popularity, politicized psychoanalysis as well as the disagreements within the profession.

In 1978, Marcel Jaeger noted that France had more than 130,000 psychiatric hospital beds, that more than a million people had something to do with psychiatry, and that a third of the generally ill were believed to suffer from some psychosomatic or psychiatric ailment. Because, as some French analysts told me, all medically trained psychoanalysts had hospital connections, they tended to get entangled in the power struggles of hospitals.

To the extent that the outcome of such struggles had to do with power politics, hospital politics and university politics as well could not be separated from the larger political realm. It was useful to maintain friendly relations with specific government agencies, and those who already had them had everything to gain from supporting the status quo—that is, from keeping their political allies in power. (Most of the officials they dealt with were career bureaucrats.) When they succeeded, of course, it was evidence of their conservatism.

In the course of such activities, French analysts learned also to cooperate with theoretical opponents from other associations, even to the point of sending them patients. German analysts, on the other hand, whether of the DPV or the DPG, were strictly loyal not only to their fellow members but to their general political attitudes; referrals went to like-minded people. Thus in Paris institutional problems helped blur theoretical lines, although the polemics did become more heated. In Germany, they were increasingly geared to investigations of the Nazi past and to global politics. When Parisian Freudians got into these issues they treated them abstractly, mostly addressing phenomena of individual and collective amnesia and moving into abstruse philosophical realms (Cabestan, 1982; Rigoulet, 1978). Or they made fun of all the analysts, in such books as *Les fils de Freud sont fatigués* (1977) and *L'Effet 'Yau de Poêle* (1979), among others. The many amusing verbal pyrotechnics defy description—a coming together of intellectual invention, the use of alliteration and metaphor, theoretical breadth, classical range, and sheer verve. A number of them were translated or commented on in *Psyche* and after a certain time lag crossed the ocean, to be taken up, for the most part, by the deconstructionists.

Political Tides and Tidal Waves

The Freudians as citizens of specific countries inevitably were involved in the political discourse of their own milieus. However, since psychoanalysts spend their days listening to and thinking about the motivations of their patients, many tend to personalize their politics, to psychoanalyze political leaders. And because they are experts in human behavior, most of them at times feel qualified to make sweeping political judgments. As descendants of Freud they frequently subscribe to his humanist aims and often have publicly supported progressive causes.

Freud, we recall, had not been politically astute—he called off the Dresden congress only a week before the beginning of the First World War, and he left Vienna after the Anschluss rather than before. We recall, also, that his ingenious psychoanalytic explanations for politicians' acts were given without examining the questions in any detail. For the most part, his global analyses were taken up by lay people who were not politically sophisticated.

The "rule of abstinence" and the fact that candidates are dependent upon their supervisors and continue to identify with them even after graduation account for the generally apolitical atmosphere in the Freudians' institutes. Nevertheless, institutional politics (most blatant when, at moments of splits, candidates follow their "masters") not only mirror theoretical positions but subsume general attitudes and beliefs, which also reflect national political discussions and trends. For instance, at the Vienna meetings in 1971—a few years after the college students had had their revolts—analytic candidates protested arbitrary criteria of admissions and training, secret and ad hoc decisions, and the training programs themselves. The students have continued to question organizational procedures, but though their questions have emanated from larger political issues, they have tended to end up as institutional ones. The candidates' bylaws and procedures are curiously similar to those of their elders in the IPA. This is not to say that Freudians are or ought to be political tabula rasa, but only that their political positions tend to remain unexamined. Maybe, like Freud, they are Social Democrats by disposition and too busy to keep on top of events.

When differences on political issues have erupted at IPA congresses and at precongress meetings, conflicts for the most part are expressed in terms of organizational questions—where to meet next, whether to admit a somewhat authoritarian society, whether to hold a peace rally. These issues, however, do mirror some of the political left-right splits of the various milieus and center on how best to further democracy and how to fight anti-Semitism, repression, and prejudice.

The Hamburg congress in 1985—the first one on German soil since 1932—dramatized the political problems. Emigré analysts, in particular, wondered whether their official return to Germany would be interpreted as condoning the extermination of six million Jews or, in more personal terms, whether they might be betraying the memory of the parents, grandparents, or other relatives killed in concentration camps. They questioned whether they could possibly have enough trust in their German colleagues to work through their conflicts with them. Among German Freudians, on the other hand, those with a "clean past" were divided on whether to try to recall the murky history of the reconstitution of their institutes, whether to play down the opportunism of some of their mentors, how to deal with feelings of guilt (conscious and unconscious), and whether to shoulder blame and ask for forgiveness.

German psychoanalysts with a questionable past, or a questionable analysis, who insisted that the statute of limitations ought to be applied forty years after the Nazis had been defeated, reportedly wanted to use the congress to gain international recognition and bandage old wounds rather than open them up. But those candidates who thought their elders were too authoritarian were afraid of an (unconscious) resurgence of Nazi ideology—in them and in themselves because of early influences—and insisted on complete openness. Because children identify with their fathers, and candidates must work through this early identification with their analyst, they held, only an absolutely thorough psychoanalysis could "cure" them. Afraid that they might have incorporated the unanalyzed prejudices of their "analyst fathers," they now expected to study the impact of Freud's mass psychology on individuals.

Mortimer Ostow (1985b) compared the Nazi phenomenon to other apocalyptic movements. They "attract the identificatory tendencies of the borderline and the psychotic individual," he stated, "so that he feels anchored in reality and thereby combats the anxiety that his psychotic dissociation evokes" (p. 13). Ostow hoped to diffuse the tensions induced by prejudice through advising opinion makers of the catastrophic consequences of apocalyptic thinking. Other Freudians spoke of the consequences of "autistic encapsulation"—the consequence of terror and the locus of inner drama—of the death wishes accompanying the inability to mourn and of the "shameful silences" induced by the need to forget.

The London analyst Hanna Segal and the American psychiatrist John Mack addressed the "impending apocalypse" at a political rally. They assumed that people who believe in the effectiveness of deterrence rather than unilateral disarmament are advocates of war, and they talked of destructive weapons as extensions of primitive omnipotence and of the paranoid mechanisms of leaders that might make them "push the button." Essentially, they delivered disarmament speeches, though it was not clear whether the disarmament was to be unilateral. But their remarks did not lead to a viable dialogue. For they concentrated on the evils being perpetrated by Great Britain and the United States while stating that the Soviet Union was reacting mainly to Western aggression. There was no mention of the danger of nuclear weapons in such hands as Pakistan or Libya. The statement that "we are preparing for a war against an external enemy in order to face internal problems" and that "preparedness for war makes us more paranoid," expressing the wish to "self-destruct," not only reduced politics to psychology but reminded one of calls for peace by Bertrand Russell and earlier peace movements. (In Vienna, in 1971, the Freudians had questioned how psychoanalysis might add to our knowledge about the deepest layers of human anxiety that produce the aggression leading to war.) The analysts who came to this meeting were not prepared to challenge the facts or the arguments. Two years later in Montreal, however, few people attended the peace rally that was now part of the official program. A number of speakers repeated the arguments against deterrence and called for negotiations, which were already in progress. It also was stated that "the United States fantasizes the USSR as the aggressor" and that the rarefied atmosphere in which nuclear scientists and politicians work together strengthens the power of their illness—their need to hold on to childhood omnipotence. (At a meeting of "Psychoanalysts for Peace" in Zurich in April 1983, a young analyst passed his hat around to collect money for arms for Nicaragua. No one seemed to find it odd that, as George Orwell might have said, peace was being promoted by war.) This is not the place to discuss the merit of these political views, but merely to indicate that the kind of fusion of politics and psychoanalysis made by some Freudians cannot resolve either short-term or long-term problems of realpolitik.

Both the Hamburg and Montreal rallies were attuned to the Germans' radical psychoanalysis, as practiced at Horst-Eberhard Richter's Psychoanalytic Institute in Giessen. Richter's group therapy with students, however, had other roots. Basically, he stressed, correctly, that German children must be raised in a less authoritarian fashion and with more tolerance. In the process, he expected to educate people to avoid wars as well as Nazi-like atrocities (1982a). But he stretched psychoanalysis politically when he "psychoanalyzed" leaders like Willy Brandt (he was conciliatory toward the East) and Franz-Josef Strauss (he had an enemy-friend perspective), and compared their rivalries to those between Alexander Haig and Caspar Weinberger. This led him to conclude, for example, that people play out their personal attitudes in their politics by retiring increasingly behind abstract systems and technology—for instance, in their arguments about the stationing of SS 20s and Pershing missiles (pp. 34–37). In another of his many publications, Richter (1982b) attributed the Freudians' reluctance to engage in political activities to the "rule of abstinence" and to the fact that those who are doctors (all Americans and over half of the Germans) consider neutrality an irrevocable ethical commandment.

In addition to Richter's group and the Parins', Klaus Horn of the Sigmund-Freud-Institut has organized political and social scientists around psychological issues. They meet once a year to discuss the dangers of bureaucratization, personal relationships to peace and war, and the impact of leaders' personalities on realpolitik (Horn and Senghaas-Knobloch, 1983, p. 16). Furthermore, these psychologists address questions of power and of powerlessness, and—given their geographic location—are more upset than people outside Germany when they come up against dictatorial tendencies (Horn, 1985a). After the accident at Chernobyl this group met to discuss the threat of annihilation from *all* sources (*Psyche*, in July 1987, printed some of the contributions).

But the main thrust of Freudian politics in Germany is peace, which has become a slogan of the left. In this vein, the Anglo-Saxons' denunciations of their own leaders has automatically triggered simplistic parallels between depictions of President Reagan and Chancellor Kohl, and between German and American political parties.[4]

Just as the German Freudians were steeped in the peace politics of their culture, so their French colleagues—whose Socialist government was pursuing former Gaullist foreign policies—were opposed to appeasement and neutralism. In fact, almost none of them came to the Hamburg or Montreal rallies: they backed IPA President Adam Limentani and Vice President Chasseguet-Smirgel who had voted against including peace rallies in the official congress program. (They defended their decision at the open meeting that concluded the Hamburg congress.)

The South American Freudians seemed to "mediate": their fears of oppression belonged to another arena. As eager for peace as their German colleagues and leery of U.S. "imperialism," a number of them—though afraid of the ramifications and the terror of nonliberal regimes—reminded the participants of the dangers of Soviet expansionism. Some of them remembered their own "internal emigration" (the term used for clandestine activities) and the fear they lived under were they to accept an "untrustworthy" patient, one who might denounce his analyst to the authorities for engaging in a "subversive" activity. These Freudians dreaded a leftist dictatorship as much as one on the right, for in a society that prohibits freedom of expression, psychoanalysis has no place. To practice at all might lead to reprisals. On the other hand, when such societies do allow psychoanalysis, they often try to turn it to their own ends—by asking Freudians to explain the behavior of prisoners, to "advise" torturers, or to question dissidents.

In sum, psychoanalytic explanations of politics are riddled with paradoxes: linking political events to the psychic defense mechanisms of leaders means that concrete problems must be played down; advocating humanistic goals, such as the eradication of wars, aggression, or totalitarian regimes, makes the discourse ideological and too abstract for implementation; and by expecting to convince individuals to pursue these indisputably desirable goals, psychoanalysts to some extent will compromise their neutrality. What, then, is to be done?

Freud, of course, also did not know what to do about creating peace on earth. And Erik Erikson, who in *Ghandi's Truth* (1969) came out for nonviolent resistance and who is now vaguely associated with the American peace movement, concluded rather pessimistically at the Vienna congress that in order to survive people apparently need not only enemies but also a certain amount of aggression. Unfortunately, the Freudians are no more adept at politics than are other private citizens. As for psychoanalysis, it does best when exposing the neurotic impediments to an open mind.

In the political sphere, then, the Freudians have not gone beyond Freud, who ended his "Reflections upon War and Death" with an equivocation: "*Si vis pacem, para bellum*. If you desire peace, prepare for war. It would be timely to paraphrase it: *Si vis vitam, para mortem*. If you would endure life, be prepared for death" (*S.E.*, 14:300).

Conclusion

Where is psychoanalysis now, and where is it going in its own development and in its resonance in other fields of knowledge? The Boston Freudian Stanford Gifford (1985) held that its youthful, revolutionary era, when it appealed mostly to intellectual rebels, is over—subject to an inevitable metamorphosis that one may welcome or deplore. Of course, American psychoanalysis has declined in popularity, and its fortunes have turned. But just as people, to paraphrase Daniel Bell on Marxism, have to live through their own *Kronstadt*—that is, through the loss of illusion—so psychoanalysis everywhere will lose in influence after its initial (exaggerated) promises have not been fulfilled. Then its ideas seem to inspire "lesser" therapies while psychoanalysts devote themselves to their "elite" patients and to research.

During periods of flowering, leading Freudians tended to work at enlarging both theory and therapy, in the course of which they inevitably fueled the idealistic and humanistic aims of their particular society. At that time, as we have noted, not only doctors but anthropologists, sociologists, psychologists, and political scientists borrowed Freudian ideas. Fields like ethnopsychoanalysis and psychohistory, in fact, began to legitimate themselves only after psychoanalytic thought achieved a certain amount of visibility. This could not occur before the society had reached an advanced level of well-being—

that is, before there was at least a small middle class, and before the political climate had become fairly liberal. Occasionally, this has happened during a phase of liberation in a repressive society, such as Hungary, Chile, or Argentina, when psychoanalysis had a chance to emerge from "internal emigration" to create some sort of free space for itself. (Under repressive conditions, as in Nazi Germany or even Yugoslavia, psychoanalysis could be manipulated by those in power or coupled to behavior therapy, thereby making it psychoanalysis in name only.) And before it could serve feminist or Marxist ends, a large sector of the society had to be conversant with notions of the unconscious, and the society had to be able to withstand massive internal protest.

Consequently, the place accorded to psychoanalysis varies from country to country. In America, where it had its earliest success, classical analysis now seems to be in its furthest stage of decline. But this is a decline only in relation to early exaggerated hopes, since Freudian ideas are everywhere. It is now taken for granted that some of the symptoms of neurotic behavior may be relieved. The critics of psychoanalysis, however, who accept nothing less than a total "cure," never are satisfied, even when patients in treatment get better or reach a plateau. They expect them to attain so-called normality, a state neither Freud nor anyone else ever has been able to define adequately. But there is a kind of backhanded success in the fact that psychoanalysis did pave the way for its bastard offspring—that is, for quick-fix therapies that temporarily at least are being hailed as superior replacements.

I have indicated earlier that psychoanalytic history has been constantly updated to further specific themes, recasting Freud as hero or impostor, genius or imitator. I also have shown that the rise and fall in the popularity of psychoanalysis in line with its pertinence and adaptability to events and preoccupations of a given time could be gauged by the number and types of applications it engendered.

Taken together, the inroads of psychoanalysis into history, anthropology, psychology, and sociology have had an impact beyond the academy and have penetrated every recess of modern culture. In American universities, acceptance has been accompanied by rejection. Psychoanalysis has been incorporated into women's and literary studies, but even when social work and psychology students are taught only that "Freud was wrong," in one way or another they learn something about psychoanalysis. Many students during the past decade have been introduced to Freud via deconstruction. This endeavor originally was located in departments of French and comparative literature, but it soon spread into philosophy—Jacques Derrida's own discipline. There, among other strategic readings, the Freudian hermeneuticists, the anti-Freudian Popperians, and the "scientific" Freudians were displaced or, in deconstructionist language, "decentered."

In a recent collection edited by Joseph H. Smith and William Kerrigan, *Pragmatism's Freud: The Moral Disposition of Psychoanalysis* (1986), the philosopher Richard Rorty argued that Freud fits into the "story of decentering-as-mechanization." Rorty noted that Hume had treated ideas as mental atoms whose arrangement *was* the self, but unlike Freud, he had not changed our self-image (pp. 2–4). Most philosophers, it appears, have been upset by Freud's partitioning of the self, have rejected the threatening picture of quasi-selves lurking beneath consciousness, and have preferred to believe that a single body contains a single self.[1] But Rorty found that Freud's "revisionary account of human dignity" allows each of us to "tailor a coherent self-image . . . and then use it to tinker with our behavior"—behavior that neither furthers nor hinders human solidarity (p. 19). Rorty's view of philosophy clearly was influenced by deconstructionist theories, which themselves were influenced by Derrida's critique of Lacan.

The Post-Lacanian Era

The achievements of the classical analysts contributed to such fields as psychosomatics and literature, but the impact of la psychanalyse on the Parisian public was due to Lacan. In fact, his philosophical ideas were aimed at large audiences while he denounced the establishment Freudians. As Clara Malraux once told me, people who listened to Lacan (including herself) often did not understand what he was saying and were outraged by some of the silences and attacks on opponents in his open seminars. Yet they went to hear him and to observe him: he put on the best show in town. His outrageous behavior provided unexpected excitement, and his statements always left his listeners in intellectual suspense, mulling over what he had meant and wondering what they could get out of them for their "self-analyses." In such a climate, there was little need for books explaining Lacan, although the French wrote volumes that incorporated his ideas and others that disputed them.[2] And there was the gossip surrounding Lacan's defectors. One analyst was a scoundrel, it was said, one a conniver; another "never saw a schizophrenic. One counted the suicides of one, the hospitalizations of the other . . . the unresolved transference to his analyst of yet another. . . . If one believed the rumors, ninety percent of Parisian analysts should have been disqualified" (Clément, ([1978] 1987).

In this climate, it was unlikely even after Lacan died that anyone in France would proclaim him the most important thinker since Descartes and the most innovative one since Nietzsche and Freud, as Ellie Ragland-Sullivan recently did in America (1986, p. ix). Still, by "moving psychoanalysis into the street," he probably was the most influential psychoanalyst since Freud. French classical Freudians, who now are dealing with the aftermath of "Lacanism" and who were influenced by his presence if not his philosophy, are currently reevaluating *all* of psychoanalysis and are particularly concerned with the future of the therapy. But so are the Lacanians.

By 1986, there were at least fourteen Lacanian "leaders," each claiming to be the true successor. Some of them, such as Serge Leclaire and Didier Anzieu, appeared to be moving closer to the classical Freudians; others, like Françoise Dolto and Jacques-Alain Miller, were holding their own ground. Their many publications flourished. In addition to the monthly newsletter of the *Ecole de la Cause Freudienne*, *L'Âne*, and *Ornicar?* there were *Le Cout freudien*, *Le Discours Psychanalytique*, *Cahiers de lectures freudiennes*, *Confrontation*, *Psychanalystes: le politique et l'exclusion du feminin*, *Littoral*, *Scilicet*, the proceedings of the meetings of the Cartels Constituants de l'Analyse Freudienne, *Inceste: Nouvelle revue d'ethnopsychiatrie*, and *Etudes freudiennes*, among others.

While all these publications were full of philosophical and literary excursions, they usually were meant to illuminate the therapy, and, except for medicine and psychiatry, they were not sponsored by academic departments. The publications themselves exemplified the existing confusion, which also was palpable at the many conferences set up by psychoanalysts who hoped to organize this chaos. Thus the Association Fondation Rocinante, most of whose members are South American Lacanians who moved to Paris to escape repression in their countries, organized an international interdisciplinary conference on "Psychoanalysis under Terrorism." To judge from the proceedings, edited by Heitor O'Dwyer de Macedo (1988), Lacanian language was spoken by a lot of leftist analysts who seriously and eloquently were calling for an end to terrorist governments.[3]

Still, even if the members of the many small post-Lacanian factions should manage to survive by sending each other patients, it appeared doubtful that they would be able to institute a responsible means of training young analysts. The conferences, to some extent, have taken the place of Lacan's seminars: they draw up to a thousand people. And they are more democratic than Lacan's meetings insofar as they have a number of speakers and encourage heated dialogue with a participating audience.

After René Major gave up his meetings around *Confrontation,* Alain de Mijolla helped fill the gap. Starting in 1981, he organized yearly meetings in Aix-en-Provence, led by psychoanalysts and people from other disciplines, around such themes as "Suffering, Pleasure and Thought," "Languages," "Metapsychology and Philosophy," and "Body and History" (1986). De Mijolla also cofounded the International Freudian Society in 1985, and in the same year started the Association of the History of Psychoanalysis. These meetings have served to heal wounds inflicted even before the death of, and disillusion with, Lacan, and they have helped keep psychoanalysis in the news. Just as everywhere else, Parisian psychoanalysts live by their reputations. But, because of the loose organizational structures and the inherent anti-institutionalism, the French referral system is poor. Thus the French are more dependent on a good show at a public meeting, or on an interesting book than are their foreign colleagues. This need for visibility, along with the acceptance of interdisciplinarity, not only has made for the plethora of provocative readings of psychoanalytic subjects but has turned many of these analysts into fantastic intellectual performers.

Paris between the 1950s and the early 1980s resembled Freud's Vienna: psychoanalysts entered into political and intellectual debates and did not hide behind their couches. In 1974, for instance, Chasseguet-Smirgel edited a collection of essays on the "path of anti-Oedipus." Didier Anzieu, who had been analyzed by Lacan in 1949, left the SPP in 1953 and joined Pontalis in starting the Société Psychanalytique Française in 1960; then he argued that Freud had undertaken his self-analysis in order to overcome his psychotic anxieties and that he had formulated his subsequent theories to establish successive defenses against depression (Chasseguet-Smirgel, 1974, p. 167). In 1986, Anzieu, writing explicitly against Lacan, provided one of the best descriptions of the plight of post-Lacanians. He was especially upset by their clinical practices—the floating attention and the systematic silences which were supposed to elicit the patient's infantile memories but usually did not bring about the expected transformation (1986, p. 42). Anzieu questioned Lacanian techniques, which assumed that interpreting "the letters" of an analysand's language would penetrate his unconscious and "become a language game"—often at the expense of the analysand. Thus he rejoined those classical analysts who, after treating patients who had been seeing Lacanians, either found that language analysis had been counterproductive for a proper transference or that even when it had worked it had not been handled carefully enough.

François Perrier's transference, for instance, had occurred the instant he met Lacan. Together with Serge Leclaire and Wladimir Granoff, Perrier

(1985) informed us, he had been part of Lacan's governing troika. But feeling betrayed, he had turned on Lacan and wrote a humorous and incisive commentary about his trips into *Translacanie*, describing the background of the splits, the personal quarrels, and Lacan's wheelings, dealings, and indiscretions. In fact, Perrier went beyond François George (1979a, 1979b), for whom Lacan now was an intellectual crook—his former idol had clay feet.

These were only a few of the many "obituaries" of Lacan as psychoanalysts of all stripes tried to come to grips with the inevitable changes in their institutional lives. Once more, the French were expecting to distill the best of psychoanalysis, as they had in the past each time they split and regrouped. All French Freudians were rereading Freud, adding new wrinkles to the texts or reinventing him altogether. In the process, the concerns of the SPP differed more and more from those of its sister organizations in the IPA.

Mitscherlich's Heritage

Those German analysts who expected psychoanalysis to rid them of the Nazi past championed Mitscherlich's social progressivism, although some of them gradually limited themselves to seeing patients, leaving politics to the politicians. But all German analysts had to come to grips with the fact that there had been an intellectual vacuum between 1933 and 1945 and had to face what these years had done to their own psyches and their ability to relate to others. In analytic terminology, they had a great deal to work through. After they and their countrymen saw the television film *Holocaust*, however, many of these Freudians were aware that they had to deal with still more guilt, and on a daily basis. Furthermore, they realized that they would have to look more diligently for its traces in their patients and for these patients' transferences of Nazi memories onto themselves. In fact, the Holocaust became more central in philosophical and literary investigations as well, and German classical works and authors increasingly were being interpreted in relation to it. Even friendships with Jewish individuals started to be examined as expressions of philo-Semitism, as possible reaction formations to anti-Semitism.

On the other hand, the reimbursement policies mandated by the German government have been functioning as a benign big brother. It is difficult to convey the flavor of this influence, except by comparison: in America and France many possibilities for reimbursement exist, but they have not become as organized as in Germany—though not for want of trying. When reading the many massive and relevant documents, I kept thinking that only Max Weber could have provided us with the model for the ideal type of bureaucracy, since he lived as it was being constructed. At its roots, of course, are the egalitarian principles psychoanalysts on the "right" take for granted. Those on the "left," however, have wanted to extend these principles while at the same time denouncing the bureaucrats who must implement them: they are in charge of egalitarianism. But even if they were able to live up to the Weberian ideal, they also represent the dominant social class of the *Sozialstaat*.

This paradox is magnified by the realistic fear that a strong state, if led by any sort of right-winger, might easily turn into another fascist one. In that sense, German analysts take the critical stance of the Frankfurt School, and they heed Marcuse's admonitions that "the politics of mass society begin at home, with the shrinking of the ego and its subjection to the collective ideal . . . which may well mean—to live in refusal and opposition to the Establishment" (Marcuse, 1970, p. 61). So, while "rightist" Freudians assume that well-analyzed individuals will be autonomous and able to resist undue pressures, their colleagues on the "left," in line with Freud's *Group Psychology and the Analysis of the Ego*, assume that in mass society conscience, responsibility, and ego-ideal are always projected onto a leader or a government, so that individual autonomy must be actively fought for.

Inevitably, in Germany the "rightist" Freudians have focused more on clinical questions, and the "leftists" have addressed more social and political ones. Even who may seek a psychoanalysis, for example, has become a political question when taxpayers underwrite the treatment. In fact, Cremerius, Hoffmann, and Trimborn (1979) recalled that Freud had stated that there is social assistance for the poor who get sick and that the rich and powerful can buy what they want, including the peace of mind that allows them to escape debilitating neuroses. This means that the middle class alone will seek to address the nature of an illness via psychoanalysis. Cremerius then described some of his own middle-class patients, compared them to Leo Srole's American respondents, and distinguished among neurotics who don't need treatment, those who make their neuroses functional, and those who avoid role conflict through identification. He concluded that individuals whose ego and ego-ideal are linked to group ideals lack appropriate guilt feelings (p. 42). Thus, psychoanalysts, he held, ought to feel guilty when treating mostly middle-class patients, even though these are the ones who seek them out.

In view of the fact that German psychoanalysis was nonexistent in 1945, its strides during the last forty years have been miraculous. "Too much, too soon," quipped one of my informants. On the so-called right, he was among those who felt that too many badly analyzed Freudians had passed down their Nazi-induced neuroses to their candidates. And because so much of what was called psychoanalysis had really been short-term therapy, and many of the analysts themselves had been poorly analyzed, a number of Freudians stated that it was imperative to do "repair work."

But the seven analysts and five social scientists who got together in 1983 in Frankfurt to discuss *Psychoanalysis and Its Discontents* thought research was equally important. They deplored the Frankfurt institute's increasing pursuit of therapy alone after Mitscherlich's death and attacked the trend toward medicalization. They were afraid that this would transform psychoanalysis into an adjunct of the state's mental health system, at the same time depriving it of its critical edge (Lohmann, 1983). When informed that this transformation was being advocated because the state of Hessen wanted to see (therapeutic) results in return for funding the institute, they rose to the defense of psychoanalysis as a social critique. Attacking unconscious lies of (unnamed but recognizable) psychoanalysts, their unhappy relationship to power, and their frequent neglect of the countertransference, they were unaware that these issues had become important enough to be picked up by psychoanalysts throughout the country. So, when they followed up with a second critical volume, *Psychoanalysis on the Couch* (1984), they were joined by another dozen contributors and enlarged their critiques to every political topic. They were amazed by the enormous response to their concerns and by the large audiences who came to hear them talk.

Still, not too many persons psychoanalyze in the morning and become social critics in the afternoon, a practice that appears to be limited to German-speaking left-oriented Freudians. (Close collaboration with nonanalysts and students follows from it.) And, carefully and quietly, some of the German Freudians have reactivated the critical "Bernstein circles" which had been started in the 1950s in several cities and where analysts pursue such questions as the status of lay analysis and medicalization and relations to reimbursing agents. This is not to say that Freudians elsewhere are noncritical, only that their criticism either remains more private or takes the form of social protests for equality, peace, or humanity.

A Comparative Summary

In general, much of what applies to American Freudians can be said to hold true for their London colleagues, but writ small. Only American psychoanalysis was in a position to develop unimpeded by war or totalitarian interference; the Londoners were handicapped by the blitz; the French had a hiatus of six years; and the Germans' gap of twelve years was multiplied by the trauma of Hitler's legacy. These events changed the Freudians' lives. That so many of them emigrated to Anglo-Saxon territory and were influenced by prevalent social, institutional, and cultural conditions favored the spread of psychoanalytic ideas in America. In the process, the various influences on psychoanalysis, and the demands on it, led to myriads of new readings and interpretations—all of them defended and attacked. Thus it no longer is possible to speak of theoretical coherence.

After 1945, psychoanalytic research primarily originated in the Anglo-Saxon countries. But more recently, German critical-cum-psychoanalytic theory and French feminist-cum-deconstructionist psychoanalysis have been exported to the English-speaking countries. Freudian, Lacanian, and Kleinian formulations were expanded upon in South America and, in turn, came back to Paris, London, and New York in altered versions. Although some of the ensuing differences also had to do with gaps in translations and with mistranslations, such timing itself tended to be in response to specific temporal interests and biases.[4] Still, the psychoanalytic institutes that eventually formed in many cities took on their own personalities, influenced by the theories preferred by their dominant members as well as by the type of marriage worked out with psychiatrists and psychologists. Most of all, however, Freudians everywhere depended upon the press they got from satisfied patients. And nowhere did they abdicate voluntarily to emotionally easier and shorter therapies.

Steven Marcus (1984) talked of the overdetermined sequence of development within psychoanalysis, leading from Abram Kardiner's cross-cultural observations of superego formation (as indicator of cultural stability) through Erik Erikson's focus on ego identity ("'located' *in the core of the individual* and *of communal culture* due to historical accident") to Kohut's views of fragmentary and discontinuous selves (pp. 186–89). This describes the American scenario, although some would argue that theories of the self were already in the process of being replaced by the focus on object relations. But a Frenchman is more likely to see psychoanalysis as developing from Bonaparte's elaborations on Poe via Lacan to deconstructionism, or from Charcot's experiments with hysterics via Freudian psychoanalysis to Lacan, or to Fain and Marty's *psychosomatique*—depending upon whom one talks to. A German Freudian, on the other hand, would tend to deplore the early resistance to psychoanalysis ("blaming" it either for Nazi therapy in the Third Reich or for its demise), would tend to praise Mitscherlich for its revival (*Wiederaufbau*) and would—with varying degrees of reservation—uphold American ego psychology. His London counterpart would praise Jones's proselytizing and organizational skills, would point to the lively theoretical developments arising out of the controversies, and would be proud that projective identification, as elaborated by the Middle Group, eventually caught on around the world.

Every one of these reconstructions, however, plays down the cultural determination of symptomatology. In America and England the classical symptoms of hysteria seem to have been eradicated, whereas both French and German analysts keep diagnosing and treating hysterics, and 30 percent of Viennese patients are said to suffer from hysterical symptoms. But, as we know, psychoanalytic diagnoses themselves reflect cultural assumptions. Hans Lobner, a Viennese Freudian, suggested that in an ambience where a respectable woman is still expected to jump up on a chair and scream or even faint upon seeing a mouse, hysteria will be diagnosed more frequently than in a milieu where such behavior is unusual. Is the difference then between psychoanalysts or patients? Are psychoanalysts in more "traditional" societies more likely to diagnose as hysterical behavior that is "inappropriate" to men, or are women in such societies more likely to transform "inappropriate" sexual desire into hysteria? Or must psychoanalysts rethink their diagnostic categories? These are some of the soft questions which, once more, will get answers reflecting preconceived biases.

Whatever these biases may be, psychoanalysis has advanced our knowledge of subjectivity. We now know a great deal about the unconscious psychic mechanisms influencing everyday behavior and about the myriad paths such behavior may take. Thousands of studies have filled in and confirmed Freud's observations. These are the data allowing for predictions. True, such predictions are not scientifically verifiable, but the importance of verifiability once more reflects cultural assumptions. And it overlooks the fact that psychoanalysis has helped countless individuals learn to get along better with themselves and others and has altered Western child-rearing practices, family interactions, and views of morality.

What does all this mean for the future of psychoanalysis? In America, Sanford Gifford anticipates a smaller social role, less visibility, and more scientific advances by fewer persons—that is, research that may be disseminated to others in the various helping professions. Some of his colleagues expect therapeutic insights through applications of new knowledge of the self or of object relations. Most Londoners, I believe, would concur but would stress the great number of discoveries being made in the area of child development. German psychoanalysts are more likely to focus on the social impact of unconscious drives, to extrapolate to mass psychology, and, together with their "uncritical" colleagues, to establish formally a watered-down psychoanalysis as the optimal method for the treatment of mental ailments. As for the French, they are bound to find a number of innovative amalgams of classical and Lacanian therapy.

As these psychoanalytic therapies are undergoing their metamorphoses, psychoanalytic ideas will become ever more entrenched in the culture at large. But these ideas themselves are diffused by practicing psychoanalysts and are derived from reflections and generalizations based on specific experiences with patients. Since these patients, in turn, respond to their analysts' theoretical and clinical approaches, psychoanalysis on every level mirrors culturally approved assumptions. Consequently, as time goes on, each country increasingly evolves its own Freud. Sometimes this occurs with the help of anthropologists, literary critics, ethnologists, sociologists, or psychologists; at other times the influence of the media dominates.

In any event, Freudian thought in one way or another will retain its hold on the human imagination. Even if Freud's larger hopes for a better society have not been borne out and he failed to find the formula for wiping out large-scale wars and individual irrationality, he has been a dominating figure in the modern mind and has revolutionized our way of thinking. Despite widespread criticism and frequent hostility to psychoanalysis in one form or another, Freud's ideas have permeated the consciousness of humanity, including the minds of those who swear they do not possess an unconscious. Freudian psychoanalysts have helped many people and have provided most of the tools used by other helping professions. Ultimately, even if only aspiring candidates will be exploring their unconscious four to five times a week for four or more years, many of Freud's basic ideas will prevail. He supplied us with the means to explore "scientifically" the roots of our modern imagination—a conscious and unconscious imagination that has taken off in different directions, responding to cultural traditions, influences, and trends. Freud cannot be dislodged from his role as "father" of our century: no disinterested thinker any longer can deny the power of the unconscious, or the impact of both le nom and le non-du-père.

Notes

Introduction

1. I am following Karl Mannheim's (1936) theories.
2. This resulted from the inextricable connections among therapy, theory, and factors of personality, which are summarized in chapter 3.

Chapter 1, The Reception of Freud's Theories

1. Ellenberger and Sulloway were probably correct in maintaining that the vision of Freud as surrounded by enemies helped glorify him. But even if this is true, the glorification did not lessen the value of his contributions or propel psychoanalysis into the cultural mainstream.
2. See particularly Pete Gay, *Freud for Historians* (1985); Peter Loewenberg, *Decoding the Past* (1983); David James Fisher, "Rereading Freud's Civilization and Its Discontents" (1982); Dennis Klein, *The Origins of the Psychoanalytic Movement* (1981).
3. The secrecy surrounding Freud's correspondence has led to countless speculations about the content (Gay, 1988, pp. 741–46). Early releases were found to have omitted statements uncomplimentary to Freud (Rand and Torok, 1987). The publication of the complete correspondences by friends and disciples no doubt will give rise to further reinterpretations of the early Freudians' interactions, free associations, doubts, fantasies, and feelings—illuminating Freud's human qualities. By the time the entire Freud archives are opened, the hero myth may already have been destroyed.
4. The French Freudian Alain de Mijolla created the International Association for the History of Psychoanalysis (1985) so that psychoanalysts, historians, sociolo-

gists, and psychologists might present new information about the origins of psychoanalysis.

5. Inquiries focus on Freud's relation to Jung, on the latter's Aryan credentials and his purported anti-Semitism after 1933, on the Jewish origins of the majority of Viennese Freudians, or on the non-Jewish composition of early American psychoanalysis. In general, the Freudians' histories are more reverential and lean more toward psychological explanations than those of the historians. Thus the range of their interpretations is somewhat narrower, more doctrinaire, and more likely to be couched in the idiom of the immediate environment.

6. Arthur Schnitzler, a contemporary physician and popular writer, for example, wrote of a lover who had "saved" his beloved from hysterical symptoms by seducing her. Sexuality and romanticism dominated the Vienna salons, whereas the larger intellectual ferment inspired socialist ideas. In this atmosphere, the radical premises of psychoanalysis about sexual experimentation were welcome, threatening the hypocrisy that Kaiser Franz-Josef's Vienna was nurturing.

7. See, for instance, Cuddihy (1974), who claimed that Jews when suddenly allowed to leave the ghettos had problems with civility; Marthe Robert's contention (1976) that *all* Jews were obsessed by integration; or references to revisionist histories denying Austrian anti-Semitism (Nelson, 1958; Janik and Toulmin, 1973; Gay, 1978; D. Klein, 1981; Morton, 1979; Schorske, 1980; Clark, 1980).

8. The French psychoanalytic historian Elizabeth Roudinesco (1982) recently argued that Meynert was angered because Freud had looked to Charcot as his "father."

9. Schorske (1980) summarizes the frustrations and bitterness verging on despair (p. 184) that had dogged Freud during the seventeen years (rather than the customary eight) he waited to be given a professorship.

10. The first of these histories was written by Wilhelm Solms-Rödelheim (1959). The organizers of the conference on "Die vertriebene Vernunft" (1987) invited historians and psychoanalysts to examine the Hitler period, but this was in response to questions raised by the election of Kurt Waldheim to the presidency of the country rather than to a widespread wish to know.

11. Weber and von Wiese "did not understand that psychoanalysis could have helped explain social pathology." Sociologists Georg Simmel, Ferdinand Tönnies, Alfred Weber, Ernst Tröltsch, Werner Sombart, and others also ignored psychoanalysis (Cremerius, 1981a).

12. L. H. Morgan, W. Robertson Smith, and other anthropologists were expanding on it.

13. Brauns did not mention that Frankfurt's Institut für Sozialforschung, founded by Karl Grünberg in 1929 (and the *Zeitschrift für Sozialforschung*), was set up to "fuse" Freud's ideas with Marx's. But economic and political concerns in the late 1920s were so staggering, I believe, that psychoanalytic inquiries by sociologists would have been an inconceivable luxury.

14. Wilhelm Vleugels ("Zu Freud's Theorien von der Psychoanalyse," 1923–24) agreed that a mass event, by suppressing individualism, "allows" the unconscious that is shared with others to surface and dominate. He quoted Alfred Vierkandt (*Handbook for Sociology*, 1931) who felt that Freud, Vleugels, Gustave LeBon, and

Georg Simmel all failed to explain fully crowd behavior. For Vleugels himself crowd behavior "may" result from regression to the individual's previous relations to his father during early oedipal development. Othmar Spann rejected the theory of sexuality and called Freud a "sexual criminal." And Franz Wilhelm Jerusalem noted that collectivism and individualism oppose each other in medical practice and within society, that "Freud's famous Oedipus complex . . . may estrange its carrier from his own personality to [escape] to a foreign one—derived from his thought, feelings and actions" (Brauns, 1981).

15. In 1929, E. K. Knabe thought that psychoanalysis exaggerated infantile bonds and that its preoccupation with the self furthered autism. Freud's notions of sex were said to be burrowing in dirt. E. Pfenningsdorf (1930, p. 597), repeating these views, added that Freud's idea of sublimation almost frivolously derived love of God from earthly love. Others linked Freud's ideas of religion to Judaism and secularization.

16. Hale also found that no single view of the unconscious was yet accepted: in 1908 Morton Prince, Hugo Munsterberg, Pierre Janet, and Alfred Binet had debated six common definitions without reaching agreement.

17. Because Joseph Babinsky's neurological conceptions of mental afflictions gained ascendance, psychoanalysis was said to be kept out until 1925.

18. According to the German Freudian Alfred Lorenzer, Ellenberger interpreted the rivalry between Freud and Janet around two themes, the discovery of the unconscious and the model of personality: Janet's model "is close to every psychoanalytic model not based on drive theory but on ego psychology—from Hartmann to Kohut and Roy Schafer' (1984, p. 101). Lorenzer thereby contradicted those American Freudians who tended to reject Ellenberger's reading because it favored dynamic psychiatry rather than ego psychology.

19. According to Roudinesco, in 1925 Freud misunderstood Janet's rejection of constitutionalism and at the same time indicated his ambivalence toward him. Janet, however, retained the idea of the subconscious—of two personalities, one the sleepwalking double of the other. Furthermore, for Janet heredity was not one condition among others but an etiology (Roudinesco, 1982, p. 261).

20. Ellenberger stresses the fertility of thinking and experimentation of the period. He notes, also that the Franco-German war of 1871 helped intensify both French and Austrian chauvinism, which militated against intellectual exchange and perpetuated existing prejudices.

21. Ellenberger, for example, who found that for Bernheim hypnosis "was the effect of suggestion, . . . the aptitude to transform an idea into an act," considered him an important link in the chain of dynamic psychiatry. Roudinesco maintained that Freud did not pay much attention to the rivalry between Charcot and Bernheim. According to her, Charcot and Bernheim broke over their concrete empirical methods, and their differences inspired Freud to mediate between their ideas, separating neurological and psychic factors and thus discovering the transference, the use of catharsis, and then free association (1982, pp. 55–57).

22. Although Freud published *Studies on Hysteria* in 1895, Breuer's encounter with Anna O. dated back to 1880. See particularly Gay (1988, pp. 63–69).

23. Michel Foucault's "glance" gained much currency after the publication of *Madness and Civilization* (New York: Pantheon, 1961) and *The Birth of the Clinic* (New York: Pantheon, 1963).

Chapter 2, From Informal Group to Formal Structures

1. Rank had written a psychoanalytic paper, *The Artist*, before meeting Freud in 1905, although it was not published until 1907. After he joined the army, in 1915, the *Minutes* stop, although fragmentary and "unintelligible" records do exist. There are no records of the earlier meetings.
2. The Adlerians were rarely mentioned after 1911, and neither were the Jungians or the Munich group after 1914, although individual Freudians did not necessarily lose touch with them.
3. According to Reichmayr and Wiesbauer, Adlerians tended to reduce theory to slogans, such as "socialist education," "education for class consciousness," "autonomous class-conscious proletarians," and "community consciousness," apparently because their ends were clearer than the means of achieving them.
4. These were Dr. Georg Wanke, director of a sanatorium in the Harz Mountains, Dr. Stegman of Dresden, Dr. Otto Juliusberger of Jena, Dr. Warda from Blankenberg in Thuringia, L. Röhmheld of Württemberg, A. Muthmann of Bad Nassau, E. Bloch of Kattowitz, and J. Marcinowki of Haus Sielbeck in Holstein.
5. Jones reported early on that Göring had been friendly and "approachable." Yet, according to "a deceased member," he suggested at one point that the psychoanalysts, as a birthday present for the Führer, "join the NSDAP, the German National Socialist Workers Party (Brainin and Kaminer, 1982).
6. Among the fifteen founding physicians were A. A. Brill, George H. Kirby, Maurice Karpas, C. P. Oberndorf, L. Bish, Frederic J. Farnell, Ernest M. Poate, J. Rosenbloom, William C. Garvin, and Charles Ricksher.
7. These were John T. MacCurdy, a student at Johns Hopkins Medical School; Adolf Meyer, clinical director of the Insane Hospital at Worcester; James Jackson Putnam, a distinguished specialist in nervous diseases; G. Lane Taneyhill, a Johns Hopkins instructor in neurology; A. A. Young from Omaha, who had studied in Zurich; and Ernest Jones.
8. Even theologians and religious sects like the Emmanuel movement adapted psychoanalysis to their own ends (Michel, 1984).
9. Horney moved to New York two years later. Alexander had come to the University of Chicago in 1930 as visiting professor of psychoanalysis and settled there after 1932. His institute was independent of the local psychoanalytic association.
10. Freud used this formulation half in jest, in his letter of Dec. 18, 1924, admonishing Groddeck against isolating himself from the psychoanalytic society.

Chapter 3, From Therapy to Theory

1. The publication of previously unknown letters and of notes from his school days (K. Eissler et al., 1974; Kästle, 1987; Roth, 1987; Mijolla, 1987) and the burgeoning interest in the history of psychoanalysis have led to new hypotheses about the

years before *The Interpretation of Dreams:* why Freud continued to include physiological/biological factors in his thinking, and why he abandoned or bracketed them for a while. The literature on the "Project," especially in *Psyche, Etudes freudiennes,* and various new journals, has grown enormously.

2. Freud considered this his first psychoanalytic case.

3. Essays on psychoanalytic history appear frequently in *Psyche.*

4. Phillip Rieff, in his introduction to the "History" (1963b), summarized how Adler's simplifications and Jung's return to religion took psychoanalysis out of the consulting room—that is, away from meticulous observation—the former in the service of traditional morals, the latter of Marxist idealism. Rieff, arguing that psychoanalysis is a therapy, criticized American analysts for failing to develop their science beyond Freud.

5. We recall the problem of translating *Trieb* and the fact that Freud tended to prefer this term for primarily psychic processes and *Instinkt* for primarily biological ones, although over the years his usage changed. The translation in the *Standard Edition* by James Strachey was faulted by Lacan in the 1950s and more so by Bruno Bettelheim, in *Freud and Man's Soul* (1982).

6. Wilhelm Reich had had similar ideas in the 1920s. Essentially, he postulated his "impulsive character" as a transitional stage between neuroses and psychoses (the older disciples all objected). This still was perceived as an elaboration of Freudian principle, but his character analysis, focusing on "resistance" and on orgiastic potency, lost him Freud's support even before he had fully elaborated his sex-economic concepts (Sharaf, 1983).

7. Kohut allegedly had indicated this specific approach. See chapter 11.

8. Only five of the twelve essays were ever published. These include "Drives and Their Vicissitudes" (1915), "Über Verdrängung" (1915), and "Mourning and Melancholia" (1916–17). In 1983, Ilse Grubrich-Simitis (1987) discovered a draft of Freud's twelfth metapsychological paper, "A Phylogenetic Fantasy."

9. American ego psychology would focus on "The Ego and the Id" and on ambivalences in the superego—its functions, self-observation, criticism, punishment, and the construction of ideal goals.

Chapter 4, Promises to Culture

1. After the *Project for a Scientific Psychology* (1895), Freud's works were no longer as grounded in Newtonian physics and in universal laws governing the exchange of energy, stimuli, and responses, or constancy and inertia, but these principles nevertheless continued to color his anthropological inquiries.

2. Freud himself mentions their influence in "Reflections upon War and Death" (1915) and *Totem and Taboo* (1913).

Chapter 5, Psychosomatic Medicine

1. By the 1940s when psychoanalysis had established itself, many psychiatrists were seeking a more or less rigorous psychoanalytic training, which also helped them get better jobs.

2. Mesmer, who had not received much attention in his native Germany, had gathered disciples in France. The Marquis de Puysegur, a follower of Mesmer, allegedly cured many patients. And by 1789, the Strasbourg Society of Magnetizers had over two hundred members. After its French success, mesmerism returned to Germany, where it appealed to German romanticism and promised to reveal the mysteries of the human soul.

3. French, who had been analyzed in Vienna, used psychoanalytic views of libido to explain both the production and the displacement of psychic energy. The argument advanced by Harvard physiologist Walter B. Cannon (in *Bodily Changes in Pain, Hunger, Fear and Rage*—1915) that emotions could substantially alter bodily functions (Dunbar, 1943, pp. 645–48) was more acceptable.

4. M. H. Göring had considered two sessions a week for four months optimal; Felix Boehm had found between forty-one and seventy-five visits insufficient; others had recommended thirteen sessions over four to six weeks. But they were referring to polyclinics serving the working class, Middendorp stated, which aimed to improve functioning at work, at home, and in social situations rather than to analyze the neurotic core.

5. In America, Robert E. Gould (1965) among others also found working-class patients to be more uneasy with psychoanalysis than middle-class patients.

6. Psychiatrists, however, continue to think psychoanalytically insofar as they routinely check on childhood trauma when taking patients' histories; and they address psychological problems, even when treatment is nonpsychoanalytic.

Chapter 6, Education

1. This was three years after Freud's "Three Essays on Sexuality" (1905) and a year before "Analysis of the Phobia of a Five-Year-Old Boy" (1909).

2. Hug-Hellmuth and her sister reared the latter's illegitimate son in a nonrepressive way. When he reached adolescence, the boy apparently was unable to take frustration. After his mother's untimely death in 1915, he engaged in all sorts of asocial behavior, so that Hug-Hellmuth, his guardian, in desperation put him into a home for delinquents. In 1924, he escaped and broke into her home to steal money once again. When Hug-Hellmuth screamed, he panicked and strangled her.

3. Leonard Seif, a neurologist, joined the Jungians in 1913 and the Adlerians in 1922. Seif had created his own school of *Individualpsychologie* in Munich, which Marie Bonaparte long before had dismissed as *Seifenblasen* (soap bubbles). Geoffrey Cocks (1985) noted that in 1941 Seif's center in Munich had recorded a total of 93 sessions for sixty-six families, a sharp drop from 2.6 sessions per family between 1922 and 1939 (p. 188).

4. Letter from M. H. Göring to Hitler, September 1940, on the occasion of the meeting on "Psyche and Performance" of the German Medical Association for Psychotherapy (Grunert, 1984).

5. Robert Jay Lifton in *The Nazi Doctors: Medical Killings and the Psychology of Genocide* (New York: Basic Books, 1986) deals with all the doctors' and psychiatrists' roles under the Nazis but does not single out the Freudians from the other therapists.

6. The majority of former "Nazi analysts" supported Mitscherlich's plans for re-instructing the population, although they were angry that he had broken ranks by denouncing the Nazi doctors at the Nuremberg trials.

7. In 1949 Mahler had postulated that schizophrenia, like infantile psychosis, was either autistic or symbiotic in origin, and by 1955 she (with Gosliner) hypothesized that infants' symbiosis is a universal human condition and separation-modification a normal developmental process.

8. Spotnitz, I believe, did not mention increasing funding opportunities, themselves responses to ideological and social concerns, or the fact that research on young children seemed to have progressed as far as it could.

9. This term is used for the reeducation of groups of former Nazis as well as delinquents.

10. Personal communications and comments at meetings.

Chapter 7, *The Psychology of Women*

1. See the recent analysis by Nellie Thompson (1987b) on the numbers of women who joined the early movement, on their clinical and theoretical contributions, and on their subsequent access to leadership positions, especially as training analysts.

2. Women analysts were far from alone in extrapolating from the new breed of women who had become "taxi-drivers, elevator boys and streetcar conductors, who had taken to boyish hairdos"; and they were said to be the forerunners of "a new period of Amazonism," and were reasserting "their original state of freedom" (Deutsch, 1944).

3. Nellie Thompson (1987a), analyzing Deutsch's female psychology, idealization of motherhood, and attribution of narcissism, passivity, and masochism to the "feminine" woman, suggests that the role of identification and her own personal development both enhanced and inhibited Deutsch's theories.

4. In the following generations few women, particularly in America, became leaders in the most prestigious institutes. This was not simply because of the prejudice against them but also because it was more difficult for women to enter medical school, so that the pool was exceedingly small.

5. In her introduction to *Sexuality in the Field of Vision* (1987), Jacqueline Rose brilliantly demonstrates that "a radical Freudianism always has to argue that the social produces the misery of the psychic in a one-way process, which utterly divests the psychic of its own mechanisms and drives. . . . Idealization of the unconscious and externalisation of the event have gone together in the attempt to construct a political Freud" (p. 9).

6. Phyllis Greenacre (1950) is also cited frequently as picking up on Abraham's notions of the possible links between vaginal and anal erotism in infancy as roots of later perversions.

7. Along with a few dozen psychoanalysts and political thinkers, these feminists contributed to a *Festschrift* for Mitscherlich-Nielsen (Brede et al., eds., 1987).

8. See also the books by two Freudians, Reuben Fine (1987) and, in a more philosophical and literary vein, Martin S. Bergmann (1987).

Chapter 8, Literature and Criticism

1. Freud was clearly talking about the fate of males, although he was working almost exclusively with women suffering from hysteria.
2. The historian and psychoanalyst David James Fisher (1976) provides a particularly full picture of Freud's admiring though ambivalent relationship with Rolland. See also *Letters of Sigmund Freud: The Letters of Sigmund Freud and Arnold Zweig*.
3. Following Saussurean linguistic theory, with which his listeners were thoroughly familiar, Lacan postulates a dynamic relationship between the components of every linguistic sign, and thus between sound image (signifier) and concept (signified), between language (*langue*) and word (parole).
4. Ten years later, in 1987, Shoshana Felman reintroduced Lacan's thought. Although she talks to the originality of all of his works, she stresses his links to the classic texts.
5. For an overview of Derrida's approach and influence, see, for instance, Smith and Kerrigan (1984), and Derrida ([1967] 1974, [1967], 1978).
6. Peter Brooks (1987) summarized the issues in deconstructionist terms. He stated that "psychoanalysis is not an arbitrarily chosen intertext, in that crossing the boundaries from one territory to the other both confirms and complicates our understanding of how mind reformulates the real, how it constructs the necessary fictions by which we dream, desire, interpret, indeed by which we constitute ourselves as human subjects. The detour through psychoanalysis forces the critic to respond to the erotics of form, that is, to an engagement with the psychic investments of rhetoric, the dramas of desire played out in tropes" (p. 348).
7. Julia Kristeva ([1983] 1987), whose background in deconstruction is indisputable, and who for many years followed Lacan but then became a classical Freudian, has been particularly intrigued with bridging the gap among these schools. See also her many essays in edited collections on deconstructionist literature.
8. In Hungary, Ferenczi continues to be lionized, and fairy tales, such as Pinocchio or Little Red Ridinghood, recently have been psychoanalyzed in the traditional manner in conjunction with, and in order to enrich, clinical material.
9. See also Deleuze and Parnet, *Dialogues* (1987).
10. The Germans are no different from others in looking first to their own literary traditions. In Italy, for instance, Anna-Maria Accerboni is writing a biography of Edoardo Weiss who introduced psychoanalysis to Italy (he was also the model of Italo Svevo's popular novel *The Confessions of Zeno*). See also Speziale Bagliacca (1974, 1980).
11. See, for instance, Hans Borchers (1987).
12. Peter Dettmering (1979) contains the best of such German examinations of literature. Topics are about Musil's fantasy of the Doppelgänger, Doderer's "Demons," Rilke, Kafka, and Peter Handke, as well as about the painter Edvard Munch and about Henry James and Coleridge.
13. Among others, see Gion Condrau, ed. (1979): Heinrich Mettler (1979, pp. 863–50); Claus von Eck, "Psychoanalytiker deuten Gestalten und Werke der Literatur" (1979, pp. 851–-67); Peter Dettmering (1979, pp. 868–75); Sebastian Goeppert, "Psychoanalytische Kunst und Literaturkritik" (1979, pp. 1156–63).
14. S. Bernfeld wrote a script for another such film which was never produced.

15. See Michael Worbs (1983), as well as many other contributions to the Kasslers' and Freiburgers' journals.
16. This beautifully printed publication, however, was less showy and provocative than its French counterparts, *L'Âne* or *Ornicar?*, and the contributions stayed especially close to Lacan's own language.
17. See, for instance, *Our Lady of the Flowers.*
18. Among the most recent proliferation of studies, some primarily emphasizing work with patients, and others literary comparisons, see, for instance, Patrick Mahony (1987); Herbert Rosenfeld (1987); Gilbert J. Rose (1987); Peter L. Rudnytsky (1987); and Shlomith Rimmon-Kenan, ed. (1987).

Chapter 9, *The Organizational Network*

1. In a letter Jones wrote to Marie Bonaparte in 1944 he appears to have been most concerned about preserving unity (Torok, 1984).
2. The Chilean analyst Juan Pablo Jiménez (1987) described how analysts who function within a repressive regime and themselves question the legitimacy of the authorities are able to deal with patients: they must confront their own problems along with those of their patients in the transference and countertransference, and they must face the realistic situation of specific patients, counseling one to emigrate, another to choose psychotherapy, and another to undergo an analysis. Politics must be kept out of the analytic situation, although the working through of political components is furthered by interpretation, thus strengthening the analytic dyad.
3. In New York, for instance, Freudian training is offered to psychologists, social workers, and sometimes others by "lesser" institutes, such as the New York Freudian Society, the New York University Postdoctoral Program in Psychotherapy and Psychoanalysis, and the Postgraduate Center for Mental Health. These have their equivalents around the rest of the country (Lichtenberg, 1984, pp. 137–52).
4. De Boor (1977) argued that there were only about 1,500 psychoanalysts, psychotherapists, and child therapists and 600 candidates in later stages of training in the entire country, working partly in institutes, in private practice, and as training analysts. Consequently, the actual number of fully available analysts to treat potential patients was found to be 1,152—an average ratio of 1 for every 31,960 people. *That* was why therapeutic training rather than research had to be pushed, de Boor maintained.
5. Although in other countries aspiring analysts also must work as psychiatric residents in addition to undertaking a psychoanalytic training—with two cases, supervision, and so on—the Austrian pay scale makes the process a great deal more onerous.
6. Entry into medical school is by examination and costs are fairly low, so that it is relatively easy to combine psychoanalytic and psychiatric training. In France, physicians may take advantage of various national reimbursement laws when they sign the requisite forms (Castroce-Loray, 1973).
7. Among them are the *Revue Française de Psychanalyse*, the official journal of the SPP, the *Nouvelle Revue de Psychanalyse* of the SFP, *Topique*, the publication of the Quatrième Groupe, and the newsletters, bulletins, and publications of the major

Lacanians (including *L'Âne* and *Ornicar?*, *La coute*). There are the proceedings of regular and occasional meetings, the special issues of *Confrontation*, such as *Geopsychanalyse*, the publications by Alain de Mijolla, Conrad Stein's *Etudes freudiennes*, the Collège des psychanalystes' *Psychanalystes*, and the *Nouvelle revue d'ethnopsychiatrie*.

8. Two years before then, at their congress in Jerusalem in 1977, Robert S. Wallerstein had reported on the ongoing inquiry ("Perspectives on Psychoanalytic Training around the World," *International Journal of Psychoanalysis* 59 [1978]: 477–502).

Chapter 10, *The Cultural Unconscious in National Costume*

1. Robert Merton has found that those scientists who have achieved renown will gain even more prestige as a result of their reputation.
2. A similar clinic was being set up by Johannes Cremerius in Munich, and another one by Horst-Eberhard Richter in Giessen.
3. See, for instance, Eckstädt and Klüwer (1982); Kutter (1977); Horn (1970); Dahmer et al. (1973); Brede (1986).
4. Rittmeister and his actress wife had been Communists, so that even Göring's name, it was said, could not shield them.
5. Fritz Morgenthaler's ethnopsychoanalysis in New Guinea followed similar lines, although later on he also contributed articles on homosexuality.
6. It may be accidental that the study of the Agnis, though carried out in the 1960s, was first published in 1971, around the time Parin supported the radical contingent among the Zurich psychoanalytic candidates in their move to leave the association.
7. Erdheim's examples relied largely on his own work in Mexico.
8. The anthropologist George Devereux, Erdheim stated, exploited this state to "extricate the dialectic between 'transference' and 'counter-transference'" which the fear of the foreign culture had induced. Because in *Moses and Monotheism*, for example, Freud spoke of the "archaic inheritance" as "the inheritance of memory traces of ancestors' experiences, unrelated to direct communication and influence of upbringing through example," he was perceived by Erdheim to have followed Lamarck—as quoted from *Moses and Monotheism* (1939). And this influence, together with the manifestations of repetition neuroses, were said to have led to the charge that psychoanalysis is ahistorical.
9. Sigmund Freud's *Group Psychology and the Analysis of the Ego*, *The Future of an Illusion*, and *Civilization and Its Discontents* also were postulated as critiques of institutions (family, church, school).
10. It was at that time also, in 1958, that Sartre, tempted by the large sum of money he was offered, accepted an invitation from the American director John Huston to write a screenplay on Freud. Sartre's script, however, and its many subsequent versions were too long (nine hours), philosophical, and ultimately boring. Thus it was published but never produced. See especially the introduction to Sartre's published script by Pontalis (1986).
11. See, for instance, Jean Laplanche [1970] (1976); in the introduction the translator, Jeffrey Mehlman, maintains that "the thrust of the French reading is that *until* we

grasp the poetics of Freud's work, the general economy of that work . . . will escape us." He then goes on to demonstrate how this approach and Lacan's work are indispensable to deconstructionist literary critics.

12. Socially, Lacan notes, the individual's position and status derive from the father's family name, and his prohibitions are as lawful as is the incest taboo. These facts inextricably link the father's *nom* and his *non*.

13. See, for instance, Satow (1979); Sennett (1977); Smith-Rosenberg (1972); Malcom (1981); Masson (1984); Lieberman (1985); Grosskurth (1986); Stannard (1980); Isbister (1985).

14. It is informative to note that he did not consider Kernberg worthy of a chapter (he does not have an organized set of coherent theoretical formulations) and did not include Benjamin B. Rubinstein (he must be credited with analyses and clarifications of basic psychoanalytic concepts rather than with clinical and theoretical modifications; Eagle, 1984, p. 5).

15. Psychologists too were underscoring the scientificity of their work and, aided by the American Psychological Association, about half of whose fifty thousand members do some type of clinical and applied psychology, were getting more favorable hearings from the public than the Freudians.

Chapter 11, Theoretical Innovations

1. See, for instance, the comments on American culture by Schick (1968); Deutsch ([1945] 1973); Hartmann (1939).

2. In a superficial way, objects are people and object relations are interpersonal relationships, although these concepts refer to unconsciously "internalized" meanings and potential interpretations inducing the subject to behave in a certain way.

3. The English translation, for instance, *Jenseits des Lustprinzips* into "Beyond the Pleasure Principle," it has been argued, fails to render Freud's meaning correctly and yet is taken at face value. The crucial word here is *jenseits*, which could be translated as "on the other side of," which also could imply "on the other side of life."

4. They also noted that conformity arises in adolescence and stated that questions of mass psychology and fascism are rooted at this juncture. But they did not explain how they got from observations of specific adolescents to social phenomena.

5. Here, Segal summarizes Klein, *International Journal of Psychoanalysis* 16 (1935): 145–75.

6. According to Kernberg (1976), "internal factors such as internal sensory stimuli from the highest level central nervous system (that is, "motivations") either determine overt response or control the threshold of the response to external stimuli; external factors, in turn, may activate internal factors."

7. At the Jerusalem congress in 1984 Kernberg explained, for instance, that while object relations always refer to the relationship with a significant other, for Fairbairn this represented the shift from "infantile" to "mature" dependence allowing for cooperation with a perceived separate object; for Jacobson it was the ability to acquire "true object relationships"; and for Alice Balint it was the replacement of "egoistic love" with "altruistic love."

Chapter 12, Psychoanalysis and Politics

1. Loewenberg (1983, p. 26) concluded that Fromm and Adorno erroneously had analyzed Nazism alone. Adorno and his team (1950) investigated the authoritarian person in a broadly based and extensive inquiry. Such persons, they found, are oriented toward power on a dominance-submission dimension, and therefore are arrogant and condescending to inferiors and servile and obsequious to superiors.
2. After Jones was informed of her arrest, he conferred with Anna Freud in Vienna and Otto Fenichel in Prague, and hoped for her quick release. But the German Freudians helped only a very little, mostly because they listened to Boehm, who, it was thought, feared that interference by the DPG might lead to the organization's dissolution.
3. Thus he reprinted Adorno's ([1951] 1970) attacks against the so-called psychology of fascism—that is, against the conflation of Freud's views of hypnosis and mass psychology (because Hitler had managed to hypnotize the masses).
4. The December issue of *Psyche*, 1984, was dedicated to means of avoiding an atomic war: Peter Widmer, "Zum Problem des Todestriebs"; Klaus Horn, "Wie kommen wir zu Intoleranz gegenüber Rüstung und Krieg"; Horst Eberhard Richter, "Die Verdrängung des Todes und die 'Krankheit' Atomrüstung."

Conclusion

1. Rorty ranged over philosophy and literature from Plato through Davidson, from Kant through Nietzsche, from Descartes to contemporaries, and from Aristotelian to Baconian views of the nature of knowledge. Other contributors in this volume—Annette Baier, David Damrosch, Gordon Braden, James W. Earl, and Richard King—along with the editors Smith, a psychoanalyst, and Kerrigan, a professor of English, took issues with, or complemented, Rorty's argument.
2. Anika Lemaire (1977) was one of the few introductions for the French. For Americans, see, for example, Turkle (1978); Schneiderman (1980); Bär (1974); Kurzweil (1980, pp. 135–64).
3. This volume provides insights into the dilemmas of the psychoanalysts living in, for instance, Brazil or Argentina. In response to critics of psychoanalysis who maintain that "the *favela* needs proteins, not therapy," or that "poor people's orality needs nourishment rather than words," the conference participants debated whether it is better to shiver with guilt by treating only patients from a selected elite or to feed on ideology; whether psychoanalysis can remain European or must address "the political aspects of psychoanalysis" and take seriously the religious and magical beliefs of poor clients; and whether educational psychologists working in the *favelas* may be more effective than psychoanalysts (O'Dwyer deMacedo, 1988, pp. 68–69).
4. See, in particular, Bruno Bettelheim (1983) who held that when Freud's *Trieb* was translated into "instinct" rather than "drive," when *Abwehrmechanismen* became "defenses," and *Besetzungen* turned into "cathexes," Freud's meaning was distorted in a more scientific direction than he intended.

References

Abel, T. M., Metraux, R.; and Roll, S. [1974] 1987. *Psychotherapy and Culture.* Albuquerque: University of New Mexico Press.

Abelove, H. 1986. Freud, Male Homosexuality and the Americans. *Dissent,* Winter, 59–69.

Abraham, H. C., and Freud, E. L. 1965. *Sigmund Freud/Karl Abraham: Briefe 1907 bis 1926.* Frankfurt: S. Fischer. In English. *The Letters of Sigmund Freud and Karl Abraham.* New York: Basic Books.

Abraham, K. 1922. Manifestations of the Female Castration complex. *International Journal of Psychoanalysis* 3:1–29.

Abraham, N., and Torok, M. [1976] 1986. *Le verbier de l'homme aux loups.* Paris: Aubier Flammiron. In English. *The Wolf Man's Magic World.* Minneapolis: University of Minnesota Press.

Adler, A. 1929. *Menschenkenntnis.* Leipzig: N.p.

———. 1951. *Pratique et Théorie de la psychologie individuelle.* Paris: N.p.

Adorno, T. W. 1951. *Minima Moralia: Reflektionen aus dem beschädigten Leben.* Frankfurt: Suhrkamp.

———. [1955] 1972. Zum Verhältniss von Soziologie und Psychologie. *Theodor W. Adorno: Gesammelte Schriften I.* Frankfurt: Suhrkamp, 43–92.

———. [1970] 1984. *Aesthetic Theory.* London: Routledge and Kegan Paul.

———. [1951] 1970. Die Freudsche Theorie und die Struktur der faschistischen Propaganda. *Psyche* 24:486–509.

Adorno, T. W., et al. 1950. *The Authoritarian Personality.* New York: Norton.

Aichhorn, A. [1925] 1935. *Wayward Youth.* New York: Viking.

331

Alexander, F. [1930] 1970. Der theoretische Lehrgang. In *Zehn Jahre Berliner Institut.* Meisenheim: Anton Hain, 54–58.

———. 1957. *Psychoanalysis and Psychotherapy.* London: Allen and Unwin.

———. 1962. The Development of Psychosomatic Medicine. *Psychosomatic Medicine* 24:13–24.

Alexander, F., French, T. M., and Pollock, G. H. 1968. *Psychosomatic Specificity.* Vol. 1, *Experimental Study and Results.* Chicago and London: University of Chicago Press.

Alexander, F., and Staub, H. 1929. Der Verbrecher und seine Richter. In *Psychoanalyse und Justiz.* Ed. T. Moser. Frankfurt: Suhrkamp, 1971.

Annonces et informations. 1975. *Ornicar?,* no. 7:119.

Anzieu, D. 1982. Comment devient-on Melanie Klein? *L'archaique: Nouvelle Revue de Psychanalyse,* no. 26:235–51.

———. 1986. *Une peau pour les pensées.* Paris: Clancier-Guenard.

Argelander, H. 1983. Der Weg Alexander Mitscherlich's. *Psyche* 37, no. 4: 292–97.

Arlow, J. A. 1979. Metaphor and the Psychoanalytic Situation. *Psychoanalytic Quarterly* 48:363–85.

Arlow, J. A., and Brenner, C. 1964. *Psychoanalytic Concepts and Structural Theory.* New York: International Universities Press.

Ashbach, C., and Schermer, V. 1987. Interactive and Group Dimensions of Kleinian Theory: Notes toward a Paradigm Shift. *Journal of the Melanie Klein Society,* no. 5: 43–68.

Auden, W. [1977] 1983. Psychology and Art Today. In *Literature and Psychoanalysis.* Ed. E. Kurzweil and W. Phillips. New York: Columbia University Press.

Aulagnier, P. 1985. Quelqun a tué quelque chose. *Topique,* nos. 35–36:265–95.

Bär, E. 1974. Understanding Lacan. *Psychoanalysis and Contemporary Science,* no. 3: 473–544.

Bagliacca, R. S. 1974. Monsieur Bovary c'est moi. *Nuovi Argumenti,* nos. 38–39: 207–55.

———. 1980. Lear, Cordelia, Kent, and the Fool: A Psychoanalytical Interpretation. *International Review of Psychoanalysis* 7:413–28.

Bak, R. C. 1968. The Phallic Woman: The Ubiquitous Fantasy in Perversions. *Psychoanalytic Study of the Child* 23:15–36.

Balint, M. 1968. Die Struktur der "Training-cum-Research" Gruppen und deren Auswirkungen auf die Medizin. *Jahrbuch der Psychoanalyse.* Vol. 5. Bern: Hans Huber, 125–46.

Balmary, M. 1979. *Psychoanalyzing Psychoanalysis: Freud and the Hidden Fault of the Father.* Baltimore: Johns Hopkins University Press.

Barande, I., and Barande, R. 1975. *L'Histoire de la psychanalyse en France.* Paris: Edouard Privat.

Barker, R. L. 1982. *The Business of Psychotherapy.* New York: Columbia University Press.

Barrett, W. 1947. Writers and Madness. *Partisan Review* 14:5–22.

Barthes, R. 1967. *Système de la Mode.* Paris; Editions du Seuil.

Bateson, G., and Mead, M. 1948. *Balinese Character.* New York: Academy of Sciences.

Baudrillard, J. 1971. Le corps ou le charnier de signes. *Topiques* 3, no. 6:75–107.

Baumeyer F. 1971. Zur Geschichte der Psychoanalyse in Deutschland. 60 Jahre

Deutsche Psychoanalytische Gesellschaft. *Zur Psychosomatischen Med. Psychoanalyse* 17:203–40.

Bekanntmachungen. 1976. Deutsches Ärzteblatt. *Information*, no. 6, September-October, 1634–36.

Benedict, R. 1934. *Patterns of Culture.* Boston: Houghton Mifflin.

Beres, D. 1971. Character Formation. *Psychoanalytic Study of the Child* 26:1–9. (Quote from E. Glover, The Neurotic Character. *British Journal of Medical Psychology* 5 [1925], pt. 4.)

Berger, P. 1963. *Invitation to Sociology.* New York: Doubleday.

———. 1981. *Sociology Reinterpreted.* New York: Doubleday/Anchor.

Bergler, E. 1934. The Psychoanalysis of the Uncanny. *International Journal of Psychoanalysis* 15, nos. 2–3:215–44.

———. 1951. The Mirror of Self-Knowledge. In *Psychoanalysis and Culture: Essays in Honor of Geza Roheim.* Ed. G. Wilbur and W. Muensterberger. New York: International Universities Press, 319–26.

Bergman, A., and Ellman, S. 1985. Symbiosis and Separation-Individuation. In *Beyond Freud: A Study of Modern Psychoanalytic Theories.* Ed. J. Reppen. New York: Analytic Press, 231–56.

Bergmann, M. S. 1987. *The Anatomy of Loving.* New York: Columbia University Press.

Bernfeld, S. [1925] 1973. *Sysiphus, or the Limits of Education.* Berkeley: University of California.

———. 1930. "Neuer Geist" contra "Nihilismus": Die Psychologie und ihr Publikum. *Die Psychoanalytische Bewegung,* 2:105–22.

———. 1931. *Trieb und Tradition im Jugendalter: Kulturpsychologische Studien an Tagebüchern.* Leipzig: J. A. Barth.

———. [1935] 1969. On Simple Male Adolescence. *Seminars in Psychiatry* 1, no. 1:113–26.

———. 1962. On Psychoanalytic Training. *Psychoanalytic Quarterly* 31, no. 4:453–62. In German. Über die psychoanalytische Ausbildung. *Psyche* 38 (1984): 437–59.

Bernfeld, S., and Cassirer, S. 1973. Freud's Early Childhood. In *Freud as We Knew Him.* Ed. H. M. Ruitenbeck. Detroit: Wayne State University Press.

Bernheim, H. 1884. *De la suggestion dans l'état hypnotique et dans l'état de veille.* Paris: Doin.

Bernheimer, C., and Kahane, C., eds. 1985. *In Dora's Case: Freud-History-Feminism.* New York: Columbia University Press.

Bettelheim, B. 1983. *Freud and Man's Soul.* New York: Knopf.

Bianchedi, E. T.; Antar, R.; Fernancez Bravo de Posetti, M. R.; Grassano de Piccolo, E.; Miravcent, I.; Pistiner de Cortinas, L.; Scalozub de Boschan, L. T.; and Waserman, M. 1984. Beyond Freudian Metapsychology. *International Journal of Psychoanalysis* 65:389–97.

Bion, W. R. 1970. *Attention and Interpretation: A Scientific Approach to Insight in Psychoanalysis.* London: Tavistock.

Bloch, E. 1959. *Das Prinzip Hoffnung.* Frankfurt: Suhrkamp.

Bloom, H. 1986. Freud, the Greatest Modern Writer. *New York Times,* Jan. 26, pp. 1, 26, 27.

Blos, P. 1962. *On Adolescence.* New York: Free Press.

————. 1979. *The Adolescent Passage*. New York: International Universities Press.

Bollas, C. 1987. *The Shadow of the Object: Psychoanalysis of the Unthought Known*. New York: Columbia University Press.

Bonaparte, M. 1941. Poe and the Function of Literature. *Psychoanalytic Quarterly* 10:116–30.

Borchers, H. 1987. *Freud und die amerikanische Literatur (1920–1949): Zur Rezeption der Psychoanalyse in den literarischen Zeitschriften und den Werken von Aiken, Lewisohn und Dell*. Munich: W. Fink.

Bowlby, J. 1960. Grief and Mourning in Early Infancy. *Psychoanalytic Study of the Child* 15:9–52.

————. [1969] 1980. *Attachment and Loss*. Vol. 1, *Attachment*. New York: Basic Books.

————. 1970. *Treatment or Diagnosis*. London: Tavistock.

————. 1979. Psychoanalysis as Art and Science. *International Review of Psychoanalysis* 6:3–14.

Brainin, E., and Kaminer, I. 1982. Psychoanalyse in Hitlerdeutschland. *Psyche* 36, no. 11:989–1012.

Brauns, H. D. 1981. Die Rezeption der Psychoanalyse in der Soziologie. In *Die Rezeption der Psychoanalyse*. Ed. J. Cremerius. Frankfurt: Suhrkamp, 31–133.

Bräutigam, W. 1984. Rückblick auf das Jahr 1942. Betrachtungen eines psychoanalytischen Ausbildungskandidaten des Berliner Instituts der Kriegsjahre. *Psyche* 38:905–14.

Brecht, K.; Friedrich, V.; Hermanns, L. M.; Kaminer, I. J.; and Jülich, D. H., eds. 1985. *Hier geht das Leben auf eine sehr merkwürdige Weise weiter . . . .* Hamburg: Verlag Michael Kellner, 110–15.

Brede, K. 1972. *Sozioanalyse psychosomatischer Störungen*. Frankfurt: Athenaeum.

————. 1980. *Einführung in die psychosomatische Medizin*. Frankfurt: Syndicat.

————. 1986. *Individuum und Arbeit*. Frankfurt: Campus.

Brede, K.; Fehlhaber, H.; Lohmann, H.-M.; Michaelis, D.; and Zeul, M. 1987. *Festschrift: Befreiung zum Widerstand*. Frankfurt: Fischer.

Breger, L. 1981. *Freud's Unfinished Journey*. London: Routledge and Kegan Paul.

Brenner, C. 1974. On the Nature and Development of Affects: A Unified Theory. *Psychoanalytic Quarterly* 43:532–56.

Bril, J. 1983. *Le masque ou le père ambigu*. Paris: Payot.

Brill, A. A., ed. 1938. *The Basic Writings of Sigmund Freud*. New York: Random House, Modern Library.

Brodthage, H., and Hoffmann, S. O. 1981. Die Rezeption der Psychoanalyse in der Psychologie im deutschsprachigen Raum bis 1933. In *Die Rezeption der Psychoanalyse*. Ed. J. Cremerius. Frankfurt: Suhrkamp, 135–253.

Bromberg, N. 1960. Totalitarian Ideology as a Defense Technique. In *The Psychoanalytic Study of Society*. Ed. W. Muensterberger and S. Axelrod. New York: International Universities Press.

Brome, V. 1978. *Jung: Man and Myth*. New York: Atheneum.

Brooks, P. 1987. The Idea of Psychoanalytic Literary Criticism. *Critical Inquiry* 13, no. 2:334–48.

Bulletin of the International Psycho-Analytical Association. *International Journal of Psychoanalysis* 15 (1934):486; 30 (1949): 178–208; 57 (1976): 181–256; 63 (1982): 102–36.

Bychowski, G. 1948. *Dictators and Disciples.* New York: International Universities Press.

Cabestan, P. 1982. Freud et les communistes. *Cahiers Confrontations,* no. 7:171–79.

Carotenuto, A. 1982. *A Secret Symmetry: Sabina Spielrein between Jung and Freud.* New York: Pantheon.

Carsky, M., and Ellman, S. 1985. Otto Kernberg: Psychoanalysis and Object Relations Theory: The Beginnings of an Integrative Approach. In *Beyond Freud.* Ed. J. Reppen. Hillsdale, N.J.: Analytic Press, 257–96.

Caruso, I. 1980. *Dokumentation.* Fall, 1979–80, p. 1.

Carz Hummel, W. 1987. Gen Italien! Jugend und Reifung im "Taugenichts." *Psyche* 41, no. 2:148–72.

Castel, R. 1973. *Le psychanalysme.* Paris: Maspero.

———. 1980. Le Phénomène "psy" et la société française. *le débat,* no. 1:27–38.

Castel, R., Castel, A., and Lovell, A. [1979] 1982. *The Psychiatric Society.* New York: Columbia University Press.

Castoriadis-Aulagnier, P. 1981. *La violence de l'interprétation.* Paris: Presses Universitaires de France.

Castroce-Loray, A. 1973. *Rapport avec le public et politiques de gestion des caisses d'allocation familiales.* Paris: Université de Paris et Caisse nationale des allocations familiales.

Chabot, C. B. 1982. *Freud on Schreber: Psychoanalytic Theory and the Critical Act.* Amherst: University of Massachusetts Press.

Chasseguet-Smirgel, J. 1970. *Female Sexuality.* Ann Arbor: University of Michigan Press.

———. 1974. *Les chemins de l'anti-oedipe.* Paris: Privat.

———. 1981. Une première Introduction de la Psychanalyse en France et sa difficulté. *Revue Française de Psychanalyse* 45:1383–87.

———. 1984. *Creativity and Perversion.* New York: Norton.

———. 1985. *The Ego Ideal.* New York: Norton.

———. 1986. *Sexuality and Mind: The Role of the Father and the Mother in the Psyche.* New York: New York University Press.

———. 1987. Une tentative de solution perverse chez une femme et son échec. Paper presented at the meetings of the IPA, July.

Chodorow, N. 1978. *The Reproduction of Mothering: Psychoanalysis and the Sociology of Gender.* Berkeley: University of California Press.

Cixous, H. [1975] 1980. Demystifications. In *New French Feminisms.* Amherst: University of Massachusetts Press, 90–98.

Cixous, H., and Clement, C., eds. 1986. *The Newly Born Woman.* Minneapolis: University of Minnesota Press.

Clark, R. 1980. *Freud: The Man and the Cause.* New York: Random House.

Clément, C. [1978] 1987. *The Weary Sons of Freud.* New York: Verso.

———. [1981] 1983. *The Lives and Legends of Jacques Lacan.* New York: Columbia University Press.

Cocks, G. C. 1985. *Psychoanalysis in the Third Reich: The Göring Institut.* New York: Oxford University Press.

Coleman, E. 1985. From "Dear Lou" to *Code Name "Mary"*: A Glorious Tradition. Paper presented at a meeting of the Freudian Society.

Condrau, G., ed. 1979. *Die Psychologie des 20. Jahrhunderts*. Zurich: Kindler.

Coser, L. 1974. *Greedy Institutions: Patterns of Undivided Commitment*. New York: Free Press.

———. 1984. *Refugee Scholars in America*. New Haven: Yale University Press.

Cournut, J. 1979. Eclaircissements succincts à l'intention de ceux et celles qui pensent que les fils de Freud sont fatigués. *Les Temps modernes* 34, no. 392:1440–52.

Cremerius, J. 1979. Robert Musil, Poeta Doctus: The Dilemma of the Learned Poet after Freud. *Sigmund Freud House Bulletin* 3, no. 2:20–45.

———. 1981a. Die Präsenz des Dritten in der Psychoanalyse: Zur Problematik der Fremdfinanzierung. *Psyche* 35:1–41.

———, ed. 1981b. *Die Rezeption der Psychoanalyse*. Frankfurt: Suhrkamp.

———. 1981c. Zur Krankenfinanzierung der Psychoanalysen. *Psyche* 35, no. 1:1–41.

———. 1982. Die Bedeutung des Dissidenten für die Psychoanalyse. *Psyche* 36, no. 6:481–514.

———. 1987. Deutsche Literatur nach Freud. *Psyche* 41, no. 1:39–53.

Cremerius, J., Hoffmann, S. O., and Trimborn, W. 1979. *Psychoanalyse, Über-Ich und soziale Schicht: Die psychoanalytische Behandlung der Reichen, der Mächtigen und der sozial Schwachen*. Munich: Kindler.

Cremerius, J.; Mauser, W.; Pietzcker, C.; and Wyatt, F.; eds. 1981. *Freiburger literaturpsychologische Gespräche I*. Frankfurt: Peter D. Lang.

Crews, F. 1985. The Future of an Illusion. *New Republic*, Jan. 21, pp. 28–33.

Cuddihy, J. M. 1974. *The Ordeal of Civility: Freud, Marx, Lévi-Strauss and the Jewish Struggle with Modernity*. New York: Basic Books.

Curtius, M. 1986. *Erotische Fantasien bei Thomas Mann*. Königstein: Athenaeum.

Dahmer, H. 1982. *Libido und Gesellschaft*. Frankfurt: Suhrkamp.

Dahmer, H.; Leithäuser, J.; Lorenzer, A.; Horn, K.; and Sonneman, U. 1973. *Das Elend der Psychoanalyse-Kritik*. Frankfurt: Athenaeum.

Dalsimer, K. 1986. *Female Adolescence: Psychoanalytic Reflections on Literature*. New Haven: Yale University Press.

Dalton, E. 1978. Myshkin's Epilepsy. *Partisan Review* 45:595–610.

Daws, D., and Boston, M., eds. 1977. *The Child Psychotherapist and Problems of Young People*. London: Wildwood House.

de Boor, C. 1974. *Jahresbericht*. Frankfurt: Sigmund-Freud-Institut.

———. 1975. *Jahresbericht*. Frankfurt: Sigmund-Freud-Institut.

———. 1976. *Jahresbericht*. Frankfurt: Sigmund-Freud-Institut.

———. 1977. *Information*, no. 7. Frankfurt: Sigmund-Freud-Institut.

———. 1981. Begrüssung. *Psychoanalyse und Justiz*. Proceedings of a meeting at the Sigmund-Freud-Institut, Frankfurt, Dec. 4 and 5.

———. 1982. Soziotherapie mit Delinquenten. Typed draft.

Decker, H. S. 1977. *Freud in Germany*. New York: International Universities Press.

Deleuze, G. [1969] 1979. The Schizophrenic and Language: Surface and Depth in Lewis Carroll and Antonin Artaud. In *Textual Strategies*. Ed. J. V. Harari. Ithaca: Cornell University Press, 277–95.

Deleuze, G., and Guattari, F. [1972] 1977. *Anti-Oedipus: Capitalism and Schizophrenia.* New York: Viking.

Deleuze, G., and Parnet, C. 1987. *Dialogues.* New York: Columbia University Press.

Derrida, J. [1967] 1974. *Of Grammatology.* Baltimore: Johns Hopkins University Press.

———. [1967] 1978. *Writing and Difference.* Chicago: Chicago University Press.

Dettmering, P. 1979. Psychologisch und psychoanalytisch beeinflusste Interpretationsmethoden in der Literaturwissenschaft. In *Psychologie des 20. Jahrhunderts,* 15. Zurich: Kindler, 868–75.

———. 1981. *Psychoanalyse als Instrument der Literaturwissenschaft.* Frankfurt: Fachbuchhandlung der Psychologen.

———. 1983. Literatur als Selbstbefreiungsversuch. *Fragmente: Schriftenreihe zur Psychoanalyse* 7–8:15–39.

———. 1984. *Literatur, Psychoanalyse, Film.* Stuttgart: Frommann-Holzboog.

Deutsch, F. 1922. Zur Bilding des Konversionssymptoms. *Zeitschrift für Psychoanalyse,* 10. Vienna: Internationale, 380–414.

Deutsch, H. [1945] 1973. *The Psychology of Women.* New York: Bantam.

Devereux, G. 1951. The Primal Scene and Juvenile Heterosexuality in Mohave Society. In *Psychoanalysis and Culture: Essays in Honor of Geza Roheim.* Ed. G. B. Wilbur and W. Muensterberger. New York: International Universities Press.

Diatkine, R. 1985. La psychanalyse devant l'autisme infantile précoce. *Topique,* nos. 35–36:25–46.

Dilman, I. 1984. *Freud and the Mind.* Oxford: Basil Blackwell.

Döhmann-Höh, G., ed. 1981. *Die neuen Narzissmustheorien: Zurück ins Paradies?* Frankfurt: Syndikat.

Dolto, F. 1982. *Seminaire de psychanalyse d'enfants.* Paris: Editions du Seuil.

———. 1984. *L'image inconsciente du corps.* Paris: Editions du Seuil.

Doolittle, H. 1956. *Tribute to Freud.* New York: New Directions.

Douglas, M. 1982. *The Active Voice.* London: Routledge and Kegan Paul.

Dräger, K. 1971. Bemerkungen zu den Zeitumständen und zum Schicksal der Psychoanalyse und der Psychotherapie in Deutschland zwischen 1933 und 1949. *Psyche* 25:255–68.

Dührssen, A. 1962. Katamnestische Ergebnisse bei 1004 Patienten nach analytischer Psychotherapie. *Zeitschrift für psychosomatische Medizin* 8:94–113.

Dunbar, F. 1943. *Psychosomatic Diagnosis.* New York: Höber.

Eagle, M. N. 1984. *Recent Developments in Psychoanalysis.* Cambridge: Harvard University Press.

Eck, Claus D., von. 1979. Psychoanalytiker deuten Werke der Literatur. In *Die Psychoanalyse des 20. Jahrhunderts,* 15. Zurich: Kindler, 851–67.

Eckstädt, A., and Klüwer, R., eds. 1982. *Zeit allein heilt keine Wunden.* Frankfurt: Suhrkamp.

Ehebald, U. 1977. Überlegungen eines Psychoanalytikers zu den Problemen der Durchführung psychoanalytischer Behandlung in der kassenärztlichen Versorgung. *Referat der DPV-Tagung.* Cologne, October 18.

Eigen, M. 1985. Toward Bion's Starting Point: Between Catastrophe and Faith. *International Journal of Psychoanalysis* 66:321–30.

Eissler, K. R. 1958. Goethe and Science: A Contribution to the Psychology of Goethe's

Psychosis. In *Psychoanalysis and the Social Sciences.* Ed. W. Muensterberger and S. Axelrad. New York: International Universities Press.

———. 1960. The Efficient Soldier. In *The Psychoanalytic Study of Society.* Ed. W. Muensterberger and S. Axelrad. New York: International Universities Press, 39–97.

———. 1963a. Notes on the psychoanalytic concept of cure. *Psychoanalytic Study of the Child* 18:424–63.

———. 1963b. *Goethe: A Psychoanalytic Study, 1775–1786.* Detroit: Wayne State University Press.

———. 1965. *Medical Orthodoxy and the Future of Psychoanalysis.* New York: International Universities Press.

———. 1971. *Discourse on Hamlet: A Psychoanalytic Inquiry.* New York: International Universities Press.

———. 1978. Der Psychoanalytiker und das Geld—oder die Ideologie vom persönlichen finanziellen Opfer des Patienten. In *Provokation und Toleranz: Festschrift für Alexander Mitscherlich zum 70. Geburtstag.* Ed. S. Drews et al. Frankfurt: Suhrkamp, 361–386.

———. 1986. Moses' Flüche am Berg Ebal. *Psyche* 40:1–20.

Eissler, K. R.; Freud, S.; Goeppert, S.; and Schröter, K. 1974. *Aus Freuds Sprachwelt und andere Beiträge: Jahrbuch der Psychoanalyse/Beiheft Nr. 2.* Bern: H. Huber.

Eissler, R. S.; Freud, A.; Kris, M.; and Solnit, A. J. 1977. *The Psychoanalytic Study of the Child. Psychoanalytic Assessment: The Diagnostic Profile.* New Haven: Yale University Press.

Ellenberger, H. 1970. *The Discovery of the Unconscious: The History and Evolution of Dynamic Psychiatry.* New York: Basic Books.

Ellman, R. 1984. Freud and Literary Biography. *American Scholar,* Autumn, pp. 465–78.

Elrod, N., Heinz, R., and Dahmer, H. 1978. *Der Wolf im Schafspelz: Erikson, die Ich-Psychologie und das Anpassungsproblem.* Düsseldorf: Campus.

Endleman, R. 1981. *Psyche and Society.* New York: Columbia University Press.

Engel, G. L., and Schmale, A. H., Jr. 1966. Psychoanalytic Theory of Somatic Disorder. *Journal of the American Psychoanalytic Association* 15, no. 2:344–65.

Engelhardt, K. 1976. *Psychoanalyse der strafenden Gesellschaft.* Frankfurt: Haag and Herchen.

Eppensteiner, B., Fallend, K., and Reichmayr, J. 1987. Psychoanalyse im Film (1925–26). *Psyche* 41, no. 2:129–39.

Erdheim, M. 1982. *Die gesellschaftliche Produktion von Unbewusstheit.* Frankfurt: Suhrkamp.

Erikson, E. H. 1950. *Childhood and Society.* New York: Norton.

———. 1958. *Young Man Luther: A Study in Psychoanalysis and History.* New York: Norton.

———. 1964. *Insight and Responsibility: Lectures on the Ethical Implications of Psychoanalytic Insight.* New York: Norton.

———. 1968. *Identity, Youth and Crisis.* New York: Norton.

———. 1969. *Ghandi's Truth: On the Origins of Militant Nonviolence.* New York: Norton.

———. 1985. The First Psychoanalyst. *Yale Review* 75, no. 1:63–85.

Ey, H. *L'Inconscient*. 1966. Paris: Desclée de Brouwer.

Faimberg, Haidée. 1977. The Snark was a Boojum. *International Review of Psycho-analysis* 4, no. 2:243–49.

Fairbairn, W. R. D. [1952] 1954. *Object Relations Theory of the Personality*. New York: Basic Books.

Feigenbaum, D., ed. 1930. *Character Diseases and the Neuroses*. New York: Medical Review of Reviews, March.

Felman, S. 1977. To Open the Question. *Yale French Studies. Literature and Psycho-analysis: The Question of Reading: Otherwise*, nos. 55–56.

———. 1987. *Jacques Lacan and the Adventure of Insight: Psychoanalysis in Contemporary Culture*. Cambridge: Harvard University Press.

Ferenczi, S. [1908] 1949. Psychoanalysis and Education. *International Journal of Psychoanalysis* 30:220–24.

———. 1921. *Psychoanalysis and the War Neuroses*. Vienna: International Psychoanalytical Press.

———. [1932] 1949. Confusion of Tongues between the Adult and the Child (The Language of Tenderness and of Passion). *International Journal of Psychoanalysis* 30:225–230.

———. 1955. *Final Contributions to the Problems and Methods of Psychoanalysis*. London: Maresfield Reprints.

Fetscher, I. 1983. Alexander Mitscherlich: Zur Pathologie der bundesdeutschen Gesellschaft. *Psyche* 37:298–310.

Fine, R. 1979. *A History of Psychoanalysis*. New York: Columbia University Press.

———. 1987. *The Forgotten Man: Understanding the Male Psyche*. New York: Harrington Park Press.

Fischer, P. 1986. Familienauftritte: Goethes Phantasienwelt und die Konstruktion des Werther-Romans. *Psyche* 40:527–56.

Fish, S. 1986. Withholding the missing portion: Power, meaning and persuasion in Freud's "The Wolf-Man." *Times Literary Supplement*, Aug. 29, pp. 935–38.

Fisher, C. 1965. Psychoanalytic Implications of Recent Research on Sleep and Dreaming. *American Journal of Psychoanalysis* 13:197–270.

Fisher, D. J. 1976. Sigmund Freud and Romain Roland: The Terrestrial Animal and His Great Oceanic Friend. *American Imago* 33:1–59.

———. 1982. Rereading Freud's *Civilization and Its Discontents*. In *Modern European Intellectual History*. Ed. C. LaCapra and S. L. Kaplan. Ithaca: Cornell University Press.

———. 1982–83. Lacan's Ambiguous Impact on Contemporary French Psychoanalysis. *CFC* 6:89–114.

Flader, D., Grodzicki, W.-D., and Schröter, K. 1982. *Psychoanalyse als Gespräch*. Frankfurt: Suhrkamp.

Flournoy, O. 1980. Sigmund Freud—Melanie Klein: Une Querelle Dépassé. *Revue française de Psychanalyse* 44, nos. 5–6:912–16.

Fogel, G. I., Lane, F. M., and Liebert, R. S., eds. 1986. *The Psychology of Men: New Perspectives*. New York: Basic Books.

Fornari, F., Fontori, C., and Crugnola, C. R. 1985. *Psicoanalisi in ospedale*. Milan: Raffaello Cortina.

Forrester, J. 1980. *Language and the Origins of Psychoanalysis.* New York: Columbia University Press.

Foucault, M. [1961] 1965. *Madness and Civilization.* New York: Pantheon.

———. [1973] 1975. *I, Pierre Rivière, having slaughtered my mother, my sister, and my brother . . .* New York: Pantheon.

———. [1976] 1978. *The History of Sexuality.* Vol. 1. New York: Pantheon.

Fraiberg, L., ed. 1987. *The Selected Writings of Selma Fraiberg.* Columbus: Ohio State University Press.

Freud, A. [1936] 1966. The Ego and the Mechanisms of Defense. In *The Writings of Anna Freud.* Vol. 2. New York: International Universities Press.

———. 1950. Probleme der Lehranalyse. In *Max Eitingon: In Memoriam.* Ed. M. Wulff. Jerusalem: Israel Psycho-Analytical Society.

———. 1960. Discussion of Dr. John Bowlby's Paper. *Psychoanalytic Study of the Child* 15:53–62.

———. 1977. The Symptomatology of Childhood. In *An Anthology of the Psychoanalytic Study of the Child.* Ed. R. Eissler, A. Freud, M. Kris, and A. Solnit. New Haven: Yale University Press.

———. 1980. Child Analysis as the Study of Mental Growth. In *The Course of Life: Psychoanalytic Contributions toward Understanding Personality Development.* Vol. 1, *Infancy and Childhood.* Ed. S. I. Greenspan and G. H. Pollock. Washington, D.C.: National Institutes of Mental Health, 1–10.

Freud, E. L., ed. 1960. *Letters of Sigmund Freud.* New York: Basic Books; *Briefe, 1873–1939.* 1968. Frankfurt: Fischer.

———, ed. 1968. *The Letters of Sigmund Freud and Arnold Zweig.* New York: New York University Press.

Freud, E. L., and Meng, H., eds. 1963. *Sigmund Freud/Oscar Pfister: Briefe 1909 bis 1939.* Frankfurt: Fischer.

Freud, S. 1886f. Preface to the Translation of Charcot's *Lectures on the Diseases of the Nervous System.* In *The Standard Edition of the Complete Psychological Works.* Ed. and trans. J. Strachey. 24 vols. London: Hogarth Press, 1:19–22. (Hereafter *S.E.,* vol. and page number. The letters following the years conform to *S.E.* citations.)

———. 1888–89. Preface to the Translation of Bernheim's *Suggestion. S.E.,* 1:71–85.

———. 1893e. Les Diplégies cérébrales infantiles. *Revue Neurologique* 1:177–83.

———. 1893h. On the Psychical Mechanism of Hysterical Phenomena: A Lecture. *S.E.,* 3:25–39.

———. 1895. Project for a Scientific Psychology. *S.E.,* 1:283–437.

———. 1895d. Studies on Hysteria. *S.E.,* 2:37–59.

———. 1896c. The Aetiology of Hysteria. S.E., 3:189–221.

———. 1898a. Sexuality in the Aetiology of the Neuroses. *S.E.,* 3:261–85.

———. 1900a. The Interpretation of Dreams. *S.E.,* 4–5.

———. 1901a. On Dreams. *S.E.,* 5:631–86.

———. 1901b. The Psychopathology of Everyday Life. *S.E.,* 6.

———. 1905a. On Psychotherapy. *S.E.,* 7:255–68.

———. 1905c. Jokes and their Relation to the Unconscious. *S.E.,* 8:3–238.

———. 1905d. Three Essays on the Theory of Sexuality. *S.E.,* 7:123–245.

———. 1905e. Fragment of an Analysis of a Case of Hysteria. *S.E.,* 7:1–122.

———. 1907. Obsessive Actions and Religious Practices. *S.E.,* 9:116–27.

———. 1907a. Delusions and Dreams. *S.E.*, 9:1–95.

———. 1908b. Character and Anal Erotism. *S.E.*, 9:169–75.

———. 1908e. Creative Writers and Daydreaming. *S.E.*, 9:142–53.

———. 1909b. Analysis of a Phobia in a Five-Year-Old Boy. *S.E.*, 10:1–149.

———. 1910a. Five Lectures on Psycho-Analysis. *S.E.*, 11:1–55.

———. 1910c. Leonardo da Vinci and a Memory of His Childhood. *S.E.*, 11:59–137.

———. 1910d. Die zukünftigen Chancen der psychoanalytischen Therapie. *S.E.*, 11:139–52.

———. 1910k. "Wild" Psycho-Analysis. *S.E.*, 11:219–27.

———. 1911c [1910] Psycho-Analytic Notes on an autobiographical account of a Case of Paranoia. *S.E.*, 12:3–82.

———. 1912b. On the Dynamics of Transference. *S.E.*, 12:97–108.

———. 1912e. Ratschläge für den Arzt bei der psychoanalytischen Behandlung. *S.E.*, 12:111–20.

———. 1912–13. Totem and Taboo. *S.E.*, 13:1–161.

———. 1914b. The Moses of Michelangelo. *S.E.*, 13:211–38.

———. 1914c. On Narcissism: An Introduction. *S.E.*, 14:69–102.

———. 1914d. On the History of the Psycho-Analytic Movement. *S.E.*, 14:1–66.

———. 1914g. Remembering, Repeating, and Working Through. *S.E.*, 12:145–56.

———. 1915a. Observations on Transference-Love. *S.E.*, 12:157–71.

———. 1915b. Reflections upon War and Death. *S.E.*, 14:273–300.

———. 1915c. Instincts and Their Vicissitudes. *S.E.*, 14:109–40.

———. 1915e. The Unconscious. *S.E.*, 14:161–204.

———. 1916a. On Transience. *S.E.*, 14:303–07.

———. 1916–17. Introductory Lectures on Psycho-Analysis. *S.E.*, 15:3–239; 16:243–476.

———. 1917e. Mourning and Melancholia. *S.E.*, 14:237–58.

———. 1920g. Beyond the Pleasure Principle. *S.E.*, 18:1–64.

———. 1921c. Group Psychology and the Analysis of the Ego. *S.E.*, 18:65–143.

———. 1923b. The Ego and the Id. *S.E.*, 19:1–66.

———. 1925j. Some Psychical Consequences of the Anatomical Distinction between the Sexes. *S.E.*, 19:243–58.

———. 1926d. Inhibitions, Symptoms, and Anxiety. *S.E.*, 20:75–174.

———. 1926e. On the Question of Lay Analysis. *S.E.*, 20:177–258.

———. 1927a. Postscript to the Question of Lay Analysis. *S.E.*, 20:251–58.

———. 1927c. The Future of an Illusion. *S.E.*, 21:3–56.

———. 1928b. Dostoevsky and Parricide. *S.E.*, 21:173–96.

———. 1930a. Civilization and Its Discontents. *S.E.*, 21:57–145.

———. 1930e. Address in the Goethe House. *S.E.*, 21:208–12.

———. 1931b. Female Sexuality. *S.E.*, 21:223–43.

———. 1933a. New Introductory Lectures on Psycho-Analysis. *S.E.*, 22:1–182.

———. 1933b. Why War? *S.E.*, 22:195–215.

———. 1936a. A Disturbance of Memory on the Acropolis. *S.E.*, 22:239–48.

———. 1937c. Analysis Terminable and Interminable. *S.E.*, 22:209–53.

———. 1939a. Moses and Monotheism: Three Essays. *S.E.*, 22:3–137.

———. 1941e [1926] Address to the Society of B'nai B'rith. *S.E.*, 20:272–74.

Freud, S., and Bullit, W. 1966. *Woodrow Wilson*. Boston: Houghton Mifflin.

Fromm, E. 1942. *The Fear of Freedom*. London: Routledge and Kegan Paul.

———. 1956. *The Sane Society*. London: Routledge and Kegan Paul.

———. 1970. *The Crisis of Psychoanalysis*. Greenwich: Fawcett.

Füchtner, H. 1984. Traurige Psychotropen. *Psyche* 38, no. 7:605–26.

Furer, M. 1967. Some developmental aspects of the superego. *International Journal of Psychoanalysis* 48:277–80.

Furtos, J., and Roussillon, R. 1972. "L'Anti-Oedipe" Essay d'explication. *Esprit* 40, no. 418:817–34.

Galenson, E., and Roiphe, H. 1976. Some Suggested Revisions concerning Early Female Development. *Journal of the American Psychoanalytic Association* 24:193–212.

Gallop, J. 1982. *The Daughter's Seduction: Feminism and Psychoanalysis*. Ithaca: Cornell University Press.

———. 1987. Reading the Mother Tongue: Psychoanalytic Feminist Criticism. *Critical Inquiry* 13, no. 2:314–29.

Gantheret, F. 1969. Freud et la question sociopolitique. *Partisans*, no. 46:9–16.

Gardner, M. 1971. *The Wolf-Man* (With the Case of the Wolf-Man by Sigmund Freud and supplement by Ruth Mack Brunswick). New York: Basic Books.

Garma, A. 1971. Within the Realm of the Death Instinct. *International Journal of Psychoanalysis* 65:389–97.

Gay, P. 1978. *Freud, Jews and Other Germans: Masters and Victims in Modernist Culture*. New York: Oxford University Press.

———. 1985. *Freud for Historians*. New York: Oxford University Press.

———. 1987. *A Godless Jew: Freud, Atheism, and the Making of Psychoanalysis*. New Haven: Yale University Press.

———. 1988. *Freud: A Life for Our Time*. New York: Norton.

Geertz, C. 1973. *The Interpretation of Cultures*. New York: Basic Books.

Gelly, R. 1982. L'art de Michael Balint. *Revue de Médecine Psychosomatique* 24:149–69.

Gendrot, J. A. 1968. Introduction au colloque sur analyse terminée, analyse interminable. *Revue française de Psychanalyse* 32:2.

George, F. 1979a. *L'effet 'Yau de Poêle*. Paris: Hachette.

———. 1979b. Lacan ou l'effet 'yau de poêle. *Les Temps modernes* 34:1787–1894, 2038–50.

Gifford, S. 1985. Review of "*Repression*" or "Sea-change": Fenichel's Rundbriefe and the "Political Analysts" of the 1930s. *International Review of Psychoanalysis* 66:265–71.

Gill, M. M. 1982. *Analysis of Transference*. Vol. 1, *Theory and Technique*. New York: International Universities Press.

Gill, M. M., and Hoffman, I. Z. 1982. *Analysis of Transference*. Vol. 2, *Studies of Nine Audio-Recorded Psychoanalytic Sessions*. New York: International Universities Press.

Gillibert, J. 1981. L'énigme de la femme par Sarah Kofman: La femme dans les textes de Freud. *Revue française de Psychanalyse*, no. 3:579–92.

Girard, C. 1982. La Psychanalyse en Grande Bretagne. In *Histoire de la Psychanalyse*. Ed. R. Jaccard. 2 vols. Paris: Hachette, 367–72.

Goeppert, S. 1979. Psychoanalytische Kunst- und Literaturkritik. *Die Psychoanalyse des 20. Jahrhunderts*, 15. Zurich: Kindler, 1156–63.

Goffman, E. 1959. *The Presentation of Self in Everyday Life*. New York: Doubleday.

Goldberg, A. W., and Stepansky, P. E. 1984. *How Does Analysis Cure?* Chicago: Chicago University Press.

Goldstein, J. E. 1974. The Woolfs' Response to Freud: Water Spiders, Singing Canaries, and the Second Apple. *Psychoanalytic Quarterly* 43:438–76.

Gölter, W. 1983. Aspekte weiblichen Schreibens. *Psyche* 37:642–68.

Gould, R. 1965. Dr. Strangelove or: How I Stopped Worrying about the Theory and Began Treating the Blue Collar Worker. Paper presented at the annual meetings of the American Orthopsychiatric Association.

Granoff, W. 1975. *Filiations: L'avenir du complexe d'Oedipe.* Paris: Editions du Minuit.

Green, A. 1973. *Le discours vivant.* Paris: Presses universitaires de France.

———. 1983. *Narcissisme de vie narcissisme de mort.* Paris: Editions de Minuit.

Greenacre, P. 1950. Special Problems of Early Sexual Development. *Psychoanalytic Study of the Child* 5:122–38.

———. 1955. Further Considerations Regarding Fetishism. *Psychoanalytic Study of the Child* 10:187–94.

———. 1956. *Jonathan Swift: Swift and Carroll.* New York: International Universities Press.

Greenspan, S. I., and Pollock, G. H., eds. 1980. Child Analysis as the Study of Mental Growth, by A. Freud. In *The Course of Life: Psychoanalytic Contributions toward Understanding Personality Development.* Vol. 1, *Infancy and Early Childhood.* Washington, D.C.: National Institutes of Mental Health.

Gross, E. B. 1979. Psychoanalysis as an Emerging Specialty: A Sociological Study of the Vienna Psychoanalytic Society. *Journal of the Philadelphia Association of Psychoanalysis* 6, nos. 3–4:163–74.

Grosskurth, P. 1986. *Melanie Klein: Her World and Work.* New York: Knopf.

Grossman, C. M., and Grossman, S. 1965. *The Wild Analyst: The Life and Work of Georg Groddeck.* New York: George Braziller.

Grossman, W. I., and Stewart, W. A. 1976. Penis Envy: From Childhood Wish to Developmental Metaphor. *Journal of the American Psychoanalytic Association* 24 (suppl.): 193–212.

Grotjahn, M. L. 1956. A Letter by Sigmund Freud with Recollections of His Adolescence. *Journal of the American Psychoanalytic Association* 4:644–52.

———. 1967. S. Freud and the Art of Letter Writing. *Journal of the American Medical Association* 200, no. 1:119–24.

———, ed. [1970] 1973. *Sigm. Freud–E. Weiss: Briefe zur psychoanalytischen Praxis.* Frankfurt: Fischer.

Grotstein, J. S. 1985. Wilfred R. Bion: An Odyssey into the Deep and Formless Infinite. In *Beyond Freud: A Study of Modern Psychoanalytic Theories.* Ed. J. Reppen. Hillsdale, N.J.: Analytic Press.

Grubrich-Simitis, I., ed. 1987. *A Phylogenetic Fantasy.* Cambridge: Harvard University Press.

Grünbaum, A. 1983. Freud's Theory: The Perspective of a Philosopher of Science. 1982 Presidential Address to the American Philosophical Association. In *Proceedings and Addresses of the American Philosophical Association* 57, no. 1:5–31.

———. 1984. *The Foundations of Psychoanalysis.* Berkeley: University of California Press.

Grunberger, B. 1971. *Le narcissisme.* Paris: Payot.

Grunert, J. 1984. Zur Geschichte der Psychoanalyse in München. *Psyche* 38:865–904.

Guntrip, H. 1968. *Schizoid Phenomena, Object Relations, and the Self.* London: Hogarth Press.

Haarstrich, R. 1977. Die Entwicklung der psychotherapeutischen Versorgung in der Bundesrepublik. *Tagung der Deutschen Psychoanalytischen Vereinigung*, Cologne, Oct.

Habermas, J. 1982. Die Verschlingung von Mythos und Aufklärung. In *Mythos und Aufklärung*. Ed. K. H. Bohrer. Frankfurt: Suhrkamp.

———. 1983. Mythos und Moderne. In *Begriff und Bild einer Rekonstruktion*. Ed. K. H. Bohrer. Frankfurt: Suhrkamp.

Hagemann-White, C. 1978. Die Kontroverse um die Psychoanalyse in der Frauenbewegung. *Psyche* 32:732–63.

Hale, N. G. 1971a. *Freud and the Americans*. New York: Oxford University Press.

———. 1971b. *James Jackson Putnam and Psychoanalysis*. Cambridge: Harvard University Press.

Hamilton, V. 1982. *Narcissus and Oedipus: The Children of Psychoanalysis*. London: Routledge and Kegan Paul.

———. 1985. John Bowlby: An Ethological Basis for Psychoanalysis. In *Beyond Freud: A Study of Modern Psychoanalytic Theories*. Ed. J. Reppen. Hillsdale, N.J.: Analytic Press.

Hampden-Turner, C. 1983. *Gentlemen and Tradesmen*. London: Routledge and Kegan Paul.

Haring, D. G., ed. 1948. Some Systematic Approaches to the Study of Culture and Personality. In *Personal Character and Cultural Milieu*. Syracuse: Syracuse University Press.

Harris, J., and Harris, J. 1984. *The One-Eyed Doctor Sigismund Freud: Psychological Origins of Freud's Works*. New York: Aronson.

Hartman, G. 1978. *Psychoanalysis and the Question of the Text*. Baltimore: Johns Hopkins University Press.

Hartmann, H. 1939. Psychoanalysis and the Concept of Health. *International Journal of Psychoanalysis* 20:308–21.

———. [1939] 1958. *Ego Psychology and the Problem of Adaptation*. New York: International Universities Press.

———. 1950. Technical Implications of Ego Psychology. *Psychoanalytic Quarterly* 20:31–43.

Hartmann, H., and Kris, E. 1945. The Genetic Approach in Psychoanalysis. *Psychoanalytic Study of the Child* 1:11–30.

Hartmann, H., Kris, E., and Loewenstein, R. M. 1946. Comments on the Formation of Psychic Structure. *Psychoanalytic Study of the Child* 2:11–38.

———. 1949. Notes on the Theory of Aggression. *Psychoanalytic Study of the Child* 3–4:9–46.

———. 1951. Some Psychoanalytic Comments on "Culture and Personality." In *Psychoanalysis and Culture*. Ed. G. Wilbur and W. Muensterberger. New York: International Universities Press, 3–31.

Heimann, P. 1950. On Countertransference. *International Journal of Psychoanalysis* 31:81.

———. 1969. Gedanken zum Erkenntnisprozess des Psychoanalytikers. *Psyche* 23: 2–24.

Heimonet, J.-M. *Politiques de l'écriture. Bataille/Derrida: Le sens du sacré dans la pensée française du surréalisme à nos jours*. Chapel Hill: North Carolina Studies in the Romance Languages and Literatures.

Heller, E. 1976. Observations on Psychoanalysis and Literature. In *Psychiatry and the Humanities I*. Ed. J. H. Smith. New Haven: Yale University Press, 35–50.

Hendrick, I. 1934. *Facts and Theories of Psychoanalysis*. New York: Knopf.

———. 1936. Ego Development and Certain Character Problems. *Psychoanalytic Quarterly* 5: 320–46.

Herink, R., ed. 1980. *The Psychotherapy Handbook*. New York: Meridian.

Hidas, G. 1986. "Zur Geschichte der Psychoanalyse in Ungarn." In *Psychoanalyse Heute*. Festschrift zum 60. Geburtstag von Harald Leupold-Löwenthal. Ed. H. Lobner. Vienna: Orac.

———. 1987. Die Psychoanalyse und ihre Schicksale in Ungarn. *Sigmund Freud House Bulletin* 11, no. 2: 1–12.

Hofling, G. K., and Meyers, R. 1972. Recent Discoveries in Psychoanalysis. *Archives of General Psychiatry* 26: 518–23.

Holland, N. 1964. *The Shakespearean Imagination*. New York: Macmillan.

Holzey, H. 1970. Psychoanalyse und Gesellschaft—Der Beitrag Herbert Marcuse's. *Psyche* 26: 188–207.

Honegger, M., ed. 1988. *Sigmund Freud–Georg Groddeck. Briefe über das Es*. Frankfurt: Fischer.

Hook, S., ed. 1959. *Psychoanalysis, Scientific Method and Philosophy*. New York: New York University Press.

Horn, K. 1970. *Dressur oder Erziehung? Schlagrituale und ihre gesellschaftliche Funktion*. Frankfurt: Suhrkamp.

———. 1984. Wie kommen wir zu Intoleranz gegenüber Rüstung und Krieg? *Psyche* 38, no. 12: 1983–1104.

———. 1985a. Aggression und Gewalt vom gegenwärtigen Schicksal menschlicher Expressivität. In *Aggression und Gewalt: Anthropologische und sozialwissenschaftliche Aspekte*. Ed. A. Schöpf. Würzburg: Königshausen and Neumann.

———. 1985b. *Politische Partizipation*. Bonn: Bundeszentrale für politische Bildung.

Horn, K., and Senghaas-Knobloch, E., eds. 1983. *Friedensbewegung Persönliches und Politisches*. Frankfurt: Fischer.

Horney, K. 1924. On the Genesis of the Castration Complex in Women. *International Journal of Psychoanalysis* 5: 50–65.

———. 1926. The Flight from Womanhood: The Masculinity Complex in Women as Viewed by Men and by Women. *International Journal of Psychoanalysis* 7: 324–39.

———. 1935. The Problem of Feminine Masochism. *Psychoanalytic Review* 2, no. 3: 241–57.

———. 1937. *The Neurotic Personality of Our Time*. New York: Norton.

———. 1939. *New Ways in Psychoanalysis*. New York: Norton.

Hug-Hellmuth, H. 1921. Zur Technik der Kinderanalyse. *Internationale Zeitschrift für Psychoanalyse* 7: 179–97.

Hughes, H. S. 1958. *Consciousness and Society*. New York: Vintage.

Inkeles, A., and Levinson, D. J. 1954. National Character: The Study of Modal Personality and Sociocultural Systems. In *Handbook of Social Psychology*. Vol. 4. Ed. G. Lindsay. Cambridge: Addison-Wesley, 418–506.

Irigaray, L. [1977] 1980. Demystifications. In *New French Feminisms*. Ed. E. Marks and I. Courtivron. Amherst: University of Massachusetts Press, 99–110.

————. 1986. This Sex Which Is Not One. In *The Newly Born Woman*. Ed. H. Cixoux and C. Clement. Minneapolis: University of Minnesota Press.

Isbister, J. N. 1985. *Freud: An Introduction to His Life and Work*. London: Polity Press.

Izenberg, G. N. *Existential Psychoanalysis*. Princeton: Princeton University Press.

Jaccard, R., ed. 1982. *Histoire de la psychanalyse*. 2 vols. Paris: Hachette.

Jacobson, E. 1937. Wege der weiblichen Über-Ich-Bildung. *Internationale Zeitschrift für Psychoanalyse* 23:402–12.

————. 1950. Development of the Wish for a Child in Boys. *Psychoanalytic Study of the Child* 5:139–52.

Jacoby, R. 1983. *The Repression of the Unconscious*. New York: Basic Books.

Jacquot, J. P. 1975. Le psychanalysme de Robert Castel. *Revue française de Psychanalyse* 39, no. 4:653–65.

Jaeger, M. 1978. Le désordre psychiatrique. *Les Temps modernes* 33, no. 378:1040–74.

Jameson, F. 1981. *The Political Unconscious*. Ithaca: Cornell University Press.

Janik, A., and Toulmin, S. 1973. *Wittgenstein's Vienna*. New York: Simon and Schuster.

Jiménez, J. P. 1987. Einige Überlegungen zur Praxis der Psychoanalyse im heutigen Chile. Unpublished article.

Jones, E. 1933. The Phallic Phase. *International Journal of Psychoanalysis* 14:1–33.

————. 1949. *Hamlet and Oedipus*. London: V. Gollancz.

————. 1948. The Death of Hamlet's Father. *International Journal of Psychoanalysis* 29, no. 3:174–76.

————. 1953–57. *The Life and Work of Sigmund Freud*. 3 vols. New York: Basic Books.

Joseph, E. 1979. Proceedings. *International Journal of Psychoanalysis* 60.

Julien, P. 1985. Hainamoration et réalité psychique. *Littoral*, nos. 15–16:5–19.

Jung, C. G. 1934. Zur gegenwärtigen Lage der Psychotherapie. *Zentralblatt für Psychotherapie* 7:1–16.

Kakar, S. 1982. *Shamans, Mystics and Doctors*. New York: Knopf.

Kaplan, L. 1984. *Adolescence: The Farewell to Childhood*. New York: Simon and Schuster.

————. 1987. *The Family Romance of the Impostor-Poet Thomas Chatterton*. New York: Atheneum.

Kardiner, A. 1945. *The Psychological Frontiers of Society*. New York: Columbia University Press.

Kästle, O. U. 1987. Unbekannte Freud-Texte aus den Jahren 1893–94. *Psyche* 41, no. 6:508–19.

Kernberg, O. F. 1965. Notes on Countertransference. *Journal of the American Psychoanalytic Association* 13:38–56.

————. 1975. *Borderline Conditions and Pathological Narcissism*. New York: Aronson.

————. 1976. *Object Relations Theory and Clinical Psychoanalysis*. New York: Aronson.

————. 1979. Some Implications of Object Relations Theory for Psychoanalytic Technique. *Journal of the American Psychoanalytic Association* 27 (suppl.): 207–39.

————. 1984. The Influence of Projective Identification on Countertransference.

Paper presented to the First Congress of the Sigmund Freud Center, Jerusalem, May 27–29.

———. 1986. An Ego Psychology Object-Relations Theory Approach to the Transference. Paper.

Kestemberg, E., and Jeammet, P. 1987. *Le psychodrame psychanalytique*. Paris: Presses Universitaires de France.

Kestenberg, J. S. 1985. Child Survivors of the Holocaust, Forty Years Later: Reflections and Commentary. *Journal of American Child Psychiatry* 24, no. 4:408–12.

Kestenberg, J. S., and Gampel, Y. 1985. Growing up in the Holocaust Culture. *Israel Journal of Psychiatry rel. Science* 20, nos. 1–2:129–46.

King, P. 1988. Early Divergences between the Psycho-analytical Societies in London and Vienna. In *Freud in Exile*. Ed. E. Timms and N. Segal. New Haven: Yale University Press.

Klein, D. 1981. *The Origins of the Psychoanalytic Movement*. New York: Praeger.

Klein, M. 1932. *The Psychoanalysis of Children*. London: Hogarth Press.

———. 1935. A Contribution to the Psychogenesis of Manic-Depressive States. *International Journal of Psychoanalysis* 16:145–75.

———. 1950. On the Criteria for the Termination of a Psycho-Analysis. *International Journal of Psychoanalysis* 31:78–80.

———. 1957. *Envy and Gratitude*. London: Tavistock.

Kohon, G. 1986. *The British School of Psychoanalysis*. New Haven: Yale University Press.

Kohut, H. 1971. *The Analysis of the Self: A Systematic Approach to the Psychoanalytic Treatment of Narcissistic Personality Disorders*. New York: International Universities Press.

———. 1977. *The Restoration of the Self*. New York: International Universities Press.

Kommittee für Alternativen zum Psychologengesetz. 1980. *Auseinandersetzungen zwischen Vereinsmeierei, Demokratisierung und Expertenherrschaft*. Vienna: Institut für Wissenschaft und Kunst.

Körner, J. 1980. Über das Verhältnis von Psychoanalyse und Pädagogik. *Psyche* 34:769–89.

Kovel, J. 1981. *The Age of Desire: Case Histories of a Radical Psychoanalyst*. New York: Pantheon.

Kramer, R. [1976] 1988. *Maria Montessori: A Biography*. New York: Addison-Wesley.

Krauss, H., and Wolff, R., eds. 1982. *Psychoanalytische Literaturwissenschaft und Literatursoziologie* 7. Frankfurt: Peter D. Lang.

Kris, E. 1955. Neutralization and Sublimation. *Psychoanalytic Study of the Child* 10:30–46.

———. 1956. The Personal Myth: A Problem in Psychoanalytic Technique. *Journal of the American Psychoanalytic Association* 4:653–81.

Kris, E., and Kurz, O. 1979. *Legend, Myth, and Magic in the Image of the Artist: A Historical Experiment*. New Haven: Yale University Press.

Kristeva, J. [1980] 1982. *Powers of Horror: An Essay in Abjection*. New York: Columbia University Press.

———. 1982. Psychoanalysis and the Polis. In *Politics of Interpretation*. Ed. W. J. T. Mitchell. Chicago: University of Chicago Press.

———. [1983] 1987. *Tales of Love.* New York: Columbia University Press.

Krüger-Zeul, M. 1979. Bewirkt der Film "Holocaust" eine Klimaveränderung oder bleibt er Episode? *PSA: Information,* no. 13:15–23.

———. 1986. M. Fassbinder's "Maria Braun": Liebende Frau oder Femme fatale? In *Sadomasochisten, Keusche und Romantiker: Vom Mythos neuer Sinnlichkeit.* Ed. Ulrike Heider. Hamburg: Rohwolt, 141–51.

Krüll, M. [1979] 1986. *Freud and His Father.* New York: Norton.

Kurzweil, E. 1971. The (Freudian) Congress of Vienna. *Commentary,* November, pp. 43–48.

———. 1980. *The Age of Structuralism: Lévi-Strauss to Foucault.* New York: Columbia University Press.

———. 1985. The Freudians Meet in Germany. *Partisan Review,* no. 4:387–97.

———. 1986. Interview with Julia Kristeva. *Partisan Review,* no. 2:216–26.

———. 1987a. Freud in Montreal. *Partisan Review,* no. 4:603–10.

———. 1987b. Psychoanalysis as the Macro-Micro Link. In *The Macro-Micro Link.* Ed. J. C. Alexander et al. Berkeley: University of California Press.

Kurzweil, E., and Phillips, W., eds. 1983. *Literature and Psychoanalysis.* New York: Columbia University Press.

Kutter, P., ed. 1977. *Psychoanalyse im Wandel.* Frankfurt: Suhrkamp.

———. 1981. Der Basiskonflikt der Psychosomatik und seine therapeutischen Implikationen. *Jahrbuch der Psychoanalyse* 13:93–114.

———. 1984. Zur Dynamik psychosomatischer Erkrankungen—damals und heute. *Psyche* 38, no. 6:544–62.

Kutter, P., and Roth, J. K. 1981. *Psychoanalyse an der Universität.* Munich: Kindler.

Lacan, J. [1966] 1977. *Ecrits: A Selection.* New York: Norton.

———. 1968. *The Language of the Self: The Function of Language in Psychoanalysis.* Baltimore: Johns Hopkins Press.

———. 1972. Seminar on "The Purloined Letter." French Freud. *Yale French Studies* 48:38–72.

———. 1974. *Télévision.* Paris; Editions du Seuil.

———. 1977. Desire and the Interpretation of Desire in *Hamlet. Literature and Psychoanalysis. Yale French Studies* 55–56:11–52.

Lagache, D. [1947] 1981. *La jalousie amoureuse.* Paris: Presses Universitaires de France.

Laible, E. 1987. Marie Bonapartes Beiträge zur Anwendung der Psychoanalyse auf die Anthropologie. Paper presented at a meeting on the History of Psychoanalysis, Trieste, Oct.

Lampl-de Groot, J. 1947. On the Development of the Ego and Superego. *International Journal of Psychoanalysis* 28:7–11.

Langer, M. 1985. Der Widerspruch in der Lehranalyse. In *Jenseits der Couch: Psychoanalyse als Sozialkritik.* Frankfurt: Fischer.

Langer, W. 1972. *The Mind of Hitler.* New York: Basic Books.

Langman, L. 1978. The Crises of Self and State under Late Capitalism: A Critical Perspective. *International Journal of Law and Psychiatry* 1:343–74.

Laplanche, J. [1970] 1976. *Life and Death in Psychoanalysis.* Baltimore: Johns Hopkins University Press.

———. 1982. Reconnaître la recherche psychanalytique. *Psychanalyse à l'université* 7:353–57.

Laplanche, J., and Pontalis, J.-B. [1967] 1973. *The Language of Psychoanalysis.* New York: Norton.

Lasch, C. 1978. *The Culture of Narcissism.* New York: Norton.

———. 1984. *The Minimal Self: Psychic Survival in Troubled Times.* New York: Norton.

Lax, R. F., Bach, S., and Burland, J. A., eds. 1986. *Self and Object Constancy: Clinical and Theoretical Perspectives.* New York: Guilford Press.

Leavy, S. A. 1970. John Keats' Psychology of Creative Imagination. *Psychoanalytic Quarterly* 39:173–97.

———. 1980. *The Psychoanalytic Dialogue.* New Haven: Yale University Press.

———. 1983a. Speaking in Tongues: Some Linguistic Approaches to Psychoanalysis. *Psychoanalytic Quarterly* 52:34–55.

———. 1983b. The Image and the Word: Further Reflections on Jacques Lacan. In *Interpreting Lacan.* Ed. J. H. Smith and W. Kerrigan. New Haven: Yale University Press, 3–20.

Lebovici, S. 1977. "Un institut des sciences humaines cliniques": Réponse à André Green. *Psychanalyse à l'université* 2, no. 7:537–39.

———. 1980. L'expérience du psychanalyste chez l'enfant et chez l'adulte devant le modèle de la névrose infantile et de la névrose de transfert. *Revue française de Psychanalyse* 44, nos. 5–6:733–857.

Lebovici, S., and Solnit, A. J. 1982. *La formation du psychanalyste.* Paris: Presses Universitaires de France.

Le Guen, C. 1974. *L'Oedipe Originaire.* Paris: Payot.

Leites, N. 1948. Psycho-Cultural Hypotheses about Political Acts. *World Politics* 1:102–19.

Lemaire, A. 1977. *Jacques Lacan.* London: Routledge and Kegan Paul.

Leupold-Löwenthal, H. 1981. Zur Beendigung der psychoanalytischen Behandlung. *Jahrbuch der Psychoanalyse* 12:192–203.

———. 1982. Bulletin. *International Journal of Psychoanalysis* 63:115–17.

———. 1984. Zur Geschichte der "Frage der Laienanalyse." *Psyche* 38:97–120.

Levine, D. N. 1971. *The Sociology of Georg Simmel.* Chicago: University of Chicago Press.

Lévi-Strauss, C. [1955] 1963. *Structural Anthropology.* New York: Basic Books.

Lewin, K., and Ross H. 1960. *Psychoanalytic Study in the United States.* New York: Norton.

Lichtenberg, J. D. 1984. *The Talking Cure: A Descriptive Guide to psychoanalysis.* New York: Analytic Press.

Lichtman, R. 1982. *The Producton of Desire.* New York: Free Press.

Lieberman, J. E. 1985. *Acts of Will: The Life and Work of Otto Rank.* New York: Free Press.

Lipowski, Z. J. 1977. Psychosomatic Medicine in the Seventies. *American Journal of Psychiatry* 134:235.

Lipton, S. D. 1977. The Advantage of Freud's Technique as Shown in his Analysis of the Rat Man. *International Journal of Psychoanalysis* 58:255–73.

Liss, E. 1955. Motivation in Learning. *International Study of the Child* 10:100–16.

Little, M. 1951. Countertransference and the Patient's Response to It. *International Journal of Psychoanalysis* 32:32–40.

Loch, W. 1977. Einige Thesen zu den Problemen der psychoanalytischen Facharzt-Ausbildung. Paper. *Tagung der DPV,* Cologne, Oct. 18.

———. 1983. A. Mitscherlich zur Psychologie der BRD. *Psyche* 37, no. 4:342–43.

Lockot, R. 1985. *Erinnern und Durcharbeiten: Zur Geschichte der Psychoanalyse und Psychotherapie im Nazionalsozialismus.* Frankfurt: Fischer.

Loewald, H. W. 1951. Ego and Reality. *International Journal of Psychoanalysis* 32:10–18.

Loewenberg, P. 1971. "Sigmund Freud as a Jew": A Study in Ambivalence and Courage. *Journal of the History of the Behavioral Sciences* 7, no. 4:363–69.

———. 1983. *Decoding the Past.* New York: Knopf.

Loewenstein, R. M. 1982. *Practice and Precept in Psychoanalytic Technique: Selected Papers.* Introduction by Jacob A. Arlow. New Haven: Yale University Press.

Lohmann, H. M. 1980. Psychoanalyse in Deutschland—eine Karriere im Staatsapparat? Ansichten von jenseits des Rheins. *Psyche* 34:945–57.

———, ed. 1983. *Das Unbehagen in der Psychoanalyse.* Frankfurt: Qumran.

———, ed. 1984a. *Die Psychoanalyse auf der Couch.* Frankfurt: Qumran.

———, ed. 1984b. *Psychoanalyse und Nationalsozialismus.* Frankfurt: Fischer.

Lohmann, H. M., and Rosenkötter, L. 1982. Psychoanalyse in Hitlerdeutschland. *Psyche* 36, no. 11:961–88.

Lorand, S. 1969. Reflections on the Development of Psychoanalysis in New York from 1925. *International Journal of Psychoanalysis* 50:589–95.

———. 1973. Historical Aspects and Changing Trends in Psychoanalytic Therapy. *Psychoanalytic Review* 59, no. 4:497–525.

Lorand, S., and Schneer, H. I., eds. 1961. *Adolescence.* New York: Hoeber.

Lorenz, K. 1963. *On Aggression.* New York: Bantam.

Lorenzer, A. 1973. *Sprachzerstörung und Rekonstruktion. Vorarbeiten zu einer Metatheorie der Psychoanalyse.* Frankfurt: Suhrkamp.

———. 1974. *Die Wahrheit der psychoanalytischen Erkenntnis: Ein historisch-materialistischer Entwurf.* Frankfurt: Suhrkamp.

———. 1981. *Zur Begründung einer materialistischen Sozialisationstheorie.* Frankfurt: Suhrkamp.

———. 1984. *Intimität und soziales Leid.* Frankfurt: Fischer.

Lowen, A. 1893. *Narcissism: Denial of the True Self.* New York: Macmillan.

McCannel, J. F., and McCannel, D. 1982. *The Time of the Sign: A Semiotic Interpretation of Modern Culture.* Bloomington: Indiana University Press.

McDougall, J. 1974. The Psychosoma and the Psychoanalytic Process. *International Review of Psychoanalysis* 1:437–59.

———. 1980. The Homosexual Dilemma: A Study of Female Homosexuality. In *Plea for a Measure of Abnormality.* New York: International Universities Press.

———. 1985. *Theaters of the Mind.* New York: Basic Books.

McGrath, W. J. 1985. *Freud's Discovery of Psychoanalysis.* Ithaca: Cornell University Press.

McGuire, W. 1974. *The Freud/Jung Letters*. Bollingen Series. Princeton: Princeton University Press.

Maetze, G. 1976. Psychoanalyse in Deutschland. In *Die Psychoanalyse des 20. Jahrhunderts*. Vol. 2, *Freud und die Folgen*. Zurich: Kindler, 1145–1179.

Mahler, M. S., and Gosliner, G. J. 1955. On Symbiotic Child Psychosis: Genetic, Dynamic and Restitutive Aspects. *Psychoanalytic Study of the Child*. 10:195–212.

Mahler, M. S., and McDevitt, J. D. 1979. Observations on Adaptation and Defense *in statu nascendi*. In *The Selected Papers of Margaret S. Mahler*. Vol. 2. New York: Aronson.

Mahler, M. S., Pine, F., and Bergmann, A. 1975. *The Psychological Birth of the Human Infant*. New York: Basic Books.

Mahony, P. J. 1986. *Freud and the Rat Man*. New Haven: Yale University Press.

———. 1987. *Psychoanalysis and Discourse*. London: Tavistock.

Major, R. 1982. L'amour de transfert et la passion du signifiant. In *L'amour de transfert: Etudes Freudiennes*. Paris: Evel.

Malcolm, J. 1981. *Psychoanalysis: The Impossible Profession*. New York: Vintage.

Malinowski, B. 1927. *Sex and Repression in Savage Society*. New York: Harcourt, Brace.

Mannheim, K. 1936. *Ideology and Utopia*. New York: Harcourt, Brace and World.

Mannoni, M. 1979. *La théorie comme fiction: Freud, Groddeck, Winnicott, Lacan*. Paris: Editions du Seuil.

———. 1980. *Ça n'empêche pas d'éxister*. Paris: Editions du Seuil.

Marcus, S. 1966. *The Other Victorians*. New York: Basic Books.

———. 1974. "Freud and Dora: Story, History, Case History." *Partisan Review* 41, no. 1:12–23, 89–108.

———. 1984. *Freud and the Culture of Psychoanalysis*. London: Allen and Unwin.

Marcuse, H. 1955. *Eros and Civilization*. Boston: Beacon Press.

———. 1970. The Obsolescence of the Freudian Concept of Man. In *Five Lectures*. Boston: Beacon Press, 44–61.

Marks, E., and Courtivron, E., eds. 1980. *New French Feminisms*. Amherst: University of Massachusetts Press.

Marty, P. 1958. La relation objectale allergique. *Revue française de Psychoanalyse* 22: 3–35.

———. 1968. A Major Process of Somatization: The Progressive Disorganization. *International Journal of Psychoanalysis* 49:246–49.

———. 1969. Notes cliniques et hypothèses à propos de l'economie de l'allergie. *Revue française de Psychanalyse* 33:243–53.

———. 1975. *Les mouvements individuels de vie et de la mort*. Paris: Payot.

Masson, J. M. 1984. *The Assault on Truth: Freud's Suppression of the Seduction Theory*. New York: Farrar, Straus and Giroux.

———. 1985. *The Complete Letters of Sigmund Freud to Wilhelm Fliess, 1887–1904*. Cambridge: Harvard University Press.

Maxmen, J. S. 1985. *The New Psychiatry*. New York: Morrow.

Mead, M. 1935. *Sex and Temperament in Three Primitive Societies*. New York: William Morrow.

———. 1959. Mental Health in World Perspective. In *Culture and Mental Health*. Ed. M. K. Opler. New York: Macmillan, 501–16.

Mechanic, D. 1980. *Mental Health and Social Policy*. Englewood Cliffs, N.J.: Prentice-Hall.

Meisel, P., and Kendrick, W., eds. 1985. *Bloomsbury/Freud: The Letters of James and Alix Strachey*. New York: Basic Books.

Meissner, W. W. 1966. Family Dynamics and Psychosomatic Process. *Family Process*, no. 5:142–61.

———. 1984a. *Psychoanalysis and the Religious Experience*. New Haven: Yale University Press.

———. 1984b. Clinical Differentiation on Borderline Syndromes from the Psychoses. *Psychoanalytic Review* 71, no. 2:185–210.

Menaker, E. 1982. *Otto Rank: A Rediscovered Legacy*. New York: Columbia University Press.

Meng, H., and Freud, E. L., eds. 1963. *Psychoanalysis and Faith: The Letters of Sigmund Freud and Oskar Pfister*. New York: Basic Books.

Menne, K., and Schröter, K. 1980. Soziale Herkunft—ein Hindernis für die psychoanalytische Behandlung? In *Psychoanalyse und Unterschicht*. Ed. K. Menne and K. Schröter. Frankfurt: Suhrkamp.

Mettler, H. 1979. Autoren schreiben anders: Der Einfluss der Psychoanalyse auf die moderne Literatur. In *Psychoanalyse des 20. Jahrhunderts*. Zurich: Kindler, 836–50.

Meyers, H. C. 1986. *Between Analyst and Patient: New Dimensions in Countertransference and Transference*. New York: Analytic Press.

Mezzich, J. E., and Berganza, C. E., eds. 1984. *Culture and Psychotherapy*. New York: Columbia University Press.

Michel, S. 1984. American Conscience and the Unconscious: Psychoanalysis and the Rise of Personal Religion, 1906–1963. *Psychoanalysis and Contemporary Thought* 7, no. 4:387–421.

Middendorp, V. 1956. Katamnesische Untersuchungen nach poliklinisch durchgeführter Kurztherapie. *Psyche* 10, no. 9:662–75.

Mijolla, A. de. 1982. La Psychanalyse en France, 1926–65. In *Histoire de la Psychanalyse*. Ed. R. Jaccard. Paris: Hachette.

———. 1986. *Corps et Histoire*. Paris: Société d'Editions, "Les Belles Lettres." (Contributions by J. McDougall, G. Gachelin, P. Aulagnier, O. Marty, J. Loriod, and J. Cain.)

———. 1987. A propos de la pratique psychanalytique de Freud. *La conduite de la cure: Etudes freudiennes*, no. 30:17–37.

Mijolla-Mellor, S., de. 1986. Aperçu sur de nouvelles perspectives dans la recherche psychanalytique. *Topique* 16, no. 37:163–66.

Miller, J.-A. 1976. *La scission de 1953*. Paris: Ornicar?.

———. 1977. *L'excommunication*. Paris: Ornicar?.

Miller, J. B., ed. 1973. *Psychoanalysis and Women*. Middlesex, England: Penguin.

Miller, J. W. 1983. *In Defense of the Psychological*. New York: Norton.

Millet, J. P. 1966. Psychoanalysis in the United States. In *Psychoanalytic Pioneers*. Ed. F. Alexander et al. New York: Basic Books.

Mirsky, A. 1966. Physiological, Psychological, and Social Determinants of Psychosomatic Disorders. *Bulletin, Association of Psychoanalytic Medicine* 6, no. 1:3–7.

Mitchell, J. 1974. *Psychoanalysis and Feminism*. New York: Pantheon.

————. 1984. *Women: The Longest Revolution*. New York: Pantheon.

Mitchell, J., and Rose, J. 1982. *Feminine Sexuality: Jacques Lacan and the école freudienne*. New York: Norton.

Mitscherlich, A. 1939. *Mass und Wert*. (Quoted in *Psyche* 37, no. 4 [1983].)

————. [1963] 1969. *Society without the Father*. New York: Harcourt, Brace and World.

————. 1967. *Krankheit als Konflikt: Studien zur psychosomatischen Medizin*. Vol. 2. Frankfurt: Suhrkamp.

————. [1974] 1980. Bedingungen der Chronifizierung psychosomatischer Krankheiten: Die zweifachige Abwehr. In *Einführung in die psychosomatische Medizin*. Ed. K. Brede. Frankfurt: Syndikat, 396–406.

————. 1980. *Ein Leben für die Psychoanalyse*. Frankfurt: Suhrkamp.

————. 1984. *Gesammelte Schriften*. Frankfurt: Suhrkamp.

Mitscherlich, A., and Mielke, F. 1947. *Das Diktat der Menschenverachtung*. Heidelberg: Lambert Schneider.

Mitscherlich, A., and Mitscherlich-Nielsen, M. 1967. *Die Unfähigkeit zu trauern*. Munich: Piper.

Mitscherlich, A.; Lorenzer, A.; Horn, K.; Dahmer, H.; Schwanenberg, E.; Brede, K.; and Berndt, H. 1970. On Psychoanalysis and Sociology. *International Journal of Psychoanalysis* 51:33–48.

Mitscherlich, A.; Silverman, A.; Grunberger, B.; Wangh, M.; and Hochheimer, W. 1966. Die psychologischen und sozialen Voraussetzungen des Zeitalters. *Psyche* 16, no. 5:241–316.

Mitscherlich-Nielsen, M. ed. 1972. *Sigmund Freud: Briefe*. Frankfurt: Suhrkamp.

————. 1975. Psychoanalyse und weibliche Sexualität. *Psyche* 29:769–88.

————. [1976] 1983. Psychoanalytic Notes on Kafka. In *Literature and Psychoanalysis*. Ed. E. Kurzweil and W. Phillips. New York: Columbia University Press, 270–89.

————. 1979. Die Notwendigkeit zu trauern. In *Im Kreuzfeuer: Fernsehfilm Holocaust*. Ed. P. Märtesheimer and I. Frenzel. Frankfurt: Fischer.

————. 1985. *Die friedfertige Frau*. Frankfurt: Fischer.

————. 1987a. Theorie in der Krise. *Psyche* 41, no. 11:961–68.

————. 1987b. *Erinnerungsarbeit: Zur Psychoanalyse der Unfähigkeit zu trauern*. Frankfurt: Fischer.

Moersch, E.; Kerz-Rühling, I. E.; Drews, S.; Nern, R. D.; Kennel, K.; Kelleter, R.; Rodriguez, C.; Fischer, R.; and Goldschmidt, R. 1980. Zur Psychopathologie von Herzinfarkt-Patienten. *Psyche* 34:493–587.

Morgenthaler, F. 1984. *Gespräche am sterbenden Fluss: Ethnopsychoanalyse bei den Iatmul in Papua-Neuguinea*. Ed. F. Weiss and M. Morgenthaler. Frankfurt: Fischer.

————. 1986. *Der Traum*. Frankfurt: Qumram.

Morgenthau, H., and Person, E. 1978. The Roots of Narcissism. *Partisan Review*, no. 3:337–47.

Morton, F. 1979. *A Nervous Splendour*. Boston: Little, Brown.

Moscovici, S. 1961. *La Psychanalyse et son image public*. Paris: Presses Universitaires de France.

Moser, T. 1971. *Repressive Kriminal Psychiatrie: Vom Elend einer Wissenschaft. Eine Streitschrift*. Frankfurt: Suhrkamp.

————. 1974. *Gespräche mit Eingeschlossenen*. Frankfurt: Suhrkamp.

Muck, M.; Schröter, K.; Klüwer, R.; Eberenz, U.; Kennel, K.; and Horn, K. 1974. *Information über Psychoanalyse: Theoretische therapeutische und interdisziplinäre Aspekte.* Frankfurt: Suhrkamp.

Muensterberger, W., Boyer, L. B., and Grolnick, S. A. 1984. *The Psychoanalytic Study of Society.* Vol. 10. Hillsdale, N.J.: Analytic Press.

Muslin, H. L. 1985. Heinz Kohut: Beyond the Pleasure Principle: Contributions to Psychoanalysis. In *Beyond Freud.* Ed. J. Reppen. New York: Analytic Press, 203–29.

M'Uzan M. d. 1977. *De l'art à la mort.* Paris: Gallimard.

———. 1983. Misère de l'ideal du moi. *Ideaux: Nouvelle Revue de Psychanalyse,* no. 27:273–76.

Nacht, S. 1959. *Psychoanalysis of Today.* New York: Grune and Stratton.

Nadig, M. 1986. Zur ethnopsychoanalytischen Erarbeitung des kulturellen Raums der Frau. *Psyche* 40, no. 3:193–219.

Nägele, R. 1987. *Reading after Freud: Essays on Goethe, Hölderlin, Habermas, Nietzsche, Brecht, Celan, and Freud.* New York: Columbia University Press.

Nelson, B. 1958. *Freud and the 20th Century.* New York: Meriden.

———. 1968. Scholastic Rationales of Conscience: Early modern crises of credibility and the scientific-technolocultural revolutions of the seventeenth and twentieth centuries. *Journal of the Scientific Study of Religion* 7:157–77.

Nunberg, H., and Federn, E., eds. 1962; 1967; 1974. *Minutes of the Vienna Psychoanalytic Society.* Vols. 1–3. New York: International Universities Press.

Oberndorf, C. P. 1949. Forty Years of Psycho-analytic Psychiatry. *International Journal of Psychoanalysis* 30:153–61.

———. 1951. Obituary: August Aichhorn. *International Journal of Psychoanalysis* 32:51–57.

O'Dwyer de Macedo, H., ed. 1988. *Le psychanalyste sous la terreur.* Vigneux: Editions Matrice.

Oliner, M. 1988. *Cultivating Freud's Garden in France.* New York: Jason Aronson.

Olivienstein, C. 1982. *La vie du taxomane.* Paris: PUF.

O'Shaughnessy, E. 1985. A 3 1/2-Year-Old Boy's Melancholic Identification with an Original Object. Paper presented at the IPA Congress, Hamburg.

Ostow, M. 1985a. Revisions of Psychoanalytic Theory and Practice Required by Experience with Psychiatric Drug Therapy. Paper.

———. 1985b. The Psychodynamics of the Apocalyptic. Discussion of Papers on Identification and the Nazi Phenomenon, Hamburg, July 30.

Ouzouf, M. 1980. Sondage: 65% des Française refuseraient une psychanalyse, même gratuite. *Le Nouvel Observateur,* no. 897:42–43.

Overbeck, G. 1984. *Krankheit als Anpassung: Der sozio-psychosomatische Zirkel.* Frankfurt: Suhrkamp.

Pankoff, G. 1981. *L'être-là du schizophrène.* Paris: Aubier Montaigne.

Parin, P. 1978. Warum die Psychoanalytiker so ungern zu brennenden Zeitproblemen Stellung nehmen: Eine ethnologische Betrachtung. *Psyche* 32:385–99.

———. 1984. Anpassung oder Widerstand. *Psyche* 38, no. 7:627–35.

Parin, P., Morgenthaler, F., and Parin-Matthey, G. 1963. *Die Weissen denken zu viel:*

Psychoanalytische Untersuchungen bei den Dogon in West-Afrika. Zurich: Atlantis.

———. 1971. *Fürchte deinen Nächsten wie dich selbst: Psychoanalyse und Gesellschaft am Modell der Agni in Westafrika.* Frankfurt: Suhrkamp.

Parsons, T. [1952] 1970. *Social Structure and Personality.* New York: Free Press.

Pasche, F. 1969. *A partir de Freud.* Paris: Payot.

Perner, J., and Tholen, G. C. 1983. Einleitung. *Fragmente: Schriftenreihe zur Psychoanalyse*, nos. 7–8:6–14.

Perrier, F. 1985. *Voyages extraordinaires en Translacanie.* Paris: Lieu Commun.

Person, E. S. 1978. Transvestism: New Perspectives. *Journal of the American Academy of Psychoanalysis* 6:301–23.

———. 1980. Sexuality as the Mainstay of Identity: Psychoanalytic Perspectives. In *Women: Sex and Sexuality.* Ed. C. Stimpson and E. S. Person. Chicago: University of Chicago Press.

———. 1983. Review, *Homosexualities: A Study of Diversity among Men and Women*, by A. P. Bell and M. S. Weinberg. *Journal of the American Psychoanalytic Association* 6:301–23.

Person E. S., and Ovesey, L. 1974. Transsexual Syndrome in Males. *American Journal of Psychotherapy* 28:4–20.

Peters, U. H. [1979] 1985. *Anna Freud.* New York: Schocken.

Pfennigsdorf, E. 1930. *Praktische Theologie.* Vol. 2. Gütersloh: C. Bertelsmann.

Pfister, O. 1913. *Die psychoanalytische Methode.* Leipzig: Klinkhardt.

Phillips, W., ed. 1957. *Art and Psychoanalysis.* New York: Criterion.

Pietzcker, F. 1984. *Wilhelm Busch—Schuld und Strafe in Werk und Leben.* Munich: Minerva Fachserie Psychologie.

Pines, M., ed. 1985. *Bion and Group Psychotherapy.* London: Routledge and Kegan Paul.

Pohlen, M., and Wittmann, W. 1980. *"Die Unterwelt bewegen": Versuch über Wahrnehmung und Phantasie in der Psychoanalyse.* Frankfurt: Syndikat.

Pollock, G. H. 1975. The Psychomatic Specificity Concept: Its Evolution and Re-Evaluation. *Annual of Psychoanalysis* 5:141–67.

Pontalis, J.-B. 1970. La question de la psychanalyse. *Nouvelle Revue française* 1:5–8.

Pribram, K. H., and Gill, M. M. 1976. *Freud's "Project" Re-assessed.* New York: Basic Books.

Quinn, S. 1987. *A Mind of Her Own: The Life of Karen Horney.* New York: Summit.

Radó, S. 1934. *Die Kastrationsangst des Weibes.* Vienna: Internationaler Psychoanalytischer Verlag.

Ragland-Sullivan, E. 1986. *Jacques Lacan and the Philosophy of Psychoanalysis.* Chicago: University of Illinois Press.

Rand, N., and Torok, M. 1987. The History of Psychoanalysis: History Reads Theory. *Critical Inquiry* 13:278–86.

Rangell, L. 1953. The Interchangeability of Phallus and Female Genital. *Journal of the American Psychoanalytic Association* 1:504–09.

———. 1976. Lessons from Watergate. *Psychoanalytic Quarterly* 45:37–61.

———. 1980. *The Mind of Watergate: An Exploration of the Compromise of Integrity.* New York: Norton.

Rank, O. [1907] 1932. *Art and the Artist*. New York: Tudor.

Rassial, A., and Rassial, J.-J., eds. 1981. *La psychanalyse est-elle une histoire juive? Colloque de Montpellier*. Paris: Éditions du Seuil.

Reed, G. 1983. *Candide:* Radical Simplicity and the Impact of Evil. In *Literature and Psychoanalysis*. Ed. E. Kurzweil and W. Phillips. New York: Columbia University Press, 189–200.

———. 1985. Psychoanalysis, Psychoanalysis Appropriated, Psychoanalysis Applied. *Psychoanalytic Quarterly* 54:234–69.

Reich, A. 1951. On Countertransference and the Patient's Response to It. *International Journal of Psychoanalysis* 32:25–31.

Reichmayr, J. 1986. Theoretische Annäherungen. In *Psychologie*. Ed. G. Rexilius and S. Grubitzsch. Hamburg: Rohwolt, 453–75.

Reichmayr, J., and Wiesbauer, E. 1979. Das Verhältnis von Sozialdemokratie und Psychoanalyse in Österreich zwischen 1900 und 1938. In *Beiträge zur Psychoanalyse in Österreich*. Ed. W. Huber. Vienna: Geyer Verlag.

Reik, T. [1925] 1971. Geständniszwang und Strafbedürfnis. In *Psychoanalyse und Justiz*. Ed. T. Moser. Frankfurt: Suhrkamp, 9–201.

———. 1948. *Listening with the Third Ear: The Inner Experience of a Psychoanalyst*. New York: Farrar, Straus.

———. [1949] 1957. The Three Women in a Man's Life. In *Art and Psychoanalysis*. Ed. W. Phillips. New York: Criterion, 151–64.

Reinke, E. 1987. Psychoanalytisches Verstehen im soziotherapeutischen Setting: Ein Modellprojekt mit Straftätern. *Psyche* 41, no. 10:900–14.

Reinke-Köberer, E. 1978. Zur Diskussion der weiblichen Sexualität. *Psyche* 32:695–731.

Reppen, J., ed. 1985. *Beyond Freud*. Hillsdale, N.J.: Analytic Press.

Richter, H. E. 1982a. *Zur Psychologie des Friedens*. Hamburg: Rohwolt.

———. 1982b. Psychosoziale Medizin und Prävention von Militarisierungsbereitschaft. *Psychosozial* 5, no. 1:134–145.

———. 1984. Die Verdrängung des Todes und die "Krankheit" Atomrüstung. *Psyche* 38:1105–23.

———. 1985. Als Psychoanalytiker in der Friedensbewegung. *Psyche* 39:289–300.

———. 1986. Amerikanismus, Antiamerikanismus—oder was sonst? *Psyche* 40, no. 7:583–99.

Ricoeur, P. 1970. *Freud and Philosophy*. New Haven: Yale University Press.

Rieff, P., ed. 1963a. *Sigmund Freud, Character and Culture*. New York: Collier.

———, ed. 1963b. *The History of the Psychoanalytic Movement*. New York: Collier.

Riesman, D. 1950. *The Lonely Crowd*. New Haven: Yale University Press.

Rigoulet, P. 1978, Marx, Freud et la mort. *Les Temps modernes* 33, no. 380:1525–30.

Rimmon-Kenan, S., ed. 1987. *Discourse in Psychoanalysis*. London: Methuen.

Rioch, M. J. 1970. The Work of Wilfred Bion on Groups. *Psychiatry* 33, no. 1:56–66.

Roazen, P. 1985. *Helene Deutsch: A Psychoanalyst's Life*. New York: Doubleday/Anchor.

Roazen, P.; Schoenwald, R.; Zaretzki, E.; and Gay, P. 1986. Symposium: Gay on Freud. *Psychohistory Review* 5, no. 1:81–104.

Robert, M. 1976. *From Oedipus to Moses: Freud's Jewish Identity*. Garden City, N.Y.: Doubleday/Anchor.

Rodman, F. R., ed. 1987. *The Spontaneous Gesture: Selected Letters of D. W. Winnicott.* Cambridge: Harvard University Press.

Róheim, G. 1919. *Spiegelzauber.* Leipzig and Vienna: Internationaler Psychoanalytischer Verlag.

———. 1941. Psycho-Analytic Interpretation of Culture. *International Journal of Psycho-Analysis* 22:147–69.

Roland, A., ed. 1978. *Psychoanalysis, Creativity, and Literature: A French-American Inquiry.* New York: Columbia University Press.

———. 1988. *In Search of Self in India and Japan.* Princeton: Princeton University Press.

Rorty, R. 1986. Freud and Moral Reflecton. In *Psychiatry and the Humanities.* Vol. 9, *Pragmatism's Freud: The Moral Disposition of Psychoanalysis.* Ed. J. H. Smith and W. Kerrigan. Baltimore: Johns Hopkins University Press, 2–4.

Rose, G. J. 1987. *Trauma and Mastery in Life and Art.* New Haven: Yale University Press.

Rose, J. 1985. Dora: Fragment of an Analysis. In *In Dora's Case.* Ed. C. Bernheimer and C. Kahane. New York: Columbia University Press.

———. 1986. *Sexuality in the Field of Vision.* London: Verso.

Rose, R. M. 1983. What Are We Talking about and Who Listens? A Citation Analysis of *Psychosomatic Medicine. Psychosomatic Medicine* 45, no. 5:379–94.

Rosenfeld, H. 1987. *Impasse and Interpretation.* London: Tavistock.

Rosenkötter, L., and von Schweinichen, M. 1981. Psychoanalyse als Teil der sozialen Krankenversicherung. *Psyche* 35, no. 1:42–48.

Rosolato, G. 1978. Symbol Formation. *International Journal of Psychoanalysis* 59:303–13.

Roth, M. S. 1987. *Psycho-Analysis as History: Negation and Freedom in Freud.* Ithaca: Cornell University Press.

Rothstein, A. 1985. *Models of the Mind: Their Relationship to Clinical Work.* New York: International Universities Press.

Roudinesco, E. 1982. *La Bataille de cent ans: Histoire de la psychanalyse en France.* Vol. 1. Paris: Ramsay.

———. 1986. *La Bataile de cent ans: Histoire de la psychanalyse en France.* Vol. 2. Paris: Ramsay.

Roussillon, R. 1984. Du baquet de Mesmer au "baquet" de S. Freud: Premières réflexions sur la préhistoire du cadre psychanalytique. *Revue française de Psychanalyse* 18, no. 6:1363–83.

Roustang, F. [1976] 1982. *Dire Mastery.* Baltimore: Johns Hopkins University Press.

———. 1980. *Psychoanalysis Never Lets Go.* Baltimore: Johns Hopkins University Press.

———. 1984. La psychanalyse peut-elle s'exporter? *Psychanalystes*, no. 11:3–9.

Rudnytsky, P. L. 1987. *Freud and Oedipus.* New York: Columbia University Press.

Sachs, H. 1928. Über einen Antrieb bei der Bildung des weiblichen Über-Ichs. *Internationale Zeitschrift für Psychoanalyse*, 14, no. 2:163–74.

Safouan, M. 1983. *Jacques Lacan et la question de la formation des analystes.* Paris: Editions du Seuil.

Salomé, L.-A. 1958. *In der Schule bei Freud: Tagebuch eines Jahres 1912–13*. Zurich: Max Hiehans Verlag.

Saluti, J. 1986. Kein Näherkommen: Eine Jubiläumsbetrachtung. *Werkblatt* 3, nos. 3–4:107–11.

Sandler, J. 1975. Sexual Fantasies and Sexual Theories in Childhood. In *Studies in Child Psychoanalysis: Pure and Applied*. Monograph Series of *The Psychoanalytic Study of the Child*, no. 5. New Haven: Yale University Press, 149–67.

———. 1984a. Comment presented at the first congress of the Sigmund Freud Center, Hebrew University, Jerusalem, May 27–29.

———. 1984b. Brief Notes on Concepts of Internalization and Externalization presented at the first congress of the Sigmund Freud Center, Hebrew University, Jerusalem, May 27–29.

Sartre, J.-P. [1948] 1965. *Anti-Semite and Jew*. New York: Schocken.

———. [1958] 1986. *The Freud Scenario*. Chicago: University of Chicago Press.

Satow, R. 1979. Pop Narcissism. *Psychology Today*, nos. 13–14:17.

Scaluta, J. 1987. *La Psychohistoire*. Paris: PUF.

Schafer, R. 1974. Problems in Freud's Psychology of Women. *Journal of the American Psychoanalytic Association* 22:459–85.

———. 1976. *A New Language for Psychoanalysis*. New Haven: Yale University Press.

Scharfenberg, J. 1981. Die Rezeption der Psychoanalyse in der Theologie. In *Die Rezeption der Psychoanalyse*. Ed. J. Cremerius. Frankfurt: Suhrkamp.

Schauder, C. 1982. L'évènement balintien pour le pédagogue. *Revue de Médecine Psychosomatique* 24:179–89.

Scheidt, C. E. 1986. *Die Rezeption der Psychoanalyse in der deutschsprachigen Philosophie vor 1940*. Frankfurt: Suhrkamp, 254–77.

Schick, A. 1968. The Vienna of Sigmund Freud. *Psychoanalytic Review* 55, no. 4:529–51.

Schlumberger, M. 1949. Bulletin. *International Journal of Psychoanalysis* 30:210.

Schmidl, F. 1981. *On Applied Psychoanalysis*. New York: Philosophical Library.

Schneider, G. 1985. Stellungnahme zu "Traurige Psychotropen" von Hans Füchtner in Psyche. *Psyche*, no. 7:1133–49.

Schneiderman, S. 1980. *Returning to Freud: Clinical Psychoanalysis in the School of Lacan*. New Haven: Yale University Press.

———. 1983. *Jacques Lacan: The Death of an Intellectual Hero*. Cambridge: Harvard University Press.

———. 1986. *Rat Man*. New York: New York University Press.

Schorske, C. E. 1978. Generational Tension and Cultural Change: Reflections on the Case of Vienna. *Daedalus* 107, no. 4:111–22.

———. 1980. *Fin-de-Siècle Vienna*. New York: Knopf.

Schott, H. 1985. *Zauberspiegel der Seele: Sigmund Freud und die Geschichte der Selbstanalyse*. Göttingen: Vandenhoek and Ruprecht.

Schur, M. 1955. Comments on the Metapsychology of Somatization. *Psychoanalytic Study of the Child* 10:119–64.

———. 1960. Discussion of Dr. John Bowlby's paper. *Psychoanalytic Study of the Child* 15:65–94.

———. 1972. *Freud: Living and Dying*. New York: International Universities Press.

Schuster, P. 1985. Korreferat zu A. de Blecourt. *Zeitschrift für psychoanalytische Theorie und Praxis.* 0:89–94.

Schwartzmann, J. 1971. *Die Verwahrlosung der weiblichen Jugend.* Munich: Ernst Reinhardt.

Schwidder, W. 1950–51. Mitteilungen. *Psyche* 4:382.

Segal, H. 1979. *Klein.* London: Fontana.

Sennett, R. 1977. *The Fall of Public Man.* New York: Knopf.

Sharaf, M. 1983. *Fury on Earth: A Biography of Wilhelm Reich.* New York: St. Martin's Press.

Simenauer, E. 1981. Die zweite Generation—danach: Die Wiederkehr der Verfolgermentalität in Psychoanalysen. *Jahrbuch der Psychoanalyse.* Vol. 12. Vienna: Hans Huber.

Simmel, E. 1918. *Kriegsneurosen und psychisches Trauma.* Leipzig and Munich: O. Nemnich.

Smirnoff, V. N. 1979. Regards sur la psychanalyse. *Nouvelle revue française,* no. 20: 13–58.

———. 1982. Le Contre-transfert, maladie infantile de l'analyste. *Topique,* no. 30: 5–25.

Smith, J. H., and Kerrigan, W., eds. 1984. *Taking Chances: Derrida, Psychoanalysis and Literature.* Baltimore: Johns Hopkins University Press.

———, eds. 1986. *Pragmatism's Freud: The Moral Disposition of Psychoanalysis.* Baltimore: Johns Hopkins University Press.

Smith-Rosenberg, C. 1972. The Hysterical Woman: Sex Roles in 19th Century America. *Social Research* 39:652–78.

Solms-Rödelheim, W. 1959. Psychoanalyse in Österreich. In *Handbuch der Neurosenlehre und Psychotherapie.* Vol. 3, *Spezielle Psychotherapie I.* Munich: Urban and Schwarzenberg, 1181–91.

Solnit, A. 1975. Developments in Child Psychoanalysis in the Last Twenty Years, Pure and Applied. In *The Psychoanalytic Study of the Child.* Monograph no. 5. New Haven: Yale University Press, 1–14.

Sperber, M. 1972. *Alfred Adler et la psychologie individuelle.* Paris: Gallimard.

Spiegel, L. A. 1974. Youth, Culture and Psychoanalysis. *American Imago* 31, no. 2: 206–31.

Spiro, M. E. 1965a. Religious Systems as Culturally Constituted Mechanisms. In *Content and Meaning in Cultural Anthropology.* New York: Free Press.

———. 1965b. *Children of the Kibbutz.* New York: Schocken.

———. 1982. *Oedipus in the Trobriands.* Chicago: Chicago University Press.

Spitz, R. A., and Wolf, K. M. 1946. Anaclitic Depression: An Inquiry into the Genesis of Psychiatric Conditions in Early Childhood. *Psychoanalytic Study of the Child* 2:313–42.

———. 1955. The Primal Cavity. *Psychoanalytic Study of the Child* 10:215–40.

———. 1960. Discussion of Dr. Bowlby's Paper. *Psychoanalytic Study of the Child* 15:85–94.

———. 1963. Life and the dialogue. In *Counterpoint, Libidinal Object and Subject.* Ed. H. S. Gatskill. New York: International Universities Press.

Spotnitz, H. 1961. Adolescence and Schizophrenia. In *Adolescents*. Ed. S. Lorand and H. I. Schneer. New York: Hoeber, 217–37.

Stadler, P. 1982. Triebrepräsentanz, Orientierungsreflex, Alarmreaktion: Eine Skizze zu Gegenstand und Forschungslogik der Psychosomatik. *Psyche* 36:97–122.

Stannard, D. E. 1980. *Shrinking History*. New York: Oxford University Press.

Staples, H. D., and Smarr, E. R. 1980. Bridge to Adulthood Years from Eighteen to Twenty-three. In *The Course of Life*. Vol. 2, *Latency, Adolescence and Youth*. Washington, D.C.: National Institutes of Mental Health, 477–96.

Stein, C. 1971. *L'enfant imaginaire*. Paris: Denoël.

———. 1982. D'un amour qui ferait obstacle à l'amour. *Etudes Freudiennes*, nos. 19–20:147–63.

———. 1987. *Les erinyes d'une mère: Essai sur la haine*. Quimper: Calligrammes.

Stepansky, P. E., and Goldberg, A. 1985. *Kohut's Legacy: Contributions to Self Psychology*. New York: Analytic Press.

Sterba, R. F. *Reminiscences of a Viennese Psychoanalyst*. Detroit: Wayne State University Press.

Stoller, R. J. 1964. A Contribution to the Study of Gender Identity. *International Journal of Psychoanalysis* 45:220–26.

———. 1968. *Sex and Gender*. New York: Science House.

Stone, L. 1961. *The Psychoanalytic Situation: An Examination of Its Development and Essential Nature*. New York: International Universities Press.

Storr, A. 1979. *The Art of Psychotherapy*. New York: Methuen.

Strotzka, H. 1969. *Psychotherapie und soziale Sicherheit*. Vienna: Huber.

———. 1983a. Entwicklung, Stand und Chancen—mit besonderer Berücksichtigung Österreichs. *Sozialpsychiatrie* 23, no. 2:169–84.

———. 1983b. *Fairness, Verantwortung, Fantasie*. Vienna: Franz Deuticke.

Strout, C. 1979. Henry James' Dream of the Louvre, "The Jolly Corner," and Psychological Interpretation. *Psychohistory Review* 8, nos. 1–2:47–52.

Sullivan, H. S. 1953. *The Interpersonal Theory of Psychiatry*. New York: Norton.

Sulloway, F. J. 1979. *Freud, Biologist of the Mind: Beyond the Psychoanalytic Legend*. New York: Basic Books.

Sylwan, B. 1982. Sous le seing de Georg Brandes: le cachet de Melanie Klein-Reizes. *Confrontation*, no. 8:133–52.

Takahashi, T. 1982. La psychanalyse au Japon. In *Histoire de la psychanalyse*. Ed. R. Jaccard. Paris: Hachette, 417–38.

Tholen, G. C. 1985. Dichtung und Verdichtung. *Fragmente* 17–18:4–13.

Thomä, H., and Kächele, H. 1987. *Psychoanalytic Practice*. Berlin: Springer.

Thompson, C. [1943] 1973. Penis Envy in Women. In *Psychoanalysis and Women*. Ed. J. B. Miller. Middlesex, England: Penguin, 51–84.

Thompson, N. L. 1987a. Helene Deutsch: A Life in Theory. *Psychoanalytic Quarterly* 56:317–53.

———. 1987b. Early Women Psychoanalysts. *International Revue of Psycho-Analysis* 14:391–407.

Timpanaro, S. [1974] 1985. *The Freudian Slip*. London: Verso.

Tinbergen, N. 1951. An Attempt at Synthesis. In *Study of Instinct*. New York: Oxford University Press, 101–27.

Torok, M. 1981. *Melanie Mell* avec la participation de Barbro Sylwan et Adele Covello. *Confrontation: Geopsychanalyse: rencontre franco-latino-américaine.* février: 215–42.

———. 1984. La correspondance Ferenczi-Freud. *Confrontation,* no. 12: 79–99.

Trilling, L. 1950. *The Liberal Imagination.* New York: Viking.

Turkle, S. 1978. *Psychoanalytic Politics.* New York: Basic Books.

Uexküll, J. v. [1928] 1973. *Theoretische Biologie.* Frankfurt: Suhrkamp.

Van Herik, J. 1982. *Freud on Femininity and Faith.* Berkeley: University of California Press.

Vermorel, M., and Vermorel, H. 1985. Freud Romantique. Paper presented to the International Psychoanalytic Congress, Hamburg, July 30.

Vianna, H. C. B. 1988. Psychoanalyse und Politik in Brasilien. *Psyche* 42: 997–1015.

Viderman, S. 1970. *La construction de l'espace analytique.* Paris: Gallimard.

———. 1983. La toile, la mouche et l'araignée. *Ideaux: Nouvelle Revue de Psychanalyse,* no. 27: 171–83.

Voghera, G. 1980. *Gli anni della psicoanalisi.* Pordenone: Edizioni Studio Tesi.

Vogt, R. 1986. *Psychoanalyse zwischen Mythos und Aufklärung oder Das Rätsel der Sphinx.* Frankfurt: Qumran.

Waelder R. [1949] 1951. Authoritarianism and Totalitarianism. In *Psychoanalysis and Culture.* Ed. G. V. Wilbur and W. Muensterberger. New York: International Universities Press, 11–25.

———. 1960. Characteristics of Totalitarianism. In *The Psychoanalytic Study of Society.* Vol. 1. Ed. W. Muensterberger and S. Axelrod. New York: International Universities Press, 11–25.

———. 1962. Psychoanalysis, Scientific Method and Philosophy. *Journal of the American Psychoanalytic Association* 10: 617–37.

Wallerstein, R. S. 1987. Presidential Message: Litigation. *IPA Newsletter* 19, no. 1.

Weber, S. 1982. *The Legend of Freud.* Minneapolis: University of Minnesota Press.

Weinstein, F., and Platt, G. 1973. *Psychoanalytic Sociology.* Baltimore: Johns Hopkins University Press.

Weiss, E. 1985. *Elementi di psicoanalisi.* Pordenone: Edizioni Studio Tesi.

Weiss, E., and English, O. S. 1943. *Psychosomatic Medicine.* Philadelphia: W. B. Saunders.

Weizsäcker, V. 1947. *Der Gestaltkreis.* Stuttgart: Thieme.

Wesiak, W. 1978. The role of psychoanalysis in psychosomatic and general medicine. *Sigmund Freud House Bulletin* 2, no. 1: 30–38.

Wetzel, M. 1987. Spurensicherung, *Fragmente* 17–18: 179–204.

Widmer, P. 1984. Zum Problem des Todestriebs. *Psyche* 38: 1059–82.

Wiegman, H. 1950–51. Die Klinik für psychogene Störungen Berlin Grünewald. *Psyche* 4: 389–93.

Wiesenhütter, E. 1958. Die Bedeutung individueller Konflikte für die politische Meinungsbildung. *Psyche* 12: 233–40.

Winnick, H. Z., Moses, R., and Ostow, M., eds. 1973. *Psychological Bases of War.* New York: Quadrangle.

Winnicott, D. W. [1957] 1964. *The Child and the Outside World.* London: Penguin.

———. [1960] 1986. *Home Is Where We Start From: Essays by a Psychoanalyst.* New York: Norton.

———. 1971. *Playing and Reality.* London: Tavistock.

Wirschnig, M. and Stierlin, H. 1982. *Krankheit und Familie.* Stuttgart: Klett.

Wittels, F. [1954] 1957. Heinrich von Kleist—Prussian Junker and Creative Genius. In *Art and Psychoanalysis.* Ed. W. Phillips. New York: Criterion, 165–82.

Wolff, K. 1950. *The Sociology of Georg Simmel.* New York: Free Press. (Partial translation from *Soziologie, Untersuchungen über die Formen der Vergesellschaftung.* Leipzig: Verlag von Duncker und Humboldt, 1908.)

Worbs, M. 1983. *Nervenkunst: Literatur und Psychoanalyse im Wien der Jahrhundertwende.* Frankfurt: Europäische Verlagsanstalt.

Wulff, M., ed. 1950. Aus der Frühzeit der Psychoanalyse. Talk for Freud's Eighty-first Birthday in Chwrah Psychoanalytith b/Eretz Israel. In *Max Eitingon: In Memoriam.* Jerusalem: Israel Psycho-Analytical Society.

Wyatt, F. 1981. Möglichkeiten und Grenzen der psychoanalytischen Deutung der Literatur. In *Freiburger literaturpsychologische Gespräche 1.* Ed. J. Cremerius, W. Mauser, C. Pietzcker, and F. Wyatt. Frankfurt: Lang, 7–12.

———. 1986a. The Narrative in Psychoanalysis: Psychoanalytic Notes on Storytelling, Listening, and Interpreting. In *Narrative Psychology.* Ed. T. R. Sarbin. New York: Praeger, 193–210.

———. 1986b. Aufarbeitung der Vergangenheit: Psychoanalyse unter dem Nationalsozialismus. Paper.

Ziferstein, R. 1970. Der Psychoanalytiker vor den Problemen der Gesellschaft. *Psyche* 24:541–52.

Zilboorg, G. [1930] 1970. Ausländisches Interesse am Institut. In *Zehn Jahre Berliner Psychoanalytisches Institut.* Meisenheim: Anton Hain, 66–69.

———. 1944. Masculine and Feminine. *Psychiatry* 7:257–96.

Index